Shakespeare's Drama of Exile

Palgrave Shakespeare Studies

General Editors: **Michael Dobson** and **Gail Kern Paster**

Editorial Advisory Board: **Michael Neill**, University of Auckland; **David Schalkwyk**, University of Capetown; **Lois D. Potter**, University of Delaware; **Margreta de Grazia**, Queen Mary University of London; **Peter Holland**, University of Notre Dame

Palgrave Shakespeare Studies takes Shakespeare as its focus but strives to understand the significance of his oeuvre in relation to his contemporaries, subsequent writers and historical and political contexts. By extending the scope of Shakespeare and English Renaissance Studies the series will open up the field to examinations of previously neglected aspects or sources in the period's art and thought. Titles in the *Palgrave Shakespeare Studies* series seek to understand anew both where the literary achievements of the English Renaissance came from and where they have brought us.

Titles include:

Pascale Aebischer, Edward J. Esche and Nigel Wheale (*editors*)
REMAKING SHAKESPEARE
Performance across Media, Genres and Cultures

Jane Kingsley-Smith
SHAKESPEARE'S DRAMA OF EXILE

Palgrave Shakespeare Studies
Series Standing Order ISBN 1–4039–1164–9(hardback) 1–4039–1165–7(paperback)
(*outside North America only*)

You can receive future titles in this series as they are published by placing a standing order. Please contact your bookseller or, in case of difficulty, write to us at the address below with your name and address, the title of the series and the ISBN quoted above.

Customer Services Department, Macmillan Distribution Ltd, Houndmills, Basingstoke, Hampshire RG21 6XS, England

Shakespeare's Drama of Exile

Jane Kingsley-Smith
Department of English,
University of Hull

First published 2003 by
PALGRAVE MACMILLAN
Houndmills, Basingstoke, Hampshire RG21 6XS and
175 Fifth Avenue, New York, N. Y. 10010
Companies and representatives throughout the world

PALGRAVE MACMILLAN is the global academic imprint of the Palgrave Macmillan division of St. Martin's Press, LLC and of Palgrave Macmillan Ltd. Macmillan® is a registered trademark in the United States, United Kingdom and other countries. Palgrave is a registered trademark in the European Union and other countries.

ISBN 0–333–99344–6

This book is printed on paper suitable for recycling and made from fully managed and sustained forest sources.

A catalogue record for this book is available from the British Library.

Library of Congress Cataloging-in-Publication Data

Kingsley-Smith, Jane, 1973–
    Shakespeare's drama of exile/ Jane Kingsley-Smith.
      p. cm. – (Palgrave Shakespeare studies)
    Includes bibliographical references (p.) and index.
    ISBN 0–333–99344–6
      1. Shakespeare, William 1564–1616–Criticism and interpretation. 2. Exile (Punishment) in literature. 3. Exiles in literature. I. Title. II. Series.

PR3069. E94K56 2003
822.3'3–dc21   2003046916

10   9   8   7   6   5   4   3   2   1
12   11   10   09   08   07   06   05   04   03

Printed and bound in Great Britain by
Antony Rowe Ltd, Chippenham and Eastbourne

For James

Contents

Acknowledgements

I would first like to acknowledge the financial support I received from the British Academy as a postgraduate at the Shakespeare Institute. It is from my PhD thesis that the following book derives.

To my supervisor, Stanley Wells, I extend grateful thanks for his guidance and encouragement, both in Stratford and subsequently. There cannot be many supervisors who send their students a wedding present! I would also like to thank Martin Wiggins for his wise counsel and for taking me out to lunch.

My colleagues at the University of Hull, Rowlie Wymer and Angela Leighton, have given me much-needed advice on the process of turning the thesis into a book. Jason Lawrence read the final manuscript and I am extremely grateful for his comments.

Finally, I would like to thank my parents, Margaret and Trevor Kingsley-Smith, for their generosity and patience, and James Quinn, who has believed in this book from its inception. To James, I send my love and gratitude in the hope that our own exile, creative though it has been, will not last much longer.

List of Abbreviations

The following abbreviations have been used:

Crit. Q.	*Critical Quarterly*
ELH	*English Literary History*
ELR	*English Literary Renaissance*
E. in C.	*Essays in Criticism*
F	First Folio (1623)
HLQ	*Huntington Library Quarterly*
MLQ	*Modern Language Quarterly*
MLR	*Modern Language Review*
N & Q	*Notes and Queries*
PMLA	*Publications of the Modern Language Association of America*
Q	Quarto
Ren. D.	*Renaissance Drama*
Ren. Q.	*Renaissance Quarterly*
RES	*Review of English Studies*
Sh. Q.	*Shakespeare Quarterly*
Sh. St.	*Shakespeare Studies*
Sh. S.	*Shakespeare Survey*
Sh. Y.	*Shakespeare Yearbook*
SEL	*Studies in English Literature, 1500–1900*
Stud. in Phil.	*Studies in Philology*
YES	*Year in English Studies*

All dates given for plays indicate their earliest performance according to the *Annals of English Drama 975–1700*, 3rd edn, unless specified otherwise. All dates for Shakespeare plays derive from the *Oxford Complete Works of Shakespeare*, eds Stanley Wells and Gary Taylor.

All quotations from Shakespeare are taken from the *Oxford Complete Works*.

The gates of Paradise were opened, and Lambajan averted his eyes. I stumbled through them, giddy, disoriented, lost. I was nobody, nothing. Nothing I had ever known was of use, nor could I any longer say that I knew it. I had been emptied, invalidated; I was, to use a hoary but suddenly fitting epithet, ruined. *I had fallen from grace, and the horror of it shattered the universe, like a mirror. I felt as though I, too, had shattered; as if I were falling to earth, not as myself, but as a thousand and one fragmented images of myself, trapped in shards of glass.*

The banishment of Moraes Zogoiby from *The Moor's Last Sigh* (1995) by Salman Rushdie (London: Vintage, 1996), 278–9

Introduction

According to Stephen Dedalus, exile defines the Shakespearean canon:

> The note of banishment, banishment from the heart, banishment from home, sounds uninterruptedly from *The Two Gentlemen of Verona* onward till Prospero breaks his staff, buries it certain fathoms in the earth and drowns his book.[1]

Exile recurs in the figure of the banished man, from Valentine in *The Two Gentlemen of Verona* through to Prospero in *The Tempest*. It lies embedded in the plays' poetic subtext, transformed from action into metaphor, 'banishment from the heart'. It can even, Stephen claims, provide a structure for the Shakespearean canon itself. Shakespeare leaves Stratford-upon-Avon to become a playwright and his first play pivots on exile. Only with Prospero's repeal from banishment and Shakespeare's return to Stratford is the circle completed.[2] Banishment is both the action which defines the canon and the reason for its existence.

This book concurs with Stephen Dedalus not least in that it argues for the dramatic and poetic significance of banishment in Shakespeare's work. Fourteen out of Shakespeare's 38 plays represent the banishment of one or more central characters. If we include minor characters and self-imposed exile, that number is considerably increased. The simplest explanation for this recurrence is theatrical: banishment was dramatic almost to excess. The proclamation of exile is a climactic moment on the stage whether mimed, as in *The Duchess of Malfi*, or vocally delivered. The words 'I banish you' have a direct performative power; they effect the removal of a character beyond civic or national limits, and in that moment redefine the exile, depriving him of origins, language and a name. In response, the exile utters a long, highly-wrought lament, expressive of grief, anger, despair or resignation, but above all of a recognition that the world has changed. From thence, banishment may inspire revenge or even madness. It will almost certainly require the adoption of disguise and a journey into an alien environment. Thus exile expands the horizons of the play, perhaps requiring a change of location and of social context, while the absences and separations it creates in the exile's place of origin alter the dynamics of that world.

Exile recurs across the generic landscape. In pastoral comedy, it provides a motive for wandering which leads to the reconciliation of lovers, siblings, parents and children (*The Thracian Wonder, The Maid's Metamorphosis*, John Day's *Humour Out of Breath*). The exiled protagonist is often the heir to a deposed monarch, and exile recurs frequently in the cycle of usurpation and restoration presented by history plays (Thomas Lodge's *The Wounds of Civil War*, Robert Greene's *Alphonsus, King of Aragon*). Where banishment is imposed as a punishment for crimes, its application varies widely, including cases of murder, adultery, harbouring a felon, treason and war-mongering.[3] However, tragedy most often features banishment as a motive for revenge. Webster begins *The White Devil* with Lodovico's cry of 'Banished!' thus providing not only a dramatic opening but an insight into both the revenger's alienation and the alien's revenge. Marston blurs the roles of revenger and banished man across his three greatest plays, *Antonio and Mellida, Antonio's Revenge* and *The Malcontent* which all feature banishment as a tragic fate, to be variously lamented or stoically endured.

Shakespeare was not alone in his penchant for banishment, as a later comparison with Marston will suggest. Yet there remains something rich and strange in his recurrence to exile. Again and again, he writes a scene of banishment, reworking the details of earlier plays, redirecting the emphasis from loss of language to loss of nation, from loss of the beloved to loss of self. The mystery need not be that Shakespeare had experience of banishment. The 'hopeless word of "never to return"', as Richard II puts it, could be heard in many contexts; there were exiles all around. Banishment was not only a legal punishment inflicted upon a surprising variety of subjects: the Catholic recusant, the gypsy, the vagabond, etc., but a highly metaphorical and poetic fate which men might fashion for themselves. It was in part this sense of fabrication or theatricality that inspired contemporary debate as to the meaning of banishment. When has the banished man deserved his punishment and what does he become outside the confines of society? Do the conventions of exile adequately express the reality? At what point does banishment shade into self-imposed exile and the banished man morph into the traveller, the patriot, the poet or the martyr? These questions underlie many of Shakespeare's dramas of exile and point to larger debates about the nature of the individual's relationship with society and the extent of his self-authorship.

Nevertheless, criticism has rarely addressed Shakespeare's representation of exile.[4] Whilst we appear to be fascinated by the spectacle of a marginal Shakespeare giving utterance to the suppressed voices of his society, we remain largely uninterested in the representation of marginality, *that is exile*, performed with surprising regularity on the Shakespearean stage. In the rest of this Introduction, I will examine the legend of Shakespeare-as-exile and the way in which this has distracted from banishment in his plays. I will then discuss the kinds of exile suffered in sixteenth- and seventeenth-century England and the contemporary polemic surrounding its interpretation. Finally, I will offer an overview of what I perceive to be Shakespeare's unique engagement with exile as a subject for drama.

Shakespeare in exile

In the biographical essay appended to his 1709 edition of the *Complete Works*, Nicholas Rowe describes how Shakespeare fell in with a gang who poached deer from the park of Sir Thomas Lucy of Charlecote:

> For this he was prosecuted by that gentleman, as he thought, somewhat too severely; and in order to revenge that ill usage, he made a ballad upon him. And tho' this, probably the first essay of his Poetry, be lost, yet it is said to have been so very bitter, that it redoubled the prosecution against him to that degree, that he was oblig'd to leave his business and family in *Warwickshire*, for some time, and shelter himself in *London*.

Rowe characterizes this exile as providential:

> tho' it seem'd at first to be a blemish upon his good manners, and a misfortune to him, yet it afterwards happily prov'd the occasion of exerting one of the greatest *Genius*'s that ever was known in dramatick Poetry. [5]

Despite the discrediting of Rowe by recent biographers (most notably Samuel Schoenbaum in *Shakespeare's Lives*), this story retains a powerful hold on both popular and academic conceptions of Shakespeare.

In the Oscar-winning Hollywood film, *Shakespeare in Love* (1998), directed by John Madden, Shakespeare visits a psychiatrist because he fears that he has lost his creative gift. When asked to describe his marriage, Shakespeare recalls the age difference between himself and Anne Hathaway, the unplanned pregnancy and the cooling of their relationship following the birth of twins. He concludes that 'banishment was a blessing'. Banishment from the bed was a common metaphor for the estrangement between man and wife,[6] but in the film this line may specifically allude to Rowe's theory that the dramatist was exiled from Stratford, for it also shares the biographer's providential tone. In *Shakespeare in Love*, exile from Stratford means not only that the young dramatist has a theatre and patrons to write for, but also that he exchanges Anne Hathaway for the fictional Viola de Lesseps, a bewitchingly androgynous figure who apparently inspires not only *Twelfth Night* but all of Shakespeare's star-crossed and cross-dressed heroines.

This assumption that exile is inevitably the fate of the artist, that exile makes great art, may strike us as a Romantic cliché but it continues to exert a powerful influence upon readers of Shakespeare.[7] In *The Story that the Sonnets Tell*, A. D. Wraight 'reveals' from a close reading of the sonnets that Shakespeare is Marlowe. Part of the proof offered that Marlowe faked his own death and went abroad, from whence he wrote and published under Shakespeare's name, are the so-called 'sonnets of exile':

> When we apply ourselves to a detailed and unprejudiced analysis of the major themes of the Sonnets, we are struck by the inescapable fact that by far the largest group of all deals with the theme of a journey that was undertaken in great heaviness of heart, and that represented a period of cruel separation from his former life and friends, a journey into what can only be likened to a state of exile. It is amazing, but there is no other way to describe this major event in the Poet's life.[8]

One obvious objection to the argument above and to the classification, 'sonnets of exile', is the multiplicity of images of banishment and separa-tion in English Renaissance literature, particularly, as I will argue in Chapter 1, in Petrarchan poetry. It is seriously misleading to suggest that there is no other way of accounting for these poems. And yet, Wraight's certainty serves as a powerful instance of the need to banish Shakespeare/Marlowe in order to explain his genius.

Other versions of this narrative abound. In *Ulysses*, the theory of Shakespeare as exile purports to derive from a close reading of the plays but it is primarily based on the study of Shakespearean biography.[9] Stephen uses the work to flesh out themes already traced in the detail of Shakespeare's life. Thus *Venus and Adonis* describes the deadly wound the dramatist suffered when seduced by Anne Hathaway, a form of castration which alienated him from the world. In *Hamlet*, Shakespeare mourns his dead son and the betrayal and exile which defined their relationship. Yet the purpose of this investigation seems not so much the discovery of Shakespeare, as the discovery of Stephen Dedalus. Stephen's vivid re-imagining of an isolated Shakespeare 'trudging to Romeville', of 'Christfox in leather trews, hiding, a runaway in blighted treeforks from hue and cry. Knowing no vixen, walking lonely in the chase' (244, 247), is implicitly autobiographical.[10] Prior to the National Library scene, Stephen has decided to break with Buck Mulligan, to abandon his teaching job and to quit his present home. His motive for these acts of self-alienation brings us back to the assumed contingency of art and exile; Stephen will recreate himself as an artist by denying all other definitions. Moreover, exile and betrayal will provide him with a subject for his work, just as he imagines

Shakespeare 'carr[ying] a memory in his wallet' as he trudges to London. By taking Shakespeare as the archetypal banished poet, Stephen justifies his own acts of isolation, seeming to prove that great art is the product of exile. Other critics of Shakespeare would 'banish' him in the interests of historical veracity. While there remains no evidence to suggest that Shakespeare was forced to leave Stratford, recent historicist studies of the Elizabethan and Jacobean stage have resulted in a kind of displacement of the dramatist and his canon which might be likened to banishment. This approach argues that, if Shakespeare did not feel himself to be an exile, he occupied a space which is positively liminal in contrast with the centrality he now enjoys. In *The Place of the Stage*, Steven Mullaney argues that the location of the public theatres, in the liberties or outside the city walls, associated it with other ostracized sights/sites such as the brothel, the plague hospital and the madhouse. Where Mullaney finds this marginality to have been artistically liberating, Leeds Barroll suggests that Shakespeare's dramatic career was 'fraught with unexpected difficulties which he barely surmounted [...] at a considerable cost in creative energy'.[11] For Barroll, these difficulties include not only the repeated closure of the theatres due to plague or fears of political unrest, but also the marginality of the playwright in a professional acting company, even one which had been given the King's name. As we will consider later, the theatres lay under threat of expulsion and demolition for most of Shakespeare's lifetime, with antitheatrical tracts of the period repeatedly calling for the theatre and its playwrights to be banished.

Another dimension to this historical displacement is provided by our greater understanding of the conditions of sixteenth- and seventeenth-century authorship. None of Shakespeare's plays published before 1598 appeared under his name, including the first quartos of *Titus Andronicus*, *The Taming of the Shrew*, *Romeo and Juliet* and *Richard II*, and even after that date it was by no means inevitable that Shakespeare's name would appear on the title-page. While this fact may reflect larger issues at the heart of the conception of authorship in the period, not least the absence of any authorial copyright, it also suggests the marginal status of drama as a literary genre, banished from Thomas Bodley's library. Moreover, the *collaborative* nature of performance and publication distracted then, as now, from the playwright or playwrights who produced the initial text. Shakespeare's hands-on role in the theatre may explain why he did not take more interest in the printing of his own works, allowing 18 of his plays to remain unpublished during his lifetime and those that were printed to appear unacknowledged by their parent.[12]

However, perhaps the most passionately debated argument for a marginal Shakespeare centres on the question of his religious faith. If Shakespeare were a Catholic, does this argue that he must have experienced literal or psychological exile? In *Shakespeare: The 'Lost Years'* (1985; rev.

1998), E. A. J. Honigmann re-examines old evidence and offers new material to suggest that Shakespeare acted as a schoolmaster for the Catholic Houghtons in Lancashire. The will left in 1581 by Alexander Houghton makes reference to one 'Shakeshafte', a servant whom he wishes to bestow upon his friend, Thomas Hesketh, along with playing clothes and musical instruments. The theory that this was Shakespeare meets a number of substantive objections. 'Shakeshafte' was a popular name in Lancashire at the time and there are no records to prove that it was ever used as a variant of 'Shakespeare'. Perhaps Alexander Houghton simply misspelt his servant's name. However, a more intriguing defence is offered by Eric Sams who suggests that Shakespeare took the Lancashire variant as an alias in exile. Honigmann has little time for the Shakespeare-as-exile paradigm. He explains Shakespeare's departure from Stratford as evidence of his ambition to follow a different profession to that of his father, recording that it was not unusual for boys to leave home at this age. His most fanciful conjecture is that Shakespeare's parents might have been trying to put an end to their son's relationship with Anne Hathaway.[13] But Sams proves himself much more susceptible to Shakespeare legends, particularly that of the dramatist's flight from the persecution of Sir Thomas Lucy:

> From first to last, the various sources record hatred and ill-usage [...] culminating in banishment and exile ('fly his Native Country / ...forc'd him out of his Country / ... obliged to leave his Business and Family / ... and shelter himself in London / drove him to London ... / obliged him to quit ... his native place / obliged him to quit Stratford').[14]

Sams confuses here descriptions which commend Shakespeare's exile and those which lament it, citing both the providentialist Rowe and the lachrymose John Jordan.[15] As we have seen already, the readiness of biographers and critics to ascribe banishment to Shakespeare is by no means as disinterested as Sams implies, and the legend is partly sustained by the fact that each biography bases itself on the same limited sources. However, Sams makes a new connection between persecution and exile by arguing that Shakespeare was a Catholic fugitive. He reminds us that Sir Thomas Lucy was a famous Catholic tormentor and pursuer who had tracked down John Somerville, the husband of Mary Arden's cousin, Margaret, and was the chief signatory on two documents indicting John Shakespeare for recusancy. For Sams then, the wrangle over deer-poaching belies much more dangerous grounds for enmity. Shakespeare takes refuge with a wealthy Catholic family outside Warwickshire where he assumes a Lancashire name to avoid detection.

We will shortly consider in more detail the religious context, both Protestant and Catholic, in which exile might be defined in this period. It may be as well to state now that I remain agnostic about Shakespeare's

Lancashire connection. Indeed, it will be one of the arguments of this book that Shakespeare was remarkably disengaged from the drama of Catholic exile. For the moment, Sams' argument is chiefly significant for the way in which it fuses the biographical desire to make an extraordinary narrative out of the tedious facts of Shakespeare's existence; the historical impulse to locate Shakespeare in a more dangerous and turbulent era; and the literary theoretical need to banish Shakespeare so that he might better represent the marginalized and suppressed. It could be argued that this banishment of Shakespeare is part of the tendency to universalize the poet. In a post-Heideggerian world, Shakespeare-as-exile might represent some larger perspective on the human condition. Yet Shakespeare-as-exile most often appears in the late twentieth and early twenty-first century in contexts which insist upon alienation as a social and political *injustice*, and as an experience limited to a minority. Again, we might turn to *Ulysses*. The 'Scylla and Charybdis' chapter marks Stephen's exclusion from Dublin literary life. He is not invited to a literary soirée, or asked to contribute to a new collection of Irish poems, though both are discussed in his presence. By fashioning Shakespeare as a marginal poet, Stephen creates a figure with whom he can identify, both in his exclusion and in his hopes of future glory and recognition. Moreover, when Stephen cannot make himself heard at parties or in print by speaking and writing in his own voice, he does command a certain amount of attention for his theories about Shakespeare, expressed in an idiom pieced together from Shakespearean quotation. This appropriation suggests both reverence and an aggressive iconoclasm. Stephen not only adapts the plays to his own tongue, but rewrites the biography so that it more closely reflects his own life. Nor should we underestimate the magical efficacy of banishing Shakespeare. In *Ulysses*, Stephen and his author, James Joyce, express ambivalence about the position of the Irish writer in an English literary canon. As a representative of that canon, itself synecdochic of English imperialism, Shakespeare represents a figure whom the 'marginalized' Irish poet might certainly wish to dominate and expel.

This reading of *Ulysses* owes something to the way in which post-colonialism might interpret the ambiguities of exile and this is an approach that I have considered in more detail in my chapter on *The Tempest*. In very general terms, the representation of Shakespeare and the interpretation of his works by feminism, queer theory and post-colonialism often owes some kind of debt to the Shakespeare-as-exile paradigm we have been tracing here. Shakespeare is often asked to speak for these theoretical perspectives, that is, to represent the experiences of various minority groups not only in the sixteenth and seventeenth centuries but in the present. His works can be viewed as 'attempts to explore the alternatives – alternatives to the discursive and hegemonic constructions of a dominant culture – available to the silenced voices on the margins of dominant and centralized authorities'.[16] This quotation is taken from a monograph on Joyce, a writer who paraded his alienation, but it could just as easily derive from a work of Shakespearean criticism, so familiar are we now with a Shakespeare defined by his passionate, highly anachronistic, sympathy for what is marginal. As suggested above with reference to *Ulysses*, the effect of such an identification is paradoxical. On the one hand, the act of banishing Shakespeare is a celebration of his centrality, a recognition of the need to win Shakespeare over to one's theoretical corner. Moreover, the significance, the universal representativeness, of the sixteenth-century English poet is affirmed by his ability to embody what is perceived as marginal. Shakespeare, Champion of the Outcasts, arguably serves a number of important functions in western academia. He allows us to continue celebrating and centralizing Shakespeare's plays simultaneous to the liberal pursuit of the oppressed and/or silenced voices of Shakespeare's society and of our own. Moreover, by reinventing Shakespeare as a patron of the marginal, in the wake of Stephen Dedalus, we may allay some of our anxieties about canons and canonicity, and about Shakespeare's power as a symbol of cultural and social difference.

On the other hand, there remains a subversive power to the banishment or marginalization of Shakespeare. It encourages the marginal figure to reverse the balance of power, banishèd becomes banisher, in an action that reveals the temporary and fictional nature of the difference between them. One reason why I find it strange that Shakespeare's drama of exile has received so little attention is that this exchange of banisher and banishèd is one that he frequently deployed himself, most explicitly in Coriolanus' challenge to Rome: 'I banish you', but also in other forms throughout the canon. The spectacle of banishment gives expression to society's fears of displacement but, more daringly, it hints at the contingency of identity and of place.

This section has suggested a number of reasons why critical attention has often been given to the banishment of Shakespeare and the marginality of his texts rather than to their representation of exile. In the next section, we will consider another obstacle to such discussion, namely the definition of exile itself.

Banishment in early modern England

On 16 May 1603, James I issued a proclamation against unlawful hunting:

> Forasmuch as his Majestie understandeth, that there be divers ancient & other good and necessary Lawes and statutes of this his Kingdome of England, which do inflict and impose divers grievous Corporall and pecuniary paines & punishments, extending in some cases to sentence of death (the last and greatest punishment,) and in some cases to final

exile & banishment out of their naturall Countrey for ever, upon such as unlawfully hunt or enter into any Forest, Parke, Chase, or Warren, to kill or destroy any Deere or Game [...] yet his Majestie understandeth withall, that the same good Lawes and Statutes have had (especially of late time) little or no effect ...[17]

This proclamation was only the seventh James had issued as king of England and implies a concern to demonstrate not only mastery of but respect for the English legal system. However, the new king appears to be mistaken. Banishment was not, either in common law or statute law, the penalty for the crimes he describes. James' predecessors had sometimes issued proclamations threatening banishment to the poacher. In 1548, for example, Edward VI declared that anyone convicted of hunting, chasing or killing deer in Waltham Forest who could not provide surety on their release from prison should 'abjure this our realm'.[18] Yet James appears to be harking back, not to Tudor precedent, but to the Charter of the Forest, dating from the reign of King Canute in the eleventh century, according to which a man could be outlawed or exiled, suffer the loss of hand or foot, or even be executed, for violence towards one of the king's foresters or for killing a royal deer.[19] By offering this long obsolete code as his authority for banishment, James may have deliberately obscured an unconstitutional act, namely the reinstitution of a penalty without the sanction of the Commons or the House of Lords.[20] But it is also possible that the confusion was genuine, reflecting James' perception that banishment was indeed a fundamental part of English law. Hence, this proclamation might serve as a warning to those Renaissance scholars and legal historians who have too easily written off banishment in this period, insisting that a much dis-cussed and frequently implemented punishment did not exist. James' definition of the legality of banishment encompasses law, statute and royal proclamation. By contrast, most twentieth-century readings have focused only on the first term. In the rest of this section, we will attempt to address this omission.

As legal dictionaries invariably state, banishment was not a part of English common law; it was, in an appropriate metaphor, 'unknown to the common law'.[21] An important exception to this rule was *abjuration*, the origins of which seem to lie in the older practice of outlawry. For criminals who refused to attend trial and evaded capture, outlawry was a form of punishment depriving the offender of his goods and lands, and declaring him *civiliter mortuus*, deprived of all legal rights. By the fourteenth century, due to improvements in the criminal justice system, outlawry was less frequently imposed and had lost much of its terror due to the ease with which the charge might be overturned or a pardon obtained. By the six-teenth century, Elizabeth could complain at the number of Members of Parliament who were also outlaws.[22] More serious was the related practice of abjuration. Where outlawry was usually imposed in the defendant's absence and was thus partly an expression of the law's inability to prosecute him, abjuration regarded exile as a punishment befitting the crime, and required the offender's acquiescence. The protagonist needed first to have sought sanctuary on either consecrated soil or in one of the secular liberties. Within forty days of his arrival, he would be required to confess before a coroner and then to take an oath to leave the country never to return, thus forfeiting his property and leaving his wife as a widow. His destination and his journey towards the port would be dictated to him and if he were discovered to have deviated from this route or to have returned unlicensed, he could be summarily executed.[23]

However, by the sixteenth century, abjuration too was in decline. Conscious that English abjurers might choose to join foreign armies against their native country, Henry VIII undertook a series of measures from 1530 to 1540 to prevent abjuration and to limit sanctuary. Though these measures were repealed at the beginning of James I's reign, abjuration was finally abolished in 1624.[24] Hence, in *The Third Part of the Institutes* (1644), Coke concludes that, by this act, 'such abjuration as was at the common law, founded [...] upon the priviledge [*sic*] of Sanctuary, is wholly taken away'.[25] So, from a common law perspective, the only legal form of banishment in England had been abrogated long before Shakespeare came to write.

Such a reading informs B. J. and Mary Sokol's interpretation of exile in *Shakespeare's Legal Language: A Dictionary*. They insist that banishment was 'mainly a memory' in late sixteenth-century England. Shakespeare's audience might have been familiar with banishment as a practice in Roman imperial and European medieval law, and as a punishment incurred by the poets Ovid and Dante, but such an audience could not have drawn upon any personal experience of banishment. The one exception made is the 1592/3 Act against English recusants which still used the terms of abjuration (see note 25) but this remains an exception for 'exile was not, by name, a judicial penalty in Elizabethan England'.[26] Yet such a 'common-law mentality' is deeply misleading. For, if abjuration was in decline, banishment was becoming increasingly visible as a penalty under statute law. J. H. Baker reminds us that Henry VIII passed some 677 statutes, in one reign taking up almost more space in the statute books than all the other English legislation since Magna Carta.[27] Moreover, the Tudors had established new courts which would supplement the practice of common law. The Court of Chancery in the sixteenth century dealt mainly with equity. The Star Chamber wielded both common and statute law, and implemented royal proclamations which had no power in ordinary courts.[28]

If we turn to *The First Part of the Institutes*, we find Coke defining banishment in common law *and* statutory terms. In a discussion about a wife's right to sue a writ if her husband has been banished, Coke is called upon to define banishment. He reminds his reader that

> by Law no Subiect can be exiled or banished his Countrie, whereby he shall *perdere patriam*, but by authoritie of Parliament, or in case of Abiuration, and that must be upon an ordinarie proceeding of Law ...[29]

Here, Coke recognizes the dual application of banishment: through common law and through an act of Parliament. Perhaps by placing the 'authoritie of Parliament' first, he implies the greater possibilities of banishment in statutory law than in common law and this will be central to our discussion. For, if we turn to a consideration of Elizabethan and Jacobean statutes, we find banishment being offered as a solution to a variety of crimes. In 1562, it was decreed that 'Egyptians' and 'counterfeit' Egyptians must quit the kingdom or face charges of felony. In 1585, an 'Act against Jesuits, Seminary Priests, and other such like disobedient Persons' ordered Catholic priests trained at one of the notorious colleges abroad to return there. Recusants were similarly banished in Elizabeth's 1592/3 act and expelled from London by James' act of 1605. Finally, the unreformed and unlicensed beggar, wandering minstrel and player might all be expelled from the kingdom in accordance with an act of 1597.[30] These are the main statutes regarding exile to which this book will return.

Yet the visibility of exile in sixteenth-century English law does not end here. One way of reinforcing statutes was for the monarch to issue a royal proclamation, to be carried out by the Justice of the Peace in every shire. Banishment seems to have been difficult to enforce, either because the banished subject refused to quit the country or because he or she returned illegally and could not then be identified. Hence, a number of proclamations in the years 1554–1625 are concerned with refining the process of exile.[31] However, royal proclamations also reveal a much wider application of banishment than the statutes, suggesting that this was a punishment particularly favoured by Tudor and early Stuart monarchs. Under Elizabeth, proclamations were issued for the banishment of Anabaptists, the Irish, Negroes and even those whose swords exceeded the length set down in the sumptuary laws.[32] James extended the application of this punishment to illegal hunters, to those who printed or circulated material promoting duelling (banished from the king's presence), to rebels in the shire counties (transported to Virginia) and to individuals.[33] One of the most intriguing proclamations of banishment under James is that which refers to Sir Giles Mompesson, a politician closely allied to Buckingham and Sir Francis Bacon, who was found guilty of abusing his privilege as commissioner for the licensing of inns. Mompesson escaped to France and in his absence he was stripped of his knighthood, fined £10,000 and condemned to life imprisonment. One month later, while still absent in France, the King was resolved

> in detestation of his offences, utterly to Banish and expell the said Giles Mompesson out of His Realmes of England, Scotland, and Ireland, and all other His Majesties Dominions, as a person infamous and unworthy to partake of any the comforts of his Majesties happy Government.[34]

Since Mompesson was not even in the country at the time, this proclamation implies a sentence of outlawry more than banishment. Yet it also suggests the symbolic importance accorded to banishment, such that this proclamation, though impossible to perform, might assuage the anger of Mompesson's enemies.

Having considered common law, statutes and proclamations, we might finally narrow our focus to the local ordinances which threatened banishment in the protection of a town or city. In particular, banishment seems to have been popular with a succession of Lord Mayors; not only must London defend its walls from the constant pressure outside, it must ease the pressure within by regular expulsions. In 1580, the Lord Mayor, Sir Nicholas Woodrofe, wrote to Lord Burghley enclosing draft regulations by which London might be saved from imminent inundation. Woodrofe complained of the increasing number of 'inmates' [tenants] in every house, of the 'thexceding great pestering of exempt places with multitudes of strangers & foren Artificers', of plays and playgoers, and of the practice of killing cattle in the city. His repeated plea was for the removal of these practices *outside*.[35] Across the country, the Poor Laws ordained that the wandering poor be sent from their place of residence to the parish of their birth for relief, an experience that might sometimes have been akin to exile. Yet the *Remembrancia* for the period document the increasing frustration of Privy Council and Lord Mayor in the face of 'swarmes of loose and idle vagrants' leading to regular attempts to banish beggars and to prevent their further ingress into the city.[36] Not only the begging poor were affected. In 1614, Thomas Middleton wrote to the Lord Chamberlain outlining the steps he had taken since his appointment as Mayor to curb various abuses. These included using spies to gather information about brothels in the city, with Middleton himself adopting a disguise to gain entry: 'And findinge those nurseries of villanye I punished them according to their deserts, some by carting and whippinge and verie many by Bannishment from hence.'[37]

Perhaps one reason why banishment remains relatively unexplored, not only in English Renaissance drama, but in this period of English history as a whole, is the problem of defining what was and is meant by it. Many of the measures described above are concerned with relocating the subject to what is seen as his/her rightful place. This applies not only to the subjects of the Poor Law, or to the country gentlemen who were ordered to leave the court and return to their estates, but most obviously to the Irish, Scots borderers, Negroes and 'Egyptians'. The motive for what we might call deportation (a word also in use at the time) is often economic. The draft proclamation regarding 'Negroes and blackamoors' points out that in a time of 'dearth', strangers must not be allowed to consume the relief intended for her Majesty's subjects.[38] But it is also based on a much more fundamental belief in the maintenance of 'natural' topographical (as well as hierarchical) positions which make any form of wandering a suspicious and symbolically transgressive act. It is partly for this reason that the demarcation between deportation as an enforcement of natural order and transportation as a means of redressing crime is often blurred. A proclamation for the banishment of Irishmen assumes that those wandering persons who haunt the court must be potential traitors. Such 'men of Ireland, that have these late years unnaturally served as rebels against her majesty's forces beyond the seas [...] cannot have any good meaning towards her majesty'.[39] Much more confident is James' 1617 proclamation against border and shire rebels which insists that transportation to Virginia will prevent the offenders from further infecting the realm, as well as punishing them for their heinous crimes.[40] Deportation, which might sound like a rapprochement and a return and thus quite opposite to exile, is nevertheless intended as such a loss.

There are other significant ambiguities inherent in the act of banishment. Perhaps most important is the question of enforcement or volition.[41] Although there were cases of transportation, the offender was often asked to *choose* exile. An element of volition was built into the banishment statutes – if one chose to remain in the country or returned without permission one would be liable to prosecution as a felon – and banishment was often represented as a final act of mercy.[42] However, there was also a kind of exile to be achieved by negotiation, recalling the practice of abjuration. The process of obtaining a licence to travel could involve an agreement on both sides that the offender would leave the country without further prosecution. Such exile seems to have been applied in a number of treason cases. When Edward Courtenay, Earl of Devonshire, was imprisoned for his involvement in a plot to put himself and Princess Elizabeth on the throne, Mary released him on the condition that he go into exile. In 1607, Tobie Matthew was imprisoned for converting to Roman Catholicism and was allowed to leave only on the understanding that he would subsequently travel abroad.[43] Occasionally, the monarch would change his or her mind and then the unspoken terms of exile came into dispute. Dr John Storey referred to such an agreement at his trial in 1571. Storey had occupied the position of chancellor of the dioceses of Oxford and London during Mary's reign and was notorious for his bloody persecution of English Protestants. He fled abroad following Elizabeth's succession but was captured and brought back for trial. Storey argued that he was no longer a subject of the Queen (or of English law) by mutual consent:

> For it is well knowen, that I departed this realme beynge freelye licensed therunto by the queene, who accounted me an abject and castawaye, and I came not hether agayne of myne owne accorde; but I was betrayed.[44]

The language of exile encourages such ambiguity. In Republican Rome, the term 'exsilium' was applied to both voluntary exile, chosen in avoidance of the death penalty, and banishment, imposed at a criminal trial.[45] Similarly, in English law, the terms 'exile' and 'banishment' are considered synonymous.[46] In the literature with which this chapter is concerned, there is generally no attempt to distinguish linguistically between the man exiled by royal proclamation, legal statute, 'compulsion of circumstances' or free will. Hence, Anthony Wood in *Athenae Oxonienses* (1695) speaks of 'voluntary banishment' and 'either a forced or voluntary Exile'.[47]

If exile may occur by force or mutual consent, another variable is the distance implied. While banishment could mean expulsion from one's native country, it was also implemented on a smaller scale; the word 'country' could also signify 'county'. Thus, the illegal deer hunter could be banished from his town; the unlicensed beggar could be expelled from one parish to another. Particular distances are often stipulated in relation to the monarch. In statutes passed by Elizabeth and James, Catholics were to remain at all times at least ten miles away from the monarch. Similarly, when Sir Francis Bacon was banished by James I in 1621, he was charged not to come within the 'verge' of the court, a distance of twelve miles. However, banishment from the presence of the sovereign was often a highly metaphorical suffering – a distance not easy to measure. For example, after a period of exile from the Queen's presence in 1593, Bacon re-entered the court and tried to regain his place in her favour. The Earl of Essex, who had pleaded Bacon's case to Elizabeth, related her answer:

> Your access, she saith, is as much as you can look for. If it had been in the King her father's time, a less offence than that would have made a man be banished his presence for ever. But you did come to the Court when you would yourself; and she should precipitate too much from being highly displeased with you to give you near access, such as she shows only to those that she favours extraordinarily.[48]

There was an obvious correlation between the courtier's power and his access to the sovereign's body in the reigns of Elizabeth I and James I. Under Elizabeth, this had been relatively unproblematic since those closest to the Queen's body were women. When James replaced them with male servants, the role of gentleman of the bedchamber became a highly sought-after position at court.[49] Hence, exile from that body was a literal and metaphorical disempowering of the subject. Moreover, where Elizabethan and Jacobean ideology equated sovereign and kingdom (through the theory of the King's two bodies), this exile might yet be imagined as banishment from the world. The representation of Elizabeth standing on a map of England in the Ditchley portrait (*c.*1592) and James' declaration that he united England and Scotland within his body reinforced the idea that banishment from the monarch was exile from England and hence from the world.

The indefinition of exile may be a source of ambiguity and frustration, but it is also the heart of its fascination. On the one hand, exile offers an opportunity for self-reinvention. Sixteenth- and seventeenth-century writers, whether they wrote private letters, biography, hagiography, consolation literature, poetry or drama, exploited the slippery terms of exile to transform the banished state. The lack of clear differentiation, in particular between expulsion and voluntary flight, is crucial, allowing the desire to seek one's fortunes abroad to be turned into a heroic escape from persecution, or shameful banishment from court to be recast as literary escapism. Archetypes for the experience of banishment were created, to be appropriated by dramatists in the theatre as well as by their 'real-life' counterparts. However, this rewriting of exile did not go unresisted. Many times the authority which had imposed the sentence of exile would insist upon its punitive, anti-social meaning in the face of a more heroic definition. It was also likely to point out the fictionality of the exile's reinvention. Perhaps the two most highly contested exile identities at this time are those of the religious fugitive and the banished poet/player, roles that we need to consider in more detail.

Religious exile

It has usually been assumed that the title 'Marian exiles' is accurate, that is to say that the flight of approximately eight hundred Protestants during Mary I's reign was an exile based on 'compulsion of circumstances' if not official banishment. To remain in England would inevitably lead to persecution and possibly execution. Yet Christina Garrett has argued that this flight of English Protestants, at least in the first year of Marian rule, was a voluntary act of religious colonization. She describes how plans had been made for such a journey a month after the Queen's accession to the throne (August 1553) and that these were in operation the following January before any coercive religious measures had been taken by the government.[50] Ironically, it was the state of alienation in which the English Protestants found themselves that necessitated the adoption of the exile persona. They had left behind their incomes, homes and patrons, the protection of the law and even their native language. To succeed abroad they needed foreign patronage, and yet to be a political refugee from an oppressive regime would not ensure a welcome. Indeed, Strasbourg, Frankfurt and Zurich, among other cities, had a strict policy on the political backgrounds of their refugees, denying access to those guilty of 'crimes against the state':

> It was out of this predicament [...] that the need arose for *a legend of persecution and banishment*. Hence it was that in all their supplications for shelter, these voluntary exiles became in their own phrase 'die armen vertrybnen Engellender', and 'poor banished Englishmen' they have remained in the sympathy of the world to the present day [italics mine].[51]

This legend was partly perpetuated by Protestant hagiography. In his *Acts and Monuments*, John Foxe includes exile among the tribulations suffered by English Protestants under Henry VIII and Mary I. He describes the latter's reign as one in which 'many men, women, and children were burnt, many imprisoned, and in prison starved, divers exiled, some spoiled of goods and possessions, a great number driven from house and home'.[52] But the same semiotics of exile was also used to describe the plight of English Catholics under Elizabeth I. In Nicholas Sanders' *The Rise and Growth of the Anglican Schism* (1585), Edward Rishton describes how high dignitaries of the Church were 'banished the realm' in the early years of Elizabeth's reign. As in the case of the Protestant exiles, the extent to which this removal was voluntary or enforced remains unclear.[53] Once again, the migration of a number of Elizabethan bishops and academics from Oxford and Cambridge may be seen as religious colonization. The exiles went to the universities of Paris, Padua, Salamanca and Louvain and to newly created Catholic colleges such as Rheims, Rome and Douai, where the intention was to train priests who might return to England and keep the faith alive there. The transportation of these priests, following an act of 1585,[54] may be more literally described as banishment, but again, the self-dramatizing, tragic tone in which such exile was described is reminiscent of Foxe. Rishton writes from personal experience of expulsion, testifying to the priests' reluctance to 'forsake' English Catholics (327–30). He suggests that the Church's persecutors believe they are pursuing a more humane course by banishing rather than imprisoning or executing priests. Rishton begs to differ:

> Most assuredly banishment for life is no strong proof of forbearance, and in truth is the most cruel punishment, when the condition of it is death if you return. Now the priests of God are in England by the command of their superiors, and out of their own great zeal for the salvation of souls; to them, therefore, this banishment must have been harder to bear than all torture and death itself, and to the Catholic people also, thus robbed of their priests, it must have been infinitely sad.
>
> (326)

However, the religious fugitive was not limited to the role of tragic exile/martyr. He might also recast his flight as voluntary and heroic. While Foxe laments the enforced exile of his Protestant martyrs, he also praises them for choosing to leave. In a letter to Richard Bertie and his wife, Protestants who fled England in 1554–55, Foxe praises God for 'delivering you out of that miserable land, from the danger of idolatry and fearful company of Herodians'. He goes on to argue that the choice of exile is a sign of the operation of God's grace and an indication that they are saved (the doctrines of irresistible grace and of predestination being two of the heresies for which they were persecuted). Foxe tells them:

> To forsake your country, to despise your commodities at home, to contemn riches, and to set naught by honours which the whole world hath in great reveration, for the love of the sacred gospel of Christ, are not works of the flesh, but the most assured fruits of the Holy Ghost, and undeceivable arguments of your regeneracy or new birth ...[55]

Foxe does not interpret their flight as in any way an escape from persecution (though the couple had made an enemy of Bishop Gardiner). Rather, the journey into exile is imagined as a spiritual quest, an abandoning of worldly pleasure for the sake of eternal life.

The story of Sir Thomas Copley exemplifies both the heroic and ignominious connotations of voluntary exile during Elizabeth's reign. Copley features in Robert Parsons' *Relation of a Triall between the Bishop of Evreux and the Lord Plessis Mornay*. Here, he is cited as evidence that John Jewel's *The Apology of the Church of England* (1562) has had no power to convert Catholics to Protestantism, but has rather had the opposite effect.[56] According to Parsons, Copley was a 'zealous Protestant' who found many errors in Jewel's book but, on confronting the author, received only 'trifling answers':

> Which thing made the good Gentleman to make a new resolution with himself, and to take that happy course which he did to leave his Country and many great commodities, which he enjoyed therein, to enjoy the liberty of conscience, and so both lived and died in voluntary banishment.[57]

Yet this was not the only construction put upon Copley's exile. Before taking the decision to flee, he received a letter from William Cecil, Lord Burghley, which asked Copley if he were willing to incur

> the infamy that wilful exile doth bring, to be accompted, if not a traitor, yet a companion of traitors and conspirators, a man subject to the curses and imprecations of zealous good subjects, your native countrymen, yea,

subject to lack of living by your own and thereby compelled to follow strangers for maintenance of livelihood and food? The cause must needs be of great force to induce you thereto.[58]

This letter could be read as an account of the exile's *heroic* suffering, were it not for Cecil's insistence that exile is recognized as an act of treason, to be deplored by the exile's 'native countrymen'. Even if the fugitive is not a traitor on departure, he will be forced into the company of villains; economic necessity may compel him to dark deeds.

Voluntary or enforced, motivated by religious zeal or political dissidence, the definition of exile was a central bone of contention in contemporary debates over Catholic persecution. Cecil's *The Execution of Justice in England* (1583), written nine years after his letter to Copley, extends the arguments of that letter by insisting that the Pope has been deceived by English fugitives.[59] Their support for his bull of excommunication against Elizabeth is inspired by treachery not religious conviction. Cecil writes:

Not only all the rabble of the foresaid traitors that were before fled, but also all other persons that had forsaken their native countries, being of divers conditions and qualities, some not able to live at home but in beggary, some discontented for lack of preferments, which they gaped for unworthily in universities and other places, some bankrupt merchants, some in a sort learned to contentions, being not contented to learn to obey the laws of the land, have many years, running up and down from country to country, practiced [*sic*] some in one corner, some in another, some with seeking to gather forces and money for forces, some with instigation of princes by untruths to make war upon their natural country, some with inward practices to murder the GREATEST, some with seditious writings, and very many of late with public infamous libels, full of despiteful vile terms and poisoned lies, altogether to uphold the foresaid anti-Christian and tyrannous warrant of the Pope's bill.[60]

Hence, Cecil argues that no Catholic has been persecuted for his faith but rather for the sedition and treachery practised against Elizabeth in the name of that faith. He extends this argument to the seminaries, urging his readers not to be deceived by their apparently apolitical intents in sending priests across to England. It is all part of a papal master plan, 'to nourish and bring up persons disposed naturally to sedition' and to smuggle them into England for the Queen's overthrow.[61] However, in *A True, Sincere and Modest Defense of English Catholics* (1584) William Allen insists that the Catholic exiles are quite innocent of treason. His seminarians are paragons of hard work and endurance, spending their 'long banishment in honest poverty', never accused of the least crime or disorder by their host country.[62] Allen also defends the *religious* convictions of the exiled laymen. If their exile were motivated by secular self-interest, he argues, they would certainly have succumbed to the Protestants' persuasions. Instead, the Catholic exiles remain steadfast and it is England's Protestants who are being tempted across the Channel to true faith.[63]

The interpretation of banishment was central then not only to the actual experience of English religious fugitives abroad, but also to the government policy which alternately condoned and condemned their departure, and to the way in which they were perceived by those left behind. When we turn to representations of the poet and the player in sixteenth- and seventeenth-century England, we find the same struggle to control the meaning of exile.

The banished player and poet

Before the battle between the city and the Elizabethan stage was really under way, the prohibition on playing during times of plague was referred to as banishment. In 1572, Harrison records that 'plays were banished for a time out of London, lest the resort unto them should engender a plague, or rather disperse it, being already begonne'.[64] As Harrison states, this expulsion was only temporary, part of a variety of measures intended to limit the spread of infection. However, banishment came to be used to define a more permanent and specific exclusion. In a petition of November 1596, the residents of Blackfriars protested against the erection of Burbage's theatre there. They described the original removal of the theatres, from the city into the Liberties, following a bill of 1574, as banishment:

> All players being banished by the Lord Mayor from playing within the city by reason of the great inconveniences and ill rule that followeth them, they now think to plant themselves in liberties.[65]

Similarly, 'An Act of Common Counsel for releafe of the poore ... Article 62', dated approximately 1582, declared:

> There are no enterludes allowed in London in open spectacle but in private howses only at marriages or such like, w'ch may suffise, and sute is apointed to be made that they may be likewise banished in place adioyning. Since that time and namely upon the ruine at Parise garden, sute was made to my S'rs to banishe playes wholly in the places nere London, according to the said law, letters were obtained from my S'rs to banishe them on the sabbat daies.[66]

It is difficult to say how seriously we should take the 'banishment' of the theatre. Despite official insistence that playing had been suppressed and players expelled, the celebrated legislation often had minimal effect. In *A Monster Lately Found Out* (1628), Richard Rawlidge testifies to the success of the 1582 bill but performances seem to have continued in the Liberties and inn yards of the city.[67] Even in cases of a dramatic shift, such as the removal of playhouses from the city to the Liberties, the interpretation of banishment remains problematic. Once again we are faced with the difficulty of differentiating between voluntary and enforced exile. E. K. Chambers and Virginia Gildersleeve have convincingly argued that the removal of the theatres to the Liberties around the time of the 1574 Act was voluntary and in the best interests of the companies: 'The players seem to have come to the conclusion that it would be better to be independent, as far as possible, of the risks attaching to this discretion. They turned to the easier conditions afforded by the lax county government of the suburbs.'[68]

We have, unfortunately, very little testimony as to the perceptions of the theatre-owners, playwrights and players regarding their 'banishment'. But what we do have suggests that attempts to define the banished poet/player were focused, not on the reclamation of that fate as tragic or heroic, but on determining exactly who should be expelled.[69] This was not due to a lack of precedent. Protestant apologists frequently celebrated the literature produced in exile, converting banishment into a literary as well as a divine vocation.[70] For example, John Bale wrote *The Image of Both Churches, Being an Exposition of the most Wonderful Book of Revelation of St. John the Evangelist* (1545) during a period of exile in Antwerp:

> Of such a nature is the message of this book with the other contents thereof, that from no place is it sent more freely, opened more clearly, nor told forth more boldly, than out of exile. And this should seem to be the cause thereof. In exile was it first written [...] In exile are the powers thereof most earnestly proved of them that have faith.[71]

Certainly, exile produced a number of important Protestant works. The *Geneva Bible*, translated by William Whittingham and Anthony Gilby with assistance from Coverdale (April 1560), John Ponet's *Shorte Treatise of Politicke Power* (1556) and of course Foxe's *Acts and Monuments* were all written in exile and celebrated as such. As John Hopkins put it in an elegy for Foxe: 'Thy tongue and pen the truth did still defend, / Thou banishment for Christ didst gladly bide.'[72] Exile was a state that allowed English Protestants the freedom to write and publish their work while offering a heroic, even tragic, identity which gave further prestige to that writing. Later, Elizabethan Catholics would follow their example by commanding printing-presses and celebrating literary exile.[73] However, this association between exile and literary creation was not confined to exegesis.

Legends surrounding the 'banishment' of Sir Thomas Wyatt, Sir Philip Sidney, Edmund Spenser and Sir John Harington have encouraged us to consider certain of Wyatt's poems, *Arcadia*, *The Faerie Queene* and the first English translation of Ariosto's *Orlando Furioso* as works produced in exile. Scholars continue to debate the actual situation of the artist in each case, but it is clear that one's self-invention as an exile could serve a number of important functions, not least the privileging of the outcast perspective and the tragic elevation of the poet.[74] Moreover, as in the case of the religious fugitive, 'voluntary' exile could transform the shame of banishment into an expression of artistic vocation. Following his banishment from court in 1621, Bacon appealed to the King for a pardon, for financial assistance and for permission to return to court. But to the Spanish ambassador, Count Gondomar, he reinvented his disgrace as retirement for the sake of his art:

> For myself, my age, my fortune, yea my Genius, to which I have hitherto done but scant justice, calls me now to retire from the stage of civil action and betake myself to letters, and to the instruction of the actors themselves, and the service of Posterity. In this it may be I shall find honour, and I shall pass my days as it were in the entrance halls of a better life.[75]

Similar claims have been made for the English Renaissance stage. Steven Mullaney argues that:

> When Burbage dislocated theater from the city, he established a social and cultural distance that would prove invaluable to the stagecraft of Marlowe and Shakespeare: a critical distance [...] that provided the stage with a culturally and ideologically removed vantage point from which it could reflect upon its own age with more freedom and license than had hitherto been possible.[76]

But however convincing this argument may be in hindsight, I have found no evidence to suggest that it represents a common perception at the time. Apologists for the stage tend not to dispute whether banishment is an apt punishment for dangerous or transgressive art, nor are they concerned to redefine the marginality of playing or players. The focus of their attention is given to becoming *themselves* the socially responsible power that banishes, rather than the socially pernicious outcast. This position too involved some tinkering with the definition of exile.

Plato's *Republic*, available from 1484 in Ficino's Latin translation, justifies the banishment of the artist on three main grounds. Firstly, art is seen to misrepresent both gods and heroes – Socrates objects to slanderous lies, and to the poet's questioning of social and divine justice.[77] Secondly, the affective power of poetry and drama may be a form of *moral* corruption, for anger, effeminacy, lechery or inconstancy may all be learned through the empathy inspired by representative art.[78] Related to this is the possibility that acting erodes civic identity. The multiplicity of roles the actor adopts contradicts one of the basic tenets of Socrates' ideal state: that each man has one function to perform for the benefit of all, and only one. Finally, art is said to distract man from the study of philosophy. These three points consistently inform the anti-theatrical debate in sixteenth-century England.[79] In *The Schoole of Abuse* (1579, repr. 1587), Stephen Gosson describes the Circean temptations of poetry and its ability to 'turne reasonable creatures into brute beastes'. Plato is his authority from the beginning:

> No marveyle though *Plato* shut them out of his Schoole, and banished them quite from his common wealth, as effeminate writers, unprofitable members, and utter enimies to vertue.[80]

In order to defend themselves from this Platonic curse, apologists for the stage often began by challenging the authority of Plato himself. Where Gosson argued that poets labour over what is worthless, Thomas Lodge suggests that philosophy is equally useless and 'fantasticall'. [81] In his *Defence of Poesy* (*c.* 1581), Sidney rejects Plato's authority on the basis that, elsewhere, he recommended that women be held as common property and that men enjoy homosexual relationships.[82] However, the main thrust of the apologists' arguments was that Plato had been misconstrued. Sidney quotes Julius Scaliger's description of Plato as one, 'Qua authoritate barbari quidam atque hispidi abuti velint ad poetas e republica exigendos', 'whose authority certain barbarous and uncouth men seek to use to banish poets from the commonwealth'.[83] In fact, Sidney argues, the philosopher intended to defend poetry by purging the state of scandalous misrepresentations of the gods which even pagans would find blasphemous. Sidney ends where he began by declaring Plato the most poetical of philosophers: 'So as Plato, banishing the abuse, not the thing, not banishing it, but giving due honour unto it, shall be our patron, and not our adversary.'[84]

This argument for banishing the abuse in order to save true poetry became a crusade against the poetaster. In *The Anatomie of Absurditie* (1589), Thomas Nashe condemns the ignorance that characterizes much contemporary poetry and declares of the poetaster:

> Such kind of Poets were they that *Plato* excluded from his Common wealth, and *Augustine* banished *ex civitate Dei*, which the *Romans* derided, and the *Lacedaemonians* scorned, who wold not suffer one of *Archilocus* bookes to remaine in their Countrey ... [85]

But this concession of banishment on the basis of a distinction between the socially righteous poet and the scurrilous poetaster, the Lord

Chamberlain's man and the wandering vagabond, was not without its sacrifices. If Plato is the most famous banisher in the war against poetry, then Ovid is the most famous banishee. The principal anti-theatrical pamphleteers of the period, namely John Northbrooke, Stephen Gosson, Philip Stubbes and William Prynne, all cite the banishment of Ovid as justification for the exclusion of drama from the city of London. What is perhaps more unexpected is the fact that the apologists for the stage generally concur. Thus, in his *Defence*, Lodge implies that he cannot protect Ovid from Gosson's accusations and can only point out that one man's folly should not be held against poetry as a whole: 'I abhore those poets that savor of ribaldry: I will with the zealous admit the expullcion of such enormities.'[86] In *Poetaster* (1601), Ben Jonson went further. By creating so many representative poets, from Virgil and Horace through to Crispinus and Demetrius, Jonson encouraged an audience to differentiate between them. The play condones the punishment of the poetasters and slandering satirists, but also seems to endorse the banishment of Ovid, the poet who lived an immoral life and thus debased his art. Ovid himself urges the need for discrimination between 'the high raptures of a happy Muse' and those 'jaded wits / That run a broken pace for common hire' (1.2.242–3), but it is finally Ovid, the ostensible defender of poesy, who must also be rejected. In thus casting him off, Jonson may be signalling his rejection of the Ovidian style popular in 1590s England,[87] but he is also clarifying his association with Horace and Virgil, the poets who grow in stature and authority as Ovid falls.

This need to differentiate between the true and the false artist, and thus to banish art's abuse, was, then, not simply a question of survival in the face of civic hostility. It was also bound up with the professional rivalries which inspired the so-called 'war of the theatres'. The play which may have begun the debacle, John Marston's *Histriomastix* (1599), also uses banishment to define its position in the theatrical landscape. In the sixth act, England is ruled by Poverty. The players cannot pay their tavern debts or their taxes and the Constable tells them that it is his job to 'banish idle fellowes out o'th'land'. Despite their protests that they are patronized by Sir Oliver Owlet, the players are banished.[88]

Histriomastix dramatizes a situation in which it was imperative that the professional players 'distinguish' themselves. The definition of itinerant players as social outcasts had been formalized in Elizabethan law by the Vagabond Act of 1572 which ordered vagrants and beggars to be whipped and sent back to their parishes of origin for employment. Among these were included 'juglers, pedlars, tynkers, and pety chapmen [...] fencers, bearewardes, comon players in enterludes, and minstrels ...' The player who could not prove that he performed under the auspices of a wealthy patron would be subject to this law. The subsequent Act of 1597 included banishment among its redressive measures. Any rogue who was declared dangerous or irredeemable was to be 'banished the realm or adjudged to the galleys'. Marston's players are described in act 3 as 'Proud statute rogues' and they finally fall victim to this legislation.[89]

However, the object of Marston's satire here is not simply the unlawful, itinerant player. It clearly extends to the actors of the professional companies (as opposed to the boys of the private theatres) who had the vulgarity to consider acting their trade. Where Shakespeare's *A Midsummer Night's Dream* suggests a fondness for its 'hard-handed' mechanicals, despite their lack of a classical education, Marston's Chrisogonus condemns the ignorance of Sir Oliver Owlet's men and the 'thickskin'd auditors' whom they attract. *Histriomastix* seems likely to have been written for the Middle Temple, and it certainly indulges an academic prejudice against the popular stage.[90] In particular, Chrisogonus vents his spleen against the aspiring playwright:

> O age, when every Scriveners boy shall dippe
> Prophaning quills into Thessaliaes Spring,
> When every artist prentice that hath read
> The pleasant pantry of conceipts, shall dare,
> To write as confident as *Hercules*.
> When every ballad-monger boldly writes:
> And windy froth of bottle-ale doth fill
> Their purest organ of invention:
> Yet all applauded and puft up with pryde,
> Swell in conceit, and load the Stage with stuffe,
> Rakt from the rotten imbers of stale jests:
> Which basest lines best please the vulgar sence
> Make truest rapture lose preheminence.

(273–4)

The name of the popular playwright, Posthast, reinforces this impression of plays being speedily and carelessly composed, pieced together from 'stale jests' in order to feed the voracious appetite of the popular audience. But Posthast is banished in Act 6 along with the players. As in *Poetaster*, the true poet, Chrisogonus, rises in estimation while his popular rival is expelled. The fact that this representation of Chrisogonus seems to have offended Jonson and led to the violent satire of *Poetaster* appears at least ironic since Marston and Jonson clearly shared similar prejudices against the popular stage.[91] But what *Histriomastix* and *Poetaster* also share is the tendency to explore the banishment of poetry, not in terms of its social or moral righteousness per se, but as a punishment suitable for a particular group of poets and players whom the 'legitimate' artists are most capable of identifying and of rooting out. Banishment has become a fantasy through which the 'true' playwright gains control of the popular stage.

Shakespeare's drama of exile

In the previous section, we have examined the problems that confront the historian of exile. We have also considered some of the paradigms by which banishment was debated and reinvented in sixteenth- and seventeenth-century England. What we have not done is to answer the question of why and how Shakespeare dramatized exile. One might argue that if Shakespeare was a Catholic who suffered banishment from Stratford and who came to feel the marginality of the player and playwright in London, the reason for his fascination with exile is clear enough. Yet, quite apart from the objections that might be raised to such a biographical reading (and one based on dubious historical grounds), this explanation begins to fall apart when we look at the plays. It is not simply that Shakespeare shows a marked disinclination to engage with the idea of religious exile or that he avoids any sustained identification of player/poet as exile, despite his appropriation of the other banishment paradigms explored throughout this book. What is perhaps most important about the omission of any Catholic/Protestant perspective on exile is the emphasis it throws upon the secularity of Shakespearean banishment: the concern in his plays for the local conditions of identity, that is the material, the familial, the national. This absence of a spiritual dimension to exile is most apparent if we consider Shakespeare's work in comparison with two contemporary plays, Marston's *The Malcontent* (1604) and Heywood's *A Woman Killed with Kindness* (1603).

Shakespeare and Marston seem to have shared an interest in the representation of banishment and to have approached it from similar perspectives.[92] In *As You Like It, King Lear* and *Coriolanus*, Shakespeare uses the dramatic scenario of banishment to test the Stoic principles of his characters. Likewise, in Marston's *Antonio's Revenge* (1600), the Stoic play-acting of Pandulpho is undermined by the unquenchable sorrow of exile and bereavement: 'I spake more than a god, / Yet am less than a man. / I am the miserablest soul that breathes' (4.5.51–3).[93] Exile also proves integral to both dramatists' interest in alienation – something Marston explores dramatically through his insistent disruption of the suspension of disbelief, and psychologically through the characters' confrontation with the roles they play. Thus, in *Antonio and Mellida* (1599), the banished protagonist compulsively dramatizes his self-loss by refusing to be 'Antonio'. In the first scene, he describes his own death in a shipwreck. In 2.1, he makes a spectre of himself, asking Mellida:

> Dost not behold a ghost?
> Look, look where he stalks, wrapped up in clouds of grief,
> Darting his soul upon thy wond'ring eyes.
> Look, he comes towards thee. See, he stretcheth out

His wretched arms to gird thy lovèd waist
With a most wished embrace. See'st him not yet?
Nor yet? Ha, Mellida, thou well may'st err,
For look, he walks not like Antonio,
Like that Antonio that this morning shone
In glistering habiliments of arms
To seize his love, spite of her father's spite,
But like himself, wretched and miserable,
Banished, forlorn, despairing, struck quite through
With sinking grief, rolled up in sevenfold doubles
Of plagues unvanquishable. Hark, he speaks to thee!

Mellida   Alas, I cannot hear nor see him.

(2.1.269–84)[94]

The association of exile with death, with the metamorphosis of the self, and with a paradoxical belief that this is and is not Antonio are all familiar exile tropes. What may be even more familiar here is the echo of *Hamlet*. In his argument for a date of late 1600 for both *Antonio* plays, Philip J. Finkelpearl notes similarities between this encounter and the closet scene in *Hamlet*. He also observes that, like Hamlet, Antonio is described as being 'shipped / For England'.[95] I would argue that part of Marston's indebtedness to Shakespeare is this sense of exile, and that in banishing Antonio, Marston took up a detail which Shakespeare had, for once, underplayed. After the murder of Polonius, Hamlet is ordered to depart for England, a fate which is obviously enforced if it is not specifically referred as exile. In the case of Antonio and Malevole/Altofront, Marston makes explicit an alienation that Shakespeare had left unsaid and in doing so sharpens the malcontent's satirical commentary upon the world. Indeed, we might attribute to Shakespeare the convention of Jacobean malcontent as exile.

However, in *The Malcontent*, Marston has swerved away from the Shakespearean conception of exile by placing his theme in a spiritual light. 'For hit is so that all mankynde in this warld nis but in exile and wildernesse out of his kyndely contre': that this medieval identification of the secular world as exile continued to resonate into the sixteenth and seventeenth centuries is apparent from Marston's play.[96] Consider Malevole's meditation in 4.4:

World! 'tis the only region of death, the greatest shop of the devil, the cruellest prison of men, out of the which none pass without paying their dearest breath for a fee; there's nothing perfect in it but extreme, extreme calamity, such as comes yonder.

Enter Aurelia, two halberts before and two after, supported by Celso and Ferrardo; Aurelia in base mourning attire.

Aurelia   To banishment! Lead on to banishment!

$$(4.4.26-31, 4.5.1)^{97}$$

The point that the world is a site of exile is reinforced through descriptions of Malevole himself. He is pictured as 'more discontent than Lucifer when he was thrust out of the presence' (1.1.19–20) and 'as far from any content as heaven' (21).[98] While these allusions serve to remind an audience that Malevole is really the banished Duke Altofront, they also reinforce our sense of exile as a spiritual state.

If we now turn to *A Woman Killed with Kindness*, we find further evidence of directions Shakespearean banishment might have taken. Heywood's play deals extensively with the domestic exile of an adulterous wife. This is a subject which Shakespeare considered only briefly in *Henry VI Part One* though we have a glimpse of further possibilities in *Othello* when, immediately before her death, Desdemona pleads 'O, banish me, my lord, but kill me not' (5.2.85).[99] In *A Woman Killed*, the wrathful husband is more merciful:

> Go, make thee ready in thy best attire,
> Take with thee all thy gowns, all thy apparel;
> Leave nothing that did ever call thee mistress,
> Or by whose sight being left here in the house
> I may remember such a woman by.
> Choose thee a bed and hangings for a chamber;
> Take with thee everything that hath thy mark,
> And get thee to my manor seven mile off,
> Where live. 'Tis thine; I freely give it thee.
> My tenants by shall furnish thee with wains
> To carry all thy stuff, within two hours,
> No longer, will I limit thee my sight.

$$(13.159-70)^{100}$$

But all Frankford's concern for his wife's domestic comfort cannot disguise the fact that this is banishment, defined as such by its stipulations of distance (seven miles) and of time (within two hours). Moreover, Anne's subsequent experience resembles that of many Shakespearean exiles in the loss of her name and her voice. Frankford insists that all traces of his wife be removed and enjoins a binding silence upon her: never to communicate with him or her children again. Anne passionately embraces this self-annihilation by refusing to speak for herself (16.59–64) and by urging her children never to speak her name (87–91).

The play puts a heavy emphasis on the material conditions of identity, that is on the marks of Anne's existence in her possessions and her home, her body and her children, and this theme is further reinforced by the subplot in which Charles and Susan Mountford are expelled from their ancestral home with a subsequent loss of identity.[101] But for all this emphasis upon secular authority and definition, the real focus of the play is Anne's exile from God. As Diana Henderson has shown, the adultery plot closely resembles the story of Adam and Eve's transgression and expulsion from Paradise, with the Lucifer-like Wendoll invading the Edenic marital home to the shame and banishment of both lovers.[102] Anne's sinful condition is described in terms of 'wandering' (6.151) and distance. Thus she identifies with another Biblical exile in her despair of forgiveness: 'I am as far from hoping such sweet grace / As Lucifer from heaven' (13.81–2). This distance is only resolved at the end of the play when Frankford physically travels to Anne's deathbed and symbolically cancels their division: 'thy repentant tears / Unite our souls' (17.108–9).

The general contrast I am suggesting is not simply based on absence, that is on the silence of the religious fugitive in Shakespeare's work or the lack of a larger religious paradigm to give meaning to his drama of exile. Shakespeare's banishment plays lament an identity that seemed *complete*, based as it was on familial and romantic love, civic and national vocation, honour and reputation. They explore the limitations placed on identity by these structures but do not proffer any more valuable or life-enhancing basis for existence. Such plays are sometimes overtly nationalistic. In *Richard II*, three characters lament the loss of England and what that means in terms of national identity. *King Lear* and *Cymbeline* explore the concept of a united and then disrupted Britain where exile acts as a microcosm for national dissolution. However, even at its most patriotic, Shakespearean exile is always inclusive. It is, to my mind, no coincidence that one of the sections of *Sir Thomas More* which Shakespeare seems to have been asked to write (and thus possibly the only manuscript we have in his handwriting) treats the subject of exile.[103] Sir Thomas More has been brought in to calm the Londoners who are preparing to take arms against foreigners in the 'ill May day' riots of 1517. He begins with an evocative image of the outcast foreigner:

> Imagine that you see the wretched strangers,
> Their babies at their backs, with their poor luggage
> Plodding to th'ports and coasts for transportation,
> And that you sit as kings in your desires ...

> (Add.II.D 83–6)

But rather than emphasize their strangeness or the difference in their class status, his speech works to redefine the foreigner in familiar terms and thus to bring the banisher closer to the position of banished:

Say now the King,
As he is clement if th'offender mourn,
Should so much come too short of your great trespass
As but to banish you: whither would you go?
What country, by the nature of your error,
Should give you harbour? Go you to France or Flanders,
To any German province, Spain or Portugal,
Nay, anywhere that not adheres to England –
Why, you must needs be strangers. Would you be pleased
To find a nation of such barbarous temper
That breaking out in hideous violence
Would not afford you an abode on earth,
Whet their detested knives against your throats,
Spurn you like dogs, and like as if that God
Owed not nor made not you, nor that the elements
Were not all appropriate to your comforts
But chartered unto them, what would you think
To be thus used? This is the strangers' case,
And this your mountainish inhumanity.

(137–55)

By insisting upon the inhumanity of the banisher, this speech implies the greater civility of the banished man. Foreigners may be spurned like dogs but it is the native who shows 'barbarous' and 'detested' violence. What is most interesting in this speech is its mingling of nationalist sentiment, expressed through the chauvinism it encourages about being anywhere other than England, with a kind of cultural empathy which works to dissolve those distinctions. Banishment on the stage may well have appealed to an audience for its endorsement of patriotic feeling. How terrible would it be to be forced upon the kindness of strangers, deprived of one's tongue and thus of one's humanity, to be singled out as an outcast by one's peers? As I will argue in Chapter 2, the anachronisms in *Richard II* suggest that the play was intended to frighten its audience with the loss of England and thus of themselves. However, the reach of Shakespeare's banishment plays is much broader, questioning the conditions of identity itself. The audience is consistently asked to imagine itself banished, not simply to encourage appreciation of what social and national marks of identity they possess, but to undermine their confidence in these distinctions.

Of course, Shakespeare's drama of exile is self-consciously metatheatrical. Every exile must decide how he will appear in the future: whether to adopt a disguise and perhaps a new accent, what name to call himself and what history to invent, in his estrangement from the world. But perhaps the most obsessive concern of these plays is language, wherein lies the originality of Shakespeare's representation of exile. For, no other dramatist asked so insistently what happens when the language by which the individual is known turns against him or her – through the word or 'sentence' of banishment – or explored the dilemma of transforming or adapting one's own alienated speech. In every play, the exile's language changes: in the tragedies, it is choked by densely metaphorical lamentation; in the comedies, by the smugly self-conscious Stoic or Epicurean consolation. Yet, in each case, the exile's survival depends upon the possibility of sustaining *any* language in isolation from the linguistic community. The most basic equation of Shakespearean exile is that language equals creativity and thus power. Language-loss equates to silence, impotence and death. These two possibilities, played out as comedy and tragedy, are frequently juxtaposed by Shakespeare within a single play, for example through the characters of Bolingbroke and Richard II, Hal and Falstaff, Edgar and King Lear, or Prospero and the shipwrecked men. Through this *dialogue* about exile, Shakespeare's plays examine not only the precondition of art (and thus of their own existence) but the linguistic foundations of identity.

This study will focus on eight of Shakespeare's plays that banish their protagonists.[104] In *Romeo and Juliet* (1594–95), I focus upon the tragic power of the word 'banishèd' and the lovers' attachment to Verona which renders them more susceptible to that word, comparing this scenario with the banishment of Valentine in *The Two Gentlemen of Verona* (1590–91). The association of exile with political and poetic creativity or impotence will be explored in the chapter on *Richard II* (1595). My study of *Henry IV* Parts One and Two (*c.*1597) argues that the 'tragic' banishment of Falstaff is consistently undermined by the presence of a pastoral narrative of exile centred on Prince Hal at Eastcheap. A more detailed exploration of the conventions of pastoral exile shapes the interpretation of *As You Like It* (1599) and of *King Lear* (1605) in Chapter 4. In *Coriolanus* (1608), I consider the theme of the alienated Roman, banished from his archetypal city and from Roman history, in Plutarchan, Ciceronian and Shakespearean terms. Finally, in *The Tempest* (1611), Prospero's position as exile is examined in the light of the Aristotelian maxim that the exile is either a beast or a god, and with reference to contemporary ideas about magic and colonialism. This book does not claim to offer an exhaustive account of banishment in early modern England or even in the drama of the period, but rather to explain the function of banishment in Shakespeare's plays at a literal, figurative and symbolic level, and to explore the range of meanings available to audiences familiar with the various contemporary discourses of banishment.

1

'That One Word "Banishèd"': Linguistic Crisis in *Romeo and Juliet*

Stunned at the news of Romeo's exile, Juliet utters the word 'banishèd' five times in 13 lines. If this statistic strikes us, like most statistics, as possibly illuminating but essentially dull, that is very much the attitude which directors and critics have taken to the repetition of the word. Indeed, its effects are assumed to be so fatal to an audience's involvement in the play that many directors substantially cut the speeches in which it occurs.[1] This chapter will reclaim the word 'banishèd' from such ignominy by arguing that it has a crucial dramatic role in *Romeo and Juliet*. We will begin with a brief consideration of the significance of exile in Elizabethan love poetry, including the status of 'banished', 'exile' and their variants, as clichés. We will then move on to consider how Shakespeare revivified these words to illuminate not only the lovers' response to exile but their relationship with language throughout the play. Finally, a comparison with *The Two Gentlemen of Verona* will reveal the fatal power of 'banishèd'.

The metaphor of banishment, like so much else in Elizabethan poetry, traces its immediate origins back to Petrarch. Perhaps the most enduring image of the *Rime sparse* is of the poet wandering alone in a deserted landscape. Sonnet 35 begins:

> Solo et pensoso i più deserti campi
> vo mesurando a passi tardi et lenti,
> et gli occhi porto per fuggire intenti
> ove vestigio uman la rena stampi.
>
> Altro schermo non trovo che mi scampi
> dal manifesto accorger de le genti,
> perché negli atti d'allegrezza spenti
> di fuor si legge com' io dentro avampi.

(1–8)

[Alone and filled with care, I go measuring the most deserted fields with steps delaying and slow, and I keep my eyes alert so as to flee from where any human footprint marks the sand. No other shield do I find to protect me from people's open knowing, for in my bearing, in which all happiness is extinguished, anyone can read from without how I am aflame within.][2]

The poet's lamentations are heard in silent sympathy by the trees and hills (71). Landscape and memory conspire to make Laura present when the poet recognizes traces of her in the natural world (125, 126). But elsewhere Petrarch insists that the lover's solitude is not self-imposed. By figuring absence as exile, he heightens the tension between possession and loss, characteristic of desire. The lover's plight is explicitly associated with exile, *esilio*, in sonnet 45 and song 80, but we can see this theme at its most powerful in sonnet 209. It begins with the loss of self:

> I dolci colli ov' io lasciai me stesso,
> partendo onde partir giamai non posso,
> mi vanno innanzi, et emmi ogni or a dosso
> quel caro peso ch'Amor m'à commesso.
>
> Meco di me mi meraviglio spesso
> ch' i' pur vo sempre, et non son ancor mosso
> dal bel giogo più volte indarno scosso,
> ma com' più me n'allungo et più m'appresso.

(1–8)

[The sweet hills where I left myself, when I departed from the place I can never depart from, are before me as I go, and still behind me is that sweet burden Love has entrusted to me. Within myself I am often amazed at myself, for I still go and yet have not moved from the sweet yoke that I have shaken off in vain many times, but the farther I go from it the closer I come.]

To leave a place you cannot leave, to move without moving, this is not simply an example of Petrarchan paradox or, more generally, of that mood of vacillation and of stasis which the English sonnet tradition embraced so fervently. These lines also suggest part of the appeal of exile as a metaphor in Petrarchan poetry and its English successors. Exile enforces absence from the structures by which the exile knows himself, hence he can physically leave but may feel that some aspect of himself remains. Moreover, exile intensifies the relationship between desire and death.[3] The banished man who returns to his native land fears the rigour of the law which threatens death, but he is inevitably drawn towards his own extinction. One conceit which Petrarch used to explore the danger of desire is the separation of hearts based on the *migration du coeur* tradition. This described the lover's longing for union with his beloved through the image of his heart passing into her body. Sonnet 21 offers a variation on this theme wherein the woman rejects his offering:

> Mille fiate, o dolce mia guerrera,
> per aver co' begli occhi vostri pace
> v'aggio proferto il cor, m'a voi non piace
> mirar sì basso colla mente altera;
>
> (1–4)

[A thousand times, O my sweet warrior, in order to have peace with your lovely eyes, I have offered you my heart; but it does not please you to gaze so low with your lofty mind]

As a result of the woman's rejection, the poet too scorns his heart and refuses to take it back. Yet he fears the mortal consequences of this action:

> Or s' io lo scaccio, et e' non trova in voi
> ne l'esilio infelice alcun soccorso,
> né sa star sol, né gire ov' altri il chiama,
>
> poria smarrire il suo natural corso;
> che grave colpa fia d'ambeduo noi,
> et tanto più de voi quanto più v'ama.
>
> (9–14)

[Now if I drive him away, and he does not find in you any help in his sad exile, nor can stay alone, nor go where some other calls him, his natural course of life might fail, which would be a grave fault in both of us, and so much the more yours as he loves you the more.][4]

Exile is already associated with death, as is the grief caused by despised love. To this conceit is added the physiological impossibility of surviving without a heart.

It was this banished Petrarch, the lover forever exiled from Laura, who was most familiar to Elizabethan England, but there was another. Petrarch was born in exile after his father was banished from Florence in 1301 and he spent much of his adult life perpetuating this condition by extensive travels around Europe. The Florentine seems to have taken pride in his alienation, declaring in the *Epistulae metricae* that 'I have no permanent land or sky; an inhabitant of no place, I am thus a pilgrim everywhere'.[5] While advancing exile as a crucial aspect of his autobiography, Petrarch also explored the pleasures and pains of exile in a number of consolatory letters to banished friends and in his *De vita solitaria* (1346).[6] In the latter, exile is celebrated as freedom and, more importantly, as an opportunity for study and literary endeavour. It is this belief in the eloquence of banishment that unites the two banished Petrarchs. The lover of the *Rime* is inspired to write poetry by the necessity of remembering. His consciousness of alienation from the essence of his being inspires repeated acts of self-definition as lover and as poet. More prosaically, *De vita solitaria* associates solitude with eloquence, in particular oratory. Petrarch cites Seneca and Cicero when he insists that only the man who has no interest in literature can ever really suffer exile.[7]

Since they came at Petrarch's poetry from a considerable remove, it is difficult to know what Elizabethan sonneteers knew of his literal banishment. In *A Defence of Ryme* (1603), Samuel Daniel demonstrates familiarity with a wide range of Petrarchan verse and prose, including specific references to Petrarch's moral philosophy (e.g. *De remediis utriusque fortunae*), his history of the Punic Wars (*Africa*) and his three books of Latin verse epistles (the *Epistulae metricae*).[8] Readers of Latin could have traced the theme of exile in Petrarch's work through the *Opera quae extant omnia* (Basle, 1554, 1581) but those who wished to read him in English were often dependent on manuscript translations such as Sir John Harington's *The Prayse of Private Life*. This adaptation of *De vita solitaria* (previously quoted on exile) was presented by Daniel to his patron, Margaret Clifford, some time after 1605.[9] However, difficulties of transmission are not the most significant obstacle to a familiarity with Petrarch as exile. His experience was clearly overshadowed by the dramatic expulsion of Dante. Moreover, the Petrarchan lover bewailing his *figurative* exile seems to have obtained such a purchase on the Elizabethan English imagination that any literal context might well have been forgotten.

With the passion for Englishing Petrarch, initiated by Wyatt and Surrey but flowering in the sonnet sequences of the 1590s, exile becomes a central metaphor for the lovely torment that is absence from the beloved. But while the other Petrarchan metaphors which the Elizabethans used so freely, of love-in-death, the storm-tossed ship, the beloved's eyes like sun and stars, etc., have been carefully catalogued, the Petrarchan antecedents of banishment have not been traced. This is an important omission because it means that the truism that Petrarchan conventions became debased currency in the Elizabethan period, as likely to be satirized as straightforwardly imitated, has not been extended to banishment. One of this chapter's arguments is that Petrarch's success in the creation of the exiled lover made absence such a conventional aspect of desire that it became difficult to represent any kind of literal expulsion. Moreover, when the terms which describe this estrangement become conventional, exile is no longer that experience of heightened eloquence and creativity which Petrarch imagined.

In the early 1570s, the courtier, Sir Edward Dyer, wrote a lyric called 'A Fancy' which became popular among his contemporaries: it was imitated by Fulke Greville and satirized by Robert Southwell. The poet complains of his enforced separation from a cruel mistress and, in an obvious debt to Petrarch, describes the transformation of the landscape in her absence:

> The sollitarie woodes my Cittie shall become:
> The darkest den shalbe my lodge, whereto noe light shall come:
>
> Of heban blacke my boorde, the wormes my feast shalbe,
> Wherewith my Carcasse shalbe fed, till they doe feede on mee:
>
> My wine of Niobe, my bedd the cragie rocke,
> The serpents hysse my harmony, the scritchinge owle my clock:
>
> Mine Exercise naught ells but raginge agonies,
> My bookes of spightfull fortunes foiles and drerye tragedies:

But after an extensive catalogue of these transformations, the poet begins to doubt their affective power:

> And though I seeme to use the Poets fained stile,
> To figure forth my wofull plight, my fall, and my Exile;
>
> Yet is my greefe not faind, wherein I strive and pine:
> Whoe feeleth most, shall finde it least, comparinge his with mine.

> (ll. 63–76)[10]

Dyer's rejection of poetic artifice in pursuit of a more 'genuine' language is itself conventional. What is striking is the suggestion that exile has become a cliché which can no longer be trusted to elicit sympathy from an audience. Though Dyer seems to juxtapose the 'Poet's fained stile' with the reality of 'my fall and my Exile', the latter are familiar tragic metaphors from those 'bookes of spightfull fortunes' and 'drerye tragedies' (such as *A Mirror for Magistrates*) which Dyer claims he is now doomed to read. The capitalization of 'exile', reproduced here from the Ashmolean manuscript, draws attention to the word, reinforcing its tragic resonance, but also perhaps highlighting its status as a metaphor. Hence, 'Exile' is an effect of the 'figuring forth' Dyer claims to reject. Moreover, the juxtaposition of 'Exile' with the next line 'Yet is my greefe not faind' reinforces the suggestion that the former lacks the force it once possessed to depict alienation and loss.

If we consider the context in which 'A Fancy' was written, this linguistic problem takes on a new significance. In 1571, for reasons still unknown, Dyer had fallen into disfavour with Elizabeth and departed the court. In his retirement, he wrote a number of plangent lyrics on his sufferings in exile, including this poem. As we will see in the next chapter, the pose of the banished man was frequently adopted by the dejected courtier, and to material effect. Dyer's recall to court was occasioned not by 'A Fancy' but by another lyric, 'The Songe in the Oke', which he performed for Elizabeth during her sojourn at Woodstock in 1575.[11] It features a man wandering, friendless, in a deserted landscape where he is occupied in 'endlesse plainte'. Perhaps, then, Dyer's anxiety about 'Exile' in the earlier poem reveals his trust in that metaphor's power to end 'real' banishment – a trust that would prove well placed. In general, however, Elizabethan love poetry seems to have widened the gap between the reality of exile and its status as an amatory trope. Twenty years after 'A Fancy', one of the most curious examples of this is the opening sonnet of Henry Constable's sequence, *Diana*, published in 1592. The sequence begins:

> To his absent Diana
>
> Sever'd from sweete Content, my lives sole light;
> Banisht by over-weening wit from my desire:
> This poore acceptance only I require,
> That though my fault have forc'd me from thy sight;
> Yet that thou wouldst (my sorrowes to requite)
> Review these Sonnets, pictures of thy praise;
> Wherein each woe thy wondrous worth doth raise,
> Though first thy worth bereft me of delight.
> See them forsaken: for I them forsooke,
> Forsaken first of thee, next of my sence;
> And when thou deignst on their blacke teares to looke,
> Shed not one teare my teares to recompence:
> But joy in this (though Fates gainst mee repine)
> My verse still lives, to witnes thee divine.

We might imagine behind this poem some particular instance of courtly exile, that is of the mistress denying access to the lover. However, if we read the sonnet in terms of authorial biography the theme of banishment comes into sharper focus. It was around 1590, when *Diana* is thought to have been largely completed, that Constable converted to Catholicism and went into exile in France, not to return until 1603. Perhaps a reference in the 1592 edition of *Diana* draws attention to this exile: the Epistle to the Reader refers to the sonnets being 'left as Orphans'. Moreover, when the sequence appeared in the Todd manuscript two years later it was prefaced by a poem which explicitly lamented Constable's condition: 'Englands sweete nightingale what frights thee so / As over sea to make thee take thy flight?'[12] It may be that Constable's readers, within the private circle afforded by manuscript, were encouraged to view the sonnet sequence as connected with the exile of its author. Yet there is little in the sonnets themselves to anticipate such a reading. The opening sonnet, in particular, elides any literal context. The synonyms offered for banishment – to be forced into absence, forsaken, bereft – reinforce the poetic theme while distancing the literal. Although the poet is clearly the subject of 'banisht', he renders ambiguous both who does the banishing and how it was incurred. 'Over-weening wit' could ostensibly refer to both the poet's ambition which caused him to be exiled and the lady herself. Similarly, the passive form 'my fault have forc'd me' refrains from casting the lady in the role of banisher. The extent to which banishment is deliteralized, and even depersonalized, so that in the course of the sonnet the verse *displaces* the poet as the forsaken, is significant if we recall that Constable was exiled in France at the time. If not for the poet himself, then at least for his audience, the metaphor of banishment existed at a strange remove from the facts of enforced absence.

It might be argued that Constable is a minor Elizabethan poet not renowned for his original use of poetic conceits.[13] However, if we consider the appearance of banishment in other sonnet sequences we find it occurring in witty, often allegorical contexts, not freighted with any emotional import. In *Astrophil and Stella* (*c.* 1582, pub. 1591), Cupid and Desire are threatened with banishment (46, 72), and Astrophil constructs an elaborate simile between Stella's face and the garden of the Hesperides, urging that he not be banished from those lips which surpass the Hesperidean apples (82). Samuel Daniel also uses banishment allegorically in sonnet 22 of *Delia* (1592):

> False hope prolongs my ever certaine griefe;
> Traytrous to me and faithfull to my love:
> A thousand times it promis'd me reliefe,
> Yet never any true effect I prove.
> Oft when I finde in her no trueth at all,
> I banish her, and blame her trechery:
> Yet soone againe I must her backe recall,
> As one that dyes without her company.

$$(1–8)^{14}$$

While absence remains a central theme of the sonnet sequence, and desire is still represented as temptation versus prohibition, possession versus loss, banishment is less frequently used to describe these states. It is notably lacking from the sonnets on absence in Sidney's and Shakespeare's sequences, and when Spenser refers to it in the *Amoretti* (sonnet 52), exile is one among a number of metaphors for separation; it describes a repeated leave-taking, a familiar event. Somehow exile has lost its drama.

It will be my argument throughout this book that the poet of this period who rediscovered and fully exploited the drama of exile was Shakespeare and perhaps no play exemplifies this more powerfully than *Romeo and Juliet*. Romeo's banishment should not be a surprise to the Petrarchan lover. Some enforced absence from the beloved is an essential part of the ritual of excitement and frustration. Indeed, it creates desire and allows the lover to know himself in love. But in *Romeo and Juliet*, banishment cannot be contained within the limits of the sonnet sequence or embraced as metaphor. Rather, it brings the lovers up against the limits of poetry to describe the world by showing them an experience which seems to undermine not only poetic but also civic and social commonplaces.

Critics have pondered the question of whether Shakespeare's tragedy of feuding, murder and exile was inspired by real-life events. In 1594, Sir Charles and Sir Henry Danvers fled abroad after the former had killed Henry Long in a fight at an inn. Shakespeare's patron, the Earl of Southampton, gave sanctuary to the men and it is argued that Shakespeare himself might have been at Titchfield while the fugitives were hiding there.[15] But although this event may have directed the dramatist's source-hunting, it lacks some crucial elements. If, as I am arguing here, Shakespeare was concerned with the exploding of a Petrarchan cliché, he needed a source which not only focused on the banishment of lovers but also located itself in the Petrarchan tradition.

If Shakespeare had not come across banishment as a poetic commonplace from his study of contemporary sonnets, he would certainly have found it in Arthur Brooke's *The Tragicall Historye of Romeus and Juliet* (London, 1562). Here, Brooke uses the word 'banished' with prodigality. Indeed, considering the fate of the lovers, it seems rather tasteless to bandy it around as he does. For example, early on in the poem Romeus decides to forsake Rosaline in the hope that once his eye is 'banished by absence from her sight', his passion will fade (86).[16] Another frequent use concerns the individual's emotional and physical state, e.g. the banishment of care, hope, sorrow or joy. But perhaps the most callous deployment of the metaphor occurs after Romeus has learnt of his exile. Brooke describes Romeus' recovery from despair as a result of the Friar's good counsel:

> As blackest cloudes are chaced, by winters nimble winde,
> So have his reasons chaced care out of his carefull mynde.
> As of a morning foule, ensues an evening fayre,
> So banisht hope returneth home to banish his despayre.

> (1,483–6)

Where Brooke deadens the effect of 'banished' upon Romeus by such frequent metaphorical use, Shakespeare preserves the power of the word. He only employs it to describe the fate which befalls Romeo and thus it bursts violently onto the stage:

> Some word there was, worser than Tybalt's death,
> That murdered me. I would forget it fain,
> But O, it presses to my memory
> Like damnèd guilty deeds to sinners' minds!
> 'Tybalt is dead, and Romeo banishèd'.
> That 'banishèd', that one word 'banishèd'
> Hath slain ten thousand Tybalts ...
>
> 'Romeo is banishèd' – to speak that word
> Is father, mother, Tybalt, Romeo, Juliet,
> All slain, all dead. 'Romeo is banishèd' –
> There is no end, no limit, measure, bound,
> In that word's death. No words can that woe sound.

(3.2.108–14, 122–6)

Here, banishment has escaped the lyric convention whereby it signifies the poet's Petrarchan indebtedness and his linguistic *sprezzatura* as much as the experience of absence. Banishment has become dramatic, performative, making absence present. In the rest of this chapter we will consider how the word 'banishèd' relates to a paradox about language in *Romeo and Juliet*, and, more generally, how banishment undermines the linguistic and social codes through which identity is constructed.

In *The Art of Pronuntiation* (1617), Robert Robinson contrasts the gross substance and the durability of written language with the ephemerality of the spoken word: 'though the voice be a more lively kind of speech, yet in respect it is but onely a sleight accident made of so light a substance as the ayre, so it is no sooner uttered but it is dissolved ...'[17] Composed not simply of air but of human breath, speech may also serve as a reminder of human mortality. Every utterance is shaped by the need for the speaker to take a breath; each inspiration draws him closer to his end. However, Shakespeare and his contemporaries had also inherited a definition of 'vox', the voiced sound of language, as material formed from the striking of air. The medieval grammarian, Priscian, in his *Institutio Grammaticarum*, attributed to the voice height, width and length: all properties of matter.[18] Moreover, the physicality of language could be assumed because of its ability to *affect* matter. Neoplatonic magic depended on the communication between words and things: words could raise tempests, afflict the body with sickness or health, inspire love or hatred. The lingering superstition about cursing conceived of the efficacy of certain speech acts to perform vengeance on the possessions or body of the offender.[19]

Throughout *Romeo and Juliet*, the protagonists reject 'airy' words in the search for words that matter. The 'airy' word is a commonplace, that is transient, trivial, depersonalizing. It is the speech of the marketplace, of the ancient quarrel and of Petrarchan love poetry. It is a language that expresses only the speaker's commitment to society and cannot express the individual or make him known. Words that *matter* individuate the speaker but they may also have a performative power. It is the Prince's word of banishment that not only compels Romeo into exile but also releases the fatal power of language upon the protagonists. The play explores the paradox that language can be composed of breath and yet material, transient to the ear but permanent in its effect on human flesh.

Romeo and Juliet begins with a scene of violence derived from the trivial word. The Capulet servants have deliberately sought a fight with the Montague, Abram, in a comically brief exchange. Abram merely has to say 'You lie' and the swords are drawn. As the Prince remonstrates:

> Three civil brawls bred of an airy word
> By thee, old Capulet, and Montague,
> Have thrice disturbed the quiet of our streets.
>   (1.1.86–8)

The jibe is trivial, insubstantial and borne away by the wind. The violence incited leads to bloodshed and destruction that is palpable and permanent. This juxtaposition of airy words and blows implies the triviality of the feud but it also hints at the power of 'insubstantial' language to destroy.

Later in this scene, the same concern with immaterial words is reflected in the world of Petrarchan love. Benvolio and Montague represent Romeo as the antithesis to civil violence. He is the sentimental lover, passive, solitary, melancholic. Yet Romeo recognizes the relevance of the fighting to his own experience:

> O me! What fray was here?
> Yet tell me not, for I have heard it all.
> Here's much to do with hate, but more with love.
> Why then, O brawling love, O loving hate,
> O anything of nothing first create;
> O heavy lightness, serious vanity,
> Misshapen chaos of well-seeming forms,
> Feather of lead, bright smoke, cold fire, sick health,
> Still-waking sleep, that is not what it is!
> This love feel I, that feel no love in this.
>
>   (1.1.170–9)

Romeo employs the paradox of love and violence, of wooing as waging war, which is essential to Petrarchan poetry. The love/war conceit has already been expressed in the violent and bawdy puns of Capulet's servants and it remains a constant pressure throughout the play in the love-death imagery which reaches its apotheosis in the fusion of wedding-bed and death-bed. As the prologue foretells, Romeo is right to associate love with violence. Yet the primary impact of this speech is to persuade us that Romeo's love lacks substance, that it too is bred of an 'airy word'. The anti-Petrarchan voice incipient in Benvolio reminds us that these oxymorons were dying metaphors at the time of the play's composition. They are losing their power to signify:

> The Petrarchan style aspires to pure poetry and in so aspiring becomes an airy, hyperbolic, mechanically artificial expression of unfelt and undiscriminating feelings. In this sense it is too pure ('Virtue itself turns vice, being misapplied' – 2.3.21), and when the too pure becomes too popular it turns impure, an infectious blight on the literary landscape.[20]

Mercutio is fully aware of the conventions that define Romeo as a lover: 'Now is he for the numbers that Petrarch flowed in' (2.3.36–7). What Mercutio finds particularly irksome about this style is its airy hyperbole, its elevation of frustrated desire to the status of the transcendent and divine. He tries to prove the impotence of this language by pretending to conjure Romeo with it:

> Romeo! Humours! Madman! Passion! Lover!
> Appear thou in the likeness of a sigh.
> Speak but one rhyme and I am satisfied.
> Cry but 'Ay me!' Pronounce but 'love' and 'dove'.
>
> (2.1.7–10)

The fact that Romeo does not appear might be taken as evidence of Petrarchan self-loss: 'Tut, I have lost myself. I am not here. / This is not Romeo; he's some other where' (1.2.194–5). Yet it also draws attention to the stubborn reality of human flesh (which cannot be conjured in this way) in contrast with the ethereality of the language which pretends to define it. A similar effect is created when Mercutio tries to summon the lover in Rosaline's name (17–21). We are reminded that Rosaline never appears on stage, that she exists only to be supplanted by Juliet. Indeed, by this point, Romeo has already forgotten his former love. Thus Mercutio demonstrates how ineffective Petrarchan terms are to define Romeo or his affections. He offers instead a language that brings the lover down to earth and an action that will produce physical satisfaction: 'If love be rough with you, be rough with love. / Prick love for pricking, and you beat love down' (1.4.27–8).

To some extent, Romeo also recognizes it as a failure of language that his love is not more substantial. He employs Petrarchan terms to persuade Rosaline to give up her much-prized chastity and give him some physical return for his words but laments that she will not 'stay the siege of loving terms' nor receive his 'saint-seducing gold' (1.1.209, 211).[21] Romeo's materialist ambitions are represented by an airy, transcendent idiom. However, when Romeo finds 'real love', he does not require a new language to describe the revelation that is Juliet but retains all the hyperbole and imagery of the old. For him, the language is newly validated by its discovery of substance. John Donne's *Songs and Sonnets* (published 1633) can enrich our understanding of *Romeo and Juliet* for its similar reworking of Petrarchan conventions. 'Air and Angels', which may have been written in the 1590s, describes Romeo's predicament in having all the structures of love but lacking its substance:

> Twice or thrice had I loved thee,
> Before I knew thy face or name;
> So in a voice, so in a shapeless flame,
> Angels affect us oft, and worshipped be;
> Still when, to where thou wert, I came,
> Some lovely glorious nothing I did see,
> But since my soul, whose child love is,
> Takes limbs of flesh, and else could nothing do,
> More subtle than the parent is
> Love must not be, but take a body too,
> And therefore what thou wert, and who
> I bid love ask, and now
> That it assume thy body, I allow,
> And fix itself in thy lip, eye, and brow.

$$(1-14)^{22}$$

When Romeo sees Juliet, he rejects Rosaline and calls Juliet 'beauty' and then 'love'. Moreover, Juliet reciprocates by naming Romeo 'love' and by filling out the poetic structure of a sonnet. In their conversation about Rosaline, Romeo and Benvolio frequently spoke in rhyming couplets and Romeo in quatrains. The sonnet existed here but unformed, in disparate pieces, waiting to be created between Romeo and Juliet at the Capulet feast. It is not only that Juliet is willing to match the Montague line for line. She also offers him a substantial return for his conceits. Like the saints who do not 'move', Juliet remains still so that Romeo can kiss her. The sonnet leads to action. The Petrarchan language becomes performative as the sonnet to Rosaline was meant to be.

   However, although Juliet conforms to the sonnet convention here, she is famously sceptical about the substantiating power of language. In the orchard, she defies the word that makes Romeo her enemy:

> What's in a name? That which we call a rose
> By any other word would smell as sweet.

> So Romeo would, were he not Romeo called,
> Retain that dear perfection which he owes
> Without that title. Romeo, doff thy name,
> And for that name – which is no part of thee –
> Take all myself.

(2.1.85–91)

Juliet tries to suggest that words are insubstantial, a name is no part of Romeo's anatomy and therefore it ought to be easily cast off. This desire to make their union nameless recurs in the epithalamium when she imagines the lovers finding one another without light or speech (3.2.7). The paradox inherent in Juliet's nameless fantasy is elucidated by Catherine Belsey:

> These isolated, unnamed bodies (and roses) are only imaginary. The human body is already inscribed: it has no existence as pure organism, independent of the symbolic order in which desire makes sense. In the sixteenth-century text Juliet's imagined act of love is paradoxically defined in a densely metaphoric and tightly structured instance of signifying practice [...] The text specifies a wish in a tissue of formally ordered allusions, comparisons and puns, which constitute a poem, the zenith of signification, self-conscious, artful, witty.[23]

This paradox is a crucial element in the tragedy. Where the characters appear to seek a private universe and a secret language, they are deeply conventional. Romeo values Petrarchanism because it has the weight of social as well as poetic convention behind it. It inspires the bookish terms of Lady Capulet's eulogy on Paris (1.3.83–94) and Capulet's description of Juliet grieving (3.5.130–7), and provides the father with conceits by which to lament his daughter's death (4.4.62–6). As Jill Levenson has shown, Petrarchan language is very much part of the daily intercourse of Veronese society.[24] Indeed, Juliet rejects the debased airy language of love only to opt for an even more public and impersonal word:

> Although I joy in thee,
> I have no joy of this contract tonight.
> It is too rash, too unadvised, too sudden,
> Too like the lightning which doth cease to be
> Ere one can say it lightens.

(158–62)

Juliet's use of the term 'contract', of 'rash and 'unadvised', reminds us that she is as conventional as Romeo but that her book is that of civic law rather than Petrarch's *Rime*.[25] The strongest words of love Juliet can imagine are those of matrimony, witnessed by the Church and by society. It is through this language that she will seek to define their relationship, thus strengthening their bond with the community. For, although the marriage remains private, the fact that they have entered into it within Verona's walls testifies to their definition by the city and by its rituals. Hence, the convention by which Romeo and Juliet should hate one another is legitimated by their marriage.

Act 3, scene 1, brings to a climax this question of the substantiality of language. Here, we have two performative utterances – Mercutio's curse and the Prince's sentence of exile – which radically redefine the perceived power of language in the rest of the play.

It is often argued that the death of Mercutio marks a shift from comedy to tragedy.[26] This transformation is partly effected through a curse on Capulets and Montagues: 'A plague o' both your houses. / They have made worms' meat of me. / I have it, and soundly too. Your houses!' (3.1.106–8).[27] A curse necessarily posits the incarnation of a word. Indeed, Calderwood suggests that Mercutio's 'plague' on both households is realized when it is a plague that prevents the Friar's letter from reaching Romeo.[28] More generally, Mercutio's curse reinforces the prophetic words of the prologue: 'From forth the fatal loins of these two foes / A pair of star-crossed lovers take their life' (5–6). But it is not only the prologue which determines their fate; 'fatal' (mortal, fateful) 'loins' (loins, *lines*) hints at the considerable body of literature which had already condemned Romeo and Juliet to death. For example, Brooke's *Tragicall Historye* refers to a play, now lost, as one source. A more obvious predecessor would be the French version of the story by Pierre Boaistuau, itself based on Matteo Bandello's *Romeo e Giulietta* (1554).[29] The play must end with the lovers' deaths not only because of its title, the 'lamentable tragedy', or even because of its opening sonnet, but because it carries the weight of half a century at least of mythology.

Yet Mercutio's curse is not only significant because it adds to the number of prophecies that the tragic conclusion will substantiate. It also signals the vulnerability to language from which Romeo and Juliet will suffer in this second half of the play. After Mercutio's death and Romeo's revenge, curses proliferate. When the Nurse joins Juliet in vilification of Romeo ('Shame come to Romeo'), Juliet repents at once: 'Blistered be thy tongue / For such a wish! He was not born to shame' (3.2.90–1). Juliet reclaims the essential Romeo, the rose that exists despite the name of murderer. Yet the slanders poured upon Romeo's name have already taken effect: 'Ah, poor my lord, what tongue shall smooth thy name / When I, thy three-hours wife, have mangled it?' (3.2.98–9). In both 3.2 and 3.3, words are increasingly deadly. Even a monosyllable such as 'Ay' threatens to wreak disaster on the listener. Responding to the Nurse's confused lamentation, Juliet asks:

> Hath Romeo slain himself? Say thou but 'Ay',
> And that bare vowel 'I' shall poison more

> Than the death-darting eye of cockatrice.
> I am not I if there be such an 'Ay'.

(3.2.45–8)

The word which told Juliet of Romeo's love, 'I know thou wilt say "Ay"' (2.1.132), would now poison her with his death. This transformation of 'Ay' endorses Juliet's nominalist instinct that words are too unstable and too general to describe her lover or her love. But while this multiplicity of meaning implied the insubstantiality of language before, Juliet now finds that words are reified into weapons that attack the lovers' own substance. It is no coincidence that one of the most lethal linguistic weapons in the play is the word 'banishèd'. In 3.3, Romeo accuses the Friar:

> Hadst thou no poison mixed, no sharp-ground knife,
> No sudden mean of death, though ne'er so mean,
> But 'banishèd' to kill me – 'banishèd'?
> O friar, the damnèd use that word in hell.
> Howling attends it. How hast thou the heart,
> Being a divine, a ghostly confessor,
> A sin-absolver and my friend professed,
> To mangle me with that word 'banishèd'?

(3.3.44–51)

The Prince's banishment of Romeo is the most powerfully performative speech act of the play, as Juliet testifies:

> 'Romeo is banishèd' – to speak that word
> Is father, mother, Tybalt, Romeo, Juliet,
> All slain, all dead. 'Romeo is banishèd' –
> There is no end, no limit, measure, bound,
> In that word's death. No words can that woe sound.

(3.2.122–6)

'Banishèd' in the mouth of the Prince redefined Romeo as an exile before he had left the city. All the Prince needed to say was that 'Immediately we do exile him hence' (3.1.186). This sentence of exile thus encompasses the paradox about language we have been considering: it is a composition of breath and therefore transient, but it effects an endless, inexpressible woe. In 3.3, the Friar describes banishment to Romeo in similar terms, recalling that 'A gentler judgement vanished from his lips: / Not body's death, but body's banishment' (3.3.10–11). G. Blakemore Evans gives two possible meanings for 'vanished': 'breathed out like so much air (compare "airy word" and "airy tongue")' or 'issued without possibility of recall'.[30] It is here that the insubstantiality and permanence of 'banishèd' collide.[31] As it is limitless so Romeo's exile drives him beyond all recognizable limits. As it is impossible of recall, so Romeo may be permanently lost.

On one level, 'banishèd' signifies the lovers' failure to create a private language and to release themselves from the public discourse which defined them as enemies and kept them apart. Banishment is the result of Romeo's inability to be nameless, to reconcile the warring Capulet and Montague within himself rather than participate in the feud. But 'banishèd' also makes the lovers aware of how much they are defined by and how much they depend upon Veronese linguistic and social codes. 'Banishèd' gives them a glimpse of an unfamiliar, unmapped world and they recoil from it in horror.

Earlier, it was suggested that 'banishèd' was a poetic cliché with which any Petrarchan lover ought to be familiar. Perhaps then we might locate Romeo and Juliet's responses to exile within a poetic tradition. Romeo's wish that the Friar would kill him rather than repeat that word 'banishèd' is reminiscent of *The Two Gentlemen of Verona* when Valentine bids Proteus: 'No more, unless the next word that thou speak'st / Have some malignant power upon my life' (3.1.236–7). The idea that words could kill, particularly if they enforced absence, is a commonplace in many Petrarch-inspired lyrics, for example Donne's *The Expiration* (1609):

> Go, and if that word hath not quite killed thee,
> Ease me with death, by bidding me go too.
> Oh, if it have, let my word work on me,
> And a just office on a murderer do.
> Except it be too late, to kill me so,
>   Being double dead, going, and bidding, go.
>
> (7–12)

Juliet's frantic repetition of 'banishèd', imagined as causing a general slaughter ('to speak that word / Is father, mother, Tybalt, Romeo, Juliet, / All slain, all dead') begins to look like a turning of the weapon against herself in a proleptic gesture of suicide. Moreover, for Romeo's insistence that the beloved is heaven and exclusion from her presence a kind of hell, we need look no further than *Henry VI Part Two* in which Suffolk declares,

> 'Tis not the land I care for, wert thou thence,
> A wilderness is populous enough,
> So Suffolk had thy heavenly company.
> For where thou art, there is the world itself,
> With every several pleasure in the world;
> And where thou art not, desolation.
>
> (3.2.361–6)

But there is a difference in tone between the banishment scenes of *Romeo and Juliet* and these earlier plays, a difference that relates to the use of exile conventions and of rhetoric.

In *The Two Gentlemen of Verona*, Valentine's speech on exile is characterized by its symmetry, created through the use of *parison* ('What light is light if Sylvia be not seen / What joy is joy, if Sylvia be not by' (3.1.174–5)) and through *ploche* (the repetition of 'light', 'joy' and 'Sylvia'), suggesting a measured response to exile. Moreover, the repetition of 'Sylvia' and of 'I' generates an assonance by which 'I' disappears into 'Sylvia', reinforcing the poet's argument that they cannot be separated and, at the same time, offering a kind of lyric solace. In *2 Henry VI*, Suffolk and Margaret speak in elaborately artificial conceits: Margaret's tears become 'monuments', her kiss a 'seal' or imprint, and in a repetition of the *migration du coeur* theme, the banished man carries away his beloved's heart as a 'jewel locked into the woefull'st cask / That ever did contain a thing of worth' (3.2.413–14). Moreover, the fact that Suffolk's lamentation is conducted in dialogue with Margaret, with one speaker taking up the other's rhyme and sometimes finishing the verse line, reinforces our sense of their control over language.

However, in *Romeo and Juliet*, though some of the same metaphors recur, there is a sense of linguistic failure. Juliet cannot do anything with the word 'banishèd' other than repeat it: '"Tybalt is dead and Romeo banishèd". / That "banishèd", that one word "banishèd" / Hath slain ten thousand Tybalts' (3.2.112–13). The awkward dactylic rhythm of the word, its harsh plosive and aggressively short vowels, isolate it from surrounding words; they suggest that 'banishèd' would be difficult to replace with anything else. Throughout the scene, Romeo and Juliet insist that 'banishèd' is not their word but that of the Prince, the Nurse, the Friar. Juliet fails to perform any lyrical or metaphysical trick with 'banishèd' because she refuses to incorporate it. Similarly, although Romeo quibbles frantically on 'flies/fly', he cannot make 'banishèd' into a metaphor. In fact, he explicitly rejects the Friar's argument that the Prince transmuted the sentence from death to exile, turning 'that black word "death" to banishment' (3.3.27). As far as Romeo is concerned, there is no such transformation. Banishment is 'death mistermed' (21).

Earlier, we saw how exile was commonly associated with death in Elizabethan love poetry. *Romeo and Juliet* takes this association further by endorsing the lovers' exile/death wordplay with action. When Juliet leaves the stage in 3.2, she expresses her intention to commit suicide, 'I'll to my wedding bed, / And death, not Romeo, take my maidenhead!' (136–7). Juliet will perform this scene twice, once with a sleeping potion and once with a dagger. After his exile speech, Romeo throws himself on the ground to take 'the measure of an unmade grave' (3.3.70) and shortly afterwards tries to stab himself. Moreover, Lady Montague apparently *does* die from banishment. In the final scene, Montague announces that 'Grief of my son's exile hath stopped her breath' (5.3.210).[32] We might argue that this is another of those Petrarchan conceits that is 'unmetaphored' in the course of the play.[33] Where Romeo describes love as 'A choking gall and a preserving sweet' (1.1.191), he unconsciously predicts his own death by poison and also describes the liquor which preserves Juliet from Paris. When he features love as 'Still-waking sleep, that is not what it is!' (178), he might similarly be anticipating Juliet's death-like trance. But rather than reinforcing the relevance of poetic conventions to the world, I would argue that banishment reveals to the lovers a world wherein such conventions do not apply.

When the Friar tries to offer Romeo philosophy as 'armour' to protect him from that bloody word, Romeo will not listen. He bases his objections on the difference between precept and experience: 'Thou canst not speak of that thou dost not feel' (64). However embarrassed critics are by Romeo's self-pity, this line strikes a note that is hard to ignore.[34] According to the consolation literature of the period (often based on classical texts), it was crucial that the adviser had some experience of the sufferer's grief. As Marcus Aurelius points out in a letter to his banished friend, Domitius, 'in the ende, in thinges whiche touche the sorrowes of the spyryte, and the troubles of the bodye, there is greate difference from hym that hathe *red* them, and from hym that hathe *felt* them'.[35] However, Romeo's resistance extends to all precepts about exile. He may self-consciously perform his grief, but there is a general sense that banishment for the lovers exceeds other people's definitions of it, whether poetic, philosophical, etc. Indeed, this is what they find so appalling. Their lamentations focus on the limitlessness, the indefinability, of exile: 'There is no end, no limit, measure bound / In that word's death.' When the Friar tries to reassure Romeo by reminding him that the world is 'broad and wide' (3.3.16), he chooses terms which reinforce the exile's fears. It is not simply that Romeo and Juliet fear the unknown; they are also concerned with the effects of being unknown. 'Banishèd' was described as a weapon which could 'mangle' Romeo because banishment effectively reshapes him, not only casting a blight upon his name but forcing him outside a context in which that name has meaning. Thus, we might argue that it is not love which Romeo and Juliet fear to lose by banishment but themselves.

In order to explore more fully this question of the lovers' definition, we might compare Romeo's situation with that of Valentine in *The Two Gentlemen of Verona*. It has been said of *Romeo and Juliet* that 'much of the play is actually comedy, close in kind to *The Two Gentlemen*, with which it could almost be a twin birth, the comic and tragic variations on the same theme'.[36] The derivation of both plays from the same source, Brooke's *Tragicall Historye*, partly explains this twinship. If we compare the different ways in which Shakespeare has made use of this source, to comic and tragic effect, we may be able to explain the very different attitudes expressed by

Valentine and Romeo towards banishment. Perhaps the key distinction is to be found in their attitudes towards Verona.

In *The Two Gentlemen of Verona*, Shakespeare has been notoriously careless about location. The First Folio locates the main action of the play in either Verona or Milan, while Padua and Mantua are thrown in for added confusion.[37] Editors have found various ways to emend this text and to explain its eccentricities but the play's vagueness about location does at least reflect its attitude towards travel and adventuring. At the beginning, Valentine is about to depart for Milan. He speaks scathingly of idle and 'Home-keeping youth' and entreats Proteus to seek 'the wonders of the world abroad' (1.1.2–8). Proteus' father is also concerned, arguing that Proteus 'cannot be a perfect man, / Not being tried and tutored in the world' (1.3.20–1). Thus, Proteus too is shortly dispatched from Verona to try his fortune at the Emperor's court. In this new world, both men are metamorphosed and Valentine is banished. But as the play encourages the expansion of their horizons literally and psychologically, so it takes banishment comparatively lightly. Valentine is a traveller at the court of Milan. His parents, friends and his social position are presumably all at Verona, waiting to be reclaimed.[38] Hence, his expressions of despair and self-loss are contingent upon banishment from Sylvia. Yet even this exile is quite painlessly endured until the comic structure brings about their reunion.

The contrast between this and *Romeo and Juliet* could hardly be more marked. To begin with, the tragedy is almost entirely located in Verona. Only Act 5, scene 1, occurs in Mantua and then the play is largely concerned with Romeo's preparations for a return to his native city. Nor is there any suggestion that the young Veronese might leave the city voluntarily. Travel is not associated with pleasure, education or honour as it is in the comedy. When Romeo imagines venturing to 'that vast shore washed with the farthest sea' in pursuit of Juliet (2.1.124–6), he utters a conventional metaphor; his most daring physical transgression at this point has been to climb the orchard walls! Although his name in Italian meant 'wanderer' or 'pilgrim', the closest Romeo gets to any such identity before exile is to play the pilgrim at the Capulet ball.[39] More telling is Juliet's image of Romeo as a bird which she allows to hop a little before pulling it back, 'So loving-jealous of his liberty' (2.1.222–6).

These attitudes obviously colour the way in which both plays deal with the question of elopement. In Brooke's *Tragicall Historye*, Juliet pleads to go with the banished Romeus:

> Receave me as thy servant, and the fellow of thy smart:
> Thy absence is my death, thy sight shall geve me life.
> But if perhaps thou stand in dred, to leade me as a wyfe,
> Art thou all counsellesse, canst thou no shift devise?
> What letteth, but in other weede I may my selfe disguyse?

What, shall I be the first? hath none done so ere this?
To scape the bondage of theyr frendes? thy selfe can aunswer yes.

(1,616–21)

Romeus refuses this plan for several reasons, among them that he considers
it shameful for his wife to dress up as a man (1,681–2).[40] However, in *The
Two Gentlemen of Verona*, Julia does not ask anyone's permission to disguise
herself as a page and to go off in search of Proteus. Sylvia too is quite
willing to elope with Valentine, and abandons family, friends and city for
an uncertain future with a banished man.

In writing *Romeo and Juliet*, Shakespeare returned to details in Brooke that
he had already incorporated once into *The Two Gentlemen of Verona*. Thus,
where Valentine and Sylvia's plan depends upon the use of a rope ladder
(2.4.179–80), so this is the means by which Romeo and his bride are
united. When Valentine is banished, Sylvia assumes that he is in Mantua
where Romeo too spends his exile. Finally, Sylvia tells Sir Eglamour that she
must leave Verona to escape 'a most unholy match' (4.3.30), defined in
Romeo and Juliet as Juliet's bigamous union with Paris. Yet there is one
crucial element missing. Shakespeare chose to ignore the possibility of
elopement in *Romeo and Juliet*. It does not feature in Romeo's desperate
conjectures, nor does Juliet ever suggest it, though she earlier declared that,
once married, she would 'follow thee, my lord, throughout the world'
(2.1.190).[41]

How are we to account for these differences? Obviously, generic conventions, the different teleology of comedy and tragedy, shape the action of
the plays. It has also been argued that in *Romeo and Juliet* Shakespeare
locates the death drive of tragedy within Verona itself; the ancient feud is
just one expression of the Veronese ideology which determines the lovers'
overthrow. In a penetrating analysis of the play, Susan Snyder describes the
claustrophobic atmosphere of Verona. The friar bearing the letter for
Romeo is not merely detained in the city but is locked inside a house sus-
pected of plague (5.2.8–12). The lovers conspicuously lack any space of
their own,

> Nor does a freer space seem to be imaginable for Romeo and Juliet some-
> where else. A milieu less insistently enclosing might make visually possi-
> ble the option of leaving the city together and finding a new life
> somewhere else. Instead, the play's physical dimensions only confirm
> that 'there is no world without Verona walls' (3.3.17). Verona, consti-
> tuted by the feud, asserts itself like any ideology as the only reality there
> is.[42]

But it is not only the limitations imposed on their vision of the world that
make elopement unthinkable and banishment a kind of death. This ideol-

ogy necessarily defines how the lovers view themselves and each other. Romeo and Juliet's ability to disregard the feuding between their families and their names suggests that they define themselves outside this social code. However, when it comes to elopement and banishment, the lovers reveal the extent to which their love is constructed from the civic and poetic commonplace.

In *A Midsummer Night's Dream*, Lysander and Hermia's flight from Athens is conceivable because love has altered their attitudes towards the city. Hermia explains:

> Before the time I did Lysander see
> Seemed Athens as a paradise to me.
> O then, what graces in my love do dwell,
> That he hath turned a heaven unto a hell?
>
> (1.1.204–7)

Although the prohibitions against their love have encouraged Hermia and Lysander to view Athens in a different light, these altered perspectives are also an effect of love. Elopement dramatizes the natural transference of Hermia's affections from her father to her husband, from her birthplace to an alternative society. Hermia allows Lysander to replace the world she has known. Crucially, the same cannot be said for Romeo and Juliet. At first glance, Romeo seems to follow Valentine and Suffolk by insisting that his beloved is the centre of the universe, the heaven apart from which all else is 'purgatory, torture, hell itself' (3.3.18). Thus the beloved becomes the 'home' to replace the town or city from which the lover is banished. But this poetic convention belies the actual state of Romeo's feelings, for he cannot distinguish Juliet from Verona. When the Friar tries to offer comfort, Romeo responds:

> Hang up philosophy!
> Unless philosophy can make a Juliet,
> Displant a town, reverse a prince's doom,
> It helps not, it prevails not. Talk no more.
> (3.3.57–60)

Romeo expresses here the impossibility, the unthinkability, of taking Juliet out of Verona. Why else would he need to make a new Juliet? This inability to distinguish Juliet from Verona also underlies his speech at the Capulet tomb:

> Here, here will I remain
> With worms that are thy chambermaids. O, here
> Will I set up my everlasting rest,

> And shake the yoke of inauspicious stars
> From this world-wearied flesh.

(5.3.108-12)

The speech seems to gesture towards two locations. There is Juliet's body, in the company of which Romeo is determined to die; but there is also Verona, the place from which Romeo was exiled and to which he has now returned. These two locations become confused in his mind, hence he never doubts that the 'dead' Juliet is still 'here'. Indeed, although Romeo often refers to heaven and hell, he shows very little sense of worlds eschatologically removed from his own. His comparisons are insistently secular, deriving not only from poetic convention (beloved as heaven), but also from Elizabethan travel literature (Italy as heaven).[43] That the beauties of Italy might distract men from their faith is inferred by Fynes Moryson:

> In these dayes, the Italyans have small confidence in these papall pardons and spirituall promises, and so much love their owne earth, as they will not give the seene and felt pleasures it yealdes them, for the unseene and unfelt ioyes of heaven, having a Common Proverb, [...] here is good bread and good wyne, who knowes if any such be in Paradice, the Fryers prate therof but knowe nothing.[44]

Romeo offers the same objections to the existence of a world beyond Verona: men cannot tell what lies beyond their sphere, the Friar prates but knows nothing.

In this context, Romeo's disguise as a pilgrim becomes highly ironic. An engraving by Enea Vico, dating from the mid-sixteenth century, presents the Exile wearing the costume and carrying the staff of a pilgrim. Recently, Philippa Berry has argued that the timing of the Capulet feast suggests that it was intended to celebrate St James' day, St James being the patron saint of pilgrims.[45] Hence, the fact that Romeo's name means 'wanderer' or 'pilgrim', and that he is addressed thus by Juliet ('Good pilgrim, you do wrong your hand too much ...' (1.5.96)) on such an occasion, seems to play on this association of exile and pilgrim in an ironic foreshadowing of Romeo's fate. Yet the irony is not confined to Romeo's complicity in adopting such a role, for these references also highlight the secularity of Romeo's response to banishment. The most famous exile who took on the role of pilgrim is, of course, Dante. While *La Divina Commedia* repeatedly anticipates his political exile from Florence, the pilgrim's experience of exile is more far-reaching: man's life is a kind of exile and the cruellest fate that may befall him is eternal separation from God. Hence, the *Inferno* is full of references to the inhabitants as exiled from God, as outcasts from Heaven.[46] There is little to suggest any Dantean subtext in *Romeo and Juliet*. We find perhaps the glimpse of an allusion in Romeo's insistence that the word 'banishèd' is uttered by the 'damned [...] in hell. / Howling attends it' or in his reference to 'purgatory' (3.3.47–8, 18). It is probably just coincidence that Dante sought sanctuary after his banishment in Verona. But an audience familiar with Dantean exile might well have compared this pilgrim's fixation on reunion with God through Beatrice with Romeo's desire to displace God for Juliet and his despair at the loss of the temporal world.[47]

Yet, Romeo's failure to imagine other worlds, or to view the secular from the perspective of the divine, is only one of the reasons why he cannot imagine a life for himself beyond Verona. Returning to the question of why he does not simply take Juliet into exile with him, we might argue that Juliet has been historically and socially constructed as the Other (the female Capulet) by which Romeo knows himself (the male Montague).[48] Hence, to remove Juliet from Verona is to further undermine the structures of the banished man's identity. More simply, we might argue that it is Juliet's embodiment of Veronese ideology, culture and history which partly attracted Romeo in the first place. To remove her from the city would profoundly devalue her in his eyes. But perhaps the most compelling argument is that neither lover is certain they could exist in exile. The assumption that there is only death beyond Verona's walls, death conceived as annihilation, reflects the belief that they do not exist outside Veronese social formations.[49] This is strikingly illustrated by Juliet's response to her father's threats that, unless she marries Paris, she will be disinherited and cast from the house (3.5.191–4). Rather than embracing banishment so that she might join Romeo in exile, Juliet responds with an elaborate staging of her death. This is a familiar comic convention by which children punish parental tyranny and achieve the marriages of their choice, as at the end of Marston's *Antonio and Mellida* or Middleton's *A Chaste Maid in Cheapside* (1613); its appearance here highlights *Romeo and Juliet*'s long dalliance with comedy. Yet, even without foreknowledge of the tragic conclusion, the fact that Juliet will only leave her father's house in the semblance of a corpse appears much darker in a play which defines exile as the destruction rather than the liberation of identity. Just as Romeo could not imagine Juliet leaving Verona, so Juliet can only conceive of her departure in terms of her death.

Moreover, Romeo's *experience* of banishment endorses Juliet's worst fears. Exile in Mantua is repeatedly described as fatal: we learn that Romeo noticed an apothecary's shop where one might buy poison, that he dreams of death (5.1.6–9) and that Lady Capulet plans to poison him (3.5.87–92).[50] More importantly, this death is seen as the inevitable conclusion to Romeo's social extinction through banishment. Thus the Nurse argues that Juliet should take Paris as a second husband: 'Your first is dead, or 'twere as good he were' (224). If Romeo is not here, in Verona, where Juliet may make bawdy use of him, he might as well be dead.[51]

Again, *Romeo and Juliet* forms a stark contrast with Brooke's *Tragicall Historye* and *The Two Gentlemen of Verona* in its description of the protagonist's experience of exile. In Brooke, the banished Romeus is a figure of action as well as of lamentation. He busies himself with finding a house, sending letters back to his aged father and getting to know the local gentry. This socializing is partly intended to assist Romeus in his plan to obtain a pardon from the Duke but it is also part of his ambition to endure exile stoically: 'he seeketh every way, his sorrowes to begyle' (1,742). Valentine has foreseen annihilation in the loss of Sylvia: 'She is my essence, and I leave to be / If I be not by her fair influence / Fostered, illumined, cherished, kept alive' (3.1.182–4), yet his experience in the forest contradicts these expectations. The outlaws he encounters are strangely familiar (one of them has been exiled for trying to abduct an heiress) and, more importantly, they 'recognize' Valentine:

> *First Outlaw* And partly seeing you are beautified
> With goodly shape, and by your own report
> A linguist, and a man of such perfection
> As we do in our quality much want –
>
> *Second Outlaw* Indeed because you are a banished man,
> Therefore above the rest we parley to you.
> Are you content to be our general ...
>
> (4.1.53–9)

Valentine's worth in this alternative society ironically depends on the qualities that found him a position in the Emperor's court. The First Outlaw implies that exile cannot deprive Valentine of the beauty, courtesy and education he possesses; these are more essential to him than a name. Furthermore, the Second Outlaw appreciates Valentine for the very fact that society has rejected him. Valentine's exile is transformed by the conventions of pastoral, wherein a sojourn in the forest becomes a time of contemplation (5.4.1–6). The spirit of regeneration also associated with the pastoral sojourn is clearly in evidence when not only Valentine but all the outlaws are welcomed back into society at the end.

This fundamental distinction between Romeo and his predecessors in exile brings us back to the question of language and, more specifically, to that one word 'banishèd'. The reason why Valentine seems to make such a success of banishment is because he has more than one language at his disposal. His being a 'linguist' makes him of value to the outlaws (presumably he will be able to rob foreign travellers more effectively) but it also reflects his ability to transform his exiled state into something else. It is striking that the *OED* offers this appearance of 'linguist' in *The Two Gentlemen* as the earliest usage of the word to mean one skilled in languages other than his own. This unfamiliar word might stand for the flexibility towards language (and towards what is foreign) which characterizes *The Two Gentlemen of Verona* in contrast with its xenophobic twin. Valentine is able to translate the word 'banishèd' into a term of value where Romeo and Juliet declare from the first moment they hear it that that word will be their deaths.[52]

If language is an ideological tool, then Romeo and Juliet's inability to transform the word 'banishèd' into a life-giving rather than a death-wielding metaphor might reflect the power of Veronese ideology to limit their selfhood to the confines of Verona. It also reflects, more generally, their parents' belief in the power of the word, defined as secular rather than divine. The lovers will be immortalized in the city by two golden statues. Through Juliet's effigy Montague promises:

> That whiles Verona by that name is known
> There shall no figure at such rate be set
> As that of true and faithful Juliet.

Capulet responds:

> As rich shall Romeo's by his lady's lie,
> Poor sacrifices of our enmity.

> (5.3.299–303)

In their fathers' promises, Romeo and Juliet are enclosed, not only in gold, but within a verbal structure that is both civic and poetic. As long as Verona is known by this name, as long as its history books exist, their identities will be secure. As we will see in *Coriolanus*, one of the most effective rejoinders to the word 'banishèd' is for the exile to appropriate the name of the city, to become 'Rome' or 'Verona'. This is what the Capulets and Montagues promise their children at the end of *Romeo and Juliet*. There is a bitter irony in the fact that this belief in the power of civic words is what made 'banishèd' fatal in the first place. But then, as the prologue stated, it was always going to be Romeo and Juliet's linguistic inheritance, their descent from those 'fatal loins/lines', which brought about their deaths.

2

'Still-Breeding Thoughts': *Richard II* and the Exile's Creative Failure

In an essay entitled 'The Exile as Uncreator', David Williams describes how banishment from English medieval society was associated with loss of speech. A common analogy for society was dialogue, the word-exchange of men. The banished man's exclusion from this kind of intercourse symbolized his anti-social nature. His 'silence' or wordlessness represented his opposition to the linguistic creativity that bound together the disparate elements of society and even of Creation. Williams writes:

> The exile is seen as a kind of anti-poet, the opposite of the figure of the poet at the feet of his lord, the centre of society, who binds words and weaves sounds to make language. The exile is an unbinder, an undoer, and an uncreator.[1]

In *Richard II*, the two banished men, Thomas Mowbray and Henry Bolingbroke, might fit this definition. Mowbray's response to banishment is to lament the loss of his tongue, signalling an end to poetry. Bolingbroke proves the exile's 'uncreative' power by breaking the most sacred oaths and dividing Richard II from his throne. However, there is another character who fulfils the criteria of 'an unbinder, an undoer, and an uncreator'. Richard II proves himself to be an enemy of corporate identity. He leases off England's land, levies exorbitant taxes, breaks English laws and thus alienates himself from the kingdom. Richard is not literally banished and to describe him as an exile is to blur the distinctions made throughout this book. Nevertheless, I will argue that a poetic subtext, created through literal acts of banishment, repeatedly identifies Richard as an exile. In this respect, the play anticipates *King Lear*. Both kings are banishers who find that their acts of banishment recoil against them. However, what particularly concerns me about *Richard II* is its insistence that exile is a linguistically barren state: Richard tries to reclaim his kingship and his identity through metaphor but finds that his poetry does not persuade. In this play, we see Shakespeare developing the tragic paradox of *Romeo and Juliet*: that to endure exile one requires linguistic flexibility and creativity but that, by its very nature, banishment renders the victim subject to language and anathema to poetry. For the first time, however, this perception is juxtaposed with an alternative reading: Bolingbroke's successful political manipulation of his banished state serves as a foil to the failure and self-exile of the King. In this way, *Richard II* anticipates the interplay of tragic and pastoral exile characteristic of the *Henry IV* plays and *King Lear*. This chapter will begin, then, with Richard's acts of banishment, before moving on to consider the ensuing forms of alienation endured and/or exploited by Bolingbroke, Mowbray and finally Richard himself.

The first two acts of the play centre on a seeming paradox: the man who should protect England is its chief enemy and despoiler. Richard's nobles testify to his farming of the realm, his taxation of the nobles and commons and his persecution of the nobility with a kind of exasperated wonder that a king should act thus. This wonder is partly inspired by the political consequences of such actions. For example, Richard's seizure of Bolingbroke's inheritance sets a dangerous precedent:

> Take Hereford's rights away, and take from Time
> His charters and his customary rights:
> Let not tomorrow then ensue today;
> Be not thyself, for how art thou a king
> But by fair sequence and succession?

> (2.1.196–200)

Similarly, his excessive taxation of nobles and commons is sufficient motive for rebellion (2.1.247–51). Yet Richard's actions also provoke incredulity because they are persistently figured as self-wounding. The play begins with an insistent opposition between self-perpetuating and self-consuming bodies.

In 1.2, Gloucester's widow describes the murder of her husband as a violation, not simply of honour, but of identity. Edward III, the father of Gaunt and Gloucester, is embodied through his sons. They are branches from that 'most royal root' (18), vials of his 'sacred blood' (12, 17). The spilling of that blood diminishes the essence of each son:

> Ah, Gaunt, his blood was thine! That bed, that womb,
> That mettle, that self mould that fashioned thee,
> Made him a man: and though thou liv'st and breathest,
> Yet art thou slain in him.

> (1.2.22–5)

The irony latent in this scene is that Edward's grandson, Richard II, perpetrated the crime. By sluicing Edward's blood, Richard is not only striking at the root of his aristocratic inheritance but also the source of his kingship. Although Gaunt refuses to take revenge, his elegy for England expresses the same concern for aristocratic blood and explores anxieties about continuation and self-consumption.[2] He even borrows his sister-in-law's rhetorical figure, *ploche*:

> This blessèd plot, this earth, this realm, this England,
> This nurse, this teeming womb of royal kings ...
> Is now leased out – I die pronouncing it –
> Like to a tenement or pelting farm.
> England, bound in with the triumphant sea,
> Whose rocky shore beats back the envious siege
> Of wat'ry Neptune, is now bound in with shame,
> With inky blots and rotten parchment bonds.
> That England that was wont to conquer others
> Hath made a shameful conquest of itself.
>
> (2.1.50–1, 59–66)

Here, the equivalent of Edward's blood, spilt to the diminution of all, is the English land 'leased out'. The model which shapes images of itself (Edward III and his sons) is again compromised in its self-reiteration: England no longer produces crusading knights and Richard II has produced no heir.

Furthermore, where Gloucester's widow imagined the self-consuming body as a desecration of feudal and aristocratic principles, Gaunt also recognizes it as a violation of the king's two bodies' doctrine. As defined by Edmund Plowden in his *Reports* (1571), the sovereign possesses two bodies, the body natural and the body politic. Where the former is mortal and susceptible to infirmity, the latter is eternal and immutable, containing within it land, law and people.[3] Although the possession of this divine and perfect body might serve the absolutist ambitions of kings, the theory was primarily concerned with the continuity of England, as Marie Axton explains:

> Men died and the land endured; kings died, the crown survived; individual subjects died but subjects always remained to be governed. Perhaps the lawyers were unwilling to envisage England itself as a perpetual corporation because the law had always vested land in a person. Anyway, for the purposes of law it was found necessary by 1561 to endow the Queen with two bodies: a *body natural* and a *body politic* [...] When lawyers spoke of this body politic they referred to a specific quality: the essence of *corporate perpetuity*.[4]

Any threat to this 'corporate perpetuity', for example the leasing of Crown land or the wasting of the treasury, might be figured as a danger to the king's own substance – hence Gaunt's insistence that Richard's 'deathbed is no lesser than thy land' (2.1.95).

This repeated image of the body warring against itself derives in part, then, from the political discourses which shaped the history play, *Richard II*.[5] However, it is also familiar from tragedy. The quarto title of the play, *The Tragedy of King Richard the Second*, reinforces our sense of the fatal peripeteia which attends Richard's actions. His acts of dispossession represent a political danger, but they also evoke a poetic subtext: the body warring against itself, the body *alienating* itself. This alienation is most dramatically expressed through banishment.

Richard's acts of banishment ought to reinforce the identification of king and realm, of body natural and body politic. To say 'I banish you' is to claim that he embodies land, law and people, and may withdraw these from the offender. However, in the context of his other acts of dispossession, banishment becomes an expression of the King's ruthless solipsism and of his hostility towards England's 'corporate perpetuity'. In *The Union of Two Noble Famelies of Lancastre and Yorke* (1548), Edward Hall relates the substance of Hereford's complaint against the King, that he

> litle estemed and lesse regarded the nobles and Princes of his realme, and as muche as laie in hym soughte occasions, invented causes and practised prively howe to destroye the more parte of theim: *to some threttenyng death, to other manacyng exile and banishment*, forgettyng and not remembryng what blotte it was to his honor, and what detrimente and damage it was to the publike wealthe ... [6] (italics mine)

Froissart's *Chronicle* (trans. into English 1523–25) elaborates further. While the banished Bolingbroke is in France, he is approached by another exile, Thomas Arundel, formerly Archbishop of Canterbury. Arundel persuades Bolingbroke to return and depose the King on the grounds that Richard has had Gloucester murdered and the Earl of Arundel beheaded, but also for that he has commanded

> the erle of Warwyke exyled, and you banysshed, and thus the realme of Englande is nere dysheryted of all noble men, by whome the realme shulde be susteyned: and also the kynge hath banysshed the erle of Northumberlande and the lorde Percy his sonne, bycause they spake somewhat agaynst the kynges governaunce and his counsayle. Thus they dayly encrease in doynge yvell, and none dare speke agaynst it ...[7]

Both accounts emphasize England's dependence upon the nobility for protection and honour. The king who banishes these protectors not only undermines his own sovereignty but becomes a kind of anathema to Englishness. Thus, Bolingbroke dares to declare himself 'though banished, yet a trueborn Englishman' (1.3.272), perhaps alluding to the literal and metaphorical 'foreignness' of his king.[8] Indeed, the banishment of Mowbray and Bolingbroke reverberates throughout *Richard II* more power-fully than is anticipated by Hall or Froissart, or is acknowledged by present-day critics of the play.[9] This banishment has disastrous political consequences: Richard will suffer deposition when the revenging exile seizes power. But I will also argue that, in the responses of Bolingbroke and Mowbray to banishment and particularly in their assumptions about the creativity of exile – political, linguistic or psychological – we can trace the pattern of Richard's subsequent tragedy. To perceive Richard's downfall as a kind of exile is to engage more deeply with the causes and the nature of his suffering.

At first, the conflict between Mowbray and Bolingbroke seems likely to be resolved through trial-by-combat. However, just when the fighting is intended to begin, the King suspends the action and proceeds to banish both men: Bolingbroke for ten years (later commuted to six); Mowbray for the rest of his life. The motive behind the King's intervention is obscure in Hall and Holinshed, described simply as some weighty cause.[10] Those texts that pursue the matter emphasize the threat of civil war that would attend the victory of either combatant.[11] In Shakespeare's play, the King also refers to the horror (and the self-mutilation) of civil war:

> For that our kingdom's earth should not be soiled
> With that dear blood which it hath fostèred,
> And for our eyes do hate the dire aspect
> Of civil wounds ploughed up with neighbours' swords, ...
> Therefore we banish you our territories.

(1.3.124–7, 133)

However, the weapons that Richard most seems to fear are not the combat-ants' swords but their tongues.[12] The conflict between the two dukes erupts over a charge of slander. Mowbray stands accused as a thief, a traitor and the murderer of Gloucester, and beneath these charges lies the accusation which no one quite dares to make: that Richard II ordered Gloucester's murder. The trial-by-combat will silence one slanderer or the other. If Mowbray dies, the secret dies with him in a possible ritual expiation of Richard's crime. The death of Bolingbroke would equally end his treason-ous quest for the truth. But the trial-by-combat cannot deal with both murderer and avenger: one or other will remain, empowered to speak by divine sanction. Richard perceives that the way to deal with these tongues/swords is not to allow them full expression in combat but to limit their effect. Banishment prevents either Bolingbroke or Mowbray from breathing slander against the King in English air. Indeed, Mowbray explic-itly refers to the effect of banishment upon his speech: 'Within my mouth you have enjailed my tongue' (1.3.160). Hence, where Richard was unable to make the nobles lay down their swords, he can disable their tongues through banishment – an association between exile and language-loss that recurs throughout the play.

Yet if Richard's decision to banish his nobles looks like an effective policy, chronicle history attested otherwise. In *The First Part of the Life and Raigne of King Henrie IIII* (1599), John Hayward condemns as inadequate Richard's use of exile, specifically the oaths to keep the two men apart:

> Therefore the later princes of this realme have with more safetie wholy abolished the use of abjuration and exile, and doe either by death extinguish the power, or by pardon alter the will of great offenders from entring into desperate and daungerous attempts, which men in miserie and disgrace have more vehemencie to begin, and more obstinacie to continue.[13]

It is certainly true that the practice of abjuration, as defined by its association with the rights of sanctuary, had been abolished under Henry VIII in 1530. The King had observed that many English exiles were skilled soldiers who subsequently became mercenaries and joined French armies. His alterations to sanctuary law reversed the policy of allowing criminals to leave the country by confining them indefinitely to particular safeholds.[14] This emphasis upon keeping English traitors within English bounds rather than allowing them to make dangerous alliances abroad manifested itself in the reigns of Henry VIII and Elizabeth I in a policy of extradition, previously rare in cases of treason.[15] Hayward's comments seem to reflect these facts, and yet this is by no means the end of the matter. At the time Hayward wrote, the word 'abjuration' was still a term in use to describe enforced expulsion from the kingdom under the 1592/93 Act against persistent recusants.[16] Nor, as I have shown in the Introduction, was this the only legislation which threatened banishment. While there may have been a tightening of state control over the movements of subjects and an increasing suspicion of their presence abroad, banishment remained a means of dealing with subversive and potentially treasonous elements of society. Perhaps in trying to differentiate between the Ricardian and Elizabethan reigns, elsewhere so dangerously identifiable, Hayward suggests his own emendation to English law.

It is clear in Shakespeare's *Richard II* that the King's policy is a failure. Banishment creates a powerful political enemy who responds to his 'miserie and disgrace' with the retaliation Hayward feared. More interestingly, exile provides Bolingbroke not only with the motive but with the means to take his revenge. He responds to banishment with apparent equanimity:

> Your will be done. This must my comfort be:
> That sun that warms you here shall shine on me,

> And those his golden beams to you here lent,
> Shall point on me and gild my banishment.

$$(1.3.138–41)$$

Although this reference to the sun was proverbial, it was also specifically associated with the consolation for exile.[17] In *Euphues: The Anatomy of Wit* (1578), the protagonist draws on a passage from Plutarch's *De Exilio* to console his banished friend. Euphues reminds Botonio that '*Plato* would never accompt him banished yt had the Sunne, Fire, Aire, Water, & Earth, that he had before, where he felt the Winters blast and the Summers blaze, wher ye same Sunne & the same Moone shined'.[18] However, Bolingbroke's commonplaces belie a radical intent. The image of the sun to denote kingship and the idea of gilding reminiscent of the gilded crown suggest that Bolingbroke is already imagining the transference of kingly power from Richard to himself. The suggestion that golden beams are 'lent' to Richard suggests that they may be reapportioned.

Similar use is made of Stoic consolations for exile by Gaunt in the 1597 Quarto. His utterance of perhaps the most ubiquitous aphorism, that the wise man is a citizen of the world, seems innocuous:

> All places that the eye of heaven visits
> Are to a wise man ports and happy havens.
> Teach thy necessity to reason thus:
> There is no virtue like necessity.

$$(C. 8–11)$$

We can imagine Gaunt reading this from the pages of a commonplace book, though sources in *Euphues*, Erasmus' *Apophthegmes* and Ovid's *Fasti* have also been suggested.[19] Yet, once again, the Stoic injunction to transform one's situation through philosophy takes on a treasonous aspect when Gaunt urges: 'Think not the King did banish thee, / But thou the King' (12–13). Throughout this scene, Bolingbroke has denied the efficacy of imagination, insisting that physical suffering cannot be altered by mental exertion (257–62).[20] Almost immediately, he sets about transferring the image of an exiled king from the realm of wishful thinking to the stage of English politics.

Moreover, Bolingbroke's usurpation is *facilitated* by banishment, in that, as an exile, he becomes a powerful symbol of the King's own trespasses. As in *King Lear*, when Gloucester keeps invoking the banishment of Kent to express the rottenness of Albion, so the banished Bolingbroke becomes the watchword for Richard's enemies and the man behind whom they all rally. The Duke's popularity among the commons is only enhanced by exile. His departure from the realm is that of a hero and martyr and thus damaging to Richard's kingship: 'As 'twere to banish their affects with him' (1.4.29). For the nobility, Bolingbroke's exile is compounded by the seizure of his inheritance. By this act, the King appears 'determined to perpetuate the banishment of Duke Henry' and, by extension, his alienation of English land and of the nobility itself.[21]

Under the terms of the Fugitives Act of 1570 (13 Eliz c. 3), Elizabeth could legally possess herself of the property of Catholics who fled abroad and of any other absentees who remained there six months after the expiry of their licence to travel. Sir Francis Englefield, a Catholic who fled to Spain when Elizabeth succeeded to the throne, spent long years negotiating for the return of property that the Queen had seen fit to bestow upon Leicester. Similarly, Leicester's illegitimate son, Robert Dudley, exiled in Italy under James I, negotiated for the return of his estates for almost forty years.[22] Nor would such a policy have been unfamiliar to the fourteenth-century exile. According to Hall and Holinshed, Mowbray's goods were forfeited upon his banishment.[23] Yet in both Shakespeare's sources and his play, the seizure of Bolingbroke's inheritance is an unconscionable deed. Before Gaunt's death, there is no mention of his son relinquishing property upon exile. Indeed, the King has granted Bolingbroke letters patent empowering lawyers to act on his behalf should he inherit any property during his absence (2.3.128–9). Richard has gone against his word in revoking those patents, and his actions are deplored by all. The nobles go so far as to condemn his 'robbing of the banished Duke' (2.1.262).

Bolingbroke exploits to the full this new-found charisma. His self-dramatization as dispossessed nobleman has a powerful emotional effect on others. In their first meeting since his return to England, York chastises his nephew in comic terms: 'Why have those banished and forbidden legs / Dared once to touch a dust of England's ground?' (2.3.89–90), but he makes a serious point about the implications of Bolingbroke's disobedience.[24] To return from banishment without a pardon and to do so bearing arms is 'gross rebellion and detested treason' (108). Bolingbroke counters that he has no choice without recourse to law. He appeals to York as to a father:

> Will you permit that I shall stand condemned
> A wandering vagabond, my rights and royalties
> Plucked from my arms perforce and given away
> To upstart unthrifts?

> (2.3.118–21)

In that image of the wandering vagabond, Bolingbroke tugs violently at the heartstrings of the Duke who sees his line degraded and his family shamed. There could hardly be a greater contrast between this socially outcast 'masterless man' and Gaunt's English knights.[25]

Yet this is not the limit to Bolingbroke's creative approach to banishment; he also uses it to justify the murders of Bushy and Green. In 3.1, he begins by enumerating their crimes against the kingdom but becomes more vehement rehearsing their crimes against himself, describing how he has

> ... stooped my neck under your injuries,
> And sighed my English breath in foreign clouds,
> Eating the bitter bread of banishment,
> Whilst you have fed upon my signories,
> Disparked my parks and felled my forest woods,
> From my own windows torn my household coat,
> Razed out my imprese, leaving me no sign,
> Save men's opinions and my living blood,
> To show the world I am a gentleman.
>
> (3.1.19–27)[26]

This speech is perhaps as much for the benefit of Bolingbroke's supporters on stage at this moment – York, Northumberland, Percy, Willoughby and Ross – as for his prisoners. The attack on the Duke's identity through banishment and the abuse of his status symbols at home become a model for the suffering of England itself under the bestial appetite of Richard and his flatterers. Bolingbroke comes to redeem England from her state of 'broking pawn' and from her self-alienation. To do this, the exile and the king must exchange roles. Where Bolingbroke's estates have been stripped and all signs of his status lost, so he will inflict upon Richard the stripping of his identity and the razing of his name.

In recognizing the emotive (and thus political) power of the performance of exile, Shakespeare's Bolingbroke had a notorious Elizabethan counterpart: Robert Devereux, Earl of Essex. To what extent Essex was influenced by Bolingbroke, or Bolingbroke recast to reflect his contemporary, remains a matter of conjecture. I am not proposing that Shakespeare wrote *Richard II* in support of the Earl or that, by any powers of prognostication, the dramatist anticipated Essex's disgrace. *Richard II* was written *c.* 1595; Essex only ran into serious difficulties in the summer of 1599.[27] But if Shakespeare's earliest audience/readership could not compare the 'exile' of Bolingbroke and Essex, the conspirators who gathered at the Globe Theatre on the evening of 6 February 1601 were certainly free to do so.[28]

The key text in this comparison between Bolingbroke and Essex is Hayward's *The First Part of the Life and Raigne of Henrie IIII* which was dedicated to Essex on its publication in February 1599. At this time, Essex's mission to Ireland seemed bound to end in triumph and Hayward's dedication is reckless in its praise.[29] The book was already selling well when Essex asked for the dedication to be removed but no other objections were raised against it. Even when all copies of the revised second edition were burnt according to a prohibition against works of English history (1 June 1599), *The First Part* was not singled out for special attention. Only when Essex's Irish expedition soured and rumours began circulating about his loyalty did the book come under serious investigation. Only then did analogies between Elizabeth and Richard, Essex and Bolingbroke, become treasonous.[30]

According to the *Directions for Preachers*, sent out shortly before the Earl's execution, Essex had plotted to become 'another Henry IV'.[31] In hindsight, the parallels between Bolingbroke and Essex are striking. For a time, both men enjoy a groundswell of public approval based on their ability to court the common man. In London, their influence is understood to pose a significant threat to the monarch. They leave England, surrounded by crowds of spectators and well-wishers, for a life both describe as 'exile'. They return illegally, with a rebellious aspect, to face the wrath of their sovereign. But, of all these similarities, perhaps the most striking is their self-dramatization as 'the banished man'. We have seen how, in Shakespeare's play, Bolingbroke wins the hearts of disaffected nobles by lamenting the miseries of exile. Similarly, in Hayward's history, the exiled nobles persuade one another to rebel through descriptions of this plight. Clearly, Essex was no stranger to such rhetoric. In a letter dated 14 September 1596 to Antonio Perez, he referred to military command in Ireland as a kind of banishment. Experience only confirmed this interpretation.[32] Initially, Essex had been granted a licence to return from Ireland at his own discretion but as his relationship with the Queen deteriorated and the mission became an embarrassment, this licence was revoked. Possibly Elizabeth feared the Earl would return with his Irish troops and march upon London.[33] In a letter dated 30 August 1599, Elizabeth's 'exiled servant' begged to be allowed to return to England:

> From a mind delighting in sorrow; from spirits wasted with travail, care, and grief; from a heart torn in pieces with passion; from a man that hates himself and all things that keep him alive, what service can your Majesty reap? Since my services past deserve no more than banishment and proscription into the most cursed of all countries, with what expectation or to what end shall I live longer?[34]

Even when he returned to England, this 'exile' did not end. After months of house arrest, Essex was found guilty of misconduct in Ireland and on 26 August 1600 he was permanently banished from the court. Since a considerable amount of the Earl's revenues depended on his presence there, he was now on the point of bankruptcy. He had become an exile in substance as well as in name.

Although Essex's metaphors would have had a limited audience, he may have planned to dramatize his exile by appearing in the guise of an

'Unknown Knight' at the 1600 Accession Day tilt.[35] More importantly, the staging of Shakespeare's *Richard II* on the night before the rebellion allowed the Earl to further exploit his exclusion. It has been argued that *Richard II*'s seditiousness lies not in its impact on the public but in the interpretation of the conspirators. Samuel Schoenbaum suggests that they chose this play about a successful deposition 'to buoy up their own spirits on the eve of the desperate adventure' rather than to rouse the multitude.[36] To see Bolingbroke repeal himself from exile, to watch the banished man exchange places with the king, would not only inspire Essex's company but would place the emphasis of the rebellion upon the Earl's restitution rather than Elizabeth's downfall. Essex had already deployed the plangent tones of the exile in his letters from Ireland and continued in such a vein from his pastoral seclusion, hoping to move the Queen to sympathy. Just as Bolingbroke's inheritance is seized by Richard, so Elizabeth had reclaimed a major source of Essex's income (the licence to the Farm of Sweet Wines). Perhaps Shakespeare's Bolingbroke confirmed the conspirators in their ambition to avenge the banished man.[37]

Through Bolingbroke, we see exile as a motive for rebellion and even a means to this end. To read the play as a comedy in which Bolingbroke, not Richard, is the central character is to perceive analogies between the political creativity of exile in *Richard II* and that of, for example, Prospero in *The Tempest*. The implications of Thomas Mowbray's banishment are more subtle. This exile will not return to demand vengeance, and his absence has few political ramifications.[38] The only time anyone thinks of him after 1.3 is in regard to Gloucester's murder, but by then Mowbray is dead. However, Mowbray's exile explores the tragic potential of banishment, prophesying with uncanny accuracy the fate of England's self-alienating king. In a speech on exile quite unlike anything else I have found in this period, Mowbray focuses in detail on the linguistic consequences:

> The language I have learnt these forty years,
> My native English, now I must forgo,
> And now my tongue's use is to me no more
> Than an unstringèd viol or a harp,
> Or like a cunning instrument cased up,
> Or, being open, put into his hands
> That knows no touch to tune the harmony.
> Within my mouth you have enjailed my tongue,
> Doubly portcullised with my teeth and lips,
> And dull unfeeling barren ignorance
> Is made my jailer to attend on me.
> I am too old to fawn upon a nurse,
> Too far in years to be a pupil now.

> What is thy sentence then but speechless death,
> Which robs my tongue from breathing native breath?
>
> (1.3.153–67)

Deprived of the opportunity to speak English, Mowbray insists that he will become speechless. An instrument without strings or locked in its case makes no sound; without skill, Hamlet's recorder player makes only noise.[39] But, as critics have pointed out since the nineteenth century, it is surprising that Mowbray should possess only one language.[40] Towards the end of the fourteenth century, English had displaced French as the national tongue, a response in part to the nationalist and chauvinist feeling generated by the Hundred Years' War. However, the language spoken at court since the Norman invasion, that is French, remained the more prestigious and courtly tongue, still used, along with Latin, by the clergy and the law.[41] One of the sources of *Richard II*, Froissart's *Chronicle*, makes clear that the King and some of his nobles were able to speak and read in French and since Mowbray was sent on embassies to France and Germany we would assume he was among this number.[42] The Duke's monolingualism also strikes us as a solecism in the context of the Elizabethan court, peopled as it was by distinguished linguists including the Queen herself.[43]

One explanation for Mowbray's linguistic inadequacy might be that his lament was intended to endorse '[our] native English' at a time when arguments about the vernacular's barbarousness and vulgarity, its lack of style and ornament, and its inferiority to the mellifluous classical tongues, still raged.[44] Perhaps more importantly, Mowbray's speech would deflect accusations that English no longer had any definite identity because of its reliance upon loan words and 'inkehorne termes'. In 1612, Thomas Heywood relates how 'our *English* tongue, which hath ben the most harsh, uneven, and broken language of the world, part *Dutch*, part *Irish*, *Saxon*, *Scotch*, *Welsh* and indeed a gallimaffry [*sic*] of many, but perfect in none' is now being refined by playwrights.[45] An interesting consequence of this heterogeneity seems to have been a sense of cultural estrangement. In a preface to his dictionary of 1604, Robert Cawdrey describes how

> some men seek so far for outlandish English, that they forget altogether their mothers language, so that if some of their mothers were alive, they were not able to tell, or understand what they say, and yet these fine English Clearks, will say they speak in their mother tongue; but one might well charge them, for counterfeyting the Kings English.[46]

By insisting that if he cannot speak English, he must be silent, Mowbray attests to the integrity of the language and, more generally, to its ability to define Englishness.

Modernist studies have argued that the English nation was only 'invented' in the late eighteenth to early nineteenth century.[47] Yet the nationhood of early modern England has some highly persuasive defenders. Adrian Hastings argues for a date no later than the fourteenth century and attests to the new intensity which characterized English nationalism after the Reformation. Where his argument is particularly illuminating to our reading of Shakespeare's history plays (even as those plays in turn substantiate some of his claims) is in the emphasis placed upon language:

> Ethnicities naturally turn into nations or integral elements within nations at the point when their specific vernacular moves from an oral to a written usage to the extent that it is being regularly employed for the production of a literature, and particularly for the translation of the Bible.[48]

Referring to the production of a vernacular Bible and Book of Common Prayer in the sixteenth century, Hastings asserts that 'the impact of the two books on the intensification and re-formation of English consciousness cannot be overemphasised'.[49] Shakespeare's exile makes a similar assumption; in *Richard II*, Mowbray delivers an eloquent lament for the English tongue in which language becomes a metonym for national identity. In doing so, Mowbray must ignore not only the other languages possessed by his historical counterpart but also those other languages contained within the nation he defines, not just Welsh and perhaps even Irish but the various dialects of English marginalized and designated as 'barbarous'.[50]

However, Shakespeare may also have confined Mowbray to one language in order to develop the association between exile and speechlessness explored in *Romeo and Juliet*. In the previous chapter, I argued that Valentine's success and Romeo's failure in banishment depended in part upon their linguistic abilities. Valentine is identified as a 'linguist' and given a new social role. Romeo is unable to translate the word 'banishèd' and lapses into a fatal silence. It seems likely that Shakespeare wrote *Richard II* with *Romeo and Juliet* still fresh in mind and its lingering concerns may have inspired Mowbray's lament. Consider the final lines: 'What is thy sentence then but speechless death, / Which robs my tongue from breathing native breath?' This couplet offers an extraordinarily dense interweaving of associations of exile, death, language and nationality which links the two plays. For example, the phrase 'speechless death' plays upon the convention of exile as death; 'speechless' because although banishment is verbally 'sentenced' its *fatal* meaning remains unspoken. However, 'speechless death' also includes a pun on the idea developed in the earlier tragedy that banishment causes speechlessness, that the word 'banishèd' kills language. In *Richard II*, as we saw in the trial-by-combat scene, banishment is more overtly a means of silencing one's enemies in a situation where tongues threaten violence.

Moving on to consider the last line, where banishment 'robs my tongue from breathing native breath', we notice a curious transposition of speaking and breathing whereby the tongue becomes the organ of inspiration and the speech shaped of breath becomes essential to life. This transposition serves a nationalist agenda, again in an extension of *Romeo and Juliet*. In the love tragedy, there was a powerful though implicit assumption that exile equalled death because identity was a construction of Veronese ideology. The lovers could not endure outside Verona's walls. Mowbray's speech is more explicit about the individual's social and national 'createdness' beyond which lies oblivion. To speak 'native English' and to breathe 'native breath' – these constitute life. What Mowbray's speech also reveals is a process by which national identity is perpetuated. As long as Mowbray is in England, every time he speaks he breathes in his native air and breathes out English words. Specifically, what Mowbray inhales is not just 'air' but 'breath', suggesting his incorporation into the body of England. The claustrophobia of 'this England' is attested to elsewhere in the play. Gaunt's 'sceptred isle' speech unashamedly ignores the other nations contained within its limits: it is all 'England'. Moreover, with the exception of the scene set in Wales, characters who move outside English bounds tend to disappear.[51] When Mowbray and Bolingbroke challenge one another to combat in 1.1, their apparently extravagant threats reveal the same limitations. Mowbray asserts that he would meet Bolingbroke 'were I tied to run afoot / Even to the frozen ridges of the Alps, / Or any other ground inhabitable, / Wherever Englishman durst set his foot' (1.1.63–6). Bolingbroke repeats the formula, declaring that he will fight 'Or here or elsewhere, to the furthest verge / That ever was surveyed by English eye' (93–4). Their refusal to countenance a movement beyond what is known and 'Englished' ironically anticipates their banishment while also preparing the ground for Mowbray's violent reaction to exile.

Mowbray's lament also hints at the other kinds of social and cultural difference eroded by the loss of one's tongue. In *Romeo and Juliet*, the banished Montague moves from one Italian city to another with his language (and thus his social status) ostensibly unharmed, as illustrated by his persuasion of and condescension towards the Apothecary. The banished Mowbray anticipates a more difficult interaction with the alien. To the courtier and knight, language is an ornament, an instrument of pleasure and a status symbol. To be deprived of speech equates to a fall in status where language must be used for mere survival. Mowbray will be at the mercy of his social and intellectual inferiors, personified by 'dull unfeeling barren ignorance'.[52] A similar fate is shared by Polinices in Gascoigne's translation of *Jocasta*, first performed at Gray's Inn in 1566. The exile describes his loss of language and of free speech as not simply

representative of a fall in status but as, to some extent, responsible for
that fall:

> In exile, every man, or bond or free,
> Of noble race, or meaner parentage,
> Is not in this unlike unto the slave,
> That muste of force obey to eche mans will,
> And prayse the peevishnesse of eche mans pryde.[53]

Mowbray's lament emphasizes the shame of dependence; the reference to
fawning upon a nurse presents the exile as emasculated and infantilized
(164). But to rely on 'dull unfeeling barren ignorance' threatens all hierarchical distinctions. Earlier, we saw the banished Bolingbroke threaten to
transpose the exile and the king. For Mowbray, banishment brings the fear
that the cultivated noble and the barbarian will be forced to change places,
or worse that they will become indistinguishable. These expectations are
fulfilled in *A Mirror for Magistrates*, where Mowbray in exile describes his
disgust at the rough manners of the Germans, their 'churlysh' speech, and
their refusal to differentiate between a lackey and a lord.[54]

At a time when Englishmen were increasingly forced into contact with
what was alien through the influx of 'strangers' into London, Mowbray's
anxiety about cultural differentiation seems likely to have struck a chord
with an audience all too ready to engage in anti-foreigner riots. However,
the lament also has its origins in a famous, classical experience of exile,
transcending the play's specific historical moment to ask broader questions about the relationship between exile and creativity. Relegated to the
island of Tomis in AD 8, Ovid mourned the loss of his poetic vocation, of
his name and his identity in the verse epistles *Tristia* and *Ex Ponto*.[55]
Jonathan Bate argues that Shakespeare had recourse to at least one of
these texts in his composition of *Richard II*: 'The language of exile in the
first act of *Richard II* seems to echo that of the *Tristia*, with its emphasis on
"frozen winters" spent in banishment and separation from the native
tongue.'[56] I would want to argue for a deeper resonance between the two
texts, reflected in their shared preoccupation with the exile as barbarian
and as poet.

Where Mowbray predicts a life in which he will be dependent upon his
social and cultural inferiors, Ovid describes the Getae as scarce worthy the
name of men for their savagery, their lawlessness, but above all for their
ignorance of Greek and Latin. Like Mowbray, Ovid finds himself disdained
for the attributes of 'civilization' and for his exile:

> They hold intercourse in the tongue they share; I must make myself
> understood by gestures. Here it is I that am a barbarian, understood by
> nobody; the Getae laugh stupidly at Latin words, and in my presence

they often talk maliciously about me in perfect security, perchance reproaching me with my exile.[57]

Similarly, where Shakespeare's Mowbray imagines the loss of the English tongue as an end to his music-making, in the *Tristia* exile is represented as the end of the poet's career. The linguistic sterility of relegation is Ovid's chief misery: 'My talent has been crushed by my long endurance of woes: no part of my former vigour remains' (253). But more dangerous than the loss of poetic inspiration is the impoverishment and contamination of his language:

Often I am at a loss for a word, a name, a place, and there is none who can inform me. Oft when I attempt some utterance – shameful confession! – words fail me: I have unlearned my power of speech. Thracian and Scythian tongues chatter on almost every side, and I think I could write in Getic measure. O believe me, I fear that there may be mingled with the Latin in my writings the language of the Pontus.

(155–7)

And yet, although Ovid's sufferings may have shaped Mowbray's lament, the two men do not share this experience of exile. Indeed, Shakespeare's Mowbray conspicuously does not suffer the fate 'history' assigned to him. Hall and Holinshed refer to him arriving in Venice 'where he for thoughte and melancoly deceassed'. In *A Mirror for Magistrates,* a repentant Mowbray accepts exile as his deserved punishment. When he hears of Richard's deposition he is grief-stricken and dies.[58] In Shakespeare's play, however, Carlisle describes the Duke as a crusading hero who finally 'retired himself / To Italy, and there at Venice gave / His body to that pleasant country's earth' (4.1.87–9). Far from losing his identity, Mowbray has become the archetypal English crusader, his loss of language compensated for by the eloquence of fighting for his religion. Hence, the banishment described by Mowbray's lament is not that of the speaker, nor does it illuminate Bolingbroke's experience since, as we have seen, he makes ambitious use of exile. Rather, it is the man who banished Mowbray whose experience mirrors this tragic fate.[59]

In the final section, I want to argue that Shakespeare's Richard II endures two experiences which might be defined as exile: his absence and return from Ireland, and his deposition. I will also suggest that the effect of such exile is apparent in the King's altered language. As anti-poets, Ovid and Richard II both attempt to write themselves back into society. Ovid was renowned in the Elizabethan period for having written more in exile than at any other time in his career.[60] The need to make himself present in Rome through his writing is a constant refrain. Hence, he begins letters by urging them to fly to the place from whence he is banished,[61] and calls on his readers to speak his name in Rome:

> And let someone of you, uttering Naso's name, pledge him in a bowl mingled with his own tears, and in thought of me, when he has gazed around upon all, let him say, 'Where is Naso, who was but now a part of our company?' [...] As then I pray ye may compose under Apollo's favour: keep – for this is lawful – my name among you.[62]

Mowbray anticipates this loss of language and of self but it is Richard who shares the poet's fate:

> I have no name, no title,
> No, not that name was given me at the font,
> But 'tis usurped. Alack the heavy day,
> That I have worn so many winters out
> And know not now what name to call myself!
>
> (4.1.245–9)

Like Ovid, Richard attempts to retain his identity through poetry, that is, through self-substantiating and legitimizing metaphors, and through telling stories about himself. When Ovid fears that he has lost the ability to express anything but grief, that grief becomes a form of identity. For Richard also, elegy provides a role, a form of kingship.

Perhaps the first indication that Richard has endured an experience akin to exile appears in his speech on returning from Ireland:

> Dear earth, I do salute thee with my hand,
> Though rebels wound thee with their horses' hoofs.
> As a long-parted mother with her child
> Plays fondly with her tears, and smiles in meeting,
> So, weeping, smiling, greet I thee my earth,
> And do thee favours with my royal hands.
>
> (3.2.6–11)

Simply to address the earth in this way is a convention of exile, reminiscent of a speech by the deposed and banished king in *3 Henry VI* (1591, 3.1.13–17), and recalling Bolingbroke's parting words to England in 1.3. Moreover, the terms of the greeting – the mother's reluctance to leave her child – may also hint at an enforced absence. However, the key feature of this 'exile' is arguably its location. In *Shakespeare, Spenser, and the Crisis in Ireland*, Christopher Highley suggests that for the bankrupts who went there to escape their creditors, the disaffected courtiers seeking administrative posts and the gentry seeking land, Ireland was generally considered a place of exile. This association has largely been the province of Spenserian critics who begin with Spenser's self-dramatization as an exile in *Colin Clout's Come Home Again* (1595):

> That banisht had my selfe, like wight forlore,
> Into that waste, where I was quite forgot.

$$(182-3)^{63}$$

but often conclude with an interpretation of banishment based on the political and aesthetic *liberties* it could afford. Highley argues that:

> The act of cultural self-fashioning, conducted at a distance from the English court and in a country that lacked established mechanisms for determining and policing social identity, inevitably fostered in Spenser a sense of autonomy from the structures of authority in Elizabethan England.[64]

Yet although such exile might serve the interests of the already marginalized and/or disaffected, the Irish sojourn of a king was a very different matter and it is significant that neither Elizabeth nor James made such a journey. For a monarch to be absent from his or her country inevitably brought with it the threat of enemy invasion, a problem debated by Henry V before he makes war on France (1.2.136–54). But to be absent in Ireland was more dangerous still, not simply because Elizabethans habitually associated it with barbarousness, violence, lawlessness, etc., but because Ireland was seen to pose a particularly insidious threat to English identity. The geographical distance alone was a cause of anxiety. In *Richard II*, the King describes his Irish adventure as a 'wand'ring with the Antipodes' (3.2.45), a journey to the other side of the earth, at a time when the extremities of the map were still associated with metamorphosis and death.[65] Moreover, descriptions of the English settlers in Ireland by Spenser and Sir John Davies among others, emphasized the ease with which those settlers became 'Irished', abandoning their English names, language, clothing and customs. The English seemed particularly susceptible to Irish licentiousness, casting off their inherent sense of responsibility and restraint in favour of Celtic barbarism.[66]

Richard's Irish sojourn diminishes him in his subjects' eyes. Like Colin Clout, he finds himself exiled 'Into that waste, where I was quite forgot'. Bolingbroke is the most obvious example of a man who exploits the King's absence and, in a sense, forgets Richard's authority, by returning in defiance of royal command and by mustering troops against him. York chastises his nephew for taking advantage of 'the absent time' (2.3.79) as if the kingdom had fallen into a period of interregnum. But Bolingbroke is not alone in associating Richard's journey into Ireland with the symbolic loss of the King. When no news is heard of Richard and when portents are seen predicting 'the death or fall of kings' (2.4.15), it is rumoured that Richard is dead and his army subsequently disperses. This diminution of Richard in the imagination of his subjects is fundamental to his subsequent deposition. Indeed, the King's 'wandering' in Ireland may be comparable to deposition in terms of alienation and self-loss.

Exile and deposition were often connected in the Elizabethan mind. In *3 Henry VI*, Margaret appeals to Louis of France for help thus:

> Now, therefore, be it known to noble Louis
> That Henry, sole possessor of my love,
> Is of a king become a banished man,
> And forced to live in Scotland a forlorn,
> While proud ambitious Edward, Duke of York,
> Usurps the regal title and the seat
> Of England's true-anointed lawful King.
>
> (3.3.23–9)

Even if the king were not literally exiled, his fall from the apex of Fortune's wheel to the very bottom led to his identification with other 'fallen' men such as the beggar, the madman, the exile.[67] This movement from the polarity of king and exile to their identification is one of the defining features of the medieval *De casibus* tradition upon which the tragic narratives of *A Mirror for Magistrates*, including the fall of Richard II, were modelled.[68] Moreover, Chronicle history and contemporary political theory frequently described kings as cast out, thrust out or expelled, banishment serving here as a euphemism for the deposition and even the death of kings. In *A Shorte Treatise of Politicke Power* (1556), John Ponet offers two precedents for popular rebellion:

> They deprived *King Edward* the II. because without law he killed his subjects, spoiled them of their goods, & wasted the treasure of the Realm. And upon what just causes *Richard* the II. was thrust out, and *Henry* the IV put in his place, I refer it to their own judgement.[69]

It is also arguable that the psychological effects of banishment and deposition were perceived to be dramatically similar. As represented on the Elizabethan and Jacobean stage, both states involve suffering shame, bewilderment and an amorphousness to which death is preferable. Robert P. Merrix and Carole Levin have argued for a number of structural parallels between the deposition scenes of *Edward II* (1592) and *Richard II*. Both are prefaced by banishment: that of the Bishop of Coventry in Marlowe's play and of Mowbray and Bolingbroke in Shakespeare's.[70] In fact, Coventry is

not banished but stripped of his possessions and titles, and then imprisoned (1.179–206). Nevertheless, the conclusions drawn by these critics
underline possible similarities in the experiences of deposition and exile:

> To be suddenly bereft of an identity one has had most of his life is to
> lose the comfortable borders of reality and be lost in the midst of a limit-
> less landscape. Until or unless a new identity is acquired, the victim of
> deposition remains vulnerable to his wild emotions, a situation that
> leads to frenzied attempts to create new roles, or, failing in that, to
> yearnings for death, the 'be-all and the end-all' to his anxiety.[71]

Perhaps the essential similarity between the states of deposition and exile
in Elizabethan and Jacobean drama is not only the language used to define
them but the focus upon language itself. This creation of new roles is essentially a poetic act; the exile's despair, his yearning for oblivion, is largely a
linguistic failure.

On his return from Ireland, Richard speaks a different language.[72] He is
fantastical, sentimental, morbid and, above all, loquacious. In the first part
of the play, the King demonstrated a range of registers. He was measured
and ceremonious in the formal scenes, brusque and contemptuous elsewhere. However, he appeared to take no pleasure in language, responding
with hostility and incomprehension to the long, emotional arias of
Mowbray, Gaunt and York. Hence, in response to Mowbray's lament,
Richard declares: 'It boots thee not to be compassionate. / After our sentence, plaining comes too late' (1.3.168–9). Yet on his return from Ireland,
Richard is defined by his linguistic self-indulgence, by elaborate sustained
metaphors and by the lachrymose gestures with which he dramatizes his
speech. Such is the King's verbosity at the beginning of 3.2 that Carlisle,
himself something of an orator, feels compelled to remind him that 'wise
men ne'er wail their present woes / But presently prevent the ways to wail'
(174–5).

Testaments to the novelty of Richard's speech are found throughout
Act 3. Richard ends his invocation of the pathetic fallacy with the words:
'Mock not my senseless conjuration, lords' (3.1.23), punning on the
word 'senseless' to his own detriment. Again, in 3.3, he assumes that his
audience is not sympathetic: 'Well, well, I see / I talk but idly and you
mock at me' (169–70). Perhaps most significant is Northumberland's pronouncement: 'Sorrow and grief of heart / Makes him speak fondly, like a
frantic man' (3.3.183–4). To speak frantically is to speak disconnectedly,
to babble like a madman, though such utterances could also be associated with truth. But why is Richard's speech thus 'frantic'? One answer
might be his recent sojourn in Ireland. As suggested earlier, one of the
anxieties surrounding English contact with the Irish was the contamination of the English tongue. In *A Discoverie of the True Causes why Ireland*

was never entirely subdued (1612), Davies describes the transformation of English settlers:

> Within lesse time then the Age of a man, they had no markes or differences left amongst them of that Noble nation, from which they were discended. For, as they did not only forget the English Language, & scorne the use thereof, but grew to bee ashamed of their very English Names, though they were Noble and of great Antiquity; and tooke Irish *Surnames and Nicke-names*.[73]

Moreover, in *A View of the Present State of Ireland* (*c.* 1598; published 1633), Spenser attests to the barbarity of Irish speech, its characteristic shrieks and cries, and draws particular attention to the people's 'lamentations at their burials, with despairful outcries, and immoderate wailings'.[74] To my knowledge, no one has suggested that the difference perceptible in Richard's speech might be attributable to the sound of Irish tongues. Yet the King's fascination with graves and burial is matched by a penchant for lamentation that is often described in the play by himself and others as a kind of wailing.

If not attributable to his Irish sojourn, Richard's altered language might reflect his state of exile on returning to a country that has forgotten him. In *The First Part*, Hayward describes how the King was abandoned and forsaken by 'faint souldiers and false friends':

> Thus the king, having lost both the fear and love of his subjects, disturbed and distracted in thoughts, without comfort, councell or courage, remained still in Wales, *as a stranger at home, as an exile in his owne kingdome*, not daring to goe to London, nor any man desirous to come to him; shifting still from place to place and (as it fals out to men distressed & amazed) fearing all things, but most disliking the present [italics mine].[75]

The behaviour associated here with exile, being distracted in thoughts, shifting from place to place, being amazed and afraid, reminds us of Shakespeare's Richard. The speech which causes Northumberland to describe him as 'frantic' (beginning at 3.3.142) is full of this shifting movement in which the King imagines himself as a palmer and catalogues the transformations thus required, then moves to imagine himself as a suicide, buried in an unknown grave and trampled upon by common men. Finally, he alludes to Aumerle's tears and suggests that both men become gravediggers. Another example might be Richard's vacillation over the repeal of Bolingbroke's exile:

> Oh God, oh God, that e'er this tongue of mine,
> That laid the sentence of dread banishment

On yon proud man, should take it off again
With words of sooth! O, that I were as great
As is my grief, or lesser than my name,
Or that I could forget what I have been,
Or not remember what I must be now!

(3.3.132–8)[76]

There is a smack of Hamlet in the repetition of 'Oh God' and the doubling of the last two lines which seems to offer alternatives but ultimately suggests stasis. Richard also shows a marked taste for *antimetabole*, another poetic figure based on repetition, which suggests movement but precludes anything but a return and is thus particularly appropriate to plays like *Romeo and Juliet* and *Richard II* with a strong sense of tragic inevitability.[77]

However, the insistent rise and fall of Richard's verse is also a deliberate feature of his self-dramatization. In the speech quoted above, this movement is enacted in lines 135–6. The speaking voice rises on the words 'O, that I were as great', there is a moment of suspension across the enjambement, and then a fall into 'As is my grief'. Moreover, the *idea* of greatness is quickly succeeded by the idea of diminution, by Richard as 'lesser' than he was. Perhaps the most famous instance of this movement is quoted below:

Down, down, I come like glist'ring Phaethon,
Wanting the manage of unruly jades.
In the base court: base court where kings grow base
To come at traitors' calls and do them grace.
In the base court, come down: down court, down King,
For night-owls shriek where mounting larks should sing.

(177–81)

Hockey points out that not only Richard but all the characters are prone to bursts of punning at moments of emotional intensity, particularly in grief, and this speech immediately precedes Northumberland's assertion that 'Sorrow and grief of heart makes him speak fondly, like a frantic man'. However, what Northumberland finds objectionable here is not just the emotional nakedness of the speech, or the 'unnecessary' wordplay, but Richard's embarrassing tendency to dramatize himself. From his return to England in 3.2 onwards, Richard has been far more concerned with creating images of himself than at any earlier time in the play. He consistently describes himself in the present tense: 'Dear earth, I do salute thee with my hand'; 'Down, down, I come'; 'I give this heavy weight from off my head'. Moreover, he tries to make his suffering and grief as dramatic as possible, either by suggesting to Aumerle that they fret out a pair of graves for themselves with their falling tears, or by breaking the mirror which represents the shadow of his face. This self-dramatization may be essential to the exile as a means of making himself present to his audience even as he becomes increasingly marginal.

Related to this creation of dramatic scenes in which he plays a tragic role is Richard's dependence upon metaphor. Much has been written on the relationship between the King's fall and the fall of language.[78] Of course, one of the linguistic functions over which Richard loses control is banishment: when Bolingbroke returns, he defies not only the King's authority but the power of his word. However, there is a particular kind of metaphor that Richard uses which we might associate with exile. Ronald R. Macdonald has argued that the language of divine right had always existed to cover up what was absent. The feudal society did not endow its king with divinity because his position was already inviolate and he superhuman, but because of their mutual vulnerability. The usurpation permanently marks the 'essentially secular, fabricated character of the political order'.[79] I find this idea of absence hidden and disclosed particularly resonant in the play. Richard decks himself in so much divine imagery, like the props of ceremony, because he is vulnerable. His indulgence in metaphor is easily explained as an attempt to substantiate himself, to gorge himself with meaning. The most obvious example is the 'Dear earth' speech. Here, Richard tries to bolster his kingship through divine metaphor, insisting on his identification with the sun in opposition to the night-marauding thief, Bolingbroke (3.2.43–53). Yet Richard never manages to persuade himself. After the speech in which he insists that the earth will defend him from Bolingbroke, Carlisle feels it necessary to reassure Richard, as if the latter had not expressed conviction: 'Fear not my lord. The power that made you king / Hath power to keep you king in spite of all' (26–8). Despite having just suggested that he commanded an army of heavenly angels, Richard quickly despairs when informed that he has no mere mortals to fight for him.

Images that seem to reinforce the King's possession of majesty are increasingly replaced by metaphors of emptiness. In 2.1, Richard draws attention to his sudden pallor. He explains this physiological process in monarchical terms, as the 'royal blood' chased from his 'native seat'. Although this image might anticipate Richard's deposition, he responds with a dreadful and empowering anger, threatening to decapitate the speaker, Gaunt. By contrast, four scenes later when the King turns pale he has lost the blood of twenty thousand men (3.2.72–5), leaving him 'pale and dead'. His only response now is to despair. Similarly, where Gaunt referred to the crown containing the realm of England (2.1.100–3), Richard takes this microcosmic conceit and reworks it to his own diminution:

> For within the hollow crown
> That rounds the mortal temples of a king

> Keeps Death his court; and there the antic sits,
> Scoffing his state and grinning at his pomp,
> Allowing him a breath, a little scene,
> To monarchize, be feared, and kill with looks,
> Infusing him with self and vain conceit,
> As if this flesh which walls about our life
> Were brass impregnable; and humoured thus,
> Comes at the last, and with a little pin
> Bores through his castle wall; and farewell, king.
>
> (3.2.156–66)

Richard has become merely the strutting player in Death's court. The line 'Infusing him with self and vain conceit' is an inspired comment on the King's situation. The conceits through which he has been celebrated and puffed up, in particular the microcosmic image, have encouraged the belief that he is greater than England. Rather than trying to sustain these metaphors, Richard himself applies the pin. But the application of that pin is in itself a metaphor. As Richard's identity in the world is increasingly threatened, he substantiates himself through language. Like the banished Ovid, whose *Tristia* offers numerous images of 'the banished Ovid', Richard performs his own suffering. He tells stories of tragic kings (3.2.151–6) and urges others to 'tell the lamentable fall of me' (5.1.44).

Richard does make some attempt to forge an alternative identity for himself through language. Where in Shakespeare's exile comedies, for example *As You Like It*, the exile adopts the name and costume appropriate to a lower station in life and embraces his new-found freedom, so Richard imagines a similar metamorphosis:

> What must the King do now? Must he submit?
> The King shall do it. Must he be deposed?
> The King shall be contented. Must he lose
> The name of King? A God's name, let it go.
> I'll give my jewels for a set of beads
> My gorgeous palace for an almsman's gown,
> My figured goblets for a dish of wood,
> My sceptre for a palmer's walking staff ...
>
> (3.3.142–50)

Under the pressure of banishment, Richard retains a language by which he might transform his plight. He knows the conventions of forsaking a worldly crown for a religious one, of abandoning public duty for private rest, but he cannot construct an identity for himself so compelling, so 'real', as to replace what he has lost.[80] Rather, his attempts at transformation reinforce rather than distract from the threat of annihilation posed by deposition/exile and this speech ends with thoughts of graves and death. The most famous example of this is Richard's meditation in prison. This speech exemplifies what Stanley Wells has called Richard's progression 'from lamentation to a more constructive form of thought; if we were to put it in poetic terms, we might say that he has developed from a lyrical to a metaphysical poet'.[81] Like a metaphysical poem, Richard's soliloquy originates in the need to argue, persuade or define:

> I have been studying how I may compare
> This prison where I live unto the world;
> And for because the world is populous,
> And here is not a creature but myself,
> I cannot do it. Yet I'll hammer it out.
> My brain I'll prove the female to my soul,
> My soul the father, and these two beget
> A generation of still-breeding thoughts;
> And these same thoughts people this little world
> In humours like the people of this world.
> For no thought is contented.
>
> (5.5.1–11)[82]

Helen Gardner, whose definition of a metaphysical poem I have used here, cites this soliloquy as a 'metaphysical failure' because it is merely indulgence: Richard does not persuade, and yet that is clearly the intention, as suggested by the verbs 'studying', 'hammer' and 'prove', and by the grim determination to force parallels.[83] Moreover, Richard's peopling of his prison cell is an attempt at consolation. His thoughts parade as various citizens: religious sophists, ambitious courtiers, Stoic beggars, each of whom has a perspective on his deposition/exile (5.5.11–30). The divine thoughts apply themselves to his fate, suggesting that it is easier for him to get into heaven now that he has been stripped of all worldly impediments. Yet the divines are typically divided among themselves and Richard cannot believe them. The ambitious thoughts do not accept that imprisonment will continue. Like the banished Suffolk in *2 Henry VI*, they are too proud to accept such debasement and deflect Richard from resignation while giving him no reason to hope. Finally, the Stoic thoughts in the stocks reflect on their fate with equanimity, perhaps in anticipation of Kent, and proffer Richard the most powerful form of panacea. Yet Richard finds no consolation in their advice.

Like Romeo and Juliet, Richard can find no creative way of looking at the world after banishment and cannot create a new identity for himself. This sterility appears in the image of Richard's still-breeding thoughts, 'ever-and-never-breeding at once, always bearing and yet still-born'.[84] In *Richard*

II Shakespeare builds on the fascination with language and exile intimated in *Romeo and Juliet*. He follows his subject into exile this time and allows him space in which to consider the future. Ultimately, however, banishment retains its nihilistic force, embodied – or perhaps we should say disembodied – in the repetition of that word 'nothing' which is all Richard can find to replace kingship:

> Then am I kinged again, and by and by
> Think that I am unkinged by Bolingbroke,
> And straight am nothing. But whate'er I be,
> Nor I, nor any man that but man is,
> With nothing shall be pleased till he be eased
> With being nothing.

(5.5.36–41)

Just as the cycle of banishment and usurpation established here will spill over into the *Henry IV* plays, so the characters' responses to exile anticipate the themes of political self-creation and substitution, and of languages gained and lost which define the rise of Henry V.

3
Historical-Pastoral Exile in *Henry IV* Parts One and Two[1]

The banishment of Falstaff has inspired more impassioned debate than any other banishment in Shakespeare. Yet this is an exile anticipated rather than experienced. Nor is its meaning interpreted by the victim himself – Falstaff has almost nothing to say in response. Rather, it is the banisher who recurs again and again to the significance of this action. Hal weaves an allegory around the knight; audiences and critics deconstruct that allegory but inevitably substitute their own; Falstaff sweats beneath the weight of it all. This chapter aims not to add to this symbolic burden but rather to examine the banishment of Falstaff as a companion piece to the exile experienced by Prince Hal. The latter may insist that he has 'turned away [his] former self' in the final scene, but his whole experience at Eastcheap bears comparison with other Shakespearean exiles, specifically those of the pastoral plays. We may be familiar with readings of Eastcheap as a comic subplot but I will argue that the shape of Hal's movement into and out of this underworld resembles strikingly the pastoral sojourn from which exiles in *The Two Gentlemen of Verona* and *As You Like It* emerge triumphant. By giving too much emphasis or 'compass' to the tragic, scapegoated Falstaff and ignoring the celebratory tone of Hal's return from exile, we lose the tension between elegy and eulogy in this historical-*pastoral* drama.

Before Falstaff appears on the stage, a cycle of deposition and exile has already been established, beginning in *Richard II* and continuing throughout the tetralogy. In the previous chapter, we considered the way in which the banishments of Mowbray and Bolingbroke contrast with one another and establish paradigms against which the King's own response to and experience of 'exile' may be judged. However, *Richard II* ends with an act of banishment, not yet discussed, which establishes this pattern as a defining feature of English kingship.

Bolingbroke's succession is celebrated in part as the reforging of the union between body natural and body politic, king and commonwealth. Yet in order to achieve the crown, Bolingbroke had first to sever permanently this connection. The consequences of his alienation of the two bodies and of the deconsecration of kingship are predicted with increasing foreboding towards the end of the play. Thus Richard prophesies that Bolingbroke will be deposed now that men make kings (5.1.55–8) and the Bishop of Carlisle foretells the bloody schism and self-loss that England will suffer in the Wars of the Roses (4.1.128–35). Though it is clearly incumbent upon Henry IV to create as great a contrast as possible between his legitimate kingship and the 'travesty' of Richard's reign, his banishment of Exton at the close of the play proves an ominous likeness between them.[2] Where Richard banished Mowbray for killing Gloucester, so Henry IV banishes Exton for killing Richard. Both kings displace their guilt at murdering a kinsman onto a substitute who is driven out in a ritual expiation of sin. If we do not perceive the structural analogy between these acts, the linguistic echoes render the likeness more emphatic. Mowbray is identified as the archetypal murderer and fratricide, Cain, in the first scene (1.1.104–6). In the last, Henry IV condemns Exton thus:

> The guilt of conscience take thou for thy labour,
> But neither my good word nor princely favour.
> With Cain go wander through the shades of night,
> And never show thy head by day nor light.

> (5.6.41–4)

The terms of Exton's banishment – wandering through the shades of night – also recall Mowbray's fate: 'To dwell in solemn shades of endless night' (1.3.171). *Richard II* has established a pattern of the banisher banished, creating the expectation that Henry IV will also be expelled.

Historically, as Shakespeare's audience would have known, this expectation of deposition and exile would not be fulfilled until the reign of Henry VI. Dramatically, however, it might yet be satisfied by displacement onto a substitute.[3] That Falstaff should be the intended victim of this cycle is signalled by numerous details that mark him out for banishment, not least his name.

The analogies between Shakespeare's knight and the Protestant martyr/heretic, Sir John Oldcastle, run deep within the play. There are allusions to the Lollard's rejection of transubstantiation and other doctrinal points, to his rebellion against the King and his death by burning.[4] However, of all the associations stirred by this name, not least is the doom of exile. Having escaped the Tower and been excommunicated but refusing to present himself for trial, Oldcastle remained hidden in Wales for several years and was officially proclaimed an outlaw.[5] This outlawry became banishment in John Weever's *The Mirror of Martyrs* (1601) in which Cobham is imagined as having left Elysium for a time to tell his story. He describes his exile in Wales:

> Here *Cobham* lives, O do not say he lives,
> But dying lives, or living hourly dies;

> A living death exilement always gives,
> A banished man still on his death bed lies.
> Mine high estate is low, misfortune's grave,
> My power restrain'd is now a glorious slave.

$$(1,250\text{--}5)^6$$

More interesting still is the name Shakespeare would substitute for 'Oldcastle'. In a dedicatory epistle to his friend, Sir Henry Bourchier (*c.* 1625), Dr Richard James attested to the muddle inspired by Shakespeare's choice:

> A Young Gentle Ladie of your acquaintance, having read the works of Shakespeare, made me this question: How Sir John Falstaffe, or Fastolf as it is written in the statute book of Maudlin Colledge in Oxford, where everye daye that societie were bound to make memorie of his soule, could be dead in Harrie the Fifts time and againe live in the time of Harrie the Sixt to be banisht for cowardize? Whereto I made answeare that this was one of those humours and mistakes for which Plato banisht all Poets out of his commonwealth ... [7]

In 1625, this young reader would have had substantial grounds for confusion: the First Folio applies the name 'Falstaff' to characters in both *1 Henry VI* and *Henry IV* rather than differentiating between Fastolf (a Lollard knight, described in chronicle history, who fought at Agincourt and the battle of Patay) and Falstaff (a character of Shakespeare's partial invention).[8] Even in the light of modern editorial practice which distinguishes the two, we might ask why, when forced to revise *Henry IV* Part One, Shakespeare should choose a name for his knight that so strongly recalled his own earlier creation.[9] Fastolf appears in only two scenes but distinguishes himself by fleeing from battle, thus betraying the English cause and specifically the English hero, Talbot. He is subsequently stripped of his knighthood. Yet it is not only the association of cowardice and of degraded honour that clings to the Fastolf/Falstaff name:

> *King Henry* Stain to thy countrymen, thou hear'st thy doom.
> Be packing, therefore, thou that wast a knight.
> Henceforth we banish thee on pain of death.

(1 Henry VI, 4.1.45–7)

The problem of Fastolf/Falstaff may call to Richard James' mind the banishment of the erroneous and scurrilous poet in Plato's *Republic*. Yet I would argue that the name 'Falstaff' in *Henry IV* Part One is intended to remind us of Fastolf's banishment, thus reinforcing the anticipation of exile in the second tetralogy.

Yet Falstaff's predisposition to exile is not simply latent in his name. Throughout both *Henry IV* plays, the knight is identified with a range of dramatic and social stereotypes also doomed to banishment. Though some of these are familiar from the extensive work done on Falstaff's origins, I would like to elaborate briefly on three of them: the Vice, the heretic and the courtly favourite. All three are united by their perceived method of corruption: they insinuate themselves into the company and affections of the victim, and only banishment can defeat them.

Both parts of *Henry IV* feature a persistent concern with intimacy. As Falstaff ironically declares in Part One: 'Company, villainous company, hath been the spoil of me' (3.3.9–10), and in Part Two: 'It is certain that either wise bearing or ignorant carriage is caught as men take diseases, one of another; therefore let men take heed of their company' (5.1.67–70).[10] One popular contemporary authority on the dangers of companionship was the morality play, in particular the psychomachia.[11] Ancient metaphors, such as to consort with the devil or to have 'fellowship with the unfruitful works of darkness',[12] became the literal means by which man was corrupted on stage. If not Satan then his instrument, the Vice, sought out the fellowship of the *humanum genus* to corrupt him through association. The task was made easier by the young victim's desire for society, as professed by Youth in *Lusty Juventus* (1550). Hence, the Vice figure, Hypocrisy, disguises himself as Friendship in order to 'infect him with wicked company' (l.498).[13] This possession is often explicit. In *Enough is as Good as a Feast* by W. Wager (1560), Covetous learns that Worldly Man has been converted to religion through the companionship of Enough and Heavenly Man. The Vice is threatened with banishment unless he can reverse this process (ll. 381–2). Hence, he advises Temerity, Precipitation and Inconsideration to infiltrate Worldly Man:

> Thus if you three within him once be placed,
> You shall see that Enough of him shall soon be disgraced.
> Under the name of Policy to enter I do not doubt,
> And I being enter'd Enough shall be cast out,
> For where Covetous in any place doth remain,
> There Content with Enough cannot abide certain.

> (ll. 539–44)[14]

If fellowship is the means by which the Vice will infect his victim, banishment consolidates his victory when the youth is made to expel his good counsellors. As Covetous suggests, there is fierce competition for the limited attentions and favours of the would-be corrupted. Yet banishment is also deployed at the end of the drama to punish the Vice and to secure the victim's future reformation. It is another ancient metaphor, this time for the exorcism of sin. Thus the protagonist of *Youth* (1513–14) finally casts off his tutor, Riot; in Skelton's *Magnificence* (1515), Despair and Mischief are banished by the avenging Virtues; while God's Visitation expels Pleasure from Lust in *The Trial of Treasure* (1567).[15]

In both parts of *Henry IV* the relationship between Hal and Sir John is described in terms of the Prodigal and the Vice. As Henry IV, Hal warns the Prince/Falstaff in Part One:

> Thou art violently carried away from grace. There is a devil haunts thee in the likeness of an old fat man; a tun of man is thy companion. Why dost thou converse with that [...] reverend Vice, that grey Iniquity, that father Ruffian, that Vanity in Years? [...] That villainous, abominable misleader of youth, Oldcastle; that old white-bearded Satan.
>
> (2.5.451–68)

Moreover, in pleading for his own virtues, Falstaff recognizes that the fate of the Vice was often banishment.[16] He predicts that Hal will have to choose between rival counsellors, proposing: 'there is virtue in that Oldcastle. / Him keep with; the rest banish' (433–4). Hal responds by promising that the Vice will indeed be banished (486).[17]

Such adaptation of the psychomachia plot to the English history play was by no means unprecedented. John Bale's *King Johan* (1538, rev. *c.*1558) shifts the focus of its attention from the mind and soul of the individual to the corruption of a government and of a nation. The play opens with England appealing to the King for help:

King John	... Say forth thy mynd now And show me how thou art thus becum a wedowe.
England	Thes vyle popych swyne hath clene exyled my hosband.
King John	Who ys thy hosband, telme good gentyll Yngland.
England	For soth, God hym selfe, the spowse of every sort That seke hym in fayth to ther sowlys helth and comfort.
Sedition	He ys scant honest that so many wyfes wyll have.
King John	I saye hold yowr peace and stand asyde lyke a knave. Ys God exylyd owt of this regyon? Tell me.
England	Yea, that he is, ser, yt is the much more pete.[18]

The kingdom has been infiltrated by the servants of Popery – in particular, Sedition, but also False Dissimulation, Vain Superstition, Private Wealth and Usurped Power. King Johan himself is never a target for conversion; rather, the Vice figures associate with Nobility, Civil Order and the Clergy, alienating them from their King who is excommunicated, deposed and finally poisoned. Only after Johan's death does Verity enter to rescue the kingdom: Superstition and Usurped Power will be banished, Private Wealth expelled from the monasteries and Sedition and Dissimulation will be hanged (ll. 2,441–52). Most importantly, the Pope himself will be banished. Verity addresses Nobility, Civil Order and Clergy when he says

> I charge yow, therfor, as God hath charged me,
> To gyve to your kynge hys due supremyte
> And exyle the pope thys realme for evermore.
>
> (ll. 2,358–60)[19]

The Reformation was repeatedly figured as an act of banishment.[20] When Henry VIII and Elizabeth I were excommunicated, in November 1538 and April 1570 respectively, the isolation imaginatively suffered by England as an island geographically divided from Europe, and now as an outcast from the Catholic church, was endorsed by papal rhetoric. In *Acts and Monuments*, Foxe relates word-for-word the sentence passed upon the excommunicant:

> Accursed may they be, and given body and soul to the devil. Cursed be they, he or she, in cities and towns, in fields, in ways, in paths, in houses, out of houses, and in all other places, standing, lying, or rising, walking, running, waking, sleeping, eating, drinking, and whatsoever thing they do besides. We separate them, him or her, from the threshold, and from all the good prayers of the church; from the participation of holy mass; from all sacraments, chapels, and altars; from holy bread and holy water; [...] and we give them over utterly to the power of the fiend ...[21]

Nevertheless, just as England's geographical isolation could be turned into a sign of its special grace – Daniel refers to England as 'The fairest land, that from her thrusts the rest, / As if she car'd not for the world beside, / A world within her selfe, with wonders blest'[22] – so Elizabeth's excommunication could be similarly rewritten as a mark of chastity, integrity and invulnerability.[23] Elizabeth becomes Astraea, returning from banishment in triumph to restore Justice to the kingdom, and subsequently displacing and even banishing the Pope.[24] In *King Johan*, as we have seen, the Pope is deprived of his power to banish by becoming himself subject to a kind of exile, an expulsion that effects the reunion of England with her husband, God, and makes way for Imperial Majesty at the end of the play. But such reversals of exile were not confined to drama. If we take banishment as a secular rejoinder to Papal excommunication, we find Protestant Tudor and Stuart monarchs regularly seizing the initiative by legislation that demanded the expulsion of Catholic 'heretics'.

In 1585, 'An Act against Jesuits, Seminary Priests, and other such like dis-obedient Persons' instituted various measures to protect England from the ingress of Catholics from seminaries at Douai, Rheims and Rome as well as from foreign universities. Principal among the demands of this legislation was the expulsion of Jesuits and seminary priests from the kingdom within forty days. If the offenders did not leave they would be charged with high treason and executed. Those who recanted and agreed to swear an oath of obedience to the Queen were still perceived as pernicious:

> If any Person so submitting himself, as aforesaid, do at any Time within the Space of ten Years after such Submission made, come within ten Miles of such Place where her Majesty shall be, without especial Licence from her Majesty [...] then and from thenceforth such Person shall take no Benefit of his said Submission, but that the same Submission shall be void as if the same had never been.[25]

Such legislation reveals not only the danger that the monarch might be cor-rupted by the heretical views of the Catholic, but that his or her life might be threatened. The Pope had granted dispensation to any Catholic who assassi-nated England's Protestant Queen. Similarly, after the discovery of the Gunpowder Plot, James I took steps to protect himself from contact with Catholics. 'An Act to prevent and avoid Dangers which grow by Popish Recusants' (1605) warned that 'the Repair of such evil-affected Persons to the Court, or to the City of *London*, may be very dangerous to his Majesty's Person', a danger prevented if they were instead confined to their private houses in the country. The Act demands that all known recusants and those who have not been to church for three months must now live and remain outside a ten-mile radius of London or else face a fine of one hundred pounds.

Thus, in *Henry IV* Part Two, when Henry V commands Falstaff 'Not to come near our person by ten mile' (5.5.65), his terms reproduce the detail of Shakespeare's sources, but they also allude to a contemporary political and religious conflict between the monarch and the heretic.[26] This associa-tion is strengthened by the shadowy presence of Oldcastle in the plays. According to various historical accounts, Henry V called the knight before him and tried to make him recant. In *Henry IV* Part One, there is a hint of this when Falstaff rejects the Prince's 'damnable iteration' (glossed by Samuel Johnson as 'a wicked trick of repeating and applying holy texts'[27]) and further depicts the Prince as a heretic: 'I'll be damned for never a king's son in Christendom' (1.2.96–7). But, as the Lord Chief Justice insists in Part Two, the corruption/conversion does not flow one way. At this meeting, Oldcastle was also condemned for trying to convert his king to Lollardy,[28] a danger perhaps glimpsed in the terms of Falstaff's banishment.

This association between the companionship of the Vice and the infec-tion of the heretic brings us to another character fated to banishment, one shaped by facets of both preceding types, namely the courtly favourite. *Henry IV* Parts One and Two has a significant relationship with a group of history plays in the 1590s dramatizing the 'weak king dilemma'.[29] Or perhaps we should say that Hal has a significant relationship with these plays since his own pretence at weakness might almost be informed by that tradition. The plot centres upon the insinuation of a young and ambitious courtier into the affections of the king – a relationship which poses a complex threat. The new counsellor may morally corrupt the king, pandering to his weaknesses and distracting him from the serious business of kingship. His pre-eminence at court may destroy the balance of power, in particular the delicate relationship between monarch and nobles. More subtly, the courtier may be responsible for an alteration in public perceptions of the king, thus undermining the legitimacy and stability of his rule – a prologue to rebellion. Such plays invariably feature banishment as a simple solution to this complex threat. In *The Conspiracy of Charles, Duke of Byron*, Henry IV, King of France, banishes La Fin for creating dissension at court, commanding: 'Away and tempt me not' (1.1.162). Greene's *James IV* (*c.* 1590) ends with the King promising to 'Exile, torment, and punish' Ateukin and his fellows for their encouragement of his 'sins and youthly pomp' (5.6.157, 201–2).[30]

An audience at the first performances of Shakespeare's *Henry IV* would probably have been aware of the historical and dramatic precedents for banishment as a means of dividing the king and his favourite. However, they might also have been sensitive to the political manoeuvring shown to inspire such an action. In *Edward II*, Piers Gaveston fulfils all the criteria outlined above for the pernicious favourite. He 'corrupts' the King by encouraging Edward's lascivious and homoerotic desires, distracting him from domestic and foreign policy and destroying the relationship between King and peers (2.5, 4.150). Gaveston is subsequently recalled from exile, only to be banished, recalled and once more expelled. However, the motives behind this pattern are hardly disinterested; Digangi argues that Mortimer has constructed a rhetoric of sodomy to justify the expulsion of his own political enemy.[31] Similarly, in *Richard II*, Shakespeare has Bolingbroke condemn the favourites for corrupting the King and destroying the royal bed (3.1.11–5), while executing them for manifest reasons of his own. In fact, the favourites play such a marginal role in *Richard II* that they are barely differentiated and easily mislaid.[32] It is not until the *Henry IV* plays that Shakespeare consistently foregrounds the relationship between a king and his favourite and, even here, the danger is easily contained. Hal persuades his father, if repeatedly, that tales of his debauchery are false and spread by his enemies. Moreover, the nobles, usually the most powerful force behind the expulsion of the parasitical favourite, can find no common enemy in Falstaff, generally referring to him with half-amused contempt. Even after Henry IV's death, when they express their fears of a future given up to hierarchical inversion (5.2.18), their main concern is with the personality or 'temper' of Prince Hal and his hatred of the Lord Chief Justice rather than with any perceived influence Falstaff might have.

What then does Falstaff's banishment mean? Centuries of critical disagreement would suggest there is no simple answer. The types of the Vice, heretic and courtly favourite offer persuasive analogues which might have been perceived by an original audience. However, there are other symbolic and allegorical readings of Falstaff's banishment which claim to illuminate this action. As Falstaff embodies corrupt kingship, the nation's moral sins, Carnival vs. Lent, rebelliousness or false report, he must be ritually cast off.[33] The distinction I would want to make here is between the threat of an individual and the threat of a relationship. Falstaff is not banished from England (and therefore cannot represent the expiation of a *nation's* sins) but from the presence of the King:

> Presume not that I am the thing I was,
> For God doth know, so shall the world perceive,
> That I have turned away my former self;
> So will I those that kept me company.
> When thou dost hear I am as I have been,
> Approach me, and thou shalt be as thou wast,
> The tutor and the feeder of my riots.
> Till then I banish thee, on pain of death,
> As I have done the rest of my misleaders,
> Not to come near our person by ten mile.

(Part Two, 5.5.56–65)

In the context of Shakespearean banishment, this sentence is uniquely personal. Even in *King Lear*, where a father banishes his daughter, Cordelia's expulsion from the King's sight and from his flesh is represented as an act to protect the realm from barbarism. Falstaff, however, is not perceived as a threat to the nation per se. Although he is obliquely associated with the rebel cause,[34] he is also asked to lead an army on behalf of Henry IV at both the battle of Shrewsbury and the forest of Gaultres. There is no need to expel the barbarian, merely to keep him away from Hal.[35]

In Henry V's banishment speech, the King presents himself as in absolute control of his reformation. Falstaff can return to being his riotous tutor only if the King has resumed his former role as pupil. If Henry then suffers a relapse, *it will not have been effected by Falstaff.* Yet the identification of the knight as Hal's 'misleader' may undermine our sense of the King's exigency, implying that he has been transformed before under this influence. The strong lure exerted by Falstaff is suggested throughout both plays: in Hal's pleasure at the Gad's Hill caper; his collusion with the lie that Falstaff killed Hotspur; his desire to go back to the tavern in Part Two. On one level, then, the danger lies in the bewitching presence of Falstaff under whose influence Hal has 'daffed the world aside / And bid it pass' (Part One, 4.1.96–7). And yet Hal seems too self-aware and Falstaff too deceived to play the roles of Prodigal and Vice. If we look again at the sentence of banishment, the main function of Falstaff's exile is not to effect a change in the King but to *reflect* it: 'For God doth know, so shall the world perceive, / That I have turned away my former self.' The banishment of Falstaff and the others is the dramatic embodiment of an intangible, psychological action already past. Falstaff must be made a spectacle of, hence the public humiliation meted out to him, so that the 'alteration' in Henry is seen and known.

The banishment of Falstaff is an important aspect in the larger drama of Hal's reformation: Henry V casts out Misrule and embraces Justice in a sequence reminiscent of the morality play.[36] However, banishment is not simply part of the plot; it is also essential to the public reception of Hal's transformation. Both Henry IV and Hal refer to luminescent, royal, spectacular majesty being produced by its distinction from what is dull, plebeian and banal. Thus, Hal insists in Part One:

> Yet herein will I imitate the sun,
> Who doth permit the base contagious clouds
> To smother up his beauty from the world,
> That when he please again to be himself,
> Being wanted he may be more wondered at
> By breaking through the foul and ugly mists
> Of vapours that did seem to strangle him.

> (1.2.194–200)

Although the danger of infection is there in the 'base *contagious* clouds', Hal perceives Falstaff and Eastcheap as a foil to his greatness. When Henry IV uses these images of sun-king vs. cloudy men, he assumes a different balance of power than that which informs his son's analogy. Hal assumes that he can actively transform the way people think of him; Henry IV insists that, apart from theatricality, the only weapon of the king in a public relations war is rarity. Richard II, for example, was too common:

> Heard, not regarded, seen but with such eyes
> As, sick and blunted with community,
> Afford no extraordinary gaze
> Such as is bent on sun-like majesty
> When it shines seldom in admiring eyes,
> But rather drowsed and hung their eyelids down,
> Slept in his face, and rendered such aspect

As cloudy men use to their adversaries,
Being with his presence glutted, gorged, and full.

(Part One, 3.3.76–84)

Henry IV makes the king's charisma not only dependent upon the rarity of public appearances but also upon the will of the spectator. It is up to the king's subjects to 'afford' him a particular kind of gaze. This is a point perhaps unintentionally conceded by Edward Forset in *A Comparative Discourse of the Bodies Natural and Politique* (1606):

> So when the person of a Prince is looked upon (wheron we doe seldome gaze enough) our inward cogitations filled with a reverence of the regall maiestie feared in that flesh (otherwise as infirme and full of imperfections as other is) *ought to surmount all sensuall conceits* (scant thinking of any humane nature) but *making an infinit difference betweene that body*, so (as it were) glorified with the presence, representation & in dwelling of that supreme or exalted eminencie, *and other ordinarie persons, which yet doeth consist materially of the same substance, and perhaps endued by nature with equall graces* [italics mine].[37]

Forset claims at first an inherent connection between the king's appearance and his divine substance. To look upon the king is to think upon his 'regall maiestie'. Indeed, he implies in parenthesis that one's apprehension of majesty would be increased if one had greater freedom to look. But Forset goes on to undermine his own assumption about the king's inherent charisma by stating that the spectator *ought* to ignore the 'sensuall' body of the king and its possible imperfections. In fact, he points out, it may be hard to differentiate between the king and the commoner where both are of the same substance and may possess 'equall graces'. Forset suggests that it is the subject's responsibility to correct his vision. This lesson in gazing on majesty is one that Falstaff has never learnt. It is here perhaps that we come closest to understanding the implications of that intimacy between Falstaff and the Prince that the latter would destroy through banishment.[38] Falstaff threatens to become the heckler at the reformation spectacle who will show how the puppets dally behind the scenes. When he looks on the King he sees his Eastcheap companion, the one with a taste for small beer and an intimate acquaintance with Poins' wardrobe. At his coronation, Hal's body is possessed by majesty and invested with the body politic, but to Falstaff this is little different from his own performance with a cushion on his head. He greets Henry V as 'King Hal', signifying his rejection of Hal's alteration.[39]

Banishment is, then, a part of Hal's reformation spectacle and an act to police the interpretation of that spectacle. But Hal cannot have it all his own way. As we have seen in *Richard II*, the banisher also suffers loss and perhaps a transformation beyond his power to control. There is plenty of

Tudor and Stuart testimony to the sufferings of the courtier expelled from the presence of the monarch. We find it not only in private letters but in the formulation of policy. In his essay 'The Charge Touching Duels' (1614), Francis Bacon argues that the punishment of exile must act as a powerful disincentive to duelling, for such absence strips a man of honour and condemns him to a Cain-like isolation:

> The fountain of honour is the King, and his aspect and the access to his person continueth honour in life, and to be banished from his presence is one of the greatest eclipses of honour that can be [...] I think there is no man that hath any good blood in him will commit an act that shall cast him into that darkness, that he may not behold his Sovereign's face.[40]

This may be to the sovereign's advantage: his or her attributes appear more rare and wonderful from the removed perspective of the exile; the wretchedness displayed by the banished courtier confirms the power of the royal presence. But there is also the implied threat that the monarch suffers diminution through his courtier's exile. In July 1592, while Raleigh and Elizabeth Throckmorton were imprisoned in the Tower as punishment for their secret marriage, Raleigh wrote a letter to Sir Robert Cecil:

> My heart was never broken till this day, that I hear the Queen goes away so far of [*sic*], – whom I have followed so many years with so great love and desire, in so many journeys, and am now left behind her, in a dark prison all alone [...] I that was wont to behold her riding like *Alexander*, hunting like *Diana*, walking like *Venus*, the gentle wind blowing her fair hair about her pure cheeks, like a nymph; sometime siting [*sic*] in the shade like a Goddess; sometime singing like an angell; sometime playing like *Orpheus*.[41]

Raleigh probably assumed that Cecil would read this passage to the Queen. His compliments are finely worded not only in their classical allusions but in the suggestion that the knight constructs these identities for the Queen. Raleigh appeals to Elizabeth's vanity as well as to her pity for his recall from banishment. Moreover, he cunningly reverses the traditional positions of banisher and banished. In the knight's presence, the Queen became Alexander or Diana through his perception of her. Removed from Raleigh's gaze, Elizabeth becomes less superlative, less mythically great, an exile from herself.

Something like this happens to Hal at the end of the play. Whether or not we read his banishment of Falstaff as a form of self-mutilation (the loss of 'what is free and vital and pleasurable in life'[42]), the knight's absence deprives us of a particular perspective on the king: Hal has banished the figure who undermined his authority but testified to his humanity.[43] One of the key alterations which Kenneth Branagh makes to the text of *Henry V* for his film version (1989) seems intended to recapture this Falstaffian perspective. At first, the use of flashbacks from *Henry IV* Parts One and Two appears to heighten the pathos of Falstaff's exile and to present it from the knight's perspective. By meshing together lines from both plays, reassigning them to different speakers and changing the context in which they are spoken, Falstaff is allowed to react more immediately and more passionately to the threat of banishment. Thus, the speech in which he urges: 'Banish not him thy Harry's company. / Banish plump Jack, and banish all the world' (Part One, 2.5.478–85) is spoken as a desperate plea, outside the context of play-acting which gave it an air of mockery.[44] Similarly, where the play gives Falstaff no response to Hal's 'I do; I will' (486), Branagh's knight expostulates in pain, incredulity and words transposed from a scene with Justice Shallow: 'But we have heard the chimes at midnight, Master Harry ... Jesus, the days that we have seen' (Part Two, 3.2.211–12, 215–16). Hal responds: 'I know thee not old man' (5.5.47) and Falstaff staggers back. The shot of his stricken face dissolves into his dead face, implying causality.[45] However, for all the attention given to Falstaff, the pathos created is explicitly framed by Henry's apparently greater sorrow, with the camera constantly moving from banished to banisher. Even before death, Falstaff has become increasingly unreal – a phantom who haunts the memories of his Eastcheap associates and the King – until he is finally consigned to the montage at the end of the film which gathers together all those whom Henry V has 'lost' in the course of his career. Ironically, the banishment of Falstaff appears to *humanize* Henry V through the conflict, nostalgia and regret it allows him to reveal.

I would argue that this transfer of attention and sympathy from the banished knight to the banisher-king is also a feature of audience responses to *Henry IV* Part Two. Shakespeare does not represent the knight in exile and the tone of Falstaff's response to banishment is ambiguous: will he live to fight another day, showing that resilience which enabled him to leap up from the battle of Shrewsbury unharmed? The Epilogue suggests so, declaring that the knight's recall from exile is in the audience's power: 'If you be not too much cloyed with fat meat, our humble author will continue the story with Sir John in it' (24–6). However, the main factor working to delimit the tragic significance of this action is the presence of a comic narrative of exile throughout Parts One and Two in which Hal is the protagonist. The moment when Falstaff is banished, and Hal diminished in the audience's perceptions, is also the high-point in a kind of pastoral comedy in which the exiled Prince throws off his shepherd's weeds, abandons the swains who gave him succour, and resumes his natural shape. By offering a pastoral reading of exile to compete with the tragic version – by juxtaposing Hal's experience of marginality with that of Falstaff – Shakespeare complicates our responses and offers us two competing notions of Hal's transformation.

In Shakespeare's main sources for *Henry IV*, Hal was literally exiled. He idled his time at the Eastcheap tavern as a result of being expelled from the Privy Council, replaced by his brother, Clarence, as president, and 'banisht [...] the court'.[46] The incident behind this banishment, namely the blow Hal struck against the Lord Chief Justice for imprisoning his friend, is discussed more than once in Part Two (1.2.194–7, 5.2.67–71), but no reference is made to Hal's subsequent exile. The nearest allusion occurs in Part One when the King chastises his son:

> Thy place in Council thou hast rudely lost –
> Which by thy younger brother is supplied –
> And art almost an alien to the hearts
> Of all the court and princes of my blood.

(3.2.32–5)

The term 'alien' hints at the banishment in Shakespeare's sources. However, the omission of any more explicit reference to Hal as exile does not detract from the fact that the Prince's sojourn in Eastcheap resembles at many points the experience of exile – to be enjoyed rather than endured – in Shakespeare's pastoral plays.

From *Richard II* onwards, it is repeatedly stressed that Hal is not where he should be: we find him in the subplot rather than the main plot, the comical rather than the historical world. However, at the beginning of *Henry IV* Part One, Hal informs us that this error will be rectified and that which was lost will be found. In attributing this kind of structure to his experience, Hal defines it as not just comedy but romance, a genre renowned for its ability to displace and recover lost heirs. This is not the first indication of such generic leanings. We seem almost to have stumbled upon the faery kingdom of *A Midsummer Night's Dream* when, in the first scene of the play, Henry confesses his envy of Northumberland's son:

> ... who is the theme of honour's tongue,
> Amongst a grove the very straightest plant,
> Who is sweet Fortune's minion and her pride –
> Whilst I by looking on the praise of him
> See riot and dishonour stain the brow
> Of my young Harry. O, that it could be proved
> That some night-tripping fairy had exchanged
> In cradle clothes our children where they lay,
> And called mine Percy, his Plantagenet!

(1.1.80–8)

A 'changeling' was a fairy child put in the place of a human child but often distinguishable by its sickliness or some mark of deformity; hence the 'stain' of riot and dishonour on Hal's brow. Henry's fantasy that his true son is displaced is an obvious expression of his own sense of illegitimacy. The fact that his son appears unworthy of the crown reflects the substitution that left Henry IV on the throne instead of Richard II – both father and son are effectively changelings. Perhaps also there is a sense behind this speech of a lost ideal of kingship from which both father and son are exiled. In *A Midsummer Night's Dream*, the human child has been transported from the human world to the faery; in *Henry IV* Part One, king and heir have fallen from the magical to a degenerate world where kingship relies on theatre for its dazzling effect. But what is perhaps most interesting about this foundling drama is Hal's collusion with it. The Prince loses himself in the tavern at Eastcheap and then stages the revelation of his true identity. Several times in both plays, Henry IV and Hal 'lose' and 'find' one another.[47]

In *Exile and Change in Renaissance Literature*, A. Bartlett Giamatti dedicates a chapter to the foundling children of Spenser's *Faerie Queene*, a category which includes Arthur, the Redcross knight, Satyrane, Pastorella and Artegall. These foundlings (and the term includes the changeling) are often described by Spenser as 'exiled'.[48] Giamatti explains:

> The children were translated in order to be trained, removed in order that they could rediscover themselves or be reborn, because only by distance could they acquire the flexibility necessary for identity. Exile is the precondition for self-consciousness, culturally or individually.[49]

Hal too might be seen as alienating himself to experience the 'barbarous' or 'primitive' – those whose limited language-use he ridicules and whose pleasures he condemns – before casting it off in a supremely artistic act of self-civilization. To what extent Hal is dramatized as gaining self-knowledge through exile is a moot point. But there is an implied 'self-consciousness' in his ability to stand outside his identity as a prince and to mock it when in the tavern, or to detach himself from Eastcheap and scorn its 'idleness' when thoughts of power possess him. This doubleness may not endear Hal to us but it serves to powerful political effect in *Henry V* – we might remember that Machiavelli was an exile. Indeed, to lose one's native origins and wander in the wilderness before overcoming the primitive and achieving civility is adjudged by Giamatti a particularly Renaissance condition:

> Both Petrarch, the individual, and humanism, the dominant elite culture of Europe for the next three centuries, had to assert exile, whether from secular antiquity and its ethics or scriptural Paradise and

its bliss, in order to refashion, or revive, or give rebirth to, or regain, what had once been purer, holier, or simply more whole.[50]

Again, we might associate this idea of a debased present compared to an idealized past with Hal's inheritance of the crown. To reject his tarnished right to it by journeying into exile from whence he can reconstruct his kingship as a miracle is to some extent to try to reclaim 'what had once been purer, holier, or simply more whole'.

This pattern of loss and recovery, emphasizing the opposition between barbarism and culture, is also characteristic of pastoral. Responding to the question: 'What is pastoral convention?', Paul Alpers refers back to the word's original Latin root, that is 'convenire', to come together:

> Pastoral convenings are characteristically occasions for songs and colloquies that *express and thereby seek to redress separation, absence, or loss* [italics mine.][51]

Pastoral plays such as *As You Like It* deploy this convention to create both structure and tone. Here, the majority of characters have been displaced – deprived of power, wealth and love – but come together in the greenwood. However, pastoral *interludes* may recur in comedy, history and tragedy: any play that deals, however perfunctorily, with the loss of power and social position. In Shakespeare's history plays, such an interlude may be confined to a single scene or even a single speech. Thus, in *2 Henry VI*, Alexander Iden meditates on the tranquillity of his walled garden as compared with living 'turmoilèd' at court (4.9.14–15) but proves only too eager to profit from the death of Cade and take his place there. Shakespeare's kings seem most often to dream in pastoral, imagining a period of respite in a sea of troubles, as when Henry VI sits on his molehill and contemplates the idyllic life of a shepherd (*3 Henry VI*, 2.5.1–54).[52] Whether this pastoral moment is simply intended to point a contrast between worlds, or to create pathos, to offer consolation for exile or to facilitate the return to power, will vary depending upon the other generic term at work here, i.e. whether it is 'tragical' or 'comical' history. Hal seems confident that he can bend his drama towards 'comical' history, using his sojourn in the Eastcheap tavern as a foil to the achievement of greatness. However, like the disempowered figures described above, Hal seems initially to be seeking redress for 'separation, absence or loss'. Whether or not we refer back to the sources' account of literal exile, there is in Part One a repeated emphasis on Hal as alien from his social class, from his ancestors (3.2.30–1), and from his father (1.3.229). He too has lost his place in the world but finds in the tavern at Eastcheap an alternative father and a sense of community. He takes pride, though mingled with disdain, in the fact that he can so easily win the hearts of these men: 'I am sworn brother to a leash of drawers [...] when I

am King of England I shall command all the good lads of Eastcheap'
(2.5.6–7, 13–14).

The world of Eastcheap is obviously not pastoral in any sense that an
Elizabethan audience would have recognized. It lacks shepherds, the
natural landscape, love intrigues and singing competitions, among other
conventions of the pastoral idyll. And yet it has attracted critical attention
as such. Most famously, William Empson included *Henry IV* in *Some
Versions of Pastoral*, citing the double plot as an expression of the pastoral
trick of 'making you feel the play deals with life as a whole', and taking
Falstaff as an example of his comic or low characters who unexpectedly
imply profound or difficult ideas: putting the complex into the simple.[53]
Thomas McFarland also focuses his pastoral critique on Falstaff, arguing
that the knight is the focus of the play's nostalgia: 'an outcast from a pastoral realm'.[54] However, it is with Hal as an outcast *within* a pastoral realm,
created in part by Falstaff, that I am mainly concerned here. In the next
chapter, we will consider in more detail Shakespeare's definition of pastoral
exile with regard to *As You Like It* and *King Lear* – but Hal's experience
anticipates in many ways the consolations there afforded to the exile.

Part One begins with Hal scorning Falstaff's query about the time: 'What
a devil hast thou to do with the time of day?' (1.2.6), a response which
anticipates Orlando's famous declaration in *As You Like It*: 'There's no clock
in the forest' (3.2.294–5). This timelessness serves in part as a satiric
comment on the obsession with time which characterizes the main plot:
Hotspur may refer contemptuously to the 'nimble-footed madcap Prince of
Wales, / And his comrades that daffed the world aside / And bid it pass'
(4.1.95–7) but he is killed by his own impatience. However, this attitude
towards time also serves as a consolation to the exile. In an essay written in
1957, Joseph Wittlin coins the word '*destiempo*' to describe the exile: 'a
man who has been deprived of his time [...] of the time which now passes
in his country'.[55] According to Wittlin, this has either tragic or comic consequences. The exile may be in danger of living only in the past, 'pining for
trifling things whose real or alleged charm has gone for ever' (105). Yet this
temporal displacement may also be a creative blessing:

> Everyone who is too passionately rooted in his time may become its
> slave, may become a prisoner of his time. [...] Only a *destiempo* can be
> really free.
>
> (107)

While Hal clearly remains conscious of the time that passes in his father's
world, he also enjoys a pleasurable languor exiled from that time. His
freedom from it allows him to create an alternative historical epoch beginning with obscurity, followed by the revelation of his greatness and ending
beyond the limits of *Henry IV* in the legend of Henry V.

The delight which Eastcheap seems to foster in artifice and disguise might also be associated with the pastoral world, particularly as Hal's passion is to mingle among his social inferiors. He may not be able to perform the role of the shepherd but his repertoire contains a convincing highwayman and tapster. Again, the pleasures of disguise are one of the principal consolations offered to the exile, whether they desire to pursue their original course (Kent) or to suspend their banished identity in favour of something more expansive (Rosalind). Such disguise involves not merely a change in external appearance but also a change in language, and this is where the experience of Eastcheap most closely mimics pastoral's consolations for exile. In Part One, Hal celebrates his ability to pick up the jargon of the drawer, a language which makes it possible for him to mingle among them and to become their 'sworn brother' (2.5.5–21). As we saw in our comparison of *Romeo and Juliet* with *The Two Gentlemen of Verona*, one of the crucial distinctions to be made between the tragic and comic/pastoral responses to exile is the *possibility* of language. But it is not just Valentine with whom we might align Hal in his multilingual triumph. In *As You Like It*, Orlando discovers new tongues in the trees of the forest of Arden. The significance of language in all three plays takes us back to Giamatti's argument about the foundling who leaves his origins, confronts the primitive, and is then recivilized. Shakespeare's pastoral is invariably a place where learning is to be achieved and, with that, ambitions of a particularly worldly kind.[56]

At the beginning of *As You Like It*, Orlando yearns to take up his rightful position in the world but fears that not only his brother's malice but his own lack of education will prevent him. When Oliver will not listen to Orlando, the latter seizes him by the throat and threatens to rip out his tongue, a threat that reveals not only Orlando's mistrust of his own eloquence but also his desire to destroy that possessed by his brother (1.1.55–8). However, when Orlando and Adam enter the forest, Arden seems to take on the savagery of which the former would accuse himself; it is an 'uncouth forest' (2.6.6) of predatory animals in which he expects to meet only what is savage. Against this backdrop, Orlando begins to identify himself with civility. Paradoxically, once he has penetrated further into the forest Orlando discovers that it provides a society far more cultured than that he has left behind. Here, the linguistic tragedy of exile is referred to but averted. When Touchstone finds his witticisms falling upon deaf ears, he laments this condition to Audrey:

> When a man's verses cannot be understood, nor a man's good wit sec-
> onded with the forward child, understanding, it strikes a man more dead
> than a great reckoning in a little room. Truly, I would the gods had
> made thee poetical.
>
> (3.3.9–13)

Touchstone's forebear, an exile whose wit was famously wasted upon 'savages', is Ovid. As the fool tells Audrey: 'I am here with thee and thy goats as the most capricious poet honest Ovid was among the Goths' (3.3.5–6). But if Touchstone's wit is misunderstood by the natives, there are plenty of courtiers around to appreciate him. This is also the precondition for Orlando's linguistic development. The language of Arden is profoundly familiar. It is still presumably French, the exiles' native tongue, and its mode is literary: the language of pastoral romance. Both Lodge's *Rosalynde* and Shakespeare's *As You Like It* presume the reader/spectator to be familiar with pastoral language and conventions. In the romance, Ganimede spies familiar characters engraved in the trees which he takes to be the work of shepherds. Aliena replies:

> No doubt [...] this poesie is the passion of some perplexed shepheard, that being enamoured of some faire and beautifull Shepheardesse, suffered some sharpe repulse, and therefore complained of the crueltie of his Mistris.[57]

Just as the trees' language can be understood, so the significance of any carving in trees is easily accessible. When Orlando comes to Arden, he finds that trees are already linguistic artefacts and animals partly allegorical through the conventions of pastoral. He responds to the wordiness of this forest and to its literary antecedents by following pastoral tradition and composing his own verses. This in itself is an expression of his transformation. In *Rosalynde*, Rosader is adept at poetry before he enters Arden. When Rosalynde rewards him for his victory at wrestling, he thanks her by immediately composing a 'sonnet' of two quatrains and a couplet (172). At the same point in Shakespeare's play, Orlando not only fails to write a poem but is struck dumb, reduced to 'a quintain, a mere lifeless block' (1.2.240). This is not a moment of realism intruding upon pastoral artifice so much as a deliberate alteration of the source to highlight Orlando's linguistic transformation. The eloquence Orlando discovers through his encounter with Arden and his tutor, Ganimede, is not merely important for his chances of wooing Rosalind. It is also essential to his renewed claim to civility, nobility and power so that he emerges from the forest, not merely recognized as his father's son but as the heir to a dukedom!

In *Henry IV*, Hal's sojourn in Eastcheap appears to share something of this pastoral fantasy of exile. The main objection to such a reading is not the absence of shepherds or the immorality of Eastcheap, but the nature of Hal's transformation. Empson writes:

> From seeing the two sorts of people [rich and poor] combined like this you thought better of both; the best parts of both were used. The effect was in some degree to combine in the reader or author the merits of the two sorts; he was made to mirror in himself more completely the effective elements of the society he lived in.[58]

Something like this process seems to occur within Shakespeare's protagonists who discover the values of simplicity while clinging fast to their own taste for sophistication. Walter Davis argues that Elizabethan pastoral is a site for the dramatization of an ideal self:

> This central aspect of the action is always made explicit by the disguise that the hero must assume before he can enter the pastoral land. He must, in effect, relinquish his identity and become someone else. He must strip off his proper clothing, change his name, and put on the clothes and manners of a shepherd. But that 'someone else' is really an image of the person that he, the hero, might become. Moreover, since the pastoral life expresses explicit ideas of value, the pastoral disguise signifies not only the discovery of a new aspect of the self, but the conscious acceptance of new values as well.[59]

What neither critic explores is how this ideal vision is affected by the courtier's abandonment of his pastoral garb and subsequent return to the court or city. No matter how convincing Duke Senior is on the benefits of suffering the penalties of Adam, he hastens back to court at the first opportunity. In Shakespearean pastoral in particular, the encounter between courtier and shepherd is rarely what it seems. For example, Orlando learns courtly manners from a duke and is almost never conversant with shepherds. Valentine among the outlaws was actually surrounded by courtiers, mirror images of himself. Poor Tom is not the 'thing itself' but yet another courtier, disguised this time by nakedness. To what extent has any interaction with the simple man taken place? What can have been learned?

In *Henry IV*, Shakespeare uses the pastoral connotations of Hal's exile to assuage some of the anxiety created by the banishment of Falstaff. We are distracted by the celebratory pattern of exile and restitution being enacted simultaneous to Falstaff's expulsion. Moreover, Hal's rejection of the knight can be seen as a necessary aspect of the pastoral conclusion in which shepherds and princes part company. What appears unnecessary is the contempt Hal expresses for his pastoral experience, suggesting that there has been no cultural and social rapprochement and even that the whole experience has been faked.[60] Such a rejection of pastoral finds expression in Warwick's speech in Part Two. Here, the Earl imposes a providential, essentially comic structure on the Prince's experience at Eastcheap, implying that the interaction between prince and commoners is to the former's benefit. However, the terms in which he expresses this idea militate against the social harmony we expect from pastoral:

> The Prince but studies his companions
> Like a strange tongue, wherein, to gain the language,
> 'Tis needful that the most immodest word

Be looked upon and learnt; which once attained,
Your highness knows, comes to no further use
But to be known and hated; so, like gross terms,
The Prince will in the perfectness of time
Cast off his followers, and their memory
Shall as a pattern or a measure live
By which his grace must mete the lives of other,
Turning past evils to advantages.

(4.3.68–78)

The language which Hal put on as part of his sojourn among the
common people, analogous to the pastoral transformation into the
habit, customs and speech of a shepherd, seems to exclude all the virtuous content which pastoral assumes. This language is only 'immodest
word[s]' and 'gross terms'. Hence, Hal will learn which words to avoid
and which people to shun in the future.[61] This language lesson is aptly
demonstrated in the banishment scene when Hal not only rejects the
'gross term' that is Falstaff (with special reference to the knight's girth)
but also the language they had previously shared. There is a hint of the
Falstaffian in his joke about the grave gaping for the knight (53), but the
speech maintains an oddly prissy, Malvolian tone. The last time Hal
adopted such language was in the play-acting scene at the Eastcheap
tavern when he and Falstaff *derided* the moral and social snobbery thus
expressed.

In order to explain this transformation, we might compare Warwick's
speech above with Mowbray's lament for his lost language in *Richard II*
(1.3.148–67).[62] At first, they appear to be opposite perspectives on the
same experience. The tragic exile laments the loss of his only tongue
where the comic prince assimilates other dialects and rejects them as
quickly. However, the distinction here is not simply generic but seems
determined in part by the differing concepts of national identity which
define the exiles. Mowbray fears the class implications of exile – the
immersion in an inverted hierarchy where 'dull unfeeling barren ignorance' will claim ascendancy over him – yet this prejudice is largely
obscured by chauvinism. He laments the loss of the English tongue in
contrast with the barbarousness of the stranger. *English* is here; the wild
and uncultivated beyond. However, somewhere between *Richard II* and
Henry IV the 'foreign' has been lost. Just as the reign of Henry IV requires
the King to look inside rather than outside the realm for enemies, so the
foreigners whom the exile might fear are no more than English-speakers
at the heart of London, differentiated by class and dialect. What Henry
IV fears on the accession of his son is not the contamination of England
by foreigners, but an invasion of ruffians spilling across the borders of
the court:

> Down, royal state! All you sage counsellors, hence!
> And to the English court assemble now
> From every region, apes of idleness!
>
> (Part Two, 4.3.249–51)

The terms of national identity have shrunk since *Richard II*. Where Mowbray lamented the loss of the English tongue, Hal learns 'barbarous' tongues for pleasure. Where Bolingbroke, Mowbray and Richard II all lose England, Falstaff is only banished ten miles from the English court. Where banishment is perceived as a means of preserving England from civil war in *Richard II*, the map of *Henry IV* is a palimpsest of different boundary lines – even the divisions between England, Scotland and Wales are no longer clear through the tangle of rebel alliances – such that banishment no longer has the power to convey or withhold national identity. The nation-fortress bound in by the silver sea is reduced to the sphere of the court defined, in even smaller terms, as the space around the king's body.

Shakespeare's history plays commonly define nationalism in terms of self and foreigner (most often England vs. France) but there is also a recurrent emphasis on the boundary between the classes, particularly after the first two *Henry VI* plays:

> It is as though Shakespeare set out to cancel the popular ideology with which his cycle of history plays began, as though he wanted to efface, alienate, even demonize all signs of commoner participation in the political nation. The less privileged classes may still have had a place in his audience, but they had lost their place in his representation of England.[63]

Helgerson's metaphors are primed to explore the banishment of Falstaff and he applies them liberally to what he calls Shakespeare's gentrification of himself and of the theatre by the expulsion of the comic and popular represented by Falstaff. This class antagonism has serious implications for the banishment of Falstaff and the exile of Hal at the historical-pastoral level we have explored. For, if the play's characters come to rely upon a sense of exclusiveness for their identity, on the need to protect the borders of privilege and thus to defend the nation from the poverty here continually associated with civil war (Part Two, 4.1.32–5), then a conflict of interests with the pastoral subtext is inevitable. Although pastoral dictates a separation of the classes at the end, it creates at least a temporary fantasy of social harmony and reciprocity. As I have suggested, Shakespearean pastoral is rather more suspicious of such an interface and tends to place courtiers in the positions of both simple and complex man. However, when the pastoral meets the historical in a play where national identity is under threat from within, the pastoral sojourn is further debased and even misappropriated.

Shakespeare rewrites the meaning of exile throughout the second tetralogy and in *Henry V* we find it once more the subject of debate. Nim, for example, perceives that the King has vented his ill-will against Falstaff (2.1.116) and might be blamed for his death, but on the other hand the Falstaff/Hal era could not last and needs to be understood as part of Hal's transformation: 'He passes some humours and careers' (2.1.121). For an interpretation of Hal's comic exile, we need look no further than Henry V himself for explication. In 1.2, the King responds with studied vehemence to the Dauphin's gift of tennis balls:

> And we understand him well,
> How he comes o'er us with our wilder days,
> Not measuring what use we made of them.
> We never valued this poor seat of England,
> And therefore, living hence, did give ourself
> To barbarous licence – as 'tis ever common
> That men are merriest when they are from home.
> But tell the Dauphin I will keep my state,
> Be like a king, and show my sail of greatness
> When I do rouse me in my throne of France.
> For that I have laid by my majesty
> And plodded like a man for working days,
> But I will rise there with so full a glory
> That I will dazzle all the eyes of France ...

> (1.2.266–79)

This speech is both familiar and extraordinary. It uses the same theatrical model as Hal's reformation in the *Henry IV* plays, emphasizing the banal and plebeian ('plodded', 'working days') as a foil to the luminous and dazzling ascent to majesty. It adopts once again a providentialist tone which we might associate with pastoral transformation. However, here the obscurity from which the true king will emerge is both England and English kingship! Henry's suggestion that 'We never valued this poor seat of England' may be ironic, but the antithesis implied between 'this poor seat' and 'my throne of France' suggests otherwise. Perhaps also the association of England, rather than simply Eastcheap, with 'barbarous licence' disturbs us, recalling that unease surrounding the civility of England and the English tongue ubiquitous in the early sixteenth century. Most intriguing, however, is the question of Hal's 'living hence'. At first, this suggests the marginality of his state in those wilder days when he lived outside the court or 'seat' of England. As we have argued previously, to be outside the court is essentially to be 'barbarous'. However, the whole meaning of the speech seems to contrast England and France; France is the King's true home, from which he is displaced. Just as Hal threw off his obscurity at the end of *Henry IV* Part Two to leave the barbarous forever and become king, so Henry V abandons his obscure position as King of England to find his destiny in France. What we have here is a king who repeatedly denies that he belongs anywhere.

Thus, to look back on the *Henry IV* plays from the perspective of *Henry V* suggests a deeper unity between the expulsion of Falstaff and the comic exile of Prince Hal. Both actions prophesy the loss of any final resting-place, origin, even nation, for England's king. Exile will again prove the precondition to Henry V's self-invention, this time as the hero of Agincourt. Moreover, the King's rejection of England as 'barbarous' in favour of the majesty of France prefaces a kind of transformation – through exile and return – by which England redefines itself as a great nation.[64] In Burgundy's final speech, France, the 'best garden of the world', has been rendered wild and savage, needing to be cultivated by the now more civilized English (5.2.23–67). However, the success of Henry and his kingdom is ultimately predicated on loss, fulfilling the prophecy we mentioned at the beginning of the chapter: that after the deposition, exile and murder of Richard II, England's kings are doomed to remain in exile. Falstaff may have looked like the royal scapegoat but he is only one in a variety of shapes taken by the successful King's self-alienation, an alienation that is simultaneously comic and tragic.

4

'Hereafter, in a Better World than This': the End of Exile in *As You Like It* and *King Lear*[1]

Plato	... Our home is elsewhere and it draws us like a magnet.
Socrates	... Our home may be elsewhere, but we are condemned to exile, to live here with our fellow exiles.

Art and Eros, Iris Murdoch[2]

In the plays we have considered so far, there has been little sense of the exile among exiles. Such encounters are usually confined to the fearful imaginings of the newly banished. However, in *As You Like It* and *King Lear*, the exile is almost never alone. The comedy features an outcast duke, a banished heiress, gentlemen outlaws in voluntary exile, a fugitive youth and his exiled brother, all of whom are brought together in Arden. In *King Lear*, the exile count is so excessive – with Kent and Cordelia banished, Lear and Gloucester cast out and Edgar in flight for his life – that Leo Salingar defines the play as 'largely a fable about alienation'.[3] Yet even this alienation is also shared: the exiles recognize each other's suffering and huddle together on the heath. This emptying out of society only for it to reform in a natural landscape is one of the pastoral conventions which shape both *As You Like It* and *King Lear*. However, far from endorsing a simple, idyllic view of the outcast society, familiar from Robin Hood ballads, both plays express considerable anxiety as to what living with one's fellow exiles might mean. This chapter will explore the anxiety of shared exile, before considering how classical consolations are invoked to assuage it. We will consider to what extent the exile society (always a potential oxymoron) represents a real alternative to the civility from which it is excluded. Finally, it will be argued that the movement from *As You Like It* to *King Lear* involves a broadening of Shakespeare's conception of exile: in the comedy, no man is really banished while in *King Lear* exile is a fate no man escapes.

Exile is often the means by which courtiers and shepherds meet in a bucolic landscape in Renaissance pastoral romance and drama. A person of high birth – most often a duke or the heir to a kingdom – is banished for some unjust cause or deposed and forced into exile, often with his relatives and supporters (*Humour out of Breath, The Foure Prentices of London*). Other crimes punishable by exile include loving a person of unequal rank (*Menaphon, The Rare Triumphs of Love and Fortune*) or inspiring the envy of an enemy at court (*Mucedorus, The Maid's Metamorphosis*). Subsequently, by wandering, by shipwreck and occasionally by choice, the exile enters a pastoral landscape where shepherds offer succour and a new way of life. If disguise has not been necessitated by threatened execution or by the perils of the journey, it will often be adopted now. It is inevitable that the young exile will find love in the forest, and the pastoral sojourn ends with the reconciliation of family members and/or former enemies, often preceding a betrothal. At this point the exiles are enabled to return to society.

By the beginning of the seventeenth century, the association between exile and pastoral had proven a long and fruitful one. In Theocritus' first *Idyll*, the inspiration for western pastoral literature, shepherds gather to hear Thyrsis lament the death of Daphnis. They come together to mourn their loss in a psychologically redressive movement from isolation to a recognition of shared human suffering. However, it was Virgil who made banishment the cause for this lament. In his first *Eclogue*, Meliboeus deplores his expulsion from his homeland:

> But we must go hence – some to the thirsty Africans, some to reach Scythia and Crete's swift Oaxes, and the Britons, wholly sundered from all the world. Ah, shall I ever, long years hence, look again on my country's bounds ...[4]

The pastoral tradition that subsequently developed was attuned to the woes of the exile and constructed to offer him comfort, but it also depended upon banishment for its motive, even for its plot. This is particularly apparent in the mode's development from classical lyric to Renaissance drama.

In sixteenth-century England, the espousal of pastoral and exile was renewed through the influence of various narrative and dramatic traditions. At the heart of the Greek romance tradition was the 'separation romance', recurring in the form of the protagonist's separation from his wife by mistaken death in *Apollonius of Tyre*, the lovers' flight from their parents' wrath in *Clitophon and Leucippe* or the abandonment at birth of the protagonists of *Daphnis and Chloe*.[5] The popularity of translations of Greek romance in the sixteenth century has been well documented, and it is not surprising that pastoral drama should appropriate this pattern, often in the form of exile.[6] Another possible influence is the secular romance drama which developed in the Middle Ages, influenced by Greek romance but also by English and Continental folk tales. Leo Salingar offers as examples three early Elizabethan romances, *Clyomon and Clamydes* (1570), *Common Conditions* (1576) and *The Rare Triumphes of Love and Fortune* (1582), whose motifs of a banished father and of an outcast heroine may derive from this medieval tradition.[7] Finally, the frequency of exile in the chivalric romance, as exemplified by Spenser's *Faerie Queene* in which 'wandering' resonates on a literal, psychological, moral and religious level, may also partly account for the development of pastoral from lyric to drama.[8]

Yet the configuration of exile and pastoral was not without its points of conflict. The movement from Virgil's Meliboeus to Shakespeare's Duke Senior requires a shift in location: Meliboeus laments the loss of a pastoral homeland; the protagonists of Renaissance pastoral are exiles from the court. This reversal was probably necessary to the continued resonance of pastoral conventions across the centuries and across different cultures in which man is essentially imagined to belong in a garden rather than in a city.[9] Although the natural landscape might initially appear strange or hostile to the courtier, there was a sense in which he had come home. In one of the most famous sixteenth-century formulations of this idea, Thomas Starkey's *Dialogue Between Reginald Pole and Thomas Lupset* (c.1534), Pole argues that true civility is only to be found outside the city:

> We see [...] now in our days, those men which live out of cities and towns, and have fewest laws to be governed by, live better than others do in their goodly cities never so well build [sic] and inhabited, governed with so many laws for common. You see by experience in great cities most vice, most subtlety and craft; and, contrary, ever in the rude country most study of virtue, and very true simplicity [...] Therefore if this be civil life and order – to live in cities and towns with so much vice and misorder – meseem man should not be born thereto, but rather to life in the wild forest, there more following the study of virtue, as it is said men did in the golden age wherein man lived according to his natural dignity.[10]

Lupset responds that the fault is not in the town or city itself but in man, and that the wise have a responsibility to remain there and to proffer guidance: 'For like as by the persuasion of wise men in the beginning men were brought from their rudeness and bestial life to this civility so natural to man, so by like wisdom they must be contained and kept therein' (28). This dialogue exemplifies a debate that would continue to rage throughout the sixteenth and seventeenth centuries: where Pole celebrates man's rude origins as his most natural and virtuous state, Lupset condemns the bestial life in favour of the natural civility of society. The definition of the Golden Age in particular remained a vexed question.[11] Did it represent an ideal form of society capable of creating virtue in man or did it actually represent the *absence* of such civilizing structures without which man might return to a prelapsarian innocence? In the popular comedy, *Mucedorus*, the Golden Age is defined in opposition to nature through the myth of Orpheus. While banished in the forest, the eponymous hero encounters a wild man who threatens to kill him. Rather than respond with violence, Mucedorus relies upon the civilizing power of language: he tells a story about the use of eloquence to redeem the forest-dwelling savage:

> Behold, one Orpheus came, as poets tell,
> And them from rudeness unto reason brought,
> Who led by reason, some forsook the woods,
> Instead of caves they built them castles strong,
> Cities and towns were founded by them then.
> Glad were they, they found such ease,
> And in the end they grew to perfect amity.
> Weighing their former wickedness,
> They termed the time wherein they lived then
> A Golden Age, a goodly Golden Age.
> Now, Bremo, for so I hear thee called,
> If men which lived tofore as thou dost now,
> Wily in wood, addicted all to spoil,
> Returned were by worthy Orpheus' means,
> Let me like Orpheus cause thee to return
> From murder, bloodshed and like cruelty.

$$(4.2.79–94)^{12}$$

To follow Orpheus from the caves into the city is not simply to be civilized but, paradoxically, to return to nature defined as the original state of mankind. As far as Mucedorus is concerned, Bremo's living 'wily in wood' is a perversion of man's natural condition rather than an expression of it. Thus the harmony which characterizes the relationship between man and the natural world in pastoral is here transferred, via the Orphic melody, to the perfect amity of man and city. I would argue that the tension described here reflects not just the Renaissance debate about primitivism but the perspective of the exile: Mucedorus' appropriation of Orpheus is far from unbiased for he has recently been banished from the court. We are left with a vision of the pastoral sojourn as *both* exile and home.

Shakespearean pastoral begins with the premise that the natural world, however unfamiliar or savage, is *kinder* than the society left behind. At the beginning of *As You Like It*, Duke Senior's exile is envisaged not as absence but as home-coming: 'there they live like the old Robin Hood of England [...] and fleet the time carelessly as they did in the golden world' (1.1.111–13) and Celia is quick to reverse the terms of exile: 'Now go we in content, / To liberty and not to banishment' (1.3.136–7). In *King Lear* also, Kent insists that either 'Friendship' in the Quarto or 'Freedom' in the Folio 'lives hence, and banishment is here' (Q 1.171, F 1.1.180) in a clear echo of the usual pastoral movement from alienation to companionship, oppression to liberty. And yet, Shakespearean pastoral also insists that the most legitimate society is that created in the town or city, that this is where human abilities will flourish and are most worthy of execution, that the exile desires civilization and yearns to know himself civilized once more. This assumption is not simply necessitated by the structural convention described above by which the play must end with the emergence from the greenwood and the return to society.[13] Rather, it informs the plays at a deeper level, sometimes to surprising effect.

In both *As You Like It* and *King Lear* the characters' (and perhaps the audience's) expectations of a pastoral idyll are deliberately flouted for an enforced encounter with what is initially perceived as the non-civilized, even savage. For example, when Orlando stumbles upon the woodland feast of the deposed Duke and his men, he sees barbarity everywhere. Courtesy is clearly not appropriate in this wild and desert place so he draws his sword. Orlando's reasoning here would have been familiar to Shakespeare's audience. The word 'savage' derives from the Latin for forest, 'silva', and woodland was generally assumed to be the haunt of wild beasts and of violent, lawless criminals. The location of the forest in which Orlando finds himself may have sharpened such associations. From the early seventeenth century onwards, concern was expressed over the large number of landless poor – some of whom supported themselves, like Duke Senior's men, by poaching animals and stealing timber – who lived illegally in the forest of Arden.[14] When the Duke points out Orlando's solecism in threatening violence, the latter eagerly defends himself: 'yet am I inland bred, / And know some nurture' (2.7.96–7). Yet he remains unconvinced of the exiles' civility:

> If ever you have looked on better days,
> If ever been where bells have knolled to church,
> If ever sat at any good man's feast,
> If ever from your eyelids wiped a tear,
> And know what 'tis to pity, and be pitied,
> Let gentleness my strong enforcement be.
>
> (113–18)[15]

Orlando's speech is ironic in the context of life in Arden for at least two reasons. Firstly, the experiences he takes to imply civility have all lately been found in Arden: Jaques has wiped a tear from his eye over the fate of the deer (2.1.65–6); they are at this moment enjoying a good man's feast; the Duke has mentioned the possibility of sermons in stones (2.1.17); and we will shortly be introduced to Sir Oliver Martext, the hedge-priest. Secondly, Orlando's sojourn in the forest will ultimately furnish him with the 'cultivation' he has lacked. Indeed, as we saw in the previous chapter, Arden could be considered the making of Orlando. Yet what the youth sees before him remains a group of outcasts, in rough, forest garb, whose behaviour only partially contradicts the savagery of their surroundings. Of course, Orlando's speech above is uttered not simply as a reproach but as an attempt to draw the outcasts together, not only 'if you have known this' but 'as you have known it'. It is perhaps as an acceptance of shared misery ('Thou seest we are not all alone unhappy' (136)) that the Duke repeats Orlando's terms word-for-word, despite his earlier insistence on Arden's superiority to the 'envious court' (2.1.1–17). Yet perhaps our main impression is not of Orlando's callowness but of his sensitivity – as a man who has suffered marginality and exile – to the play's disquieting hint that the 'golden days' of Arden cannot compare to the 'better days' of civic/courtly life.

Something similar happens in *King Lear*. There is an intriguing disparity, this time in retrospect, between the pastoral conventions of Lear's experience on the heath and the other characters' responses to it. It has been argued that the heath scene might yet represent the regeneration associated with Renaissance pastoral:

> When Lear leaves the warmth, the society, the 'civilization' of Gloucester's castle he might seem to be leaving behind him all of the little that is left to make life bearable. But the retreat into the isolated darkness of his own mind is also a descent into the seed-bed of a new life; for the individual mind is seen here as the place from which a man's most important qualities and relationships draw the whole of their potential.[16]

However, it is notable that from the perspectives of Cordelia and Kent, the play's most overtly pastoral exiles, the heath and its associates are straightforwardly wretched and debasing. Cordelia laments the suffering of her father on the heath with the words: 'wast thou fain, poor father, / To hovel thee with swine and rogues forlorn / In short and musty straw?' (21.36–8). The term 'rogue', as Linda Woodbridge points out, derives from 'rogue literature' in which it signified both the rural poor and the urban con-artist, with the implication that all vagrants were to some extent counterfeit and therefore undeserving of charity. While this meaning of 'rogue' might attribute to Cordelia an unnatural percipience into the actual condition of Poor Tom, it seems more likely that the word should be taken in its general, opprobrious sense: 'a dishonest, unprincipled person, a rascal' (*OED*). The use of 'forlorn' to mean 'morally lost, depraved' further reinforces Cordelia's sense of shame and even contempt for her father's outcast company.[17] If this seems uncharacteristic of Cordelia, we might remember the disgust Poor Tom inspired in Kent who 'Shunned [his] abhorred society' (24.207), and even perhaps the doubts Edgar expresses about his transformation: 'a semblance / That very dogs disdained' (24.184–5). There is a glimpse here of what else it might mean to live among the outcasts and to identify oneself with them.

These are not the only examples of such anxiety in *As You Like It* and *King Lear*. But they must at least share the stage with arguments intended to assuage the shame and suffering of banishment. The classical tradition of the consolation for exile (*consolatio ad exulem*) dates largely from the first century AD when some of the most famous classical exiles – Seneca, Epictetus, Dio Chrysostom and Ovid – met their fate. All but the last of those named were Stoics and the prevalence of Stoic consolations for exile reflects the policy of the Emperors Vespasian and Domitian to meet Stoic republicanism with banishment.[18] However, the consolation for exile, a derivative of consolations for the death of a loved one, was not simply inspired by experience but provided an ideal form in which the Stoic philosophy might find expression.[19] One of the most important examples is Seneca's letter to his mother, *Ad Helviam*, written during his exile on Corsica (AD 41–49). He reassures her that, despite the poverty, disgrace and contempt attendant upon exile, banishment has had no power to make him wretched:

> External circumstances have very little importance either for good or for evil: the wise man is neither elated by prosperity nor depressed by adversity; for he has always endeavoured to depend chiefly upon himself and to derive all his joys from himself.[20]

Cicero reiterates this point in his *Paradoxa Stoicorum*. He describes how the man who is not subject to Fortune but has achieved constancy of mind will not fear death or exile.[21] If he has not already embraced such liberty, then exile is the ideal opportunity to discover it – when his family and friends, home, wealth and position in society are all lost to him. The exile's happiness will no longer be dependent upon external circumstances but upon his own attitude of mind.

However, classical consolations for exile also promised a less austere, punitive kind of liberty. In *De Exilio*, Plutarch describes banishment as a release:

> For nature hath permitted us to go and walk through the world loose and at liberty: but we for our parts imprison ourselves, and we may thank ourselves that we are pent up in straight rooms, that we be housed and kept within walls; thus of our own accord we leap into close and narrow places.[22]

He goes on to expound the pleasures of retirement from public duties and from the hurly-burly of civic life, leaving man free to pursue his own intellectual ambitions.[23] There is, then, more than a touch of Epicureanism in the Stoic consolation, particularly in the emphasis on the pleasures of renouncing ambition and secluding oneself from public life. Seneca himself referred to man's 'wandering and unquiet' mind which 'spreads itself abroad and sends forth its thoughts into all regions, known or unknown, being nomadic, impatient of repose, and loving novelty beyond everything else'.[24] Perhaps the most oft-repeated dictum about exile in the English Renaissance is Socrates' assertion that the wise man is a citizen of the world.[25]

Sixteenth-century consolations for exile tend to combine the Stoic and 'Epicurean'[26] perspectives on banishment with no sense of potential conflict. For example, in the section on banishment in *Cardanus Comforte*, Cardan makes the Stoic point that only man's imagination can make him miserable, but goes on to argue that the exile might equally imagine his fate as a voluntary journey taken for pleasure and lists its pedagogical advantages. He insists that all those who 'invented anye excellent knowledge' were travellers and points out that a man's native country often fails to appreciate him: 'Thus we see that exile is not onely good, but also glorious, chiefly to a wise and Learned man.'[27] Here, we can trace not only the influence of an 'Epicurean' strain of *consolatio ad exulem* but contemporary tracts propounding, in the face of much hostility, the civilizing effects of foreign travel. A sixteenth-century writer who managed to produce both a Stoic consolation and a defence of travel is Justus Lipsius, one of the foremost neo-Stoics of the period. In *De Constantia libri duo* (trans. into English 1594), Charles Langius tries to weaken the exile's attachment to the external world:

> How much better is it that thine affection were as firmly setled to the obtaining of wisedome? That thou shouldest walke through her fertile fields? That thou wouldest search out the very fountaine of all humaine perturbations? That thou wouldest erect fortes and bulwarks wherwith thou mightest be able to withstand and repulse the furious assaules of lustes?[28]

But in an essay on travel, *Epistola de Peregrinatione italica* (trans. into English 1592), Lipsius suggests that to some travellers it is given 'to seek, to search, to learne, and to attaine to true pollicie, and wisedome, (which is traveling indeede)'.[29] He declares of Italy that if the traveller 'be not rauished with delight' on seeing it, 'I shall take him but for some stocke or stone'. Cicero famously attacked the Stoic's destruction of emotional and physical ties: 'For when the soul is deprived of emotion, what difference is there [...] between man and a stock or stone.'[30] This anti-Stoic reference is not what we might expect from the author of *De Constantia*. Yet the themes of travel as liberty and self-fulfilment are also common to both of Lipsius' works. In the *Epistola* he argues that a man's virtue and intelligence naturally dictate severance from his homeland. He lists biblical patriarchs, classical philosophers, mythical Greek heroes and comparatively recent English kings who have travelled abroad, making no distinction between voluntary travellers and exiles such as Noah, Hercules and Aeneas. In an echo of Plutarch, Lipsius writes:

> These men thinke it a great staine and dishonour to the libertie which nature hath geven them (to be *Cosmopolites*, that is Cytizens of the whole world) and yet to bee restrained within the narrowe precincts of a little countrie, as poor prisoners kept in a close place, or sillie birds cooped up in a narrowe pen.[31]

Such liberty also recurs as a consolation for banishment in *De Constantia*.[32]

However, it is not simply in the didactic prose literature of the period that we find a colloquy of Stoic and 'Epicurean' perspectives on exile. Renaissance pastoral romance provides its exiles with many such platitudes. It may be that this consolation is worked out structurally: Valentine finds a Lucretian pleasure in his solitude: 'This shadowy desert, unfrequented woods, / I better brook than flourishing peopled towns' (5.4.2–3), and the achievement of the Stoic exile is often rewarded. Yet Arcadia's consolations are often more explicit. If not literally carved on the trees, the Stoic message is conveyed through the observations of the self-sufficient and self-contented shepherd. As Thomas Lodge's Coridon, a model for Shakespeare's Corin, states:

> Envie stirres not us, wee covet not to climbe, our desires mount not above our degrees, nor our thoughts above our fortunes. Care cannot harbour in our cottages, nor doo our homely couches know broken slumbers: as we exceede not in diet, so we have inough to satisfie: and Mistres I have so much Latin, *Satis est quod sufficit* [Sufficient is enough].[33]

The Stoic's invulnerability to Fortune inevitably appeals to the exile whose sufferings are often blamed upon that capricious goddess.[34] Moreover, the pastoral life of simplicity and resignation promises to assuage grief and loss. It is partly in this spirit that the exile assumes pastoral garb: 'with my cloathes I will change my thoughts; for being poorelie attired I will be meanelie minded, and measure my actions by my present estate, not by former fortunes.'[35]

Nevertheless, the philosophy embodied by the pastoral lifestyle is not without its pleasures, even for the shepherd:

> [He] may find sensual delight, as well as moral contentment, by merely satisfying his needs; by discarding the obsessive luxury and laborious

comfort of 'high life' for simple living, with its homespun clothes, homely furnishings, and unseasoned meals.[36]

A greater range of pleasures, for example the delights of disguise and role-play, freedom from the working-day world, etc. is also implied through the blurring of exile and travel. For example, in the anonymous play *Common Conditions* the banished Sedmond urges his sister, Clarisia, to overcome her fatigue by imagining that it is the weariness of the traveller. She responds:

> But, brother! we are no travellers, that useth day by day
> To range abroad in foreign lands, to trace the beaten way.
> We are constrained through very force, to fly from native soil;
> We are compelled though cruelty to undertake this toil.
> The traveller may keep the way that likes him best to go;
> We are constrained to shroud ourselves in woods for fear of foe.
> Then, brother, tell me whether he or we do take most pain,
> Considering: when he please, he may return to home again![37]

However, this is a distinction that it is increasingly difficult to make in the consoling world of pastoral, as we will see later in the case of Jaques, both exile and traveller.

Inevitably, pastoral romance prioritizes the 'Epicurean' over the Stoic consolation. The shape of pastoral with its movement into and out of the greenwood and its corresponding assumption that men belong, at least for the time being, in cities, requires the exile to remain susceptible to the influence of Fortune when she once more smiles upon him, to the delights of companionship and society, and to the allurements of love. When we turn to *As You Like It* and *King Lear*, we find that Shakespeare has included both Stoic and 'Epicurean' consolations for exile within his plays but accorded them varying degrees of success. In general, the more effective the consolation of exile the less sense we have of an exile society.

In *Shakespeare's Pastoral Comedy*, McFarland suggests that the situation at the start of *As You Like It* 'could [...] as well serve for a tragedy as for a comedy' (98). While I agree that 'the forces of bitterness and alienation' unleashed by banishment suggest a parallel between *As You Like It* and *King Lear* and darken the later comedies (99, 101), what I find remarkable about *As You Like It* is the ease with which that darkness is vitiated. This is particularly apparent if we return to Shakespeare's main source for the play, *Rosalynde*. While still at court, Lodge's heroine thinks of her father's exile as an irreversible blight:

> The blossomes of thy youth are mixt with the frostes of envie, and the hope of thy ensuing frutes perish in the bud. Thy father is by *Torismond* banisht from the crowne, & thou the unhappie daughter of a King

detained captive, living as disquited [*sic*] in thy thoughts, as thy father
discontented in his exile.

(174)[38]

When banished herself, Rosalynde suffers from bouts of depression and
anxiety and thus decides to remain chaste:

For that thou art an exile, and banished from the Court: whose distresse,
as it is appeased with patience, so it woulde bee renewed with amorous
passions. Have minde on thy forepassed fortunes, feare the worst, and
intangle not thy self with present fancies.

(204)

In contrast, Shakespeare's Rosalind expresses discontent at her father's exile
and at her subsequent banishment (1.2.3–6, 1.3.92) but this distress barely
outlasts her preparations for flight. It does not recur in Arden.

If Shakespeare takes banishment less seriously than Lodge, I would argue
that this is partly because the play's consolations are more powerful. He has
created a court so claustrophobic and alienating that any escape from it would
be a release. Hence, Duke Senior's exile in the forest of Arden is perceived as
liberty and is, in some cases, freely chosen: 'many young gentlemen flock to
him every day, and fleet the time carelessly, as they did in the golden world.'
However, the consolations of this new world are not as straightforward as
Charles suggests. In Golding's translation of Ovid's *Metamorphoses* (1567) the
golden-age landscape streams with milk and wine, and honey pours from the
trees, thus precluding the need for hunting or farming.[39] Shakespeare's Arden
comes as something of a disappointment. It is a post-Saturnine, post-lapsarian
world where men suffer from their exposure to the elements, hunt for their
food and mourn their condition. Yet, if the landscape of exile is not the idyll
where men rediscover their original innocence, it need not remain a savage
wilderness which supports only beasts: it may be civilized, and the exile
redeemed by his efforts.

Enforced sufferance of a harsh and deserted landscape is a scenario to which
Stoic philosophers returned again and again. Thus, in *De Providentia*, Seneca
describes how the German tribes and nomads who live along the Danube,
outside 'Roman civilization', are oppressed by eternal winter and a barren soil:

They keep off the rain with thatch or leaves, they range over ice-bound
marshes, and hunt wild beasts for food. Are they unhappy, do you think?
There is no unhappiness for those whom habit has brought back to
nature. For what they begin from necessity becomes gradually a pleasure.[40]

Seneca imagines the universe as a book wherein man may read the secrets
of creation and of his own place in the universe. As long as the exile can

look upon the heavens it does not matter upon which soil he treads.[41] The harshness of the Arden landscape seems to prompt Duke Senior to meditate in this Stoic vein. He opens Act Two and our first entrance into Arden thus:

> Now, my co-mates and brothers in exile,
> Hath not old custom made this life more sweet
> Than that of painted pomp? Are not these woods
> More free from peril than the envious court?
> Here feel we not the penalty of Adam,
> The seasons' difference, as the icy fang
> And churlish chiding of the winter's wind,
> Which when it bites and blows upon my body
> Even till I shrink with cold, I smile, and say
> 'This is no flattery. These are counsellors
> That feelingly persuade me what I am.'
> Sweet are the uses of adversity
> Which, like the toad, ugly and venomous,
> Wears yet a precious jewel in his head;
> And this our life, exempt from public haunt,
> Finds tongues in trees, books in the running brooks,
> Sermons in stones, and good in everything.

(2.1.1–17)

For Duke Senior, as for the German tribes, custom has dulled the pain of exile until the deprivations of this life seem natural (and even pleasurable). The insecurity and paranoia of the court are contrasted with the predictability of life in the forest; the simplicity and honesty of that forest strips man and court life of their pretensions.

Yet although Duke Senior's monologue sounds as if it has been pieced together from a book of Stoic commonplaces, it is not as exemplary as it pretends. We see glimmers of Epicureanism perhaps in the pleasures of being 'exempt from public haunt', while the idea of gaining profit through a pedagogical approach to the landscape might just as easily suggest travel literature as the Stoic's withdrawal from his environment. The context in which these remarks are uttered represents a deeper challenge. The self-consciousness of Duke Senior's philosophizing identifies him with the Senecan Stoic, but the response of his audience creates unease.[42] Amiens congratulates the Duke in a manner that suggests no absence of flatterers in Arden and his gestures of deference contradict the brotherliness to which the Duke alludes. More emphatic is the sense of Stoicism as a style, an act of translation, a form of rhetoric which the Duke has studied and now performs. Throughout this book we have looked at the need for the exile to find the right language for banishment. Here, the Duke seems to have struck upon it and to have borrowed an identity for himself which pays lip-service to a kind of renunciation he has certainly not performed. Aspects of life in Arden imitate court life: not merely the sway the Duke still holds over his followers but the pastimes of hunting and feasting. Yet, within the context of pastoral drama (and *As You Like It* is an extremely self-conscious pastoral), the Duke's role-playing must bear worldly if not philosophical fruit. Stoic resignation proves the deposed ruler worthy of power. Thus, in *The Maid's Metamorphosis* (1600), Phoebus congratulates Aramanthus for his patient suffering of exile:

> Grave *Aramanthus*, now I see thy face
> I call to minde, how tedious a long space
> Thou hast frequented these sad desarts here,
> Thy time imployed, in heedfull minde I beare:
> The patient sufferance of thy former wrong,
> Thy poore estate, and sharpe exile so long.

> (Act 5, G3)[43]

Phoebus proceeds to reward him with a place among the Muses as long as he lives, and with fame when he dies. He also decides that it is time for Aramanthus to be reunited with his daughter, supposed drowned, but now revealed to be the play's heroine, Eurymine. Duke Senior too rediscovers his daughter, finds a son-in-law and reclaims his dukedom with dazzling speed.

Whether or not we read Duke Senior's speech as deliberately unconvincing, it remains an essential part of the exile's claim to civility. The Duke's self-consolation reminds an audience of a tradition of classical literature which in itself testifies to his education and thus to his civility. But perhaps more importantly, the Duke is here given an opportunity to civilize the landscape. In general, the foresters make little impact on the forest. Like Prospero, Duke Senior is confined to a cave. He does not cultivate or control the landscape except, that is, through language. The above-quoted speech allows him to civilize Arden by turning it into a familiar topography of wisdom, eloquence and piety. In fact, this is mainly how the Duke and his court transform the pastoral world, turning its scenes into emblems that they may moralize at their pleasure, thus distancing the reality of that world. The First Lord explains how Jaques moralized the spectacle of the weeping deer 'into a thousand similes' (2.1.45). The animals, the natural landscape, the natives, all serve as matter for the exiles' melancholy and for the expression of their cultural superiority through literary rather than pragmatic means. Only Orlando literalizes the Duke's metaphors by carving his language into the trees. One verse he composes is of particular interest:

> Why should this a desert be?
> For it is unpeopled? No.
> Tongues I'll hang on every tree,
> That shall civil sayings show.

> (3.2.122–5)[44]

Orlando's assumption about the forest is startling because we know that Arden is by no means uninhabited. Even if we exclude the temporary residents, there are shepherds, Audrey, William and the 'native' Ganimede living alongside the woodland court. Earlier Duke Senior referred to the deer's home as a 'desert city' (2.1.23), peopled by animals, on the basis that there were no real citizens.[45] We are perhaps reminded of Prospero's assumption that the island upon which he lands was uninhabited until his arrival, despite the fact that it bore the imprint of Ariel and Caliban (1.2.282–5). Perhaps in these moments we hear echoes of the argument, common to discussions of the colonization of Ireland and of America, that the land seized was 'unpeopled', not because it was not owned by anyone but because it did not bear any marks of cultivation (one of Batman's definitions of a 'Desert' is lands 'that be not sowen') or because the natives were considered too 'savage' to signify.[46] Appropriately, Duke Senior's reference to the 'desert city' anticipates Jaques' criticism that he has usurped the forest and killed the natives (61–3).

However, the main import of Orlando's carving in the trees is not to civilize those who might read his lines, but to prove his own civility through language. The compulsion to educate and redeem is characteristic of other pastoral exiles. For example, at the end of *The Two Gentlemen of Verona*, Valentine proudly presents his outlaw band to the Duke: 'They are reformèd, civil, full of good, / And fit for great employment, worthy lord' (5.4.154–5). These are men who only a short while before had expressed no repentance, one of whom had murdered because the mood took him. Charles in Heywood's *The Foure Prentices of London* (*c*. 1600) faces a similar challenge as the leader of a group of Italian banditti. His attempts to impose laws upon them are met with the riposte that, if the banditti had wanted to keep laws, they would not have been forced out into the country.[47] Charles' ambitions reflect the *exile*'s need to prove his 'sociability' by civilizing others:

> I'le make these villaines worke in severall trades,
> And in these Forrests make a Common-wealth.
> When them to civil nurture I can bring,
> They shal proclaim me of these mountains King.

(185)

The antecedents of this assumption may well lie in tales of medieval outlawry, most notably the Robin Hood ballads, in which the outlaw leader defines a new society in opposition to the old by establishing his own set of rules. In Anthony Munday's Robin Hood play, *The Downfall of Robert, Earl of Huntingdon* (1598), Robin asks his company to vow their allegiance to six articles read out by Little John advocating chastity, the defence of maids, widows, orphans and the poor, and the persecution of priest, usurer and clerk (1,328–61).[48] There is some interesting evidence to suggest that this was literally an aspect of outlaw life with criminal bands imposing fines or forfeiture while their leaders adopted regal prerogatives. John Bellamy concludes that these acts of imitation not only parodied Plantagenet rule but existed as a challenge to that government: 'They were acts of a rival system of justice, one which was considered by those who concocted it as more fair and less uncertain than the king's.'[49] In medieval legend, this alternative justice magically replaces the old, corrupt system when the outlaw (and his law) are welcomed back into society. In *The Tale of Gamelyn*, an important source for *Rosalynde* and thus indirectly for *As You Like It*,[50] Gamelyn interrupts a trial and proceeds to hang the Justice, the sheriff and the twelve corrupt jurymen. His actions are subsequently sanctioned by the King who makes Gamelyn 'Chef Iustice of al his fre forest' (892).[51]

As You Like It shares the same impulses as this tradition though it lacks any explicit law-giving scene. But why does this exile society seem to progress no further? It is neither as court-focused/exile-fixated as Lodge's *Rosalynde* nor as consciously progressive and utopian as the Robin Hood and *Gamelyn* narratives. One explanation may derive from the powerful Lethean effect of the travel-literature perspective on exile. The non-native inhabitants of Arden are not so much exiles as cultural tourists. In 2.7, Jaques condemns the Fool thus:

> And in his brain,
> Which is as dry as the remainder biscuit
> After a voyage, he hath strange places crammed
> With observation, the which he vents
> In mangled forms.

> (38–42)

This is not only a criticism that Ganimede will make about Jaques himself (and thus one of the many similarities between the two fools); it represents the *modus operandi* for all of the exiles in *As You Like It* who find in one another emblems illustrating moral precepts, *tableaux vivants* and an almost equal measure of profit and entertainment, such as was promised to the traveller from his observations of the strange and exotic. Rosalind and Celia immediately translate exile into voluntary travel, declaring: 'Now go we in content, / To liberty, and not to banishment' (1.3.136–7). Though the journey is tiring and they arrive in Arden hungry and depressed, no further mention is made of banishment. Touchstone deplores their condition but remarks that 'travellers', not exiles, must be content (2.4.15–16). That the shame of banishment has given way to the fiction of the exile-as-traveller is evident from Ganimede's encounter with Jaques. The latter has been boasting about his melancholy, fashioned from 'the sundry contemplation of my travels' (4.1.15–19, 17). Ganimede responds:

A traveller! By my faith, you have great reason to be sad. I fear you have sold your own lands to see other men's. Then to have seen much and to have nothing is to have rich eyes and poor hands.

(4.1.20–3)

Then, ignoring Orlando's greeting, he continues:

Farewell, Monsieur Traveller. Look you lisp, and wear strange suits; disable all the benefits of your own country; be out of love with your nativity, and almost chide God for making you that countenance you are, or I will scarce think you have swam in a gondola.

(31–6)

This is not simply throwaway satire, familiar from the dire warnings against travel propagated by Ascham's *The Scholemaster* or the banished Earl in *The Unfortunate Traveller*.[52] It is dramatically consistent for Ganimede to speak thus. Firstly, this critique endorses his invented history. The youth has apparently never left the forest but still received a superfluity of education and 'experience', suggesting the redundancy of travel. Moreover, his criticism of Jaques is appropriate to his position as a landowner. However, we are also invited to remember that this is Rosalind, forcibly deprived of her birthright and ejected from her home. While this history might reinforce the antipathy felt for the traveller, it reveals a surprising hypocrisy in our heroine. She wears the 'strange suits' of male attire. Knowing that her father is in the forest, indeed having met him, Rosalind continues in her disguise as if 'out of love with [her] nativity'. Nor can she still plead necessity since the dangers that required disguise are past. Rather, Rosalind as Ganimede pursues the same voluntary alienation for which s/he criticizes the traveller.

Towards its close, *As You Like It* takes some important steps towards the establishment of an alternative society. All the marriages performed under the auspices of Hymen suggest the community's rebirth – this act of union in Shakespearean comedy usually takes place outside the greenwood. Moreover, Jaques' ark metaphor: 'There is sure another flood toward, and these couples are all coming to the ark' (5.4.35–6), reminds us of the exile of Noah and his family in order that they might begin society in a less corrupt form (though the journey is made to sound more like a pleasure jaunt than a biblical catastrophe). The suggestion of a new society might also be implied by the transgression of certain boundaries previously established in the forest: the pastoral and the sylvan communities have come together, Touchstone the courtier marries Audrey the country wench etc.

Nevertheless, we are still a long way from the outlaw society of Robin Hood literature, and the promise shown here is not fulfilled. No sooner have the marriages been consecrated than the woodland society prepares to move back to the court. For all the play's attempts to console the exile with images of his own fitness for society, it is unthinkable that he should wish to remain outcast and we are meant to feel the strain Jaques' choice places upon the festive conclusion. The most to be said in its favour is that banishment is a means of embracing civility. Where Rosalind plays at being an outcast, exile is an opportunity for Orlando to *commit* himself to society. His transformation in the forest is a process which replicates the stages he should have passed through in society: recognition of his birth, education, patronage, marriage and inheritance. The ultimate consolation for exile, the subject's return to civilization, finally undermines all its other ameliorations by insisting that the natural landscape is no place for such exiles. Six years later, when Shakespeare came to write *King Lear*, it was the destruction of all such consolations that allowed for a deeper exploration of the society of exiles.

Most critics accept *King Lear*'s debt to the pastoral mode even if the exact nature of that debt remains disputed. Is the play 'the greatest anti-pastoral ever penned', as Maynard Mack argues, or can even its most violent divergences finally be reconciled within the pastoral framework?[53] The consolations for exile afforded by *King Lear* might reinforce the argument for *Lear* as pastoral. As I have argued, they enshrine many of the precepts about man's relationship with the natural landscape, ideas of civility and savagery and so on, that we might define as fundamental to the pastoral mode.[54] Hence, the failure of these consolations to dull the exile's grief in *King Lear* is not enough to annul the play's debt to pastoral romance. Rather, what I perceive as the crucial distinction between the response to exile in *As You Like It* and *King Lear* (and between the two plays' commitment to pastoral) is the way in which this question is addressed structurally. Shakespeare does not only kill the characters whom pastoral (and Nahum Tate) would have married off and promoted to new positions of power and eminence. He aborts the cycle of exile and return by refusing to allow his outcasts to reach a place that they recognize as 'home'. *King Lear* discovers and subsequently endorses a wider perception of exile than could be accommodated by this pastoral structure, though something of the pastoral's yearning for reconciliation and harmony remains resonant throughout the play.

Banishment in the opening scene of *King Lear* focuses our attention on the redrawing of boundaries, not just those between the different parts of Albion, or Jacobean England and Scotland,[55] but between an idealized culture and a savage wilderness. When we first encounter Lear, he seems utterly confident in his own power and centrality. Presiding over the map of Albion, he is reminiscent of the *Genesis* God presiding over Creation and wielding division as a creative power. Just as in the beginning all was good, so in Lear's fantasy Albion is uniformly fair. The portion bestowed on Gonoril is supposedly full of 'shady forests and wide skirted meads' (1.59). Regan's share too is 'no less in space, validity, and pleasure / Than that confirmed on Gonoril' (76–7). In fact, Lear's map does not allow for anything but fecundity, reflecting the King's fantasy of himself as beloved, virtuous and bountiful. Although Cordelia's 'ingratitude' threatens this conception of Lear as king and father, with its implication that there is a world elsewhere, banishment allows Lear to restate his original position. He first identifies her as an alien by likening her to the 'barbarous Scythian' or the cannibal who devours his own family (1.109–13). He then banishes her:

> Here I disclaim all my paternal care,
> Propinquity, and property of blood,
> And as a stranger to my heart and me
> Hold thee from this for ever.
>
> (106–9)

This gesture is clarified a few lines later when Lear declares: 'So be my grave my peace as here I give / Her father's heart from her' (117–18).[56] It is then literalized in the banishment of Cordelia from his sight and only then in the withdrawal of her portion of the kingdom and the subsequent redivision of the map. Since Lear identifies himself and Albion as an idealized, cultured landscape, to leave his sight is to go into the wilderness. Indeed, he drives Cordelia off the map of humanity as he knows it, presenting her to Burgundy as a creature entirely transformed, 'Unfriended, new-adopted to our hate, / Covered with our curse and strangered with our oath' (193–4).

Yet Lear's boundary-drawing is threatened almost at once. France, himself a potential Other, rewrites the banishment of Cordelia through a series of paradoxes:

> Fairest Cordelia, that art most rich, being poor;
> Most choice, forsaken; and most loved, despised:
> Thee and thy virtues here I seize upon.
> Be it lawful, I take up what's cast away.
> Gods, gods! 'Tis strange that from their cold'st neglect
> My love should kindle to inflamed respect.
>
> (241–6)

France not only reverses Lear's value judgement upon Cordelia (and upon the outcast in general), he also rewrites the conclusion of Lear's curse, promising: 'Thou losest here, a better where to find' (252). Kent too attempts to erase the demarcations Lear establishes in this first scene. The adviser who offered Lear an image of himself as ideal king, father, master and patron (1.131–4) now suggests that the man who banished Cordelia is not only foolish but monstrous. Kent will not be diminished by exile, reduced to a 'hated back', a 'banished trunk', but will remain himself: 'Thus Kent, O princes, bids you all adieu; / He'll shape his old course in a country new' (176–7).

A quest for liberty, exile as a precondition to falling in love, social-climbing through marginalization: this is pastoral exile at its most life-enhancing. Cordelia and Kent think in terms of 'Epicurean' consolations and their imaginings are given form, to the extent that Cordelia does find love in exile and Kent proves fidelity to his master.[57] And yet, the nurturant pastoral landscape in which this reversal of exile conventionally found expression is startlingly absent, particularly if we compare Shakespeare's play with *The True Chronicle Historie of King Leir* (*c.* 1590; published 1605). In the latter, we follow Cordella to France where we find the royal couple enjoying a day-trip at the coast, playfully disguised as 'countrye folk' (scene 24). It is here that they meet Leir and Perillus, despairing of this savage and apparently sterile landscape, until Cordella transforms it through her loving response to Leir and the revelation of a banquet.[58] Like a Proserpine figure, Cordella makes the landscape suddenly bloom. Shakespeare's omission of this scene has a number of important implications. Firstly, he never dramatizes the scenes of pastoral exile in France and thus we are deprived of the experience of exile as liberty, love and self-fulfilment. The flexibility and imagination with which the exiles respond to banishment does not bear pastoral fruit. Perhaps more importantly, Shakespeare has ignored the shift in location by which France might symbolize exile and Albion home, preferring to conflate the two. Thus, Leir laments his exile: 'Ah, Brittayne, I shall never see thee more, / That hast unkindly banished thy King: / And yet not thou dost make me to complayne, / But they which were more neere to me then thou' (2,136–9). When the landscape of France is identified as sterile and hostile, when Leir fears that he and Perillus will starve (24.2,113–19), there is at least some comfort in the fact that they are strangers there. The kingdom does not owe Leir anything. By contrast, Shakespeare does not cast abroad for a barren landscape. Rather, he locates wilderness, exposure and starvation *within* Lear's kingdom.

For all its bleakness, the heath in *King Lear* suggests both pastoral and anti-pastoral features. The harshness of the landscape seems to abrogate the convention of a harmonious relationship between man and nature, and yet Lear suggests that 'The tempest will not give me leave to ponder / On things would hurt me more' (10.23–4). The storm appears symbolic of the disorder in Lear's mind as if it were some manifestation of the pathetic fallacy particularly common in pastoral elegy. Yet, at the same time, the violence of the heath drives Lear to distraction – this disordering of the mind being an expression of its capacity to deconstruct social, topographical, even cosmic, hierarchies. We are forced to ask ourselves whether the 'pastoral' heath offers a superior world to that corrupt civilization which Lear and his fellow outcasts have left behind. Wild animals are found in both locations and it appears that Lear has less to fear from the 'cub-drawn bear [...], the lion and the belly-pinched wolf' (8.11–12) than from his monstrous daughters, yet there are urgent calls throughout the play for Lear to come in out of the storm. For all the Fool's adherence to the bitter power of satire to strip away man's pretensions, the heath represents a suffering he will not countenance.

It may be that the contrast between country and city is always an uneasy one in Shakespearean comedy. A. Stuart Daley argues that in *As You Like It*: 'All the major dramatic elements agree in denying moral superiority to the countryside. It follows, therefore, that the play cannot be understood in terms of an antithesis between court and country.'[59] Daley is concerned to refute certain critical readings which, I agree, have tended to idealize the landscape of Arden. Yet the audience is required to expect such an antithesis: the meaning of Arden is created from the disappointment and readjustment of both characters and audience to the absence of a golden world. This is even more true of the 'hard pastoral' landscapes of *Cymbeline* and *King Lear*:

> An inhospitable court is succeeded not by its antithesis, a welcoming pastoral home, but rather by the inhospitality of nature. Both texts thus resist and problematize the pastoral agenda of replacing a defective civilized world (whose defects are signalled in part by the contamination of a home by evil stepmother and daughters respectively) with an ideal natural one.[60]

King Lear makes some attempts to follow the philosophical patterns that we saw in *As You Like It* which promised that man might be redeemed through his efforts to transform this uncivilized world. Where Duke Senior relished 'the churlish chiding of the winter's wind' because of the self-knowledge it promoted, so Lear insists that the experience of wind and rain proves his flatterers false: 'They told me I was everything; 'tis a lie, I am not ague-proof' (20.99–103). Like the forest of Arden, the heath is a Stoic landscape which forces renunciation upon its inhabitants.[61] As the minimum required for existence, it compels the exile to live in a more restricted way and thus better to understand his own essential needs.[62] However, we argued earlier that the Duke's Stoic moralizing of the landscape was only partly convincing. His imaginative act of transforming Arden into a kind of civility by overlaying the landscape with 'tongues in trees, books in the running brooks', etc. is also a means of distancing himself from it. Art, specifically allegory, evades Nature, just as to perform the role of Stoic may actually be to distance oneself from the fact of Exile. Our interpretation of this avoidance of reality will vary: does man need to be rescued from nature by art, bearing in mind that Lear's unmediated experience results in his madness? There is something in the very bleakness of the heath which requires man to allegorize it, thus to distinguish his humanity from the undifferentiating chaos in which the king, the lugged bear, the wolf and the beggar all whirl about. The Gentleman who reports back to Kent describes how Lear

> tears his white hair,
> Which the impetuous blasts, with eyeless rage,
> Catch in their fury and make nothing of;
> Strives in his little world of man to outstorm
> The to-and-fro-conflicting wind and rain.

> (8.6–10)

To what extent Lear is complicit with the elements or battling against them, whether the storm's purpose is to punish or to avenge him – these are questions which remain unanswered.

King Lear invokes both Stoic and Epicurean consolations for exile, juxtaposing a kind of exilic wish-fulfilment (through Cordelia, Kent and Edgar) with a more punitive but nonetheless potentially regenerative suffering. Yet the play consistently resists these perspectives. The meaning of the storm is not easily resolved nor the heath imaginatively civilized. None of the consolations for exile can really assuage the grief of the victims. Moreover, the temporary confusion of civil versus wilderness which was usually resolved at the end of pastoral romance or drama remains permanent. Indeed, Shakespeare consistently conflates the identification of exile and home, such that the abortive structure of *King Lear* (in which none of the exiles returns from his journey) comes to seem the fulfilment of some larger philosophical perspective. In the rest of this chapter, we will examine in detail the nature of the exclusion suffered by each main character, thence to consider more fully the endlessness of exile in *King Lear*.

One of the main alterations Shakespeare made to *The True Chronicle Historie* was to intensify the experience of exile. Unlike their counterparts, Cordelia and Kent are banished, while Lear's experience of exile darkens from tragi-comedy to tragedy.[63] In *The True Chronicle Historie*, the King refers to himself as 'banished' (24.2,137). Ejected by Gonorill and nearly murdered by Ragan, he seeks refuge in France where he apostrophizes his lost country. In Shakespeare's play, Lear never leaves Albion but he is more completely exiled than any of those upon whom an official sentence has been passed. At first the King is complicit in his own displacement. He admits the need to confer the kingdom upon 'younger years' and is preparing for retirement with Cordelia. Yet he quickly becomes the victim of his own acts of banishment when he empowers Gonoril and Regan. Their policy of marginalization begins with Gonoril's order that her servants treat Lear with a 'weary negligence' (3.12, 22–3), extends to the stripping of Lear's retinue, and ends with his being physically shut out, left to wander the deserted heath in a thunderstorm. According to his own definition of exile, he finds himself part of the savage, the barbarous, the Wild. Crucially, he is not outside Albion but at its centre. Lear is finally brought to confront the fantasy that was his kingdom and thus the fantasy of his own identity as king and father. The landscape is not that lush pastoral idyll he imagined but a barren waste, its inhabitants half-naked men such as Poor Tom, shivering in a hovel. Such were Lear's subjects, dependent upon his munificence, but men of whose existence he had no knowledge: 'O, I have ta'en / Too little care of this' (11.29–30).

Although Lear's personal experience of exile is significant, its meaning is also generated through the play's other outcasts. There is an obvious comparison to be made between Lear and Gloucester. For Gloucester, the journey into exile begins with a sense of the irrelevance of age. The letter Edmund has contrived reads: 'I begin to find an idle and fond bondage in the oppression of aged tyranny, who sways not as it hath power but as it is suffered' (2.47–50). When Gloucester's 'treachery' is discovered, his title is stripped from him with his estate and all his goods. The plucking out of his eyes casts him into a dark, animalistic world: 'Go thrust him out at gates, and let him smell / His way to Dover' (14.91–2). Neither Lear nor Gloucester is able to adapt to the transformations that beset them for they insist on permanent and universally-acknowledged identities in a world that recognizes no such thing. Hence, transformation is a form of torture (4.262–3). However, the most important identification Lear makes is between himself and Gloucester's son, Edgar.[64]

Unlike Kent and Cordelia, Edgar is not banished but pursued:

> I heard myself proclaimed,
> And by the happy hollow of a tree
> Escaped the hunt. No port is free, no place
> That guard and most unusual vigilance
> Does not attend my taking.
>
> (7.167–71)

The reference to his being 'proclaimed' might suggest that Edgar is now an outlaw. From the eleventh century onwards in England the defendant accused of treason or felony would be called to face trial via the proclamation of exigents issued at five successive county courts.[65] If he failed to appear he would be proclaimed an outlaw, meaning that he was deprived of all legal rights, property and land and that he might be killed on sight.[66]

This would certainly explain Edgar's terror of capture. Yet outlawry most often expressed the Law's inability to bring the accused to trial, while Gloucester repeatedly declares that Edgar will not escape – Cornwall's proclamation will bring 'the murderous caitiff to the stake' (6.62).[67] Perhaps, then, the hints of outlawry, including Gloucester's reference to Edgar as 'outlawed from my blood' (11.154), are less a comment on the defendant's legal status than part of his dramatic identity as symbolic (and composite) outcast. Similarly, the reference to Edgar as 'banished' (21.88) is not 'a factual error' but part of this exile archetype.[68] Self-conscious about his status as outlaw/banished man, Edgar creates Poor Tom:

> My face I'll grime with filth,
> Blanket my loins, elf all my hair with knots,
> And with presented nakedness outface
> The wind and persecution of the sky.
> The country gives me proof and precedent
> Of Bedlam beggars who with roaring voices
> Strike in their numbed and mortified bare arms
> Pins, wooden pricks, nails, sprigs of rosemary,
> And with this horrible object from low farms,
> Poor pelting villages, sheep-cotes and mills,
> Sometime with lunatic bans, sometime with prayers
> Enforce their charity. 'Poor Tuelygod, Poor Tom!'
> That's something yet. Edgar I nothing am.

> (7.175–87)

There are elements in Edgar's experience which suggest the playfulness of pastoral exile. Yet if his choice of costume brings him closer to nature, it also strikes a discordant note. While a fall in status was conventional, from princess to shepherdess, from earl to servant, Edgar provokes both fear and revulsion in his identity as the semi-naked beggar possessed by devils.[69] Edgar's counterpart in the *Arcadia*, Leonatus, does not adopt any disguise but becomes a private soldier. He is on the point of promotion when he abandons this career to protect his blinded father.[70] In contrast, Edgar chooses to parade the wretchedness of his condition and the stigmatization of his life. As Carroll suggests: 'The name of loss and exile, of suffering and abasement, is Poor Tom.'[71]

One response to the question of why Edgar adopts such a pose has been to identify him as the fugitive Catholic.[72] In *The Catholicism of Shakespeare's Plays*, Peter Milward quotes a striking passage from a letter by Edmund Campion (1580):

> I cannot long escape the hands of the heretics; the enemy have so many eyes, so many tongues, so many scouts and crafts. I am in apparel to

myself very ridiculous; I often change my name also [...] Threatening edicts come forth against us daily.[73]

There are obvious parallels here with Edgar's humiliating disguise and false name, and with his continued self-reinvention. Fear and alienation are the common condition of both persecuted Catholic and pursued nobleman. Twenty-five years after Campion's letter, when Shakespeare wrote *King Lear*, 'threatening edicts' had been issued (1585, 1603) which meant torture and execution to Catholics discovered within the realm. Moreover, in the final scene, Edgar refers to 'The bloody proclamation [...] / That followed me so near' (24.180–1). In 1605, this proclamation was more likely to recall anti-Catholic legislation than the fourteenth-century process of outlawry. And yet there are some important distinctions to be made between Edgar's plight and that of the fugitive Catholic. In particular, the explicit intention of the anti-Catholic bills was not to encourage martyrdom but rather to force Catholic priests to leave the country. The proclamations referred to above (and the laws which they expressed) *banished* English Catholics, offering them a certain time-period within which to leave the country before prosecuting them for felony. Similarly, in 1585, 1603, 1606 and 1618, large numbers of Catholic priests who had been held in prison for years were transported.[74] By contrast, Edgar is only prevented from leaving the country by the fact that the ports are barred against him. His desire to leave suggests another contrast with the Catholic priest. As we saw in the memoirs of Edward Rishton, the Jesuit often resisted exile or transportation because it would mean abandoning his English congregation.[75] Campion puts on his disguise so that he may remain in the country, moving from one Catholic household to another. Although Edgar ends up using his disguise to minister to his father, preventing Gloucester's damnable suicide, this was never his intention. In fact, it is Kent, determined to serve Lear despite the death sentence which hangs over him, who more closely resembles the Catholic fugitive.

The argument for Edgar-as-Catholic then remains intriguing but conjectural.[76] What Edgar's self-invention as Poor Tom does smack of is that more general self-dramatizing tendency we have observed in the historical exiles throughout this book, a tendency that is partly a response to the loss of identity and status suffered through exile. While Shakespeare may have drawn upon accounts of the extremities to which Catholic priests were brought in his creation of the archetypal outcast, a more obvious source for Edgar's transformation is the discourse of vagrancy.[77] Not only were Bedlam beggars frequently put on display within the hospital, they were also described in theatrical terms – renowned for adopting a particular costume, rhetoric and gestures, even mutilating themselves, to 'enforce charity'.[78] Edgar's self-inflicted wounds as Bedlam beggar reflect his desire for mortification, perhaps out of guilt at his father's rejection, certainly out of shame for his condition.[79] Yet the importance of his disguise is as much the impact it has on others as its meaning for himself. It requires an audience.

The remarkable reaction Poor Tom inspires in King Lear is thrown into relief if we compare it with the encounter between Timon and Apemantus in the wilderness outside Athens.[80] Apemantus hears that Timon has turned misanthrope, specifically that 'Thou dost affect my manners, and dost use them' (4.3.200). Yet Timon's imitation of Apemantus only reinforces his sense of estrangement (4.3.220–2). In *King Lear*, the beggar is seen to offer some previously unattained insight into the human condition. In *Timon of Athens*, the self-exiled man rejects any human identification at all and would purge himself of humanity. Moreover, Apemantus is too low a man for Timon to imitate. Fortune has never smiled upon this Athenian and hence he cannot imagine the magnitude of Timon's loss, one 'Who had the world as my confectionary, / The mouths, the tongues, the eyes and hearts of men' (261–2). Where Lear debases himself to the level of Poor Tom but sees no debasement, Timon insists upon hierarchy. He may detest men and himself but he remains superior to Apemantus and proud of their difference (278–9).

By contrast, Lear's confrontation with Poor Tom echoes the pastoral encounter between the complex and the simple man. At first, Lear understands Poor Tom only as an emblem of his own suffering, interpreting his nakedness: 'Hast thou given all to thy two daughters, / And art thou come to this?' (11.43–4). But the significance he attaches to Poor Tom becomes increasingly expansive. The mad beggar is a version of the simple, unaccommodated man, a *reductio ad absurdum* and yet universal. Where the pastoral exile will often put on shepherd's garb to signal his philosophical transformation, Lear takes off his clothing that he might better imitate the 'poor, bare, forked man'. More importantly, Lear describes Poor Tom as his 'philosopher' (11.141, 162) and specifically as a 'most learnèd Theban' (144) and 'good Athenian' (166). These references may express Lear's identification of Poor Tom as a fellow exile. Banishment had frequently been the philosopher's fate in imperial Rome, as recalled by Sidney in his *Defence of Poesy*,[81] while it was also commonplace to suggest that exile created philosophers. Dio Chrysostom describes how, when banished, he put on 'humble attire' and began to wander:

> And the men whom I met, on catching sight of me, would sometimes call me a tramp and sometimes a beggar, though some did call me a philosopher. From thus it came about gradually and without any planning or any self-conceit on my part that I acquired this name [...] For many would approach me and ask what was my opinion about good and evil. As a result I was forced to think about these matters that I might be able to answer my questioners.[82]

While Lear may perceive in Poor Tom the generic exile-philosopher, F. G. Butler has persuasively argued that the King has a specific philosopher in mind: Diogenes the Cynic.[83] Again, the spectacle presented by Poor Tom is uppermost in Lear's thoughts. The Cynics, in other ways similar to the Stoics, were famous for their ragged, dirty appearance, and for their insistence on living in accordance with nature even in the midst of the city. Butler argues that Lear's recognition of Poor Tom as 'unaccommodated man' and the value he subsequently sets upon this naturalness in the face of his own sophistication reflects accounts of Diogenes' life and beliefs, perhaps familiar to Shakespeare from Erasmus' *Apophthegmes* translated by Nicholas Udall (1542).[84] Thus, Lear's insistence that Poor Tom is a 'philosopher' is not an expression of derangement so much as an inspiration. Lear perceives that such a man might offer him consolation, not just for exile (though Diogenes had supposedly been banished from Athens), but for his suffering throughout the play.

Nevertheless, Poor Tom's embodiment of the Cynic philosophy, like Duke Senior's performance of Stoicism, is only partial. He may strip himself down to the essential man (Edgar is literally homeless and reduced to begging) but he remains perceptible to the audience as Edgar in disguise and a representative of artifice both in the simple fact of that disguise and perhaps in the pastoral tradition it implies. As such, Edgar occupies a curious position in the art versus nature debate. For all his representative power as natural man, he is also the play's most artful and civilizing presence. He switches between different disguises to lead his blinded father, verbally creates the plane of Dover Cliff beneath Gloucester's feet, and fakes a *deus ex machina*. For Lear, too, he represents the hope of a new society. If we refer back to the pattern, perceived in *As You Like It*, of characters attempting to prove their civility not only over the landscape but over its inhabitants through the imposition of 'civil sayings', we may find further traces of pastoral artifice in *King Lear*.

Throughout the play, the Fool has offered Lear abundant aphorisms, expressed through prose, rhyme and song, by which to re-evaluate his behaviour and to attain self-knowledge. With the entrance of Poor Tom, however, the Fool finds his role increasingly usurped:

> Take heed o'th' foul fiend; obey thy parents; keep thy word justly; swear not; commit not with man's sworn spouse: set not thy sweet heart on proud array.

> Let not the creaking of shoes nor the rustlings of silks betray thy poor heart to women. Keep thy foot out of brothel, thy hand out of placket, thy pen from lender's book, and defy the foul fiend.

> (11.73–5, 85–8)

The first quotation has been referred to as a parody of the Ten Commandments, but I see no reason why it should not be interpreted as one of Poor Tom's utterances in defiance of the fiend.[85] From the frightening incoherence of his devil-speak, these 'civilizing' words are heard. *King Lear*'s outcasts are reminded of the original Christian blueprint for society bestowed upon the exiles at Mount Sinai. What Lear does with Poor Tom's 'civil sayings', in an echo of the law-giving scenes of *Gamelyn* and *The Downfall of Robert, Earl of Huntingdon*, is to try to establish justice.

The trial scene only appears in the Quarto. Perhaps Shakespeare judged it unnecessary given the later exploration of injustice in 4.6. Perhaps this 'ensemble in madness' with its cues for laughter distracted from the pathos of Lear's condition.[86] On paper at least, the scene extends the pastoral conventions of *King Lear*. Again, there is a sense in which the outcast subconsciously attempts to define himself back into society (and it is significant that they have moved out of the storm into the hovel) by claiming to dispense justice. In the trial scene, Poor Tom's authority is reflected in his position as 'most learned justicer' and the Fool, 'Thou sapient sir', becomes his partner (13.16–17). They are to sit on the Bench so that Lear may bring his daughters to trial. Obviously, there is parodic potential in having a madman and a fool reverenced as judges by a king. However, like the medieval outlaw's imposition of justice, this scene is not simply a parody of legal procedures in the 'real world'. It offers a reassertion of values through the vices it condemns: cruelty, ingratitude, destruction of bonds, bribery and corruption (13.48).

Nevertheless, as an expression of order and civility the scene clearly fails. Lear's justices will not sit still; he has to ask them twice to occupy the place of authority. One of the accused manages to escape. The trial falls into disarray when Lear becomes increasingly wild, Edgar begins to lose his composure as Poor Tom, and the court is imaginatively invaded by barking dogs. In fact, Lear's main difficulty is to keep anyone's attention on the business at hand. Each man is so preoccupied with his own mania that he has no thought for the needs of any other, or for the principle of justice. Hence, a scene which might have worked to suggest the reformulation of society exemplifies the extent to which it has broken down. At this point the trial scene appears suspended between genres: comic in its anticipation of the restitution of society, and tragic in its failure to achieve that ordering and in its foreshadowing of the catastrophe at Dover.

To a greater extent than its comic predecessor, *King Lear* provides glimpses of an alternative society. The exiles on the heath do not huddle together simply for warmth. Rather, Lear finds a new tone of compassion for the Fool and Poor Tom, while Kent and Gloucester, though dismayed at the company Lear now keeps, indulge his whims. After the heath, Dover becomes the focus of fresh hopes. Not only is it the site of Cordelia's landing and a centre for resistance (8.27, 13.84–5), it was also associated with a famous victory over barbarism. According to Holinshed's *Chronicles*, in the reign of Brute, Corineus killed the giant, Gogmagog, by throwing him over Dover cliff, thus marking the re-imposition of civility upon a barbarous land. Finally, even though the battle has been lost, Lear imagines an idyll based solely on himself and Cordelia (24.8–19). Michael Long writes emotively of the exiles' return from the heath to this fantasy of communal life: 'new and fresh words of civilization have arisen'.[87] Yet these attempts at civility, from the trial scene to Lear's experience in prison, prove consistently abortive. Even at the very end of the play, the new government of Albion has yet to be decided.

There are various reasons for the play's failure to establish an alternative society. Not least of these is its failure to draw all its exiles back into a circle, beginning with the Fool. Although Kent urges him to accompany Lear to Dover (13.93–4), the Fool never reappears. Whether an oversight on Shakespeare's part or the casual dismissal of one who had served his purpose (and was doubling as Cordelia),[88] this absence contributes to a sense of continued alienation which the Dover reunion might have been expected to dispel. Gloucester is another character who disappears before the end of the play. Although his presence at Dover coincides with that of Lear and Cordelia (23.0), he never makes contact with them. He dies offstage, a mere figure of Edgar's speech. Yet perhaps the most important character excluded from recognition and reconciliation at the end of the play is Kent. When Cordelia asks him to resume his former shape in Scene 21, the Earl refuses: 'Yet to be known shortens my made intent. / My boon I make it that you know me not / Till time and I think meet' (9–11). We are made to expect a pastoral scene of revelation when Kent will throw off his disguise and reveal the service he has performed for his master. Yet this plan proves abortive in three ways. Firstly, Kent's secret plot to assist Lear seems to be destroyed when Cordelia's forces lose the final battle. He appears then only to bid the King farewell (his heart apparently broken). Secondly, Edgar ruins the surprise by revealing Kent's identity. He describes his encounter with an anonymous man who recounted to him Lear and Gloucester's sufferings. When Albany asks the man's identity, Edgar replies:

> Kent, sir, the banished Kent, who in disguise
> Followed his enemy king, and did him service
> Improper for a slave.

> (24.216–18)[89]

The revelation of Kent's identity is surely his own, and a crucial part of the exile's readmission into society. Yet the terrible bathos which greets his entrance ten lines later is only partly Edgar's fault. Reeling from the news of Gonoril and Regan's deaths, Albany regrets the reception the Earl must receive: 'the time will not allow / The compliment that very manners urges'

(228–9). When Kent does appear and asks to see the King, Albany remembers what he had forgotten, to the further neglect of the exile. Kent does not expect to inspire a general wonder here. It is to the King that he is determined to reveal himself. Yet the anticlimactic nature of his reception expresses how irrelevant to the tragedy he has become as other dramas upstage his own transformation from Caius to Kent. Most importantly, he cannot make himself known to Lear because the latter is no longer capable of recognizing him:

> Lear Are not you Kent?
>
> Kent The same, your servant Kent. Where is your servant Caius?
>
> Lear He's a good fellow, I can tell you that.
>   He'll strike, and quickly too. He's dead and rotten.
>
> Kent No, my good lord, I am the very man –
>
> Lear I'll see that straight.
>
> Kent That from your first of difference and decay
>   Have followed your sad steps.
>
> Lear You're welcome hither.

> (24.277–84)

We are reminded that Dover is a port: a point of entry back into Albion, but also the beginning of other journeys. And what becomes painfully clear at the end of *King Lear* is that the exile's alienation has not ended. Lear's return to sanity from the turmoil and self-loss suffered on the heath depended upon the recognition offered by Cordelia. Through his daughter, he knew himself and his kingdom once again (21.50–84).[90] Without her, he wanders into a despairing solipsism where no one can reach him. With Lear thus lost, Kent cannot return from exile.

In Guillaume Du Vair's treatise, *The Moral Philosophie of the Stoicks* (published in English 1598), he reinterprets a familiar apophthegm:

> Every place in the world is a wise man's country, or rather no place at all is his country. For his habitation is in heaven whither he aspireth after he hath passed the time here beneath of his sorrowful pilgrimage; making his abode in cities and provinces, as travellers in Innes and hostelries.[91]

The restless structure of *King Lear*, with characters continually moving from one abode to another, seems to reflect this perception of mankind's 'sorrowful pilgrimage'. It is a state created through the play's acts of banishment yet it attains a larger significance, representing not simply 'the expulsion of the good',[92] but a sense of exile as mankind's inevitable fate.

However, if we recall the distinction made by Clarisia in *Common Conditions*, we will remember that exile could be distinguished from travel by the possibility of closure: the traveller may return home. Du Vair makes a similar assumption by insisting that mankind passes through the external world before finally attaining celestial rest. This state of displacement from heaven might be described as exile but it is a pastoral exile, re-imagined as travel because it must end in return.

King Lear also seems to end with exile as travel. While the play has paid little heed to the consolations for exile afforded by travel literature – the initial 'cosmopolitan' optimism of Kent and Cordelia is not developed – in the final scene we find references to the exile undertaking the journey towards death. On Lear's behalf, Kent insists: 'Vex not his ghost. O let him pass' (307). He asks the same thing for himself a few lines later: 'I have a journey, sir, shortly to go: / My master calls and I must not say no' (315–16). There remains an emphasis on the translation of exile into home-coming through this metaphor of travel. And yet Shakespeare seems far less convinced by this end to exile than Du Vair or even Boethius.

In *The Consolation of Philosophy*, the banished and imprisoned author is challenged by Philosophy to redefine the terms of his exile. Boethius' home is not to be found in the external world but is defined as the kingdom of God from which no man can be exiled.[93] In a metaphor which inspired Dante's *Divina Commedia*, Philosophy promises to lead Boethius out of exile to the attaining of this final home:

> I wyll shewe unto the, the waye that maye brynge the home, to the knowledge of true blessednes and felicitie. And I wyll fasten fethers or resones in thy mynde, wherby it may ryse up in helth, so that after thou hast cast awaye all trouble of worldly and temporall thynges, thou mayst reuert and turne into thy countrye safe and sounde, by my leding, by my path way and by my steppes.[94]

Boethius makes no mention of the kingdom of God as heaven, nor does he require the exile to ask for divine intercession to get there. Similarly, *King Lear* makes no reference to heaven as the exile's point of return. Perhaps both Boethius' consolation and Shakespeare's play reflect too strongly the pagan influences upon them to make the identification of heaven as haven explicit. And yet, *King Lear* seems to me far more ambivalent in tone than either Du Vair or Boethius. It is partly for this reason that I think we must reject the Catholic interpretation of *King Lear* as 'the play of his most calcu-lated to touch the hearts of a Catholic audience with its feeling of pity and its message of patience'.[95] For there is no sense that the exile's suffering will be rewarded. In the Quarto, Lear dies certain in the knowledge that he will never see Cordelia again: 'O, thou wilt come no more' (302). His cry of 'Break heart, I prithee break' is a long way from Milward's inspiring pattern of Christian patience. It expresses the exile's longing for an end to alienation from the source of love and identity, without suggesting that that source is divine or that it might be regained through death. Perhaps in Kent's last words there is a stronger sense of reconciliation: he will continue to follow (that is, travel in the wake of and remain loyal to) his master. Yet he does not express any spiritual sense of reconciliation or return. *King Lear* is undoubtedly the most nihilistic of Shakespeare's banishment plays for it cannot imagine an end to exile. In this respect the play may realize a strain of scepticism perceptible throughout the canon. There is a remarkable absence of *Christian* consolations for exile in Shakespeare's work. Rather, the plays consistently displace heaven with a secular world, declaring with Romeo: 'Heaven is here' and risking the condemnation of the Friar in their pursuit of earthly satisfaction.

A final comparison of *As You Like It* and *King Lear* suggests how dependent the comic vision of exile is upon worldly consolations, meaning not only the 'Epicurean' tradition of consoling exile but the literary tradition of a pastoral return. Perhaps there are glimpses of a more spiritual perspective in Le Beau's desire to meet Orlando in 'a better world than this' (1.2.274). When Arden turns out not to be that better world we have a sense of the characters' exclusion from some desired realm. However, in *King Lear*, the inadequacy of pastoral consolations and the avoidance of return open up a new vista of meaning where exile has become a condition endemic to humanity but without the consoling fiction of heaven as haven.

To conclude, we might relate this absence of heaven to the scepticism with which the pastoral landscape is often treated in Shakespeare's plays. Most medieval accounts of life-as-exile pivot on the distinction between the secular and the divine worlds. In one place, man is endlessly tossed about, finding nothing upon which to rely and suffering perpetual torment; in the other world he finds recognition, love, peace. In Shakespeare's *As You Like It* and *King Lear*, the assumed polarity between natural landscape and city/court is frequently undermined. It is not simply that Shakespeare's plays tend to desire civilization more than the pastoral idyll; rather that idyll simply does not exist in *As You Like It*, *Cymbeline*, *King Lear* or *The Tempest*. In a mode that so lends itself to Platonic, Christian or even pagan transcendentalism, Shakespeare's refusal to idealize the pastoral landscape may represent a larger refutation. In *King Lear*, Shakespeare refuses to bring his exiles home. He leaves us with a vision of mankind, represented by the abjuring king, the outlawed beggar, the alienated Fool and the banished nobleman on the heath. This is exile not travel.

5
Coriolanus: the Banishment of Rome

> | | |
> |---|---|
> | *Sabinus* | But these our times |
>
>   *Sabinus*   But these our times
>   Are not the same, Arruntius.
>   *Arruntius*   Times? The men,
>   The men are not the same: 'tis we are base,
>   Poor, and degenerate from th'exalted strain
>   Of our great fathers. Where is now the soul
>   Of godlike Cato? – he, that durst be good
>   When Caesar durst be evil; and had power,
>   As not to live his slave, to die his master.
>   Or where the constant Brutus, that (being proof
>   Against all charm of benefits) did strike
>   So brave a blow into the monster's heart
>   That sought unkindly to captive his country?
>   O, they are fled the light ...
>   There's nothing Roman in us.
>
>   *Sejanus His Fall* (1603), Ben Jonson (1.85–97, 102)[1]

Arruntius speaks like an exile. His use of the *ubi sunt* motif, recalling Anglo-Saxon poems such as *The Wanderer*, creates a sense of disorientation in Rome. The city may be profoundly familiar – Romanitas is inscribed in the history, rituals, language and architecture of the city – yet no one is Roman. It was inevitable that a dramatist already concerned with the representation of banishment and exile should have been drawn to this Roman setting. To be Roman was one of the strongest cultural identities on the Elizabethan and Jacobean stage and part of its dramatic appeal was the spectacle of its disruption. Alienation was built into the Roman 'character': alienation from the achievements of ancestors (particularly fathers), from a glorious historical moment, from a just political system, from the possibility of greatness. Thus banishment was not only a famous punishment in Roman law and a feature of many heroic biographies; it was also a kind of unmetaphoring of the Roman condition. In *Coriolanus*, we find Shakespearean exile at its most political. The expulsion of a man publicly celebrated as the embodiment of Romanitas symbolizes the city's adherence to a different value system and paves the way for future innovation while raising important questions about the integrity of Roman democracy. Shakespeare's historical sources frequently used examples of banishment for political comment. However, in *Coriolanus*, we are also concerned with the Roman's alienation *within* Rome and it is this public and private tragedy that Shakespeare explores through banishment.

From the beginning of the play it is clear that the word 'Rome' has become severed from a shared and stable meaning. The Republic has only recently been established; in Act 1 we hear of the creation of the tribunes. Rome is in transition and as the political structure of the city changes, so 'Rome' alters semantically. Before Menenius proffers his body politic analogy, the plebeians have worked out for themselves the reciprocity upon which Rome is founded: 'The leanness that afflicts us, the object of our misery, is as an inventory to particularize their abundance; our sufferance is a gain to them' (1.1.18–23). Their response is not merely to demand corn, or to seek revenge on the patricians, but to insist upon their Romanness. The storming of the Capitol represents both an appropriation of patrician power and their movement from an ideologically marginal position to the centre of Rome. Similarly, the franchise they gain through the appointment of the tribunes is directed towards these 'Roman' aspirations. As one of the tribunes asks, 'What is the city but the people?' (3.1.199). By contrast, the patricians defend an aristocratic and conservative conception of Rome that excludes the plebeians. This Rome is defined by the code of Romanitas, the virtues of constancy, honour, martial skill, courage and self-sacrifice, virtues that the plebeians are consistently declared to lack. According to Menenius, Rome is as far beyond the plebeians' reach as heaven (1.1.66–7). Their rebellion cannot hope to affect the state whose 'course will on / The way it takes, cracking ten thousand curbs / Of more strong link asunder than can ever / Appear in your impediment' (67–70). Hence, the word 'Rome' defines only the patricians. The few occasions when it is used by them to embrace a shared civic identity occur when the plebeians are required to fight, as at Corioli (1.7.2), or when they are required to offer praise (2.1.159).[2] The concerns of both sides are for a time subsumed in rituals of collective identity. The man who makes this possible is Rome's champion, Coriolanus.

Coriolanus' significance for Rome is expressed through eulogies, uttered in private and public, and also performed as rites of appropriation by which 'Rome must know / The value of her own' (1.10.20–1). After the battle at Corioli, Cominius looks forward to uniting the city in wonder at the hero's exploits. He imagines the scene:

> Where senators shall mingle tears with smiles,
> Where great patricians shall attend and shrug,

I'th'end admire; where ladies shall be frighted
And, gladly quaked, hear more; where the dull tribunes,
That with the fusty plebeians hate thine honours,
Shall say against their hearts 'We thank the gods
Our Rome hath such a soldier.'

(1.10.3–9)

Cominius recognizes divisions in Rome – the insouciant, grudging patricians; the tribunes and plebeians joined in hatred of the hero – but
Coriolanus' achievements are seen to reunite the city. Indeed, it could be
argued that the ritual depends on difference. As Michael Long summarizes:

> [Coriolanus] must live as they dare not. He must be in actuality what they
> can only behold in dream. While they can live in the actual and not very
> wonderful city of Rome, he must inhabit the institutional fiction of it
> which they have in their minds. He must excite them with displays of an
> excellence to which their earthbound souls cannot and dare not aspire.[3]

However, Coriolanus himself increasingly denies the plebeians' participa-
tion in this fantasy. From the first scene, he castigates them as inimical to
Rome for their inconstancy (1.1.180–2), their materialism (1.6.4–8), and
their cowardice (2.3.52–5). As he sharpens the contrast between himself
and the plebeians,[4] Coriolanus becomes increasingly adamant that the
latter do not belong in Rome:

I would they were barbarians, as they are,
Though in Rome littered; not Romans, as they are not,
Though calved i'th'porch o'th'Capitol.

(3.1.237–9)

References to the plebeians as 'slaves' imply their alienation along class
lines while hinting that they might literally be 'barbarians'.[5]

Coriolanus is the protagonist of a seductive fiction about Rome, a fiction
which, like Menenius' fable, intends to distract the plebeians from their
empty bellies and to glorify their subjection. Yet the hero is such an out-
spoken adherent of aristocratic Rome that when he is not uniting the city
in a heroic pageant, he is dividing it even to the point of rebellion. Like
Menenius' fable which *reminds* the plebeians of their hunger, Coriolanus
inadvertently helps to focus the plebeians' grievances and to shape their
responses. For example, in the first scene, the plebeians recognize Caius
Martius as their enemy and plot his assassination as part of their rebellion.
But they are also intrigued by his hatred of them. If Martius can be an
'enemy to the people' (8), 'a very dog to the commonalty' (27) and yet be

fêted as a great Roman hero and patriot, the plebeians are left with a definition of country that completely excludes them. In the course of the play, Coriolanus makes it increasingly apparent that he does not recognize the plebeians as Romans, thus inspiring them to redefine the city by taking political power and banishing their enemy.

The banishment of Coriolanus is the scene of the plebeians' greatest triumph and a critical moment in the redefinition of Rome. Until Sicinius' pronouncement at 3.3.105, various methods of punishment have been proposed for the tyrant and traitor, including execution or a public fine. Banishment is deemed appropriate because of its association with tyranny: within living memory the Tarquins were thus expelled. However, Shakespeare makes the choice of banishment particularly resonant by dramatizing the conflict between plebeians and Coriolanus in spatial terms. In 3.1, Coriolanus and the senators are making their way to the marketplace after the hero's supposed election as consul. With this political office, Coriolanus is moving further into the heart of the city, here signified by his physical progression into Rome. But he is stopped on both counts by the tribunes who tell him that the consulship has been revoked and insist that he go no further. Sicinius suggests that Coriolanus has lost his way in Rome:

> If you will pass
> To where you are bound, you must enquire your way,
> Which you are out of, with a gentler spirit.
>
> (56–8)

The tribunes have taken it on themselves to prevent Coriolanus' advancement. More importantly, the image of Coriolanus as lost in Rome, requiring directions as if he were a stranger, suggests the alienation and wandering of the exile.

The banishment of Coriolanus in 3.3 completes the movement of the plebeians from the margins to the heart of the city. His enmity to the people now makes him an enemy to Rome, in defiance of patrician definitions of the city. Boundaries are dramatically redrawn by the hero's expulsion from the city walls. But it is through the language of banishment that this plebeian appropriation of Rome and 'Rome' is most apparent:

> In the name o'th'people,
> And in the power of us the tribunes, we
> E'en from this instant banish him our city
> In peril of precipitation
> From off the rock Tarpeian, never more
> To enter our Rome gates. I'th'people's name
> I say it shall be so.
>
> (3.1.103–9)

Sicinius' use of the phrases 'in the name o' th' people', 'our city' and 'our Rome' goes unchallenged. The word 'Rome' has finally been wrested from the word-store of the patricians. Moreover, as if to reinforce this linguistic reversal of power, Sicinius suggests that the plebeians follow Coriolanus to the gates of Rome and use his own invective against him (142–4). This is particularly ironic if we remember that Coriolanus' insults centred on the plebeians' 'un-Romanness' and their barbarity, terms which now apply to the banished man.

Yet this account of Coriolanus' banishment in 3.3 leaves out one crucial element. The hero does not simply disappear into the night, as he does in Plutarch.[6] Rather, Shakespeare's Coriolanus has some parting words for Rome:

> You common cry of curs, whose breath I hate
> As reek o'th'rotten fens, whose loves I prize
> As the dead carcasses of unburied men
> That do corrupt my air. I banish you.

> (3.3.124–7)

Coriolanus' banishment of Rome works on a number of levels. It is a form of linguistic self-assertion – Coriolanus always wants to have the last word – as well as an expression of political defiance. It goes on to hint at Rome's potentially tragic self-alienation in banishing its hero (131–7). But perhaps most importantly, it challenges the redefinition of Rome that the tribunes seem now to have achieved. Simply by uttering the sentence of exile, Coriolanus reclaims banishment for the patricians and once again makes the people subject to patrician law. There is also an implication in his reference to the plebeians' stinking breath that he can prove them traitors. Earlier references in the play to foul breath served to emphasize the plebeians' materiality and to denigrate their political power since their 'voices' were synonymous with votes.[7] However, in *2 Henry VI*, foul breath and banishment are associated with treason. The King banishes Suffolk thus: 'He shall not breathe infection in this air/ But three days longer, on the pain of death' (3.2.291–2). The foul breath of the plebeian is also the treasonous language of the traitor. Thus Coriolanus displaces both banishment and treason onto the plebeians. If we look at the other insults with which Coriolanus envenoms the sentence of exile, we find that these too reinforce the plebeians' supposed anti-social, extra-social nature. 'Cur' signifies a vicious, perhaps mongrel dog, more likely to be a stray than a domestic animal. 'Rotten fens' suggests a landscape beyond the walls of the city, unsuitable for human habitation (as the settlers at the Jamestown colony had already discovered!). The corpses of unburied men imply expulsion from Roman custom, from the city of Rome and even from the Roman conception of an afterlife.[8] *Titus Andronicus* begins with the welcoming of Titus' dead sons into the family vault and ends with the denial of funereal rites to Tamora's corpse and the injunction: 'throw her forth [i.e. outside of Rome] to beasts and birds of prey' (5.3.197). In this final gesture, Lucius hopes at last to make the distinction between the noble Roman and the barbarous Goth clear. However, the most significant reversal that Coriolanus performs as banisher is the transformation of Rome into a place of exile. Such a reversal is central to Shakespeare's representation of banishment in earlier plays, neatly summarized by Kent's 'Freedom lives hence, and banishment is here', but Shakespeare may have found a source for this particular instance in Cicero's *Paradoxa Stoicorum*.[9]

In 58 BC, Cicero was banished from Rome by the consul, P. Clodius. In Paradox IV of the *Paradoxa Stoicorum*, he defies banishment by reversing the positions of banisher and banished. Cicero argues that Clodius' acts have proven him a criminal, an enemy of the people, and a man worthy of exile. The fact that he has not been banished but remains in the city does not make him any less of an outcast, for the true citizen should be distinguished by character and conduct not by race or locality.[10] Coriolanus' banishment of the plebeians makes the same point: that one may remain in Rome and still be an exile and a traitor. He also seems to respond to Cicero's suggestion that action not location defines the true citizen. As we have seen, Coriolanus identifies the plebeians as barbarians whether or not they were born and bred in Rome. More generally, he argues that Rome cannot distinguish between friend and enemy, and thus banishes its 'defenders' (3.3.132). The First Watchman outside the Volscian camp appears to concur. He asks Menenius how he can ask for mercy, 'when you have pushed out your gates the very defender of them, and in a violent popular ignorance given your enemy your shield' (5.2.41–4). The word 'enemy' here could refer to both the Volscians and the Roman plebeians and reflects the play's persistent blurring of friend and foe.[11]

However, the most Ciceronian of the play's arguments is its redefinition of Rome. Cicero makes a qualitative judgement of what is and is not a state in order to deny the possibility of exile:

> For what is a state? every collection even of uncivilized savages? every multitude even of runaways and robbers gathered into one place? Not so, you will certainly say. Therefore our community was not a state at a time when laws had no force in it, when the courts of justice were abased, when ancestral custom had been overthrown, when the officers of government had been exiled and the name of the senate was unknown in the commonwealth.

> (279)

This situation, of ancestral custom overturned and government usurped by 'uncivilized savages', reflects Coriolanus' version of events in Rome.

Perhaps more importantly, Cicero suggests that his banishment *created* a situation of alienation and anarchy: 'everybody thinks that with my departure the commonwealth went into exile' (283). Coriolanus' declaration 'I banish you' suggests that he too leaves *Rome* in exile.

In the scenes which follow Coriolanus' banishment, perceptions of the city are once again divided along class lines. According to the tribunes, Rome in Coriolanus' absence is characterized by a new peace and prosperity (4.6.1–9). But for Volumnia, Virgilia and Menenius, Rome is degraded (and perhaps self-alienated) by the shameful ingratitude it has shown its hero (4.2.20–2, 30, 40–5). In 3.1, Menenius anticipated Coriolanus' punishment with the words

> Now the good gods forbid
> That our renownèd Rome, whose gratitude
> Towards her deservèd children is enrolled
> In Jove's own book, like an unnatural dam
> Should now eat up her own!
> (291–5)

But although this may be new to Menenius, ingratitude seems to have been one of the primary characteristics of Rome in Elizabethan and Jacobean literature. In his survey of 'Roman' plays from 1585 to 1635, Clifford Ronan describes ingratitude as a major source of factionalism: 'Whether it be Rome toward its citizens or disaffected citizens toward Rome, each party jealously guards its power, casting the opponent as a being lethally unthankful.'[12] This is particularly true of Shakespeare's work: Ronan notes that the Roman plays and *Timon of Athens* account for 60 per cent of Shakespeare's use of the words 'ingrate', 'ungrateful' and 'ingratitude'. In *Coriolanus*, these words are frequently associated with the hero's banishment. At Antium, Coriolanus himself describes the 'painful service' performed for his 'thankless country' (4.5.71) and Aufidius concurs, referring to 'ungrateful Rome' (131).[13]

If banishment reveals Rome's capacity for ingratitude, it also hints at its famous capacity for envy. In *The Consent of Time* (1590), Lodowick Lloyd describes how Coriolanus

> profited *Rome* in divers services, in subduing the *Volscans*, in winning the citie *Corioles*, he invaded the *Antiates*, and often repressed the insolencie of the people, insomuch that the *Romanes* having many warres in those dayes, thus *Corolianus* [sic] was at them all: for there was no battell fought, no warre enterprised, but *Coriolanus* returned from thence with fame and honour. But his vertue and renowme gate him much envie: for hereby hee was banished *Rome* by the *Ediles* & *Tribunes* of the people, against the *Patricians* will ...[14]

Plutarch's *Lives* includes numerous examples of great men banished for their greatness. His 'Life of Aristides' tells of the Athenian, famed for justice and honour, whose reputation earned him the people's displeasure. He was banished by them 'with the Ostracismon: disguising the envie they bare to his glory with the name of feare of tyranny'.[15] In his account of how Damon, the tutor of Pericles, was ostracized because the people resented his wisdom, Plutarch explains that this exile is only practised against those 'in estimacion above the common people, either in fame, nobility, or eloquence' (353). He continues,

> to geve it an honest cloke, they sayd it was onely a pulling downe and tying shorte, of to much greatnesse and authority, exceeding farre the maner and countenance of a popular state. But to tell you truly, it was none otherwise, then a gentle meane to qualify the peoples envy against some private person: which envy bred no malice to him whose greatnes did offende them, but onely tended to the banishing of him for tenne yeares.

> (357)

Ostracism began in Athens from about 508 BC and spread to Argos, Megara and Miletus, until dying out in the fourth century. It seems to have been intended for the banishment of an unpopular prominent citizen though it may also have served to prevent civil war when conflict arose between two powerful statesmen. The banished man would leave the city for ten years, but without the loss of property or citizenship; when he returned it was without disgrace.[16] However, for Plutarch and hence for many of the Elizabethan and Jacobean writers influenced by his work, ostracism came to represent the injustices of Athenian democracy, a system in which there was apparently no place for the extraordinary or gifted. In *The Governour* (1531), Sir Thomas Elyot describes the instability of this 'monstre with many heades', such that 'often tymes they banyssed or slewe the best citezins, which by their vertue and wisdome had moste profited to the publike weale'.[17] In 1613, Thomas Milles argued that Coriolanus' inability to live in a democracy was a sign of his greatness.[18] Viewed from the perspective of Elyot's *The Governour*, Coriolanus' banishment could even be regarded as a sign of his extreme civility.

Contemporary criticism has usually focused upon Coriolanus' anti-social nature as the motive for his banishment.[19] Thus, Janette Dillon writes: 'It is clear that Coriolanus's banishment is the logical consequence of his inward solitariness, and this inward solitariness is itself not a characteristic developed by particular events, but inherent in his nature.'[20] The precedent for such a critique is found in Plutarch who observes that 'all men that are wilfully geven to a selfe opinion & obstinate minde, and who will never yeld to others reason, but to their owne: remaine without companie, & forsaken of all men' (245). While Plutarch predicts the 'banishment' of any man so flawed, he does consider Coriolanus' upbringing to be a factor in the formation of his character:

> For lacke of education, he was so cholericke and impacient, that he would yeld to no living creature: which made him churlishe, uncivill, and altogether unfit for any mans conversation.
>
> (237)

A historicized version of this argument is taken up by critics who see Coriolanus as defective for a particular age, lacking for example the skills of political cunning and adaptability required by the city-state. As Patricia Meszaros puts it, he is 'caught in the historical process, the passing of an era'.[21] However, while it is true that other characters repeatedly comment upon Coriolanus' anti-social qualities (3.1.255–60, 322–5), and the play provides many examples of his 'inability' to function effectively in a political sphere, there is no simple equation in Shakespeare's play between anti-social qualities and banishment. The individualism which Coriolanus represents was once thought profoundly Roman. Nor is it always clear who banishes whom. To what extent has Coriolanus rejected Rome and desired banishment?

Plutarch hints that the hero has *chosen* obstinacy. Coriolanus apparently believes that his refusal to yield supremacy to anyone is 'a token of magnanimitie' (245); his being 'wilfully given to a selfe opinion' implies self-determination. Dillon too concedes that Coriolanus' response to banishment suggests 'it is already more deeply rooted in his will than the mere judgement of man can make it'.[22] Late twentieth-century criticism has produced some important work on Coriolanus' deliberate opposition to society, whether to the reciprocity upon which all communal relations are founded, or to a particular regime. Janet Adelman suggests that Coriolanus' insistence on the dignity of starvation signifies his desire to be independent of the world and particularly of his mother. His refusal to feed is related to his refusal to ask for anything.[23] Locating *Coriolanus* within a Jacobean context, Shannon Miller argues that the protagonist's opposition to plebeian culture reflects James I's autocratic stance. Both Coriolanus and the King insist upon the absolute authority of the ruling elite against the commons' 'ancient' rights. For Miller, the play is a 'textual negotiation of the political tensions of the period' in which the hero's banishment is a subversive expression of anti-monarchical feeling.[24]

Yet it is important to remember that Coriolanus' alienation from Rome is at least partly occasioned by the values which make him Roman. His achievements are part of an aristocratic fantasy of the private, self-sufficient body.[25] This individualism is apparent not only in his military career when at Corioli he stands 'alone / To answer all the city' (1.5.22–3), but also in public life when he refuses to trade kindness and the showing of his wounds for votes (2.3.113–17). Throughout the play, these values are admired by the patricians who themselves frequently denigrate the mutual dependency of that many-headed monster, the plebeian class. And yet the patricians reject Coriolanus' heroic individualism in favour of political cooperation. They give the plebeians corn to stop them rioting; they provide tribunes to represent their opinions; they allow Coriolanus' consulship to be revoked and the patrician to stand trial. Where the patricians' hypocrisy is most apparent is in their insistence that Coriolanus become an actor in the marketplace. In order to be elected consul (and to prevent further rebellion), there are gestures of humility he must enact and words to go with them. Volumnia unflinchingly promotes diplomacy at the expense of truth and integrity. Her son must speak:

> Not by your own instruction, nor by th'matter
> Which your heart prompts you, but with such words
> That are but roted in your tongue, though but
> Bastards and syllables of no allowance
> To your bosom's truth.

>   (3.2.54–8)

This is, of course, the kind of performance frequently required of the exile: not just the creation of a different role but the utterance of 'foreign' words, though strangers to his heart. As such, Coriolanus' failure here anticipates the disastrous consequences of his attempt to remain himself in exile, particularly in Corioli where his refusal to adapt his language to his surroundings proves fatal. Yet this speech also alludes to a more pervasive sense of alienation, perhaps inherent in Roman citizenship.

In his *De Officiis*, Cicero, like Volumnia, argues that the constant man should be prepared to change his role in society if the state requires it. His principle of 'decorum', the foundation of a morally good life, requires man to act in consistency with his two characters: one, universally shared by mankind, based on the Stoic ideal of man as dignified, self-sufficient, constant, and following the dictates of Reason; the other individual and encompassing particular talents and personality traits. Cicero writes:

> We must so act as not to oppose the universal laws of human nature, but, while safeguarding those, to follow the bent of our own particular nature [...] For it is of no avail to fight against one's nature or to aim at what is impossible of attainment.[26]

However, men must also seek to 'make the interest of each individual and of the whole body politic identical' (293). When the two cannot be reconciled, the individual must adapt to the state's requirements.

Coriolanus' dilemma could be seen to reflect the contradiction at the heart of Ciceronian decorum. The hero's insistence on 'mine own truth' at the expense of social role-play exposes the violence that might spring up between man's two characters. Yet this conflict also expresses the irreconcilability of two Stoic doctrines of constancy, the Ciceronian and the Senecan.[27] Where Ciceronian decorum posits an ideal of consistency in playing one's individual and yet socially appointed role, Senecan constancy is a heroic ideal characterized by immutability and self-sufficiency. Miles suggests that Coriolanus is viewed from both perspectives in the play. The patricians imagine that he plays a role for the state in the Ciceronian fashion; Coriolanus' definition of his own steadfastness and self-consistency is analogous to that of the Senecan *sapientis*. The conflict emerges in the scene where Coriolanus must humbly ask the plebeians for their forgiveness and for the consulship. For Volumnia, her son's self-betrayal is necessary to his political career and hence there is a consistency in this change. However, for Coriolanus, the acting of a different role would destroy the integrity of his whole personality, reflected in the image of each bodily part rebelling against the other (3.2.112–20). Coriolanus responds 'Rather say I play / The man I am' (14–15), refusing to act, while implying that, as the patricians believe, his career has been based on the performance of a particular role. The distinction lies in the commitment with which Coriolanus has played his part:

> The man who despises acting comes to define his own moral code in terms of theatrical decorum. He has found an appropriate part, identified himself totally with it, and plays it with such unalterable consistency that he cannot step outside it [...] he endows decorum with the heroic absoluteness of Senecan *constantia sapientis*.[28]

Ironically, Coriolanus has taken Ciceronian precepts on choosing a suitable role in society to Senecan and anti-social extremes. By investing his role with greater conviction, he becomes anathema to the state and is banished.

James Holstun describes Coriolanus' banishment as 'unique in Shakespeare', largely for the absence of any epiphanic quality. For Coriolanus,

> exile brings neither the Edenic green world it brings in the comedies and romances nor the elemental landscapes of tragic exile. More important, it does not bring their perspectival wisdom to Coriolanus; as he leaves Rome, he quite accurately predicts that Rome, will hear 'never of me aught/ But what is like me formerly' (IV.I.52–3).[29]

While this is true to some extent, it also oversimplifies both Coriolanus' immediate response to banishment and his experience of exile.

Banishment brings intimations of the hero's irrelevance to Rome and thus a fragmentary understanding of the 'createdness' and the contingency of identity. For the ruling class, Romanitas is politically expedient, promoting the valour, loyalty and self-immolation of the people.[30] For the plebeians, it is an inspiring fable, a fantasy of valour and fame, extraneous to everyday life. Until exile, Coriolanus fails to recognize that Rome is a place that only exists in his mind. This revelation allows him to defy the sentence of exile. If he is uncivil, it is for that cankered city which debases his idealized Rome. If he is anti-social, it is by the judgement of a society to which he has no wish to belong: 'Despising / For you the city, thus I turn my back' (3.3.137–8). And yet Coriolanus' existence beyond Rome, his *experience* rather than his anticipation of exile, proves resistant to the rhetorical flourishes by which he has previously transformed his fate.

How to be a Roman and an exile? The Ciceronian argument that Rome was not a state when it banished the true citizen only holds in a context of passive resistance. The exile must Stoically endure his suffering and await recall. He will be welcomed back to the city with greater fame and glory than before his exile. Plutarch also commends this approach, congratulating Scipio on his response to banishment:

> For he would not come against his contry with ensignes displaied, nether would he solicite straunge nations and mighty kings to come with force, and their ayde, to destroy the citie, the which he had beautified with so many spoyles and triumphes.[31]

To threaten the city which banished you is to destroy the distinctions between exile and tyrant, state and non-state, which, in the Ciceronian reading, could actually reinforce your identity as a Roman. To 'solicite strange nations' is finally to signal one's own strangeness or foreignness and thus to justify the sentence of exile. At first, Coriolanus seems to follow this advice. His quiet demeanour and Stoic platitudes on leaving Rome suggest that he will be satisfied with a linguistic and philosophical revenge, with 'I banish you', swiftly followed by a gratifyingly obsequious reconciliation with Rome (4.1.16).

However, this is not a perspective which Coriolanus is able to sustain beyond the city walls. Once outside, in the time which elapses between 4.1 and 4.4, he formulates an alternative response to exile that had abundant historical precedents in both Ciceronian and Plutarchan narratives. According to this theory, the only way to overcome the alienation which the Roman feels, even before banishment, in a democracy which does not know how to value him is to gain political control over the city or even to destroy it completely. Such an act would be profoundly Roman. According to the custom of renaming the hero after the city he has conquered, the outcast would become 'Romanus'. Moreover, to destroy the city is paradoxically to exemplify the Roman character of self-sufficiency, bloody self-assertion and obsessive self-definition through Rome. Finally, it might even reflect the Roman's patriotic fervour. For example, in *The Wounds of Civil War* (1588), Scilla promises revenge upon the city that has overlooked him for the generalship. However, the speech in which he anticipates Rome's destruction is equally concerned to celebrate its beauty:

> *Scilla* This Capitol wherein your glories shine
> Was ne'er so press'd and throng'd with scarlet gowns,
> As Rome shall be with heaps of slaughter'd souls
> Before that Scilla yield his titles up.
> I'll make her streets that peer into the clouds,
> Burnish'd with gold and ivory pillars fair,
> Shining with jasper, jet and ebony,
> All like the palace of the morning sun,
> To swim within a sea of purple blood
> Before I lose the name of General.

> (1.1.214–23)[32]

This is a kind of bloody blazon, expressing the Roman's desire to possess and deface the city. As a banished man, Scilla makes good his promise – the scarlet robes of the Senate do bleed into the streets (5.1.5–7) – and yet his behaviour remains characteristically Roman. Looking back on Scilla's reign, the conspirators in Jonson's *Catiline* (1611) recall a golden age when Romans massacred their own kind without distinction. Women and children, old men and pregnant wives all fell. The living were piled up in heaps with the dead (1.1.229–53).[33] Coriolanus' desire for vengeance is characterized by the same exorbitance; it will be 'as spacious as between / The young'st and oldest thing' (4.6.69–70). More specifically, Aufidius promises:

> Worthy Martius,
> Had we no other quarrel else to Rome but that
> Thou art thence banished, we would muster all
> From twelve to seventy, and, pouring war
> Into the bowels of ungrateful Rome,
> Like a bold flood o'erbear't.

> (127–32)

Not only the absence of distinctions between young and old, male and female, but the fact that Coriolanus offers his country to the Volscian soldiers to prey upon suggests the indiscriminateness of his fury.

Attempts have sometimes been made to defend Coriolanus by arguing that, in the light of contemporary condemnations of democracy which characterized the tribunes as evil and popular rule as chaotic misrule, his invasion might have been seen as an attempt to rescue his country. Clifford Huffman cites *Titus Andronicus* and *Macbeth* as a warning that Shakespeare's plays do not uniformly condemn the citizen's invasion of his country with foreign troops.[34] In fact, the location of *Coriolanus* within a context of Shakespearean invasions will yield a far more condemnatory portrait of the hero than Huffman acknowledges. For example, in *Titus Andronicus*, Lucius is banished for an attempt to rescue two of his brothers from execution. When he tells his father the news, Titus responds:

> O happy man, they have befriended thee!
> Why, foolish Lucius, dost thou not perceive
> That Rome is but a wilderness of tigers?
> Tigers must prey, and Rome affords no prey
> But me and mine. How happy art thou then
> From these devourers to be banishèd!

> (3.1.51–6)

This reversal of city and wilderness is one of Shakespeare's earliest uses of a trope that recurs throughout his banishment plays.[35] Similarly, the idea of Rome devouring its citizens anticipates *Coriolanus* (3.1.291–5). But Lucius is not simply to forsake his family or his birthplace; Titus asks him to return with an army of Goths in order to avenge his family (3.1.284–6) and Lucius adds a patriotic motive, arguing that the invasion will deliver Rome from tyranny. Indeed, he tells the Goths that he has letters expressing Rome's hatred of the emperor 'And how desirous of our sight they are' (5.1.4). This context of national tragedy enables Lucius to justify his invasion of the city. Before a crowd of Romans, he first describes the sufferings of the Andronici and then moves on to his own personal and apparently patriotic motives for revenge:

> Lastly myself, unkindly banishèd,
> The gates shut on me, and turned weeping out
> To beg relief among Rome's enemies,
> Who drowned their enmity in my true tears
> And oped their arms to embrace me as a friend.
> I am the turned-forth, be it known to you,
> That have preserved her welfare in my blood,
> And from her bosom took the enemy's point,
> Sheathing the steel in my advent'rous body.
> Alas, you know I am no vaunter, I.
> My scars can witness, dumb although they are,

> That my report is just and full of truth.
> But soft, methinks I do digress too much,
> Citing my worthless praise. O, pardon me,
> For when no friends are by, men praise themselves.
>
> (103–17)

In this speech, Lucius reveals himself to be a sophisticated rhetorician. He takes on the highly emotive role of banished man to prove that he is not a traitor, but rather a hero and martyr. The exile's tears and lamentations express patriotic fervour, while his insistence that banishment was unjust and unkind partly absolves him of any unpatriotic deed. Moreover, Lucius deliberately blurs the distinction between making a league with the Goths and fighting on behalf of Rome. He follows his father's example of reversing city and wilderness to hint that a Goth army might rescue Rome from barbarousness. Hence, the exile and traitor who leads that army may yet be a true patriot and worthy emperor.

The first of Shakespeare's Roman plays teases us with anticipations of the last.[36] Indeed, Lucius is described as one 'Who threats in course of this revenge to do / As much as ever Coriolanus did' (4.4.67–8). In both cases, revenge consists of words rather than actions but there is a startling difference in the Romans' use of rhetoric so that Lucius insinuates himself back into the heart of Rome and Coriolanus argues his way into death. In fact, Lucius' speech would have been an ideal model for Coriolanus had he returned to Rome after the abortive invasion. Like Lucius, he has a tale to tell of unjust and cruel banishment. He can even be moved to lyricism on this subject as is hinted by his response to Virgilia's greeting: 'O, a kiss / Long as my exile, sweet as my revenge!' (5.3.45–6). However, Coriolanus refuses to persuade the plebeians, while Lucius, like Bolingbroke, turns this role of exile to emotive and thus political effect. More than Lucius, Coriolanus can boast to Rome that he has 'preserved her welfare in my blood', but where the latter was reluctant to show his wounds to the public, Lucius willingly displays his scars through language and perhaps gestures (113) in pursuit of political ambitions. The closest Coriolanus gets to such a speech is that delivered at the end of the play in which he boasts of taking Corioli alone (5.6.114–17), the scene of his greatest Roman triumph. Uttered in Rome, this speech would surely have confirmed the repeal of his banishment but uttered in Corioli, the eulogy becomes an elegy.

It might be argued that Coriolanus has much more in common with the vengeful invader, Alcibiades, in *Timon of Athens*.[37] The latter proffers abundant reasons for invading Athens: to avenge his banishment and to punish the Senate for their ingratitude to Timon, their profits from usury and their licentiousness. Representing himself as the scourge of this 'coward and lascivious town' (5.5.1), Alcibiades claims a patriotic motive for his invasion yet he is easily persuaded to ignore endemic Athenian corruption with the appropriate bribe (22–44). Moreover, in his immediate response to banishment he shows himself indifferent to the motives he later claims:

> Banishment!
> It comes not ill; I hate not to be banished.
> It is a cause worthy my spleen and fury,
> That I may strike at Athens.

> (3.6.109–12)

Banishment is an opportunity rather than a motive. Although it seems likely that the banishment scenes of *Timon of Athens* and *Coriolanus* were written by different dramatists,[38] in reading the latter I am continually reminded of Alcibiades' phrase: 'It is a cause worthy my spleen and fury.' Coriolanus too uses banishment to *justify* not only his violent rage against Rome and the destructiveness which has always been latent in his ambition, but his alienation.[39] Indeed, we might argue that Coriolanus' revenge is a purer form of self-expression than that of Alcibiades. The latter's revenge proves to be an astute political move in that it demonstrates to Athens how much the city needs him. In contrast, Coriolanus does not threaten Rome to improve his position there. When the city promises to 'Unshout the noise that banished Martius' (5.5.4–5), the exile has no interest in returning to reap the rewards of Rome's gratitude. Neither Shakespeare's Alcibiades nor his Coriolanus plans an invasion in the interests of the city, but their selfishness is crucially different. For Alcibiades, a grateful Athens will serve his self-aggrandizement better than a ruined one. For Coriolanus, the integrity of the identity he professes *depends* on Rome's destruction. To show mercy to Rome would be to betray himself, to refute his own claim that he carries Romanitas within.[40]

As I suggested earlier, the Roman exile has two choices. He may wait for his country to rediscover its need for him, insisting that Rome is in exile until his return, or he may choose to destroy the corrupt simulacrum of Rome so as to claim authenticity for himself. Coriolanus dallies with both possibilities but does not follow through on either one. For all his claims to self-sufficiency, he lacks the introspection which allows the Stoic to endure the injustice of exile peacefully. Yet he finds himself equally unable to take his revenge. Without wishing to give Coriolanus a Hamlet complex, I would argue that this inability to act stems from banishment (a state which curiously seems to energize Hamlet!).[41] To wait or to destroy in the name of Rome requires the exile to be certain that he still embodies Romanitas to a greater extent than anyone else – a certainty that Coriolanus appears to lose in the last two acts of the play. Holstun asserted that Coriolanus undergoes no transformation through exile: 'as he leaves Rome, he quite accurately predicts that Rome, will hear "never of me aught / But what is like me formerly" (IV.I.52–3)'. However, I would argue that the protagonist finds it increasingly difficult to be himself outside Rome. His assertion of continuous and invulnerable selfhood becomes a response to the *loss* of self. Banishment is an experience of alienation more intense than anything he imagined in Rome.

The exile we meet in 4.4 is characterized by need. Forsaken by the nobles, deprived of all but his name, 'whooped out of Rome', he appeals to Aufidius:

> Now this extremity
> Hath brought me to thy hearth. Not out of hope –
> Mistake me not – to save my life, for if
> I had feared death, of all the men i'th'world
> I would have 'voided thee, but in mere spite
> To be full quit of those my banishers
> Stand I before thee here.
>
> (79–85)

Coriolanus needs an army to destroy Rome – unlike Corioli, it will not be won alone. More importantly, he hints at other physical and emotional needs discovered through exile, this state of 'extremity'. Perhaps most significant in this speech is the reference to the 'hearth', a curiously domestic detail for the Roman warrior until we remember that he has become a wandering exile, deprived of shelter in an enemy city. Furthermore, on his first entrance into Aufidius' dwelling, Coriolanus remarks: 'A goodly house. The feast / Smells well' (5–6), suggesting his desire for both food and human company. It is worth recalling here that in the late Roman republic following the exile's departure a decree of *aquae et ignis interdictio* would be declared, literally a denial of water and fire, excluding the exile from legal protection and condemning him to death if he returned.[42]

However, perhaps most pressing is Coriolanus' need for recognition. He enters Antium 'in mean apparel, disguised and muffled' and while he wants the city to know its defeat at his hands ('"Tis I that made thy widows' (4.4.2)), he dare not remove his disguise. Disguise saves his life but it also reinforces the self-loss implied by banishment, an effect akin to death. This paradox is intensified when Coriolanus first encounters Aufidius' servants. In Plutarch's account, the servants are wary of the muffled gentleman for though 'as he thought no man could ever have knowen him for the person he was', yet 'there appeared a certaine maiestie in his countenance, and in his silence' (249). In contrast, Shakespeare's serving-men do not recognize anything extraordinary about their guest and try to turn him away, arguing with ironic insight that this is no place for him (4.5.31) and assuming that he must be a clown or a half-wit (43–4). The fact that such a mythic hero should not be perceptible through his rags may hint at Coriolanus' degradation since he was exiled,[43] but worse is to come. In Plutarch, when Aufidius fails to recognize Coriolanus without his disguise, the hero names himself. Shakespeare's Coriolanus unmuffles and waits. Embarrassingly, the Volscian who had sworn to kill him even if he came upon him in his brother's house (1.11.24–7), who has dreamt of his enemy (4.5.123–7), has no idea who this stranger is. Yet Coriolanus refuses to give his name. What Shakespeare dramatizes here is the fear that now haunts Coriolanus, that without Rome he is nothing. Once Coriolanus has named himself, Aufidius greets him with the admiration and passion that the exile needs to inspire. Yet the final commentary of the servants undercuts Coriolanus' self-discovery once more. They pretend now to have recognized him from the beginning:

Second Servingman Nay, I knew by his face that there was something in him. He had, sir, a kind of face, methought – I cannot tell how to term it.

First Servingman He had so, looking, as it were – would I were hanged but I thought there was more in him than I could think.

Second Servingman So did I, I'll be sworn. He is simply the rarest man i' th' world.

(156–63)

The joke is partly at their expense, recalling the fickle judgements of the Roman plebeians. What is most apparent, however, is the absence that they unwittingly perceive in Coriolanus. The servants falter in their descriptions of him, not merely because they lack descriptive terms but because there is nothing there to know.[44]

When his mother, wife and child enter to plead mercy for Rome, Coriolanus determines to retain the detachment of the Senecan hero, to 'stand / As if a man were author of himself / And knew no other kin' (5.3.35–7). This is the first time since his banishment that the two parties have met and both imagine themselves physically transformed by that experience. Coriolanus at first withholds recognition from his wife, arguing 'These eyes are not the same I wore in Rome' (5.3.38). Virgilia suggests that Coriolanus' kin have been so altered by grief that he may well not know them (39–40). At first, the whole dynamic of the scene revolves around the women's attempts to make Coriolanus recognize his identity as son, husband, father and Roman, and to respond like himself. But when this fails, Volumnia utters a curse which appeals to the terrible vulnerability of the exile:

Come, let us go.
This fellow had a Volscian to his mother.

> His wife is in Corioles, and this child
> Like him by chance.

(178–81)

It is these lines that bring Coriolanus, perhaps literally, to his knees. For they suggest that the alienation which lay behind Coriolanus' desire to crush Rome will only be intensified by that action.

It is no coincidence that Coriolanus' mother should be the one who threatens to disinherit him. Not only is his father dead, but Volumnia insists throughout the play that he is a warrior of her own making. Moreover, this sentence of banishment, reversing yet again the terms of exile which define Coriolanus (from traitor, to archetypal Roman, to Volscian), may recall an originary act of banishment performed by Volumnia. In *Suffocating Mothers*, Adelman describes the traumatic separation between mother and infant dictated by the sixteenth- and seventeenth-century practice of wet-nursing. She cites Stephen Guazzo's *Civile Conversation* (1586) in support of this position. Here, Annibal tells the story of an illegitimate son who, returning from battle laden with spoils, gives a richer gift to his nurse than to his mother. He explains this preference to the latter:

> You bore mee but nine monthes in your bellie, but my nursse kept mee with hir teates the space of two yeares [...] so soone as I was borne, you deprived me of your companie, and banished mee your presence, but she graciously received mee, banished as I was ...[45]

A single metaphor, though twice repeated, does not mean that we should necessarily expand our definition of banishment to include infantile loss, except that Shakespeare demonstrates a recurring interest in this conjunction, particularly in the late plays. For example, in *Cymbeline*, Posthumus' banishment from the court is consistently understood in terms of his orphanhood. In the dream sequence, his mother (known simply as Mother) describes Posthumus' birth thus:

> Lucina lent me not her aid
> But took me in my throes,
> That from me was Posthumus ripped,
> Came crying 'mongst his foes,
> A thing of pity.

(5.5.137–41)

Posthumus' subsequent banishment seems to re-enact this violent separation:

> ... To be exiled, and thrown
> From Leonati seat and cast

> From her his dearest one,
> Sweet Innogen
>
> (153–6)

The Winter's Tale shows a similar preoccupation with the violent severance of mother and child. Hermione complains that she has been barred from the presence of Mamillius and that her daughter was 'from my breast, / The innocent milk in it most innocent mouth, / Haled out to murder' (3.2.97–100). In fact, Perdita has been banished. The father, Leontes, who suffers from a kind of infantile displacement himself, performs the same action against his own children.[46]

While maternal loss and banishment are staples of the romance tradition,[47] this particular anxiety of exile is not confined to Shakespeare's late plays. Part of Lear's shock at being rejected and physically shut out by his daughters may be related to the horror of maternal abandonment. In Shakespeare's first English history play, Suffolk laments his banishment thus:

> If I depart from thee, I cannot live.
> And in thy sight to die, what were it else
> But like a pleasant slumber in thy lap?
> Here could I breathe my soul into the air,
> As mild and gentle as the cradle babe
> Dying with mother's dug between his lips;
> Where, from thy sight, I should be raging mad ...
>
> (*2 Henry VI*, 3.2.392–8)

Suffolk's pain recalls an earlier trauma which, if he cannot literally remember it, is at least recognized as a powerful emblem for the vulnerability and destitution he experiences as an exile.

In *Coriolanus*, the threat of maternal abandonment is real but it also acts as a metaphor for other kinds of alienation. Volumnia genders Rome female and consistently conflates the city and herself: if Coriolanus attacks Rome he will tread upon his mother's womb (125) with 'mother' (a familiar term for the uterus) understood as both Volumnia and the city. If Volumnia abandons him, then so does Rome: 'This fellow had a Volscian to his mother.' More importantly, this denial will extend to Roman history. It is an expression of how central a role Volumnia occupies in the representation of Romanitas that she confidently asserts her own and Virgilia's ability to confer posterity on the Roman hero. It is Volumnia's womb 'that brought thee to this world' and Virgilia's 'That brought you forth this boy to keep your name / Living to time' (125–6, 126–8). This power may be signalled in Volumnia's name:

The word *volumen* [...] means that which is rolled, a coil, whirl, wreath, fold, eddy, or a roll of writing – a book or volume or part of one (Lewis 1890). The name can be associated with the complex interior circular spaces of the female reproductive organs as well as with the religious and legal textual inscriptions that delineate the social formation.[48]

When Volumnia warns Coriolanus of the debased reputation he will win from the ruins of Rome and then threatens to deny his ancestry as a Roman, she speaks from a position of authority. Indeed, she speaks with the voice of Plutarchan history: 'The man was noble, / But with his last attempt he wiped it out ...' (146–7). Volumnia goes on to describe the infamous name that will live after Coriolanus' death, but she is nearer the source of exilic dread when she refers to him being 'wiped out'. One form of banishment invented by Augustus in the first century AD was *abolitio memoriae* by which the exile was literally erased from historical record as if he had never existed, a strategy we are familiar with perhaps from those eery photographs from Stalinist Russia in which 'seditious' figures have been deleted.[49] Shakespeare may have known nothing of this particular, rather recondite, form of Roman exile, but Coriolanus remains keenly sensitive to such danger. When at Corioli, Aufidius refuses him the title 'Coriolanus', calling him instead thief, traitor and 'boy', Martius defends his history. He boasts of past victories, curses his enemies, takes up a sword and dares a whole city to destroy him:

> Cut me to pieces, Volsces. Men and lads,
> Stain all your edges on me. 'Boy'! False hound,
> If you have writ your annals true, 'tis there
> That, like an eagle in a dove-cote, I
> Fluttered your Volscians in Corioles.
> Alone I did it. 'Boy'!

> (5.6.112–17)

Perhaps, as has sometimes been argued, Coriolanus seeks his own death. But I would suggest that it is the exile's compulsive need to define himself in the face of forgetfulness and oblivion that proves fatal. Only if the Volscians write their historical records accurately will Coriolanus become part of the myth from which he is derived and for which he has acted.

In an insightful comment on the hero's peculiarly civil and uncivil ambitions, Sicinius defines Coriolanus as one who would 'depopulate the city and / Be every man himself' (3.1.264–5). For the first three acts, Coriolanus seems confident in his ability to perform *Romanitas* and to redeem the heroic Roman archetype. But this is before exile. While banishment from Rome is at first an opportunity for heroic self-consistency and even patriotism, experience proves otherwise. The intense alienation experienced in exile undermines Coriolanus' Romanness, revealing the contingency of his identity upon other people, particularly those who will ensure his posterity. It is largely because of this vulnerability that Coriolanus cannot destroy Rome, yet that failure only weakens his position further. By allowing the city to stand, Coriolanus inadvertently endows it with some legitimacy as Rome. The greater the authority he concedes to the city, the more significant his banishment appears. Yet *Coriolanus* is not only concerned with the effect of banishment on the individual. It is no coincidence that at the end of the tragedy neither side knows anything of the other. The Romans celebrate their salvation and boisterously recall their hero, concluding their part of the play as a city comedy. Coriolanus, unaware of this reprieve to exile, meets his death as a stranger among the Volscians. The alienation experienced by *both* sides anticipates Arruntius' statement, much later on in Rome's history, that 'There's nothing Roman in us'.

6
'A World Elsewhere': Magic, Colonialism and Exile in *The Tempest*[1]

'Hence from Verona art thou banishèd / Be patient for the world is broad and wide' (3.3.15–16) – the Friar in *Romeo and Juliet* is unable to make good this consolation. The play conceives of the world as a narrow place, defined by the walls of one or two Italian cities. By contrast, in Shakespeare's late plays, for example *Pericles, The Winter's Tale, Cymbeline* and *The Tempest*, we find the exile ranging across countries and seas (imaginatively extending to continents and oceans) and through time. Towards the end of his career, Shakespeare invests dramatically in the prospect of new worlds, responding to a popular taste for the extravagant and romantic while also reflecting England's material commitment to exploration and colonization.[2] Yet a reading of *The Tempest* suggests that, in terms of Shakespearean exile, little has changed. Though older, wiser and at the other end of the Shakespearean canon, Prospero, like Romeo, imaginatively dismisses worlds that lie beyond his native place, remaining closed to their imperial or national possibilities and yearning only for his lost origins. In what is perhaps Shakespeare's final vision of banishment, he confronts the new expansiveness of the world but translates it into distance-as-loss, defined on both a horizontal and a vertical scale.[3] Thus *The Tempest* considers exile not only in terms of geographical separation, describing Claribel in Tunis as 'dwell[ing] ten leagues beyond man's life' (2.1.251–2), but also as a movement on the hierarchical ladder of creation, either upwards towards divinity or downwards towards the beast, but always away from humanity. When the Friar condemns Romeo's response to exile with the words 'Art thou a man? [...] thy wild acts denote / The unreasonable fury of a beast' (3.3.109–10), he anticipates the larger creational as well as cartographic map on which *The Tempest* locates the banished man.

Before considering *The Tempest* in detail, it is worth pausing over the expectations created by its immediate predecessor, *Cymbeline*. Here, Shakespeare seems to have rejected the old model of a Romeo or a Mowbray terrorized by the thought of linguistic and cultural loss. Posthumus was born into a state of alienation, bereft at birth of parents and siblings – banishment from Innogen only reinforces this condition. Yet he moves on. The first scene outside Britain takes place in Rome, and here we find not only a banquet attended by representatives of Italy, Holland, France and Spain, each conversing fluently (a far cry from the barbarous savages of Mowbray's earlier imaginings!) but also discussing the reputation of Posthumus himself. Hence, the exile's anxieties about the loss of name, class and reputation appear to be immediately assuaged. Posthumus has been a traveller: Giacomo saw him first in Britain; the Frenchman saw him in Orleans; he is known to the Italian, Filario, through their respective fathers. Thus he takes up the thread of previous conversations with ease while Filario throws the responsibility of generosity and courtesy not upon the stranger but upon his hosts: 'I beseech you all, be better known to this gentleman' (1.4.28–9).

Such banishment reflects the response to exile that we find most often in the tragedies of Shakespeare's successors, for example Webster and Ford. Here, exile reflects the ideological alienation from the court which created the Jacobean malcontent. To be banished from one's country is more likely to serve as an occasion for a witty set-piece on the differences of nations than for lamentation. An excellent example is the opening of Ford's tragedy, *Love's Sacrifice* (1632). Here, a distinction is made between banishment, conceived of on a national scale (to have 'the open world before you'), and Roseilli's exile, the terms of which stipulate that he depart from the court and live no less than thirty miles away (1.1.13–18).[4] Roseilli appears relieved that he is not 'banished'. Yet his subsequent decision undermines this distinction between 'banishment' and exile. He *chooses* to leave the kingdom, determining to 'bestow / Some time in learning languages abroad' (39–40). Showing admirable and un-Shakespearean *sangfroid* in the face of exile, apparently unconcerned by the threat of linguistic alienation, Roseilli discusses with the traveller, Lord Fernando, the characteristics of the Spanish, the French and the English, before settling upon England as the site of his exclusion.

Love's Sacrifice reveals several debts to Shakespearean banishment plays.[5] D'Avolos' reassurance that 'You have the open world before you' echoes the Friar's advice from *Romeo and Juliet*. The opening line of the play, 'Depart the Court?' recalls not only the beginning of Webster's *The White Devil* but a scene in *The Two Noble Kinsmen*.[6] But if Shakespeare's rhetoric of exile influenced Webster and Ford, his *interpretation* of that state, even in the Jacobean plays, remains widely different. For example, *Cymbeline* is more conflicted about exile than its initial cosmopolitanism would suggest. Innogen may declare confidently that 'there's livers out of Britain' (3.4.141) but her meeting with Giacomo registers a familiar suspicion of the stranger and his 'beastly mind' (1.6.152, 154). According to the conventions of anti-travel literature, Posthumus has been transformed by Giacomo, the stereotypical Italian Machiavel, the abuser and mis-shaper of English travellers, but it might equally be argued that he has confronted the barbarous stranger within. Exile in *Cymbeline*, whether from a virtuous ideal of Britain represented by Innogen or from the masculine *virtus* of Rome, leads to an encounter with *native* barbarity and shame.

Richard Helgerson and Jodi Mikalachki have both explored the conflict in early modern English historiography between locating the country's origins in an ancient, savage, often female prehistory, and a post-conquest identity, characterized by the masculine embrace of Roman civilization.[7] In *Cymbeline*, this conflict is decided by the King's final capitulation to Caesar and by the exiles' recognition of various debts to Rome. Thus, by 'reintegrating Britain with honor into the civilized world of empire, the romance conclusion of *Cymbeline* "romanizes" and ennobles British antiquity'.[8] However, Britain's exiled status is not simply a product of its historical and cultural alienation from Rome; it also reflects its geographical location. As Innogen suggests:

> I'th' world's volume,
> Our Britain seems as of it but not in't,
> In a great pool a swan's nest.

> (3.4.138–40)

While this recalls *Richard II*'s celebration of England as an island – the isolated jewel in the sea, defended by Neptune – it also challenges the nationalist rhetoric which would increase that isolation by alienating Britain from Rome. Later, when the Queen celebrates Britain's insularity (3.1.16–33) she contaminates the metaphor, suggesting her own destructive and violent self-interest rather than the heroic self-sufficiency celebrated by Gaunt. More importantly, however, Innogen's speech incorporates a famous Virgilian description of Britain: 'et penitus toto divisos orbe Britannos' ('and the Britons, wholly sundered from all the world').[9] As Josephine Waters Bennett testifies, there was a long tradition of reading Britain's geographical extremity as symbolic of either supernatural good or evil, the Isle of the Blest or the Isle of Devils.[10] Britain in its exile seems inevitably poised between opposing identities.

There are various distinctions that might be drawn between banishment in *Cymbeline* and in *The Tempest*. Where alienation from the empire is shunned in the former play, suggesting that national identity depends on a continued identification with Rome, in *The Tempest* we see the process of identity-formation from the other perspective. Prospero has arrived on the island as a potential representative of his culture, and even as a possible colonizer, but he rejects the opportunities offered to create an Italian empire and longs for his return to the nation. Nevertheless, both plays share a conservative perspective which directs the protagonist to value and to protect his cultural history in the face of exile. More importantly, the same axes are in place to distinguish and yet to connect the barbarous and the civilized, the bestial and the divine. This brings us to a quotation which has been thought to have inspired *Coriolanus* but whose bearing on *The Tempest* is arguably more extensive. In the *Politics*, Aristotle insists that

> he that cannot abide to live in companie, or through sufficiencie hath need of nothing, is not esteemed a part or member of a Cittie, but is either a beast or a God.[11]

In Shakespeare's last single-authored play, the question of the exile's true nature becomes increasingly urgent. As Prospero appears to be moving up the Neoplatonic scale towards divinity, doubts about the bestiality, the inhumanity of exile, keep dragging him down. It is to this subject that we need to relate the play's themes of education, magic and colonialism, for each of them reinforces Prospero's identity as an exile.

In the second scene of the play, bathos attends the revelation of Prospero's magic. Miranda responds to the shipwreck with concern but without surprise: 'If by your art, my dearest father, you have / Put the wild waters in this roar, allay them' (1.2.1–2). Where Miranda is simply complacent, Prospero appears contemptuous of his magical power. He assumes that Miranda sees in him only 'Prospero, master of a full poor cell / And thy no greater father' (19–21). For an audience, particularly one prone to superstition and occult belief, magic is the key discovery of this scene and Prospero the fulfilment of every Renaissance necromancer's dreams. Yet the characters insist that we abate our wonder; Prospero's empowerment as a magician is nothing to the revelation that he once held political sway in Europe:

> Twelve year since, Miranda, twelve year since,
> Thy father was the Duke of Milan, and
> A prince of power.
>
> (53–5)

It is this news that throws Miranda into confusion. So impossible is it that Prospero should have been Duke of Milan, that she questions whether he is, in fact, her father (55). Prospero agrees that it is scarcely imaginable that he should have been reduced from that lofty eminence to his present obscurity and explains the transformation in terms of a tragic fall. Unless he acts on the present 'auspicious star', his fortunes 'Will ever after droop' (183–5). That the magus' awe-inspiring power should be seen as ill-fortune is an ambivalence crucially dependent upon Prospero's self-image as an exile. For after twelve years Prospero remains the banished Duke of Milan. It is civilization, the political world, the West that beats in his mind, just as

Miranda will later exclaim at a 'brave new world' she mistakenly locates in Italy, echoing traces of the *Aeneid* found throughout the play.[12]

Prospero's identity as a cultural outcast is at first muted by the fact that he seems to have brought his culture with him. He describes his library as a metonym for Milan, and imaginatively displaces his dukedom with the books he so prizes. The fact that he takes these books with him into exile suggests a degree of continuity, even of wish-fulfilment.[13] Harry Berger sees exile as a corollary of Prospero's essential nature and the inevitable conclusion of his solitude in Milan:

> His being set adrift on the ocean, committed to a course which washed away the old burdensome world of civilization and translated him magically to a new world, unpeopled and unreal – this removal and isolation fulfill the process by externalizing his self-sufficient insularity.[14]

Exile appears to facilitate the achievement of Prospero's scholarly ambitions. Moreover, where in Milan he was guilty of abusing scholarship (the study of the liberal arts was intended to inspire good government, not to serve as a distraction from it), on the island Prospero dedicates himself to the education of both Miranda and Caliban. Yet, this humanist education actually seems to undermine Prospero's own claim to civility and to reinforce his alienation, as Berger's image of washing away the old civilization potentially implies. Jonathan Bate has argued that Prospero is a failed humanist even before he leaves Milan because his liberal arts have inspired evil not virtue in Antonio. This failure is more fully realized on the island when Prospero effectively 'monsters' Caliban:

> Learning language should be what makes man god-like as opposed to beast-like, but since the first effect of Caliban's education is his desire to rape Miranda, one wonders whether there is not in fact something devilish about the way in which Prospero has taught him.[15]

In fact, this 'something devilish' about Prospero has already been implied by his banishment from Milan, as Bate's Aristotelian terms suggest. We might argue, then, that education is not the source of Prospero's alienation but a possible solution to it. If he can inspire civility, he will prove his own commitment to civilization; if he can fashion a citizen out of the base substance of a Caliban, he will differentiate himself from the savage. Thus, although Prospero's attempt to educate Caliban shares a number of 'colonialist' assumptions – that the native has no language of his own; that he is 'saved' through his education by the European; that he will quickly revert to violence and lust because he is little more than a beast – this is not the only context in which to interpret his actions. The Italian duke brings culture to the stranger as much for his own benefit – to perform his own embodiment of those values – as for the recipient.[16] More simply, Prospero the exile seeks not so much to create a society as to be accepted by one. When Caliban fails to be 'civilized', that failure seems to testify to the Duke's own dubious civility, but worse, when Caliban rejects him, Prospero experiences the same pattern of betrayal and stigmatization begun in Milan. Rather than allow this rejection to identify him once again as an outcast, unfit for human society, Prospero designates Caliban as monstrous, unnatural and inhuman, and finally banishes him (1.2.345–6). Thus begins a pattern of Prospero exiling others and projecting his own supposed inhumanity onto them.

With regard to the shipwrecked men, Prospero again performs an ostensibly civilizing function by confronting them with the evil they have perpetrated, forcing them to feel guilt, and finally offering reconciliation. Yet his action takes on a much darker aspect, reflecting the exile's desire for revenge rather than his commitment to society. For much of the play it is unclear that Prospero will finally forgive his enemies: the easiest way to reclaim his dukedom would be to kill them. Moreover, the unrepentance of Antonio and Sebastian suggests that if the aim of Prospero's teaching was to inculcate virtue he has, once again, failed in his task. Rather, Prospero uses his magic to reverse the positions of banisher and banished. In *Coriolanus*, the protagonist declared 'I banish you' (3.3.127) in vengeance at his own expulsion. Prospero has the opportunity literally to banish those who banished him by forcing them to experience the full horrors of self-loss he has known.[17] In a powerful reworking of his own guilt and insecurity about what banishment implies, Prospero sets about to create on the island a landscape of exile, a place not only beyond civilized norms but located at the outermost edges of the map, perhaps the Isle of Devils, hell itself.[18] Here, the exiles suffer bewilderment and isolation: 'He hath lost his fellows, / And strays about to find 'em' (1.2.419–20). As they become increasingly disorientated, they hear noises that might be wild beasts or damned spirits, and meet monstrous shapes that might be islanders but they cannot be sure. If this exposure to 'strange shapes' makes the shipwrecked men feel vulnerable and leads them to question their position in the hierarchy of creation, that is exactly Prospero's intention for these are the questions banishment has forced him to ask himself.

In 'Prospero's Empty Grasp', John S. Hunt describes the magus as

> a dreamer trapped in the nightmare of past experience, a mind painfully detached from the life of the body, a self contemptuously separate from the entanglements of society, a cultivated person cultivating nothing.[19]

Prospero possesses a rare power to transform his state; the shapes of his imagination can be embodied through magic. Yet he unleashes a powerful anti-creative force: 'the strong-based promontory / Have I made shake, and

by the spurs plucked up / The pine and cedar; graves at my command /
Have waked their sleepers, oped, and let 'em forth' (5.1.46–9). All his
visions of beauty, kindness and utopianism finally dissolve into ugliness
and discord. As we saw in the chapter on *Richard II*, exile is often fatal to
the victim's creativity. However, in Prospero's case, this nihilistic effect is
redoubled by his transformation into a magician and a colonialist. In the
pastoral tradition, the assumption of a new role (usually that of the shepherd) facilitates the exile's acceptance of and adaptation to his fate. Even in
revenge tragedy, the protagonist adopts a disguise to better countenance
his revenge. By contrast, in *The Tempest* Shakespeare torments his character
and introduces a bitter irony to the play by insisting that even in his supposed metamorphosis Prospero remains an exile.

Magic is the attainment of the scholar who has dedicated many hours to
the contemplation of various texts. The practical demands of study, not to
mention the illicit nature of conjuring, require withdrawal and solitude.
Thus we first see Faustus in his study pursuing 'concealèd arts' from
whence he removes to a 'solitary grove' (1.1.104, 155).[20] Psychological
alienation is also required. In his *De Occulta Philosophiae* (1533), Henry
Cornelius Agrippa argued that the magus must isolate himself from the
'vulgar' uncomprehending masses and from worldly ambitions.[21]
Prospero's banishment is, then, easily identified as the prologue to his
magical arts. Indeed, in at least two other magician plays, *The Rare
Triumphes of Love and Fortune* (1589) and *The Maid's Metamorphosis* (1600),
banishment is the cause of the character's initiation into magic. But while
these plays often require magic to bring about poetic justice, they also
condemn it as dangerously anti-social. For example, in *The Rare Triumphes*,
Bomelio's magic books are denounced by Hermione as 'vile' and 'blasphemous' and subsequently burned (3.609, 1,356). It is here that the chronol-
ogy of banishment and magical empowerment begins to appear confused.
Perhaps the banishment with which the play began does not condone but
rather condemns the practice of magic, anticipating the magus' further
alienation?

In 1.2, Prospero relates, not for the first time, the banishment of Sycorax:

> This damned witch Sycorax,
> For mischiefs manifold and sorceries terrible
> To enter human hearing, from Algiers
> Thou know'st was banished.

> (264–7)

This fable is significant for a number of reasons. Firstly, Prospero assumes
that exile is a fitting punishment for Sycorax's 'sorceries'. He recognizes the
anti-social nature of magic through its anti-social fate, namely expulsion to
an 'uninhabited' island. This assumption that the witch or sorcerer should

be banished may reflect familiar biblical injunctions. For example, in Deuteronomy 18.10–12, witches, sorcerers, charmers, soothsayers and those 'yt asketh counsel of ye dead' are declared an abomination to the Lord, hence 'God doeth cast them out before thee' (12). However, contemporary European practice when Shakespeare wrote his play was to burn the magician or witch at the stake. Banishment was most often applied to the magician figuratively, as a metaphor for his state of damnation.[22] Hence, Sycorax's exile seems deliberately included to reflect upon Prospero's banishment. Her history contaminates Prospero's to the extent that we might ask, with Geraldo de Sousa, whether the magus was himself banished for practising witchcraft.[23] Prospero contrasts Sycorax's 'earthy and abhorred commands' with his own art but Shakespeare's audience must still have had doubts about the legitimacy of Prospero's 'rough magic'. The magus' description of himself waking the dead and of raising storms (5.1.41–9) echoes not only the black arts of Medea in Book 7 of Ovid's *Metamorphoses*, but the Scottish trials of 1590–91 at which a number of 'witches' were accused of raising storms to drown James VI.[24]

Yet it is not just Sycorax's association of magic and exile that disturbs Prospero. Both magicians have used their power to seize control of a territory and to bend it to their will. Indeed, there was a clear association between magic and colonialism in the magician plays of the 1580s and 1590s:

> O, what a world of profit and delight,
> Of power, of honour, of omnipotence
> Is promised to the studious artisan!
>
> (*Dr Faustus*, 1.1.55–7)

There is a sense that the world now lies open to the philosopher, a rich, fruitful and virgin territory which will yield him secrets denied to other men. Most frequently, this plunder is envisaged as material treasure. Faustus imagines fetching gold from India and orient pearl from the ocean. He will 'search all corners of the new-found world / For pleasant fruits and princely delicates' (86–7). Friar Bacon too promises his dignitaries a great feast of 'candy' and 'spices' brought from Egypt, Persia and Africa (9.256–64).[25] Yet the magician was also motivated by nationalist and imperialist aims, so that his plunder might include Egypt or Persia themselves. Hence, Faustus describes the alterations to the map of the geographical and political world that he will effect through Mephistopheles:

> By him I'll be great emperor of the world
> And make a bridge through the moving air
> To pass the ocean with a band of men;
> I'll join the hills that bind the Afric shore

And make that land continent to Spain,
And both contributory to my crown.

(1.3.105–10) [26]

Thus, before the Virginia project and before Shakespeare's *Tempest*, magical power was conventionally linked with territorial expansion and foreign conquest. However, in the figure of Sycorax, this association becomes tainted. Exile proves her unfit to live in society. Hence, the society that she creates upon the island is a kind of hell which in turn reinforces her exclusion from civilization. Prospero feels it necessary to relate, time and again, the island's improvement under his dominion because his exiled status makes such an improvement doubtful. Thus Sycorax serves as the demonic double, not simply of Prospero the magus but of Prospero the colonialist.

Exiles in English Renaissance drama invariably bewail the need to travel and specifically to *wander* outside familiar boundaries. In *The Rare Triumphes*, Bomelio addresses himself as an exile: 'Goe walke the path of plaint, goe wander wretched now / In uncoth waies, blind corners fit for such a wretch as thou ...' (3.613–14). Similarly, in *The Maid's Metamorphosis*, Eurymine describes her fate: 'Banisht, to live a fugitive alone, / In uncoth paths, and regions never knowne' (Act 1, B). The exile is not simply forced to become a traveller; rather, the exploration of unknown and possibly uninhabited regions also suggests his/her identity as a colonialist. This association between banishment, wandering and colonialism is made explicit in Peter Martyr's *De Orbe Novo Decades* (1516), an account of Spanish colonialism, translated into English by Richard Eden in 1555. [27] Of particular interest is the passage in which Martyr describes the encounter between the Spanish *conquistadores* and the native Americans under King Comogrus. The Indians have given the Spanish a sum of gold, a gift that has driven them into an undignified frenzy. Their behaviour inspires wonder and even pity in Comogrus' eldest son who asks:

> What is the matter [with] yowe Christen men, that yow soo greatly esteeme soo litle a portion of golde more then yowr owne quietnes [...] If yowre hunger of goulde bee soo insatiable that onely for the desyre yowe have therto, yowe disquiete soo many nations, and yow yowre selves also susteyne soo many calamit[i]es and incommodities, *lyving like banished men owte of yowre owne countrey*, I wyll shewe yowe a Region floweinge with goulde, where yowe may satisifie yowr raveninge appetites [italics mine]. [28]

The colonialist and the exile are seen to share a number of basic characteristics, for example both behave as if they had no home. Martyr himself describes the Spanish as 'thys wandrynge kynde of men [...] lyvynge onely by shiftes and spoyle' (116). Moreover, like Aristotle's solitary man, the

Spanish colonialists evince a kind of restless desire, an anti-social exorbitance, implied not only by their 'raveninge appetites' for gold but also by the fact that they destroy the peace of other nations through such 'raveninge'. The prince has given the Spanish a quantity of gold lest 'they shuld handle hym as they dyd other[s] whiche sought noo meanes howe to gratifie theym' (116). Indeed, such is the colonialists' innate transgressiveness that, according to the prince, they resemble 'cruell Canybales a fierce kynde of men, devourers of mans flesshe, *lyvyng withowte lawes, wanderinge, and withowte empire*' (117, italics mine).

This encounter between Spanish colonialists and Amerindian prince is remarkable in part for its reversal of the conventional positions of European and Other, noble and savage. Comogrus' son not only lectures the Spaniards in civility, he is also described by Martyr in terms reminiscent of Christ.[29] More importantly, Comogrus' son questions the most basic assumptions about the colonialist project. The avowed intention to civilize hides the restless wandering and insatiability of the banished man.[30] One might object that this is Spanish not English colonialism. The English began their colonial adventures much later than the Spanish and distinguished their humanist intentions from the so-called pure greed and viciousness of Spanish imperialism. Although we are familiar with the price paid by English colonists – starvation, disease, execution by English martial law or massacre by the natives – we do not tend to associate colonialism with the shame and self-loss of banishment. But there is evidence that the connection between colonialism and exile was already conventional in sixteenth-century England.

Before colonialism in North America became a reality, Catholics were fleeing Elizabethan England to join communities abroad, in particular the seminaries at Rome and Douai.[31] The association of this migration with the shame of exile was one of the rhetorical weapons at the government's disposal as it tried to prevent Catholics from leaving the country. In the Introduction, we saw the example of William Cecil's letter to Thomas Copley (1574) warning of the 'the infamy that wilful exile doth bring, to be accompted, if not a traitor, yet a companion of traitors and conspirators, a man subject to the curses and imprecations of zealous good subjects, your native countrymen'.[32] Cecil's image of exile is based upon his jaundiced impression of the Catholic refugees abroad. In *The Execution of Justice*, written nine years after the letter to Copley, Cecil denied that the exiles were heroes, sacrificing everything for their faith. He insisted rather that they were rebels, traitors and vagabonds whose departure from England had nothing to do with religious persecution. The same ambivalence between exile as a divine, heroic vocation and as an expression of dissoluteness and treachery appears in the context of English colonialism.

In a sermon published in 1610, William Crashaw justified the exclusion from Virginia of atheists, players and papists.[33] The Jesuit, John Floyd, responded with *The Overthrow of the Protestants Pulpit-Babels* (1612) in which he reminded Crashaw that if it had not been for papists, Britain would never have been converted to Christianity in the first place, and warned that Virginia's conversion too might depend upon Catholic intervention. According to Floyd, the Protestants are shamefully lacking in evangelical zeal:

> No *M. Crashaw*, the miseryes which the enterprize of converting Savages doth bring with it, the wanting your native soyle, friends and Gossips, wherwith now after Sermon you may be merry, the enduring hunger, cold, nakednes, danger of death, and the like, but specially the want of the new Ghospells blessing, a fayre wife, too heavy a lump of flesh to be carryed into *Virginia*; these be such curses, & such hinderances, as you may speake of.[34]

Floyd subsequently distinguishes between two kinds of banished colonialist. First, there is the priest who willingly endures the sufferings concomitant with this divine vocation. Then there is the colonist who has his mission thrust upon him. Floyd declares that those Protestant priests who do become colonists are in many instances 'the refuse of their [the Church's] Realme, whome they terme the very excrements of their swelling State' (324). Virginia's conversion depends on men presented with the choice of banishment to Virginia or the gallows. They are men conscripted in taverns, at plays, even in hedges. It was Crashaw himself who condemned the purgation of England by the deportation of such 'ruffians' to Virginia. But Floyd suggests that the Protestant Church actively promotes this. To leave England for Virginia may be a heroic expression of religious commitment but it is also an indication of one's superfluousness to the state and even of criminality.[35]

The Tempest can be seen to take an active role in the stigmatization of the colonialist project, again through its references to banishment. The wreck of the *Sea Venture*, which left Sir Thomas Gates and a number of colonists stranded in an alien landscape, was more than once described as exile.[36] This disaster was perceived by some as an expression of God's wrath at the greed and hubris underlying the colonialist enterprise. In *The Tempest*, the shipwrecked men imagine that their shipwreck/exile is also divine vengeance for a similar act of 'extravagance'. Alonso has pursued a ruthlessly expansionist foreign policy by marrying his daughter, Claribel, to the prince of Tunis, neglecting not only Claribel's feelings but also national and European concerns. As Sebastian puts it:

> Sir, you may thank yourself for this great loss,
> That would not bless our Europe with your daughter,
> But rather loose her to an African,

> Where she, at least, is banished from your eye,
> Who hath cause to wet the grief on't.

(2.1.129–33)

Claribel's banishment beyond the known world has incurred their own exile on an unmapped island and it is Alonso's anti-social ambition which is to blame.

A related plot which perhaps reinforces the immorality of colonialist ambition is Caliban's attempt to rape Miranda. The native's motive was not lust but colonialism: 'I had peopled else / This isle with Calibans' (1.2.352–3). If we recall Peter Martyr's description of the encounter between Spaniards and Comogruans it is clear that a ravenous appetite, whether for gold or female flesh, could be synonymous with colonialist ambition and the anti-social nature of the exile. The moral of the story appears to be that colonialism is dangerous, even inhuman, and it derives some of this inhumanity from its associations with exile. It might be argued then that one of the ways in which Prospero proves himself worthy of the Milanese dukedom is his rejection of this proposed union between Miranda and Caliban, despite its possibilities for extending Italy's dominions into the New World. Instead, Prospero marries her to the Neapolitan heir, training his gaze as always on the western horizon.

Prospero has bemused, irritated and confounded critics by his apparent uninterest in colonialism, an attitude in stark contrast to critics' own fascination with the colonial aspects of *The Tempest*.[37] After twelve years, he still lives in a cave by a fen and is dependent upon Caliban for providing the basic necessities of life.[38] Even if we remind ourselves not to expect empire-building from the seventeenth-century colonialist who was primarily concerned with establishing trade routes, Prospero is at best negligent in his colonialist duties and at worst hardly a colonialist at all.[39] A more obvious reading of his failure to civilize the island might be suggested by the discourses of exile. As a banished man, Prospero's ability to cultivate anything has been profoundly affected. Shamed by exile, he directs all his earth-shattering, sea-fretting magic towards exorcising this curse and returning home. And yet, like Prospero, many of the Virginia colonists had been banished to the New World. Prospero's apathy and anxiety towards the island might then reflect the experience of seventeenth-century English colonists. The discourse of colonialist-as-exile, invoked by Martyr, Floyd and others, challenges the image of a self-assured, patriarchal, even tyrannical colonialist (the archetype which does not fit Prospero's attitude to the island), and replaces it with a figure more anxious, self-doubting, and above all more marginal than has hitherto been appreciated.[40]

Shakespeare's Prospero, like Aristotle's solitary man and Floyd's colonialist, is suspended between the god and beast, uncertain whether his actions on the island are to his credit or to his shame.[41] Moreover, for all the distinctions Prospero tries to establish between the beast and the god, thus to clarify his own position in that hierarchy, the opposition will not hold. Despite Ferdinand's degradation, emasculated through the loss of his sword and the performance of menial tasks, Miranda perceives in him divinity. Yet when Ferdinand is placed on the side of the angels and Prospero shares with the couple his masque on the perfection of mankind, the opposition between the bestial and the divine is again disrupted by the imagined figure of Caliban. Prospero has managed to keep the lascivious Venus and her son, Cupid, away from the celebrations but thoughts of the darker aspects of humanity, exemplified in the rape and violence that Caliban partly represents, still intrude. Prospero's oft-expressed anxieties about pre-marital sex (4.1.14–23, 51–4) suggest his fear that even the golden couple is corruptible.

The ultimate expression of this paradox is Caliban who responds to both the beast and the god within. Caliban's human status is never fully determined; he is at first a fish, then a man-monster, rising in rank from servant-to lieutenant-monster (3.2.3, 15). Moreover, his experience with other men in the play is characterized by rejection rather than acceptance. With Stefano and Trinculo, he finds some temporary community. Yet when he refuses to obey one of Stefano's commands, the latter threatens to turn him 'out of my kingdom' (4.1.250–1). Thus, Caliban embodies Aristotle's bestial exile while offering yet another damning mirror-image of the banished Duke of Milan.[42] Nevertheless, Shakespeare establishes a parallel between Caliban and Miranda in their Neoplatonic aspiration after what is good via what is beautiful. The former declares that he has never seen a woman except for his mother and she cannot compare with Miranda's beauty (3.2.101–4). Miranda tells Ferdinand: 'I do not know / One of my sex, no woman's face remember, / Save from my glass mine own ...' (3.1.48–50), yet she cannot imagine a better man. Miranda and Caliban also make similar mistakes in their fervour. The former's naive assumption that man must always be what he appears could prove dangerous and does not escape mockery (5.1.185–7). Caliban's judgement is even more faulty when he kneels to Stefano as a god and makes 'a wonder of a poor drunkard!' (2.2.164–5). Nevertheless, his quest for divinity is also an expression of the transcendent in Caliban's nature. When he discovers his mistake in Stefano and Trinculo, Caliban adores the magician as he once did and hopes to sue for 'grace' (5.1.299).[43]

We have seen how Prospero's treatment of Caliban is informed by his desire to project alienation onto the 'native'. By designating Caliban as all that is savage and alien to the civilized Duke of Milan, Prospero seems to be rejecting that dangerous incivility within himself which banishment implies. Yet, this impulse to distinguish also implies the perception of likeness. Prospero's final acknowledgement of Caliban after so many disavowals echoes his earlier decision to recognize the humanity in himself.

In 5.1, Prospero rejoices that the shipwrecked men are finally in his power and at his mercy, but does not anticipate being merciful until Ariel intercedes with a description of the royal party's distress and with the assertion that, were he human, he would pity them. Prospero's response seems spontaneous, even impulsive. He decides to become human:

> Hast thou, which art but air, a touch, a feeling
> Of their afflictions, and shall not myself,
> One of their kind, that relish all as sharply
> Passion as they, be kindlier moved than thou art?

> (5.1.21–4)

The confusion Prospero has created on the island with men appearing to be devils, islanders and gods, comes to seem an expression of his own uncertainty about his human status. Through the 'banishment' of the shipwrecked men, Prospero has not only created the conditions for his reinstatement on the Milanese throne but has worked through his ambivalence about human identity. With his decision to recognize himself as one of their kind, Prospero proposes to drown his books and relinquish his magical power.

Indeed, the final scene is dominated by this need to embrace humanity, anticipated by Prospero's words to the still-enchanted Gonzalo: 'Mine eyes, ev'n *sociable* to the show of thine, / Fall *fellowly* drops' (5.1.62–4, italics mine). Having divested himself of his magical garb for a hat and rapier, Prospero presents himself as 'The wrongèd Duke of Milan', a 'living prince', in proof of which he clasps Alonso (109, 110). Once the Neapolitan party has accepted that Prospero, Miranda and Ferdinand are living and human, the last scene revolves around the acceptance of humanity in the other characters. Miranda's original wonder at Ferdinand is repeated when she sees Alonso and his party. She greets these men of sin, only recently restored to their senses:

> O wonder!
> How many goodly creatures are there here!
> How beauteous mankind is! O brave new world
> That has such people in't!

> (184–7)

As if the moral crimes of these men were not enough to balance such wonder, the subplot characters enter to 'represent' bestiality; Caliban is once again described as a 'plain fish' (269). Yet Prospero insists that these men be identified as human and belonging to them all in a particular sense:

> Two of these fellows you
> Must know and own. This thing of darkness I
> Acknowledge mine.

                              (277–9)

Prospero has tried to keep the bestial and divine separate, both on the island and within himself. In renouncing his magic he accepts that even this power cannot separate them. Moreover, by rejecting the magic that enabled him to transcend the everyday man, Prospero accepts his own vulnerability and mortality. He achieves this only at the price of drowning the knowledge that he was ever anything more.[44]

One of the values of reading *The Tempest* through the glass of exile is that, instead of narrowing our perspective on the text, it allows us to discuss simultaneously the play's magic, humanism and colonialism. Because ideas of exile feed into such discourses, banishment allows us to make connections which enrich and perhaps defamiliarize *The Tempest*. In a recent article, Jerry Brotton has also pursued this aim of defamiliarization. He challenges post-colonialist stereotypes and turns our attention to the Old World contexts of the play. In particular, Brotton aspires to recapture some of Prospero's ambivalence and liminality, arguing that the latter's roles as traveller, magician and Italian suggest 'a distancing of audience identification with Prospero'. He is one whom English audiences would arguably have regarded with 'fascination, but also unease'.[45] However, Brotton fails to mention Prospero's identity as an exile, despite the fact that the play consistently suggests that what is most strange and self-estranging about Prospero is his exile, an identity that encompasses these other roles. Indeed, I would argue that it is only when we understand the centrality of exile in *The Tempest* that Prospero becomes for us the truly marginal and alien figure that Shakespeare created.

Yet, even within the context of this book, Prospero stands somewhat apart from his fellow exiles. Banishment in *The Tempest* ends with scenes of pastoral triumph. Like Valentine, Hal, Orlando, and even Edgar, Prospero has achieved ambitions that would have been inconceivable in the everyday world. Moreover, the linguistic and creative power he has unleashed upon the island easily overshadows that of his dramatic contemporaries. And yet, *The Tempest* expresses grave doubts about the nature of that power and, indeed, abandons it voluntarily. Throughout this book, I have suggested that language and art are the means by which the exile endures exclusion; only at the end of his career does Shakespeare admit the possibility that art might also be a cause of alienation.

Conclusion

Edward W. Said describes exile as 'a potent, even enriching, motif of modern culture'.[1] Alienation from the possibility of belief in God or in 'society', from notions of family and even from our own individual consciousness, has been fundamental to the ways in which we have thought about ourselves in the twentieth century. Yet, for all the dependence of western culture on the facts of exile, that is, the physical displacement of artists, philosophers, etc. and their experience of alienation, exile remains profoundly unfamiliar to most of us. For Said, the literary motif has betrayed the reality it once expressed:

> Is it not true that the views of exile in literature and, moreover, in religion obscure what is truly horrendous: that exile is irremediably secular and unbearably historical; that it is produced by human beings; and that, like death but without death's ultimate mercy, it has torn millions of people from the nourishment of tradition, family, and geography?[2]

There is much here, I believe, in sympathy with Shakespeare's own dramatic meditation on exile. Hence, this final section will be concerned with addressing some of the ways in which Said's oppositions of literary versus historical, religious or secular exile can illuminate banishment in the Shakespearean canon.

Firstly, I have argued that Shakespeare was himself sensitive to the distance that literary, and especially poetic, conventions of banishment could create between the expression and the experience of exile. Petrarchanism had made mutual alienation and estrangement central to its conception of love. In *Romeo and Juliet*, Shakespeare destroys the beautiful artifice of Petrarch's banished hearts and banished eyes to reveal the barren, self-destructive anguish of exile. Something similar happens in *Coriolanus*. At first, the Roman appears to be happy with a linguistic revenge – the convention of saying that this is liberty not banishment, as popularized by Shakespeare himself. However, his attempts to realize this distinction by destroying Rome reveal its artifice. Coriolanus does not finally believe that Rome lies within him; to

174

destroy the city is to make himself a permanent stranger and exile. Again, the literary cliché offers no psychological refuge from Shakespeare's dramatic reality. Even in *As You Like It*, when Shakespeare has Touchstone identify with another literary archetype, the banished Ovid, the clown's experience ironically contradicts the paradigm he invokes.

It might further be argued that Shakespeare anticipates this anxiety about art's obfuscation of exile from the same sense of historical reality. For Said, it is the scale upon which exile has been experienced by, for example, Palestinians, Haitians, Vietnamese, Cambodians and Indian Muslims, and the irrecoverable nature of that history which makes toying with exile appear almost obscene. If sixteenth- and seventeenth-century England cannot compete with diaspora on this scale, I would argue nevertheless that part of Shakespeare's and his audience's susceptibility to exile as a dramatic theme derived from their new sense of the fragility of belonging anywhere. The Reformation and counter-Reformation inspired waves of religious exile, with conspicuous numbers of high-ranking Catholics and Protestants either leaving for or returning from the Continent upon the succession of each Tudor monarch. Whatever Shakespeare's own religious inclinations, he could number at least one Catholic fugitive among his extended family and doubtless was aware of many others. Similarly, there will have been those among his audience who knew exiles on the Continent or knew others who lived under threat of banishment from England under the recusancy laws. Nor was this the only form of dispossession for which the Reformation might be held responsible. If a member of Shakespeare's audience could not identify with the religious fugitive, he might yet recognize the danger of dispossession represented by economic hardship, a problem considerably exacerbated by the dissolution of the monasteries. With itinerant workers, unemployed soldiers, the able and disabled poor, and foreign immigrants all taking to the roads (many of them on the way to London), the possibility of one's own displacement must have seemed much closer than it once had. Towards the end of Shakespeare's dramatic career, a solution to the problem of this wandering class seemed in sight through the possibility of voluntary and enforced migration to Ireland or to Virginia. However, even before the widespread use of transportation, this could be seen as simply another form of banishment. Indeed, for Shakespeare's audience, the possibility of exile was becoming ever more varied and more distinct.

Yet, this is not to say that Shakespeare's representation of banishment is committedly historicist in the sense of representing in any detail the experience of his contemporaries. In particular, despite the persuasive arguments of a number of Catholic and/or Lancashire-based critics, Shakespeare seems to me remarkably unresponsive to the drama of Catholic exile. The only serious exception, as represented by the plays explored in this study, is the depiction of Poor Tom, though I have argued that this suggests rather a composite of banishment stereotypes than any discrete symbol for the fugitive priest. Nor have I been convinced by arguments that Shakespeare's exiles are intended to represent specific historical cases, for example the fugitive Danvers in *Romeo and Juliet* or the Earl of Essex in *As You Like It*.[3] It seems to me that one of the reasons why *Richard II* was revived before the Essex uprising was to enable the Earl's followers to make connections between the banished Bolingbroke and their banished leader. Yet, there remains little evidence to suggest that the plays were intentionally to be read as allegory. Shakespeare's history of exile derives from Plutarch, Ovid and Holinshed; its contemporaneity rests more upon the debate about the meaning of exile and its revelations about the constructedness of identity than for any particular historical detail.

This brings us back to the question of the literariness of Shakespearean exile. For, while I have argued that Shakespeare's plays often reject the artifice of exile in favour of a more immediate, emotionally raw, even inarticulate response to banishment, the pastoral comedies and romances tend to embrace and even to validate literary and philosophical conventions. Here, exile brings not only disorder but stability in the artful reconciliation of the exile with all that he has lost. Moreover, the imaginative and linguistic creativity which it is assumed the exile will require to transform his state is freely abundant. Indeed, exile eventually becomes an experience akin not merely to wish-fulfilment but to inspiration. It might be argued that the popular theory that Shakespeare was an exile, his work only possible from the vantage-point of alienation, finds partial endorsement in his own plays. Orlando learns to write poetry in the forest (though his efforts are the source of much mirth) and Rosalind educates him in the art of courtship in its amorous and political sense. Prince Hal uses the experience of exile at Eastcheap to learn languages (ostensibly with a view to perfecting his own humanist education) while, in larger terms, he fashions a story of exile and redemption very much on the pastoral model.

Shakespeare could not have written a drama of exile without expressing some conscious or unconscious debt to the tradition of exile as a literary motif, familiar from Seneca, Ovid, Boethius and so on. Moreover, as we saw in the Introduction, it is impossible to distinguish between literary and historical exile for the 'real' experience was consistently rewritten in accordance with literary paradigms. Such paradigms could inform both the Virginia Company's defence of the wreck of one of its ships – a providential exile and return – and Shakespeare's *The Tempest*. They shape not only Shakespeare's *Richard II* but Essex's appropriations of the Ovidian style in his pleading letters to Elizabeth from Ireland, and his final justification for rebellion. Yet what I have argued distinguishes Shakespearean exile from its dramatic representation by rival playwrights is the recurrence of this idea of language, imagination, artistry even, as means of enduring exile. Where the banished man or woman is allowed to speak another language, to give him- or herself another name, exile is pastoral; where he or she remains trapped in a monolingual chauvinism, clinging to an old construction of the self, banishment provides the first acts of a tragedy.

As a man whose livelihood and reputation depended upon theatrical success, one whom it is hard to believe did not take artistic pride in his work even if he betrayed no desire for authorial control, Shakespeare might be expected to celebrate the power of creativity and of language to rescue the exile from oblivion or, if it failed, to further bereave him of life. Yet the consistency with which he does so, in stark contrast to his contemporaries, suggests some deeper identification between dramatist and exile. We can only speculate about the displacement Shakespeare may have felt as he travelled between Stratford and London. Did he write in both places? Did he himself perceive the narrative of his career as a providential one in which the exile discovers his creativity and makes his fortune? Such questions are almost irresistible. Further, we might wonder if the repeated association between banishment and the loss of language/creativity, the dark side to this providential narrative, was not one which Shakespeare returns to with some kind of superstition?

Perhaps more persuasive is the possibility that this emphasis on individual creativity relates to the larger absence of any controlling Artist, that is of any Christian pattern of exile and redemption, in Shakespeare's banishment plays. One phrase that particularly struck me on reading 'Reflections on Exile' is Said's description of this fate as 'irremediably secular and unbearably historical'. Banishment in Shakespeare is a profoundly secular experience, revealing most often not only the individual's dependence upon the secular world for his definition but his passionate love for that world and his inability, even unwillingness, to perceive anything beyond it. For all the so-called immaturity of Romeo's lament on the loss of Juliet/Verona, it strikes a note that echoes throughout the canon. While it would be misleading to suggest that Shakespeare's plays urge upon their audiences a measure of psychological and ideological detachment from society so as to avoid the fate of a Romeo or a Coriolanus, they yet require that the individual be prepared to fashion himself when social constructs are withdrawn. This the artist can perform. And this he must perform for himself in the face of any other controlling artistic presence.

Theodor Adorno writes: 'For a man who no longer has a homeland, writing becomes a place to live.'[4] In Shakespeare's drama, literature provides a place in which the exile might live, through his own linguistic self-reinvention or through identification with some literary paradigm. The recurrence of this idea throughout the canon perhaps points to a larger imperative: men must be responsible for their own construction of the world, writing themselves even as they are written, for beyond these constructions lies nothingness. This worldly narrative is the only one of which Shakespeare's exiles can be assured.

Notes

Introduction

1. *Ulysses* by James Joyce (London: Penguin, 1992), 272.
2. This myth depends upon a number of dubious assumptions about Shakespeare's life and the dating of his works. It is not clear that Shakespeare ever retired from London to Stratford and the last play he wrote, also his last banishment play, was probably *The Two Noble Kinsmen*. Stephen's version, still popular with some biographers and critics, remains a narrative compelling for its sense of closure.
3. See respectively Lodovico in *The White Devil* (1612), the Duchess in Middleton's *The Revenger's Tragedy* (1606), Brishio in *A Knack to Know an Honest Man* (Anon., 1594) and D'Aumale and De Laffin in Chapman's *The Conspiracy of Charles, Duke of Byron* (1608).
4. The nearest critical works are Leslie A. Fiedler's *The Stranger in Shakespeare* (London: Croom Helm, 1973) and Janette Dillon's *Shakespeare and the Solitary Man* (Basingstoke: Macmillan – now Palgrave Macmillan, 1981). Neither critic distinguishes banishment from the other forms of alienation considered.
5. Nicholas Rowe, 'Some Account of the Life, etc., of Mr William Shakespear', (1709), repr. in *Eighteenth Century Essays on Shakespeare* ed. D. Nichol Smith (Glasgow: James MacLehose & Sons, 1903), 1–23, 3.
6. This metaphor recurs in a number of Elizabethan and Jacobean plays: in Shakespeare's *2 Henry VI*, *1 Henry IV* and *Henry VIII*, Thomas Heywood's *A Woman Killed with Kindness* (to be examined later) and John Ford's *Love's Sacrifice* (see Chapter 6). It probably originates from the legal procedure for marital separation which described the couple's alienation 'from bed and board'. See Martin Ingram, *Church Courts, Sex and Marriage in England, 1570–1640* (Cambridge: Cambridge University Press, 1987), 146.
7. More recently, Julia Kristeva has argued that 'Writing is impossible without some kind of exile' in 'A New Type of Intellectual: The Dissident' (1977), repr. in *The Kristeva Reader*, ed. Toril Moi (Oxford: Basil Blackwell, 1986), 292–300, 298.
8. *The Story that the Sonnets Tell* (London: Adam Hart, 1994), 11, 184–98.
9. The three main biographical sources upon which Joyce seems to have relied, namely Frank Harris, *The Man Shakespeare* (1909), George Brandes, *William Shakespeare: A Critical Study* (1899) and Sidney Lee, *A Life of William Shakespeare* (1898), all refer to the legend of Shakespeare as exile and quote the relevant passage from Rowe. On these debts, see William M. Schutte, *Joyce and Shakespeare: A Study in the Meaning of Ulysses* (New Haven, CT: Yale University Press, 1957), 54–5, 153–77.
10. The other biographical subject here is of course Joyce himself. Not only did he choose exile but he consistently identified himself with other exiled writers such as Dante, Giordano Bruno, Ibsen and Mangan and partly based his conception of the artist upon dispossession. See Hélène Cixous, *The Exile of James Joyce*, trans. Sally A. J. Purcell (London: John Calder, 1976).
11. *The Place of the Stage: License, Play and Power in Renaissance England* (1988; Ann Arbor: University of Michigan Press, 1995), and Leeds Barroll, *Politics, Plague*

and *Shakespeare's Theater: The Stuart Years* (Ithaca, NY and London: Cornell University Press, 1991), 13.

12. See, for example, Richard Helgerson, *Self-Crowned Laureates: Jonson, Spenser, Milton and the Literary System* (Berkeley: University of California Press, 1983); Jeffrey Masten, *Textual Intercourse: Collaboration, Authorship and Sexualities in Renaissance Drama* (Cambridge: Cambridge University Press, 1997), 12–27; Emma Smith, 'Author v. Character in Early Modern Dramatic Authorship: The Example of Thomas Kyd and *The Spanish Tragedy*', in *Medieval and Renaissance Drama*, 11 (1999), 129–42; and David Scott Kastan, *Shakespeare and the Book* (Cambridge: Cambridge University Press, 2001).

13. E. A. J. Honigmann, *Shakespeare: The 'Lost Years'* (Manchester: Manchester University Press, 1985; rev. 1998), 130.

14. Eric Sams, *The Real Shakespeare, Retrieving the Early Years 1564–1594* (New Haven, CT and London: Yale University Press, 1995), 45.

15. Jordan suggests that '[Lucy's] power was too great for poor Shakespere to contend with, and he now saw, perhaps with horror, that his youthful levity obliged him to quit his father, his fond wife, his prattling babes, and his native place'. See *Original Memoirs and Historical Accounts of the Families of Shakespeare and Hart*, ed. H. P. (1865), repr. in E. K. Chambers, *William Shakespeare: A Study of Facts and Problems* (Oxford: Clarendon Press, 1930), 2 vols, vol. 2, 293.

16. Vincent J. Cheng, *Joyce, Race and Empire* (Cambridge: Cambridge University Press, 1995), 7.

17. *Stuart Royal Proclamations*, eds James F. Larkin and Paul L. Hughes (Oxford: Clarendon Press, 1973), 2 vols, vol. 1, 14–16, 14–15.

18. *Tudor Royal Proclamations*, eds Paul L. Hughes and James F. Larkin (New Haven, CT and London: Yale University Press, 1969), 3 vols, vol. 1, no. 311.

19. *Stuart Royal Proclamations*, vol. 1, 15, fn. 1. See also John Manwood's *A Treatise and Discourse of the Lawes of the Forrest* (London, 1598; rev. 1615), 7–8.

20. See the argument put forward by W. H. Dixon in *Royal Windsor* (London, 1880), 4 vols, vol. 4, 9.

21. *Student's Blackstone: Selections from the Commentaries on the Laws of England by Sir William Blackstone*, ed. R. M. Kerr (London: John Murray, 1858), 18.

22. J. H. Baker, *An Introduction to English Legal History* (London: Butterworths, 1990), 3rd edn, 77. On the representation of the outlaw in Shakespeare, contrasted with the historical reality, see Chapter 4.

23. See Sir William Holdsworth, *A History of English Law* (London: Methuen, 1973) first pub. 1903, 5th edn, 16 vols, vol. 3, 303.

24. See Statutes 22 Hen 8 c. 14, 28 Hen 8 c. 2, 32 Hen 8 c. 12, 1 Jac 1 c. 25 & 7 and 21 Jac 1 c. 28 & 7.

25. *The Third Part of the Institutes of the Laws of England* (New York and London: Garland, 1979), 115, cap. 51. The only exception he cites is Elizabeth's Act of 1592/93 which insisted that recusants shall 'abjure this Realme of Englande and all other the Quenes Majesties Domynions for ever; And therupon shall departe out of this Realme at suche Haven and Porte, and within suche tyme as shall in that behalfe be assigned and appointed, by the saide Justices of Peace or Coroner before whom suche Abjuracion shalbe made ...' This act seems to have kept the form of abjuration – the oath to depart, the details of journey and destination – but since it was no longer dependent upon an initial place of sanctuary it did not fall foul of the 1624 Act.

26. *Shakespeare's Legal Language: A Dictionary* (London and New Brunswick, NJ: Athlone Press, 2000), 247. A much more accurate representation of the subject is

given by Leah Scragg who begins with the assertion that 'exile was not a condition remote from the everyday lives of a Renaissance audience', *Shakespeare's Mouldy Tales: Recurrent Plot Motifs in Shakespearian Drama* (London: Longman, 1992), 123–55, 123–4.

27. *An Introduction to English Legal History*, 237.
28. See G. R. Elton, *The Tudor Constitution* (Cambridge: Cambridge University Press, 1960), 150–2.
29. *The First Part of the Institutes* (1628) (New York and London: Garland, 1979), 132–3, cap. 11, lib. 2.
30. See 5 Eliz. c. 20 (1562), 27 Eliz c. 2 (1585), 34 Eliz c. 1 (1592), 3 Jac 1 c. 5 (1605) and 39 Eliz c. 4 (1597). The identification of both player and playwright as exiles is explored in more detail on pp. 19–24.
31. In 1603, James I's Parliament recognized the difficulty in enforcing the 1597 Act banishing dangerous rogues and vagabonds. The statute describes how banished men might move to other parts of the kingdom or return from abroad without it being clear that they had been banished. The statute recommends that such men be branded on the left shoulder with an 'R' and also replaces banishment with prosecution for felony, 1 Jac. 1 c. 7 (1603).
32. See *Tudor Royal Proclamations*, nos 470, 762, 804.5, 542 and 646.
33. *Stuart Royal Proclamations*, nos 132 and 168.
34. Ibid., no. 213.
35. *Remembrancia 1574–1664*, vol. 1, 40–1, letter dated 17 June 1580.
36. Ibid., vol. 2, nos 74–6.
37. Ibid., vol. 3, no. 159, letter dated 8 July 1614.
38. *Tudor Royal Proclamations*, 211, no. 804.5.
39. Ibid., 135, no. 762.
40. *Stuart Royal Proclamations*, 378, no. 168.
41. This is perhaps the key difficulty faced by any historian of exile. Paul Tabori offers as his initial definition: 'An exile is a person compelled to leave or remain outside his country of origin on account of well-founded fear of persecution for reasons of race, religion, nationality, or political opinion'. However, this definition meets with so many objections from the 'several hundred exiles and international experts' to whom it is submitted that Tabori is compelled to add: 'It does not make an essential difference whether he is expelled by physical force or whether he makes the decision to leave without such an immediate pressure', *The Anatomy of Exile: A Semantic and Historical Study* (London: Harrap, 1972), 27, 37. In a study of banishment closer to our own, Randolph Starn notes a similar problem of definition: 'There were exiles of various sorts in medieval and Renaissance Italy, and it was not easy for contemporaries to distinguish between the émigré, the outlaw, the bandit, and the stranger'. Rather than try to differentiate them himself, Starn includes those 'driven away by force or unable to make a living among enemies', *Contrary Commonwealth: The Theme of Exile in Medieval and Renaissance Italy* (Berkeley: University of California Press, 1982), xvi–xvii.
42. See in particular 'A Proclamation for the due execution of all former Lawes against Recusants' (2 June 1610) which goes into some detail about the mercy James has shown in encouraging recusants to leave his kingdom, *Stuart Royal Proclamations*, 248, no. 111.
43. See *Dictionary of National Biography: From the Earliest Times to 1900* eds Sir Leslie Stephen and Sidney Lee (London: Oxford University Press, 1921–22), vol. 13, 63–8: Matthew, Sir Tobie, p. 64.

44. See 'A Declaration of the Lyfe and Death of John Story' (1571) printed in *Somer's Tracts* (London, 1809) (New York: AMS Press, 1965), 10 vols, vol. 1, 477–87, 485.
45. The *Oxford Classical Dictionary*, eds Simon Hornblower and Antony Spawforth (Oxford: Oxford University Press, 1996), 3rd edn, 580.
46. *The Dictionary of English Law*, ed. Earl Jowitt (London: Sweet & Maxwell, 1959), 200.
47. *Athenae Oxonienses* (London: R. Knaplock, D. Midwinter & J. Tonson, 1721), 2 vols, vol. 1, 101, 170.
48. A letter from Essex to Bacon *c.*24 August 1593, repr. in *The Letters and the Life of Francis Bacon*, ed. James Spedding (London: Longmans, 1868–90), 7 vols, vol. 1, 254–5.
49. See Mario Digangi, *The Homoerotics of Early Modern Drama* (Cambridge: Cambridge University Press, 1997), 100–3.
50. *The Marian Exiles: A Study in the Origins of Elizabethan Puritanism* (Cambridge: Cambridge University Press, 1938 repr. 1966), 7. A. G. Dickens argues that Garrett's reappraisal is too sweeping and opts for a truth lying 'somewhere between the excessive optimism of the modern picture, and the old legend of hapless fugitives, weeping by the waters of Babylon', *The English Reformation* (London: B. T. Batsford, 1964), 284.
51. *The Marian Exiles*, 15.
52. *The Acts and Monuments of John Foxe*, ed. Rev. Josiah Pratt (London: Religious Tract Society, 1877), 4th edn, 8 vols, vol. 8, 624.
53. *The Rise and Growth of the Anglican Schism*, trans. and ed. David Lewis (London: Burns & Oates, 1877), bk 4, ch. 3, 261.
54. See 27 Eliz c. 2. The Act called for those mentioned to quit the realm of England within forty days or face a charge of high treason. For further provisions of the Act see the above statute or Rishton's summary in *The Rise and Growth*, bk 4, ch. 11, 332–3.
55. *Acts and Monuments*, vol. 1, 18–19. The letter has neither date nor direction.
56. Reprinted in *Athenae Oxonienses*, vol. 1, 170.
57. Ibid. Parsons makes a similar point about an employee of Jewel's, called Dr Stevens, who also queried certain allegations in Jewel's book. When the latter refused to amend them, Stevens sought the 'truth' in Catholicism, 'where only it was to be found' and went voluntarily into banishment (170).
58. Cecil's letter to Copley is reprinted in *The Other Face: Catholic Life under Elizabeth I* collected and edited by Philip Caraman (London: Longmans, Green, 1960), 141. This book includes a chapter of exile writing (140–6).
59. See *The Execution of Justice in England by William Cecil and A True, Sincere, and Modest Defense of English Catholics by William Allen*, ed. Robert M. Kingdon (Ithaca, NY: Cornell University Press, 1965), 4.
60. Ibid., 5–6.
61. Ibid., 6.
62. *A True, Sincere and Modest Defense*, 106.
63. Ibid., 106–7.
64. *Harrison's Description of England in Shakespere's Youth: 2nd and 3rd Books of his Description of Britaine* (1577), repr. by E. K. Chambers in *The Elizabethan Stage* (Oxford: Clarendon Press, 1923; repr. 1961), 4 vols, vol. 1, 281. On the expulsion of the theatre due to plague see Barroll, *Politics, Plague and Shakespeare's Theater*.
65. *The Elizabethan Stage*, vol. 1, 297–8.

66. This extract is taken from an anonymous letter thought to have been written in 1584. See the transcript of Lansdowne MS 20, no. II, reproduced in Virginia Gildersleeve, *Government Regulation of the Elizabethan Drama* (New York: Burt Franklin, 1961), 172–3.

67. *Government Regulation*, 175.

68. *The Elizabethan Stage*, vol. 1, 284, *Government Regulation*, 158.

69. An exception would be the case of Thomas Nashe who went into exile to avoid imprisonment for his part in *The Isle of Dogs* (1597). Francis Meres consoles the dramatist with the thought that 'thy banishment' is not 'like Ovid's, eternally to converse with the barbarous *Getae*', *Palladis Tamia* (1598), in *Elizabethan Critical Essays*, ed. G. Gregory Smith (London: Oxford University Press, 1904), 2 vols, vol. 2, 308–24, 324. Nashe himself defined this plight as exile in *Nashe's Lenten Stuff* (1599). Both references incline towards a tragic rather than a heroic definition of exile.

70. For many English Protestants, exile and publication were associated on a purely practical level. According to John Foxe's son, 'the most part' of the English Protestant community at Basle 'gained their livelihood by reviewing and correcting the press', *Acts and Monuments*, vol. 1, 16. Yet, such activity also recalled the origins of Protestantism, namely the dissemination of Luther's works across Europe by means of the newly invented press. Indeed, the elder Foxe suggested that 'either the pope must abolish knowledge and printing, or printing at length will root him out', vol. 3, 720.

71. *The Image of Both Churches*, in *The Select Works of John Bale*, ed. Rev. Henry Christmas (Cambridge: Cambridge University Press, 1849), 249–640, 254. The subheading of the book reads: 'Compiled by John Bale an exile also in this life for the faythfull testimonie of Jesu.'

72. See 'In Io. Foxum theologum celeberrimum cum Christo exultantem', reprinted by G. A. Williamson in *John Foxe's Book of Martyrs* (London: Secker & Warburg, 1965), xli.

73. Alison Shell argues that 'more than any other theme in English Catholic discourse, exile prompted a self-conscious addressing of the authorial role'. See her extensive work on the metaphor of exile in Catholic writings in *Catholicism, Controversy and the English Literary Imagination, 1558–1660* (Cambridge: Cambridge University Press, 1999), 169–223.

74. On the source of the legend that Wyatt was banished and a refutation of this argument see Kenneth Muir, *The Life and Letters of Sir Thomas Wyatt* (Liverpool: Liverpool University Press, 1963), 22–3; Katherine Duncan-Jones and J. Van Dorsten similarly argue that Sidney's absence from court in 1580, described as 'banishment' in his letter of 2 August, was voluntary rather than enforced in *Miscellaneous Prose of Sir Philip Sidney* (Oxford: Clarendon Press, 1973), 34–5. On Spenser's self-dramatization as the exile, Colin Clout, see my chapter on *Richard II*. In the introduction to his translation of *Orlando*, Harington himself asserted that he had been commanded to write it by the Queen during his exile from the court.

75. See Bacon's letter of 6 June 1621 translated from the Latin in *The Letters and the Life of Francis Bacon*, vol. 7, 285. In a letter to Lancelot Andrewes the following year, Bacon compared his fate and the literary endeavours it would produce with those of Cicero, Seneca and Demosthenes. These banished men apparently confirmed Bacon in his resolution 'to spend my time wholly in writing' (371–2).

76. *The Place of the Stage*, 30. Throughout his book, Mullaney is not quite consistent as to the nature of the banishment he describes. He insists upon the enforced exile of the stage, reminiscent of Plato's banishment of the arts from

the *Republic* or of Rosalind's exile in *As You Like It*, while also arguing for the theatre's deliberate and voluntary withdrawal from the city (56 and 23). The confusion of voluntary/enforced exile is paradigmatic of banishment in the period, but Mullaney makes no reference to this debate nor does he include any contemporary testimony to the stage as 'banished'.

77. *Plato's Republic*, trans. Desmond Lee (Harmondsworth: Penguin, 1987), 2nd edn, 135.
78. Ibid., 153.
79. On the polemicists' debt to Plato see Russell Fraser, *The War Against Poetry* (Princeton, NJ: Princeton University Press, 1970), 102–12. William Prynne's *Histriomastix* (1633), a vast compendium of anti-theatrical material, recurs again and again to Plato as its authority for banishment. See *Histriomastix* (New York: Garland, 1974), 368, 448, 480 and 517.
80. *Markets of Bawdrie: The Dramatic Criticism of Stephen Gosson*, ed. Arthur F. Kinney (Salzburg: Universität Salzburg, 1974), 69–120, 77.
81. *A Defence of Poetry* (1579), in *Elizabethan Critical Essays*, vol. 1, 61–86, 67.
82. *The Defence of Poesy*, in *Sir Philip Sidney*, ed. Katherine Duncan-Jones (Oxford: Oxford University Press, 1989), 239.
83. Ibid., and note, 384.
84. Ibid., 239.
85. *The Anatomie of Absurditie* in *The Works of Thomas Nashe*, ed. R. B. McKerrow (Oxford: Basil Blackwell, 1958), 5 vols, vol. 1, 1–50, 25. In *The Golden Grove* (1600), William Vaughan makes the same distinction between poetry and its abuse, concluding that 'many of our English rimers and ballet-makers deserve for their baudy sonnets & amorous allurements, to be banished ...' (London, 1608), 2nd edn, bk 3, ch. 43, n.p.
86. *Defense of Poetry*, 76.
87. This point is argued by Tom Cain in his introduction to *Poetaster* (Manchester: Manchester University Press, 1995), 23.
88. *Histriomastix*, in *The Plays of John Marston*, ed. H. Harvey Wood (Edinburgh and London: Oliver & Boyd, 1939), 3 vols, vol. 3, 299.
89. See also Tucca in *Poetaster* who says of the players: 'They are grown licentious, the rogues; libertines, flat libertines. They forget they are i'the statute' (1.2.52–4).
90. See Philip J. Finkelpearl, *John Marston of the Middle Temple* (Cambridge, MA: Harvard University Press, 1969), 119–24.
91. On the question of Jonson's objections, see James P. Bednarz, 'Representing Jonson: *Histriomastix* and the Origin of the Poets' War', *HLQ*, 54 (Winter 1991), 1–30.
92. Katherine Duncan-Jones has recently argued for a strong personal and professional relationship between the two men, to the extent that *Hamlet* and *Antonio's Revenge, Twelfth Night* and *What You Will* were written in 'close collusion'. See *Ungentle Shakespeare: Scenes from his Life* (London: Thomson Learning, 2001), 136, 145–9, 153–6.
93. *Antonio's Revenge*, ed. W. Reavley Gair (Manchester: Manchester University Press, 1978). Marston's Stoicism is discussed by Gilles D. Monsarrat in *Light from the Porch: Stoicism and English Renaissance Literature* (Paris: Didier Erudition, 1984), 151–87.
94. *Antonio and Mellida*, ed. W. Reavley Gair (Manchester: Manchester University Press, 1991). See also 4.1.1–4 in which Antonio, disguised as a mariner, shouts out to himself and then adds in his own voice: 'Vain breath, vain breath,

Antonio's lost. / He cannot find himself, not seize himself. / Alas, this that you see is not Antonio.'

95. *Antonio and Mellida*, 4.1.250–1, *John Marston of the Middle Temple*, 268–71.
96. The quotation is taken from a series of didactic tracts, B.M. MS Harley 45, f. 1.
97. *The Malcontent*, ed. George K. Hunter (Manchester: Manchester University Press, 1975).
98. Lucifer is not the only exile mentioned in the play. He is joined by allusions to Diogenes, Seneca, Ulysses and Dante. The emphasis on man's exile from heaven is echoed when Pietro responds to news of his wife's infidelity with the comment 'Good God, that men should desire / To search out that which being found kills all / Their joy of life; to taste the tree of knowledge / And then be driven from out paradise!' (3.1.15–18).
99. David Farley-Hills argues for a connection between *A Woman Killed With Kindness* and *Othello* as domestic tragedy in *Shakespeare and the Rival Playwrights* (London: Routledge, 1990), 104–35.
100. *A Woman Killed with Kindness*, ed. Brian Scobie (London: A & C Black, 1985, repr. 1998). The play may reflect contemporary practice in cases of adultery, as in the case of Henry Wriothesley's mother, Mary, Countess of Southampton, who was 'by my Lord forbydden his companye', and removed to one of his Hampshire residences where she was kept under close surveillance. See her letter dated 21 March 1580, cited by G. P. V. Akrigg, *Shakespeare and the Earl of Southampton* (London: Hamish Hamilton, 1968), 13.
101. For an excellent analysis of the interrelation of the two plots, with particular emphasis on the theme of exile, see Diana E. Henderson, 'Many Mansions: Reconstructing *A Woman Killed with Kindness*', SEL, 26 (1986), 277–94.
102. Ibid., 279–81.
103. Useful discussions of the status and, in particular, the dating of these revisions can be found in Richard Dutton's *Mastering the Revels* (Basingstoke: Macmillan – now Palgrave Macmillan, 1991), 81–6, and *Shakespeare and Sir Thomas More: Essays on the Play and its Shakespearean Interest*, ed. T. H. Howard-Hill (Cambridge: Cambridge University Press, 1989). Although Shakespeare's revision would still appear to infringe Tilney's injunctions by harping on the words 'English' and 'stranger' and by its reference to France, the overall sense of the passage, which is to blur these distinctions, might have allowed Tilney to accept it. It was not only Shakespeare as a writer of the Jack Cade rebellion which qualified him for this sensitive task, but, I would suggest, his sympathy for the exile.
104. Although, as has been argued, there is no absolute distinction between enforced and voluntary exile, the plays chosen all feature a proclamation of banishment. If we were to include characters who exile themselves, *Love's Labour's Lost*, *Macbeth* and *Pericles* would all fall within the confines of this work. If we were to treat exile more figuratively, the brothers in *The Comedy of Errors*, Lysander and Hermia in *A Midsummer Night's Dream*, Antony in *Antony and Cleopatra*, Cressida in *Troilus and Cressida*, and Camillo and Perdita in *The Winter's Tale* might also fall within the scope of this study.

Chapter 1 'That One Word "Banishèd"': Linguistic Crisis in *Romeo and Juliet*

1. Not surprisingly, these lines have fared worst in film adaptations, with Franco Zeffirelli's film (1968) cutting all of Juliet's 'banishèd' speech in 3.2 and allowing

Romeo only 13 lines from 3.3. It is notable that in Q1 *Romeo and Juliet*, although Juliet's banishment speech is reduced from 15 to seven lines, Romeo's remains largely untouched. If we accept the theory that Q1 is based on a memorial reconstruction, it seems that Shakespeare did intend his audience to hear the word 'banishèd' over and over again. See *The First Quarto Edition of Shakespeare's Romeo and Juliet* (1597) ed. Frank G. Hubbard (Madison: University of Wisconsin, 1924).

2. All quotations and translations are taken from Robert M. Durling's edition of *Petrarch's Lyric Poems: The Rime Sparse and Other Lyrics* (Cambridge, MA: Harvard University Press, 1976).

3. See Jonathan Dollimore's 'Desire is Death', in *Subject and Object in Renaissance Culture*, eds Margreta de Grazia, Maureen Quilligan and Peter Stallybrass (Cambridge: Cambridge University Press, 1996), 369–86. On the association of death and Petrarchanism in *Romeo and Juliet*, see Gayle Whittier's 'The Sonnet's Body and the Body Sonnetized in *Romeo and Juliet*', *Sh. Q.*, 40 (1989), 27–41, and Lloyd Davis, '"Death-marked Love": Desire and Presence in *Romeo and Juliet*', *Sh. S.*, 49 (1996), 57–67.

4. Sir Thomas Wyatt adapts this sonnet in 'How oft have I, my dear and cruel foe', where he makes the connection between the heart's exile and death more strongly:

> If I then it chase, nor it in you can find,
> In this exile no manner of comfort,
> Nor live alone, nor where he is called resort,
> He may wander from his natural kind.
> So shall it be great hurt unto us twain,
> And yours the loss, and mine the deadly pain.

(9–14)

Sir Thomas Wyatt: Collected Poems, ed. Joost Daalder (London: Oxford University Press, 1975), 28.

5. *Epistulae metricae*, 3.19.15–16, as translated by Gordon Braden in *Petrarchan Love and the Continental Renaissance* (New Haven, CT: Yale University Press, 1999), 4.

6. See the letters to 'Severo Apenninicola' and to Philippe de Vitry in *Rerum familiarium libri I–VIII*, trans. Aldo S. Bernardo (New York: State University of New York Press, 1975), II, 3–4, pp. 70–86, and *Rerum familiarium libri IX–XVI* (Baltimore, MD: Johns Hopkins University Press, 1982), XI, 12, pp. 35–44. Critics who have commented on the centrality of exile to Petrarch's thought include Giuseppe Mazzotta, *The Worlds of Petrarch* (Durham, NC and London: Duke University Press, 1993) and A. Bartlett Giamatti, *Exile and Change in Renaissance Literature* (New Haven, CT and London: Yale University Press, 1984).

7. *The Life of Solitude*, trans. Jacob Zeitlin (Urbana, Illinois: University of Illinois Press, 1924), bk 1, tr. 4, ch. 1, 131.

8. *Poems and A Defence of Ryme*, ed. Arthur Colby Sprague (Chicago: University of Chicago Press, 1930; repr. 1965), 141.

9. See *The Letters and Epigrams of Sir John Harington together with the Prayse of Private Life*, ed. Norman Egbert McClure (Philadelphia: University of Pennsylvania Press, 1930), 2 vols, vol. 1, 44–5.

10. *The Life and Lyrics of Sir Edward Dyer*, ed. Ralph M. Sargent (Oxford: Clarendon Press, 1935; repr. 1968).

11. Coincidentally, Woodstock had been the location of Elizabeth's own exile from court under Mary Tudor.
12. Alison Shell discusses these points in *Catholicism, Controversy and the English Literary Imagination*, 108. As we saw in the Introduction, it is impossible to rediscover the exact terms of such an exile though a document authorizing Constable's licence to travel abroad remains extant. See *The Poems of Henry Constable*, ed. Joan Grundy (Liverpool: Liverpool University Press, 1960), 49.
13. In the introduction to her edition of Constable's poems, Grundy writes: 'The materials that he handles in these sonnets are the fixities and definites of the fancy, counters [...] already in circulation, and simply moulded by him to a slightly different shape [...] There is no indication of anything in Constable's experience, real or imaginary, to which we can relate them; they exist in a vacuum, and are, in a literal sense, pseudo-statements, lacking even emotional validity' (ibid., 71).
14. *Poems and A Defence of Ryme*, 21.
15. M. C. Bradbrook, *Shakespeare: The Poet in his World* (London: Weidenfeld & Nicolson, 1978), 100–1.
16. All references to Brooke's poem are taken from Geoffrey Bullough's *Narrative and Dramatic Sources of Shakespeare*, vol. 1, 284–363.
17. *The Phonetic Writings of Robert Robinson*, ed. E. J. Dobson (London: Oxford University Press, 1957), 1–28, 4.
18. See Jane Donawerth's *Shakespeare and the Sixteenth-Century Study of Language* (Urbana: University of Illinois Press, 1984), 16–17.
19. Neil Rhodes examines the 'magical' efficacy of rhetoric to move and possess, and of satire to wound the body in *The Power of Eloquence and English Renaissance Literature* (Worcester: Harvester Wheatsheaf, 1992), 8, 19–22, 45. On contemporary attitudes towards cursing, see Keith Thomas, *Religion and the Decline of Magic* (London: Weidenfeld & Nicolson, 1971), 502–34.
20. James L. Calderwood, *Shakespearean Metadrama* (Minneapolis: University of Minnesota Press, 1971), 98. On the cliché of Petrarchanism in the play see also 'Romeo and Juliet and the Elizabethan Sonnets' by A. J. Earl, *English*, 27 (1978), 99–119, and Harry Levin, 'Form and Formality in *Romeo and Juliet*', Sh. Q., 11 (1960), 3–11.
21. Romeo uses the arguments of Shakespeare's early sonnets: 'O, she is rich in beauty, only poor / That when she dies, with beauty dies her store' (1.1.212–13). See in particular Sonnet 6 'Then let not winter's ragged hand deface ...' in which the poet urges 'Be not self-willed, for thou art much too fair / To be death's conquest and make worms thine heir' (ll. 13–14).
22. *John Donne: The Complete English Poems*, ed. A. J. Smith (Harmondsworth: Penguin, 1971).
23. Catherine Belsey, 'The Name of the Rose in *Romeo and Juliet*', YES, 23 (1993), 126–42, 131.
24. 'The Definition of Love: Shakespeare's Phrasing in *Romeo and Juliet*', Sh. St., 15 (1982), 21–36, 26.
25. Juliet's words also remind us of Brooke's moralizing prologue to his poem in which the lovers are accused of 'neglecting the authoritie and advise of parents and frendes' and of 'hastyng to most unhappye deathe'.
26. See Susan Snyder, *The Comic Matrix of Shakespeare's Tragedies* (Princeton, NJ: Princeton University Press, 1979), 57, and Nicholas Brooke, *Shakespeare's Early Tragedies* (London: Methuen, 1968), 83.

27. See M. M. Mahood, *Shakespeare's Wordplay* (London: Methuen, 1957), 69–70 on Mercutio's dying curse.
28. *Shakespearean Metadrama*, 96.
29. See G. Blakemore Evans' discussion of the sources in his introduction to *Romeo and Juliet* (Cambridge: Cambridge University Press, 1984), 6–13.
30. Ibid., 3.3.10n. 136. This usage is anticipated in *The Two Gentlemen of Verona* where Lance substitutes the word 'vanished' for 'banished' (3.1.215).
31. A similar point is made about banishment in *Richard II*. The King describes the sentence as verbal and vocal: 'The hopeless word of "never to return" / Breathe I against thee, upon pain of life' (1.3.146–7). Bolingbroke, like Juliet, wonders that any expression composed of human breath should be so lasting. When Richard grants him a reprieve of six years, Bolingbroke responds:

    > How long a time lies in one little word!
    > Four lagging winters and four wanton springs
    > End in a word: such is the breath of kings.

    > (1.3.206–8)

32. Q1 *Romeo and Juliet* adds a further casualty when Montague declares: 'Dread sovereign, my wife is dead tonight, / And young Benvolio is deceasèd too' (5.3.140–1), reprinted in *Romeo and Juliet*, ed. Jill L. Levenson (Oxford: Oxford University Press, 2000).
33. Rosalie Colie coined the term 'unmetaphoring' with regard to *Romeo and Juliet*, defining it as the 'trick of making a verbal convention part of the scene, the action, or the psychology of the play itself', *Shakespeare's Living Art* (Princeton, NJ: Princeton University Press, 1974), 145. See also Ann Pasternak Slater, 'Petrarchanism Come True in *Romeo and Juliet*', in *Images of Shakespeare*, ed. Werner Habicht et al. (London and Toronto: Associated University Presses, 1988), 129–50.
34. Pasternak Slater describes Romeo 'wallowing hysterically at news of his banishment' in 'Petrarchanism Come True', 133, while James H. Seward condemns 'the unmanliness of Romeo's behaviour' in *Tragic Vision in Romeo and Juliet* (Washington, DC: Consortium Press, 1973), 136. One of the few critics who respond sympathetically to this banishment scene is Robert O. Evans. He suggests that Shakespeare 'made Romeo's reaction to banishment appear reasonable to the audience (an easier job with an Elizabethan audience than with a modern one) by leading them to understand that Romeo and Juliet were bound by grand passion', *The Osier Cage: Rhetorical Devices in Romeo and Juliet* (Lexington: University of Kentucky Press, 1966), 54. Unfortunately, Osier does not explain why an Elizabethan audience would have responded differently to banishment.
35. *The Diall of Princes compiled by ... Don Anthony of Guevara*, trans. Thomas North (London, 1557), bk 3, ch. 34, 207.
36. Brooke, *Shakespeare's Early Tragedies*, 81.
37. For a detailed consideration of the Folio's inconsistencies as to location see Clifford Leech's introduction to *The Two Gentlemen of Verona* (London: Methuen, 1969), xv–xviii.
38. This is also true of *Mucedorus* (anon. 1590; rev. 1610). Here, the young prince travels disguised as a shepherd to a foreign court to meet his intended bride. His banishment only excludes him from a place to which he is a stranger and he may return to Valencia where his family, friends and his inheritance await. Nor

is Mucedorus long separated from Amadine for, like Sylvia, she chooses exile in the forest with him.

39. See John Florio's dictionary, *A Worlde of Wordes* (London, 1598), 333. A. J. Earl has commented on the Petrarchan origins of the identification of lover and pilgrim, referring to sonnet 16 of the *Rime*, 'Romeo and Juliet and the Elizabethan Sonnets', 115. The question of Romeo as pilgrim is considered further later on in this chapter.

40. Romeus is also afraid that Capulet will follow the lovers to take revenge and that their reputations will suffer. His anxieties are partly based on the age difference between himself and Juliet, a detail Shakespeare appears to ignore.

41. This may be a line taken from Brooke where Juliet promises 'Both me and mine I will all whole to you betake, / And following you whereso you go, my father's house forsake' (539–40).

42. 'Ideology and the Feud in *Romeo and Juliet*', *Sh. S.*, 49 (1996), 87–96, 93.

43. One text which insists upon this similarity between Italy and heaven is Thomas Coryat's *Crudities* (1611), likening Lombardy to 'the very Elysian fields, so much decantated and celebrated by the verses of Poets, or the Tempe or Paradise of the world', *Coryat's Crudities* (Glasgow: James MacLehose & Sons, 1905), 2 vols, vol. 1, 245. Ironically, Coryat also extends this comparison to Mantua (264).

44. *Shakespeare's Europe: Unpublished Chapters of Fynes Moryson's Itinerary* ed. Charles Hughes (London: Sherratt & Hughes, 1903), bk 5, ch. 1, 401–2.

45. 'Between Idolatry and Astrology: Modes of Temporal Repetition in *Romeo and Juliet*', in *A Feminist Companion to Shakespeare*, ed. Dympna Callaghan (Oxford: Blackwell, 2000), 358–72.

46. *Inferno*, IX, 91–3 and XV, 79–81 in *The Portable Dante*, trans. Mark Musa (London: Penguin, 1995). For a useful introduction to this theme in Dante's work see Giuseppe Mazzotta, 'Dante and the Virtues of Exile', in *Exile in Literature*, ed. Maria-Ines Lagos-Pope (London: Associated University Presses, 1988), 49–71.

47. Critics who find Romeo guilty of idolatry include Seward, *Tragic Vision in Romeo and Juliet*, 137, and Barbara L. Parker, *A Precious Seeing: Love and Reason in Shakespeare's Plays* (New York and London: New York University Press, 1987), 148.

48. See Coppélia Kahn's seminal article, 'Coming of Age in Verona', in *The Woman's Part: Feminist Criticism of Shakespeare*, eds Carolyn Lenz, Gayle Greene and Carol Thomas Neely (Urbana: University of Illinois Press, 1980), 171–93.

49. Snyder makes a similar point when she argues that the play demonstrates the destructive power of ideology: 'That which is necessary to give us a stable identity and a consistent view of the world is by the same token what limits and distorts us,' 'Ideology and the Feud in *Romeo and Juliet*', 95.

50. On this experience as the fulfilment of Romeo's death wish, see Marilyn L. Williamson, 'Romeo and Death', *Sh. St.*, 14 (1981), 129–37.

51. The Nurse's comments may well reflect the most familiar form of divorce in England at this time which involved a separation without the right to remarry, often on the grounds that one of the parties had deserted the other. Such a 'divorce' must often have led to bigamous second marriages.

52. While I am arguing for a marked difference between the language of *The Two Gentlemen* and *Romeo and Juliet* as a result of banishment, Peter J. Smith suggests that both plays feature a 'growing movement away from the harmless comedy of words to the increasing awareness of the potential dangers of language', *Social Shakespeare: Aspects of Renaissance Dramaturgy and Contemporary Society* (Basingstoke: Macmillan – now Palgrave Macmillan, 1995), 120–45, 133.

Chapter 2 'Still-Breeding Thoughts': *Richard II* and the Exile's Creative Failure

1. David Williams, 'The Exile as Uncreator', *Mosaic*, 8 (1975), 1–15, 8–9.
2. See Douglas M. Friedman's discussion of this speech in 'John of Gaunt and the Rhetoric of Frustration', *ELH*, 43 (1976), 279–99.
3. See Ernst H. Kantorowicz, *The King's Two Bodies: A Study in Mediaeval Political Theology* (Princeton, NJ: Princeton University Press, 1957), 7. Kantorowicz argues that, in *Richard II*, Shakespeare 'eternalized' the metaphor of the king's two bodies, making it 'the very substance and essence of one of his greatest plays' (26). His emphasis is upon the metaphor as a psychological truth about kingship rather than as an expression of competing political discourses.
4. *The Queen's Two Bodies: Drama and the Elizabethan Succession* (London: Royal Historical Society, 1977), 13–14, 26–37, 12.
5. The dialectic within the play between divine right kingship and aristocratic ideology is discussed in detail by Graham Holderness, *Shakespeare Recycled: The Making of Historical Drama* (New York and London: Harvester Wheatsheaf, 1992), 51–72.
6. *Narrative and Dramatic Sources*, vol. 3, 383.
7. *The Chronicle of Froissart translated out of French by Sir John Bourchier, Lord Berners*, ed. William Paton Ker (London: David Nutt, 1901–3), 6 vols, vol. 6, cap. CCXXXIIII, 355. Shakespeare does not refer to the banishments of Northumberland and Percy, perhaps because those of Bolingbroke and Mowbray loom so large.
8. Richard was born in France and was often called 'Richard of Bourdeaux' though, unlike *Woodstock*, Shakespeare's play makes little reference to this fact, preferring to hint at the king's symbolic foreignness.
9. Terence Hawkes is a notable exception: 'the banishment of the disaffected Bolingbroke not only precipitates the Wars of the Roses, it also initiates a social, moral, and economic disorder without parallel in the Elizabethan mind', *Shakespeare's Talking Animals: Language and Drama in Society* (London: Edward Arnold, 1973), 81.
10. See Hall's *Union* and Holinshed's *Chronicles* in *Narrative and Dramatic Sources*, vol. 3, 386 and 393 respectively.
11. See *A Mirror for Magistrates* (1559), *Narrative and Dramatic Sources*, vol. 3, 418, ll. 141–2 and 424–5, and *The Chronicle of Froissart*, vol. 6, cap. CCXXIIII, 313–15. In *The Firste Foure Bookes of the Civile Wars* (1595), Samuel Daniel suggests that banishment was an expression of Richard's fear of the ambitious Bolingbroke. In this account, an innocent Mowbray is sacrificed for the sake of the realm, *Narrative and Dramatic Sources*, 438.
12. See, for example, 1.1.190–5 and 2.1.123–4. The question of censorship and self-censorship in the play is further explored by David Norbrook, '"A Liberal Tongue": Language and Rebellion in *Richard II*', in *Shakespeare's Universe: Renaissance Ideas and Conventions*, ed. John M. Mucciolo (Aldershot: Scolar Press, 1996), 37–51, and by Paula Blank, 'Speaking Freely about Richard II', *Journal of English and Germanic Philology*, 96 (1997), 327–48.
13. *The First and Second Parts of John Hayward's The Life and Raigne of King Henrie IIII*, ed. John J. Manning (London: Royal Historical Society, 1992), 103.
14. See 22 Hen 8 c. 14, 28 Hen 8 c. 1 and 32 Hen 8 c. 3. Under the laws of sanctuary, a criminal could take refuge on consecrated ground or in certain secular sanctuaries for a period of forty days. After that time, if he confessed before the coroner, he would be required to swear an oath to abjure the realm and would

then be allowed to travel to a particular port to a particular destination. Any deviations on his journey would be punished by death. See Holdsworth's *A History of English Law*, vol. 3, 303–6.

15. See John Bellamy, *The Tudor Law of Treason: An Introduction* (London: Routledge & Kegan Paul, 1979), 88–92.

16. 'An Act to Retain the Queen's Majesty's Subjects in their due Obedience' called on persistent recusants to 'abjure this Realm of *England*' until a licence was given for their return, 34 Eliz c. 1.

17. See Morris Palmer Tilley, *A Dictionary of Proverbs in England in the Sixteenth and Seventeenth Centuries* (Ann Arbor: University of Michigan Press, 1950), S985, who traces it back to *Matthew* 5: 45, 'He maketh his sun to rise on the evil and on the good'.

18. See *Euphues* in *The Complete Works of John Lyly*, ed. R. Warwick Bond (Oxford: Clarendon Press, 1902; repr. 1973), 2 vols, vol. 1, 314. Shakespeare returns to this consolation for exile in *Cymbeline* when Innogen asks herself, 'Hath Britain all the sun that shines?', 3.4.137.

19. On the structure of Gaunt's speech as an imitation of the classical *consolatio* see Tison, 'Shakespeare's "Consolatio" for Exile', 153–4. On its sources, see Hilda H. Hulme, *Explorations in Shakespeare's Language: Some Problems of Lexical Meaning in the Dramatic Text* (London: Longman, 1962), 180–2, and T. W. Baldwin, *William Shakspere's Small Latine & Lesse Greeke* (Urbana: University of Illinois Press, 1944), 2 vols, vol. 2, 427–8.

20. Stanley Wells explores the imagination's power to console in 'The Lamentable Tale of *Richard II*', *Sh. St.* (Tokyo), 17 (1982), 1–23, 16–17.

21. *The First Part of the Life and Raigne of Henrie IIII*, 105–6.

22. See respectively Albert J. Loomie, *The Spanish Elizabethans: The English Exiles at the Court of Philip II* (New York: Fordham University Press, 1963), 18, 21 and Arthur Gould Lee's *The Son of Leicester: The Story of Sir Robert Dudley* (London: Victor Gollancz, 1964), 143 ff.

23. See Hall's *Union*, Holinshed's *Chronicles* and *A Mirror for Magistrates* in *Narrative and Dramatic Sources*, vol. 3, 387, 393 and 418, ll. 151–4.

24. Compare with the more serious tone of Augustus' banishment of Ovid in *Poetaster*: 'we exile thy feet / From all approach to our imperial court / On pain of death', 4.6.52–6.

25. The shame associated with 'vagabond', suggesting moral dissoluteness and antipathy towards society, as well as deracination and namelessness, is also resonant in *Coriolanus*, 3.3.93.

26. This reference to bitter bread as one of exile's sufferings may recall Dante's *Paradiso*: 'And you will know how salty is the taste / of others' bread, how hard the road that takes / you down and up the stairs of others' homes', c. 17, 58–60.

27. In 'Shakespeare's *Richard II* and the Essex Conspiracy', Evelyn May Albright argued that Shakespeare's *Richard II* was based on Hayward's history, suggesting that although the latter was not published until two years after the play it might have been available in manuscript, *PMLA*, 42.2 (1927), 686–720. For a thorough refutation of this argument see Ray Heffner, 'Shakespeare, Hayward, and Essex', *PMLA*, 45.2 (1930), 754–80.

28. There remains some doubt as to whether this was Shakespeare's *Richard II* or a play deriving from Hayward's *First Part*, as argued by Heffner. I follow Andrew Gurr (ed.), *King Richard II* (Cambridge: Cambridge University Press, 1984) and Leeds Barroll 'A New History for Shakespeare and His Time', *Sh. Q.*, 39 (1988), 441–64, among others, in assuming that this was Shakespeare's play.

29. Hayward described him as 'Magnus [...] & presenti iudicio, & futuri temporis expectione' ('Great [...] both in present judgement and in expectation of future time'), *The First Part*, 61.
30. On comparisons between Elizabeth and Richard, Essex and Bolingbroke see Gurr, *King Richard II*, 6–9, as well as Albright and Heffner, op. cit. For a more detailed account of the publication and suppression of Hayward's work see Manning's introduction, *The First Part*, 17–34.
31. Quoted in 'Shakespeare, Hayward, and Essex', 778–9.
32. In this letter, Essex suggests that the command in Ireland has been orchestrated by his enemies to get him away from the court. It is a fate he intends to avoid. Albright is perhaps the first critic to make the connection between Bolingbroke and Essex as exiles. Unfortunately, she insists on this letter as a possible source for *Richard II* either by moving the date of the play or suggesting that the letter's sentiments were already known: 'it may well have been that the Devereux family held strong opinions on Irish service before that time, in view of the experiences of Essex's father,' 'Shakespeare's *Richard II* and the Essex Conspiracy', 697. I will argue, on the contrary, that an association between Ireland and exile may have been conventional.
33. Robert Lacey, *Robert, Earl of Essex* (London: Weidenfeld & Nicolson, 1971), 218, 234.
34. See *Lives and Letters of the Devereux, Earls of Essex, in the Reigns of Elizabeth, James I, and Charles I 1540–1646* by W. B. Devereux (London: John Murray, 1853), 2 vols, vol. 2, 68.
35. See Richard C. McCoy, *The Rites of Knighthood: The Literature and Politics of Elizabethan Chivalry* (Berkeley and London: University of California Press, 1989), 99.
36. S. Schoenbaum, '*Richard II* and the Realities of Power' *Sh. S.*, 28 (1975), 1–13, 7. See also 'A New History for Shakespeare and His Time', 453–4.
37. Although Shakespeare's play was not printed between 1598 and 1608, and was described by a player as old and out of use in 1601, it may still have been popular. Gurr refers to the inclusion of six passages from it in the anthology, *England's Parnassus* (1600). Perhaps some of those who had seen or read the play the first time round considered it with new eyes after the Hayward/Essex farrago. The influence of Essex's fall has been detected in a number of early Jacobean tragedies, most notably Daniel's *Philotas* (1604).
38. Mowbray's son tries to suggest otherwise in *Henry IV* Part Two, 4.1.123–7.
39. This image of the stringless instrument recurs in the description of Gaunt's death: 'His tongue is now a stringless instrument. / Words, life and all, old Lancaster hath spent', 2.1.150–1.
40. See *A New Variorum Edition of Shakespeare: The Life and Death of Richard II*, ed. Matthew W. Black (Philadelphia and London: J. B. Lippincott, 1955), 69, fn. 164.
41. See *A History of the English Language* by Albert C. Baugh (London: Routledge, 1951) 3rd edn, ch. 6.
42. Froissart describes how he enjoyed easy conversation in French with Richard and at least two of his nobles, Lord Thomas Percy and Sir William Lisle. He also describes one Henry Castyde who can speak Irish as well as he speaks English and French, *The Chronicle of Froissart*, vol. 6, caps CXCVI, 131–2 and CXCVII–VIII, 147–9.
43. In the dedication to *A Worlde of Wordes*, Florio praises the 'copie and varietie of our sweete-mother-toong, which under this most Excellent well-speaking Princesse or Ladie of the worlde in all languages is growne as farre beyond that of former times, as her most flourishing raigne for all happines is beyond the

raigne of former Princes', sig. 85r. I am grateful to Jason Lawrence for drawing this to my attention.

44. See *The Triumph of the English Language: A Survey of Opinions Concerning the Vernacular from the Introduction of Printing to the Restoration* by Richard Foster Jones (London: Oxford University Press, 1953), ch. 1, and Janette Dillon, *Language and State in Medieval and Renaissance England* (Cambridge: Cambridge University Press, 1998), 141–144.

45. *An Apology for Actors* (London, 1612), bk 3, f3.

46. *A table alphabeticall, contayning and teaching the true writing, and understanding of hard usuall English words* ... (London, 1604), 'To the Reader'.

47. See Ernest Gellner, *Nations and Nationalism* (Oxford: Blackwell, 1983; repr. 1997) and Eric Hobsbawm, *Nations and Nationalism Since 1780* (Cambridge: Cambridge University Press, 1990).

48. *The Construction of Nationhood: Ethnicity, Religion and Nationalism* (Cambridge: Cambridge University Press, 1997), 12.

49. Ibid., 58. Claire McEachern places the same emphasis on the vernacular Bible as a 'cause' of the English nation in *The Poetics of English Nationhood, 1590–1612* (Cambridge: Cambridge University Press, 1996), 32.

50. On the definition of Englishness in opposition to Ireland and the Irish tongue, see Michael Neill's highly informative article, 'Broken English and Broken Irish: Nation, Language, and the Optic of Power in Shakespeare's Histories', *Sh. Q.*, 45 (1994), 1–32, 14.

51. On the absent presence of Ireland see Andrew Hadfield, '"Hitherto she ne'er could fancy him": Shakespeare's "British" Plays and the Exclusion of Ireland' in *Shakespeare and Ireland: History, Politics, Culture*, eds Mark Thornton Burnett and Ramona Wray (Basingstoke: Macmillan – now Palgrave Macmillan, 1997), 47–63.

52. Nicholas Potter argues that Mowbray laments the loss of an England defined by common speech, and by a community that includes oyster-wenches and draymen. Although this might explain why Shakespeare's Mowbray only speaks English, it does not account for his courtly assumptions about language nor his horror at being thrust into the 'common air', 1.3.150–1. See '"Like to a tenement or pelting farm": *Richard II* and the Idea of the Nation', in *Shakespeare in the New Europe*, eds Michael Hattaway, Boika Sokolova and Derek Roper (Sheffield: Sheffield Academic Press, 1994), 130–47, 136, 139, 144.

53. *The Posies* (1575), ed. John W. Cunliffe (Cambridge: Cambridge University Press, 1907), 2.1, p. 266.

54. *The Mirror for Magistrates*, ed. Lily B. Campbell (Cambridge: Cambridge University Press, 1938), 107, ll. 170–1.

55. Shakespeare could have read at least the first three books of the *Tristia* in the translation of Thomas Churchyard (London, 1572), STC 18977a and b and 18978. Further editions by the same translator appeared in 1578 and 1580. It has been argued that he must have read at least the *Metamorphoses* in the Latin original also, *Shakespeare and Ovid* (Oxford: Oxford University Press, 1993), 7–9.

56. Ibid., 167. The purgatorial descriptions of Tomis in the *Tristia* are perhaps echoed in *Richard II*'s 'To dwell in solemn shades of endless night' (1.3.171). The 'six frozen winters' (204), 'frosty Caucasus' (258) and 'December snow' (261) are conditions frequently lamented by Ovid.

57. *Tristia and Ex Ponto*, trans. Arthur Leslie Wheeler (London: Heinemann, 1924), 239, 249. In *A Mirror for Magistrates*, Mowbray is despised as a traitor when the

Germans somehow discover that he made a 'false complaynt agaynst my trusty frende', 108, l. 181.
58. *Narrative and Dramatic Sources*, vol. 3, 387, 394 and 418, l. 203.
59. Joseph Porter traces a connection between Mowbray's monolingualism and Richard's linguistic limitations in *The Drama of Speech Acts: Shakespeare's Lancastrian Tetralogy* (Berkeley and London: University of California Press, 1979), 43–6. Although I disagree with his reading of Mowbray's lament, particularly his assumption that Mowbray fears having to learn French, the relationship between Mowbray's and Richard's speechlessness is central to my argument in this chapter.
60. Jerome Cardan asks: 'And where were the bookes of wise men made more often then in banishmente? *Ovidius Naso* being in exile wrot his bookes *De tristibus, De ponto, in Ibin, Triumphus Caesaris* and *De piscibus*. So as it seemeth that in eight yeares exile, he performed more then in those fifty and foure, which before hee had lived in *Rome*', *Cardanus Comforte*, trans. the Earl of Essex (London, 1576) (Amsterdam: De Capo Press, 1969), 85.
61. *Tristia*, 3, 5, 7. Compare this with Essex's letter dated 9 September 1600, 'Haste paper to that happy presence, whence only unhappy I am banished', *Lives and Letters*, vol. 2, 120.
62. *Tristia*, 223.
63. *The Works of Edmund Spenser: A Variorum Edition*, eds Edwin Greenlaw et al. (Baltimore, MD: Johns Hopkins University Press, 1943), 9 vols, vol. 1, 153.
64. *Shakespeare, Spenser, and the Crisis in Ireland* (Cambridge: Cambridge University Press, 1997), 13–39, 39. For other considerations of Spenserian exile see Andrew Hadfield, *Literature, Politics, and National Identity* (Cambridge: Cambridge University Press, 1994), ch. 6: '"Who knows not Colin Clout?" The Permanent Exile of Edmund Spenser', and Richard McCabe, 'Edmund Spenser, Poet of Exile', *Proceedings of the British Academy*, 80 (1993), 73–103.
65. This reference to the Antipodes is also significant because it was commonly described as the social and moral antithesis to England, an allusion which became the basis of Richard Brome's play *The Antipodes* (*c*.1638) but which also occurs in Shakespeare, for example in *3 Henry VI* where York insists that Margaret is 'as opposite to every good, / As the antipodes are unto us', 1.4.134–6.
66. See Hadfield, 'Shakespeare's "British" Plays', 60–1, and Neill, 'Broken English', 9–10.
67. The reversal of fortune also works the other way. In Greene's *Alphonsus, King of Aragon* (1587), Carinus and his son, Alphonsus, were both banished from their country and from their royal inheritance. When Alphonsus successfully wins through battle what he should have inherited and more, Carinus apostrophizes, 'Oh friendly *Fortune*, now thou shewest thy power, / In raising up my sonne from banisht state, / Unto the top of thy most mightie wheele' (1913–15), *The Comicall Historie of Alphonsus, King of Aragon* (London: Oxford University Press, 1926).
68. Moody E. Prior considers the influence of medieval tragedy upon *A Mirror for Magistrates* and *Richard II* in *The Drama of Power: Studies in Shakespeare's History Plays* (Evanston, IL: Northwestern University Press, 1973), 156–82, 164–5.
69. *A Shorte Treatise of Politicke Power and of the True Obedience which Subjects owe to Kings and other Civill Governours* (London, 1556), STC 20179, 47. See also Holinshed's *Chronicles, Narrative and Dramatic Sources*, vol. 3, 397.
70. '*Richard II* and *Edward II*: The Structure of Deposition', *Sh. Y.*, 1 (1990), 1–13, 2–3.
71. Ibid., 5.

72. This is also argued by S. K. Heninger, 'The Sun-King Analogy in *Richard II*', *Sh. Q.*, 11 (1960), 319–27.
73. *A Discoverie of the True Causes* (London, 1612), 182.
74. *A View of the Present State of Ireland*, ed. W. L. Renwick (Oxford: Clarendon Press, 1970), 56. See also *Shakespeare, Spenser and the Crisis in Ireland*, 27.
75. *The First Part*, 124–5.
76. The weight that Richard attaches to the repeal of Bolingbroke's banishment reinforces the connection we considered earlier between exile and deposition. The idea of undoing exile clearly anticipates Richard's divesting himself of kingship. In his note to an earlier reference to Bolingbroke's repeal at 3.3.40, Gurr suggests that 'from this point it is Richard who moves into banishment and nameless exile'. I find this an odd moment to make the point (there are clearer examples) but obviously I applaud the sentiment.
77. See Dorothy C. Hockey, 'A World of Rhetoric in *Richard II*', *Sh. Q.*, 15 (1964), 179–91, 183–4.
78. See, for example, James L. Calderwood, '*Richard II*: Metadrama and the Fall of Speech', in *Shakespeare's History Plays: Richard II to Henry V*, ed. Graham Holderness (Basingstoke: Macmillan – now Palgrave Macmillan, 1992), 121–35 and Anne Barton, 'Shakespeare and the Limits of Language', *Sh. S.*, 24 (1971), 19–30, 22.
79. Ronald R. Macdonald, 'Uneasy Lies: Language and History in Shakespeare's Lancastrian Tetralogy', *Sh. Q.*, 35 (1984), 22–39, 23–4.
80. Men who are more successful in imagining a life beyond kingship include Shakespeare's Henry VI and Ford's Perkin Warbeck. The former insists that he carries the crown within him: 'My crown is called content – / A crown it is that seldom kings enjoy', 3.1.64–5, and gives himself up to Christian and Stoic consolation. Perkin finally reconciles himself to his loss by redefining kingship as the possession of Katherine's heart: 'Even when I fell, I stood enthroned a monarch / Of one chaste wife's troth pure and uncorrupted', *The Chronicle Historie of Perkin Warbeck* (*c.*1633), ed. Peter Ure (London: Methuen, 1968), 5.3.126–7.
81. 'The Lamentable Tale of *Richard II*', 22.
82. This soliloquy strongly suggests the influence of Marlowe's *Edward II* (*c.* 1592) on Shakespeare's play. In Marlowe's work the soon-to-be-deposed King reflects on his 'strange despairing thoughts, / Which thoughts are martyred with endless torments; / And in this torment, comfort find I none', *Edward the Second*, eds Martin Wiggins and Robert Lindsey (London: A. & C. Black, 1997), 20.79–81.
83. *The Metaphysical Poets* (Oxford: Oxford University Press, 1961), xxv–xxvi.
84. '*Richard II*: Metadrama and the Fall of Speech', 124.

Chapter 3   Historical-Pastoral Exile in *Henry IV* Parts One and Two

1. All quotations are taken from the *Oxford Complete Works* so that in Part One the name Oldcastle is used. Outside quotations I have referred to the knight as Falstaff for the sake of simplicity.
2. Naomi Conn Liebler similarly attests to the difficulty of distinguishing the two kings in *Shakespeare's Festive Tragedy: The Ritual Foundations of Genre* (London and New York: Routledge, 1995), 85.
3. See also Catherine M. Shaw's argument that Henry's guilt is displaced onto Hotspur and Falstaff through the play's 'subliminal substructure', thus effecting 'the necessary purgation, national and dramatic, before Henry V's reign of

unexampled triumph can proceed' in 'The Tragic Substructure of the *Henry IV* plays', *Sh. S.*, 38 (1985), 61–7, 62.

4. Alice-Lyle Scoufos discusses these points in detail in *Shakespeare's Typological Satire: A Study of the Falstaff–Oldcastle Problem* (Athens, Ohio: Ohio University Press, 1979), 44–69.

5. See, for example, *Acts and Monuments*, vol. 3, 323, 348.

6. Quoted from *The Oldcastle Controversy: Sir John Oldcastle Part 1 and The Famous Victories of Henry V*, eds Peter Corbin and Douglas Sedge (Manchester and New York: Manchester University Press, 1991), 223–53. Note the Petrarchan oxymoron of 'living death' in relation to banishment here, as discussed in Chapter 1.

7. The epistle and 'The Legend and Defence of the Noble Knight and Martyr, Sir John Oldcastel' are reprinted in *On the Character of Sir John Falstaff* by J. O. Halliwell (1841) (New York: AMS Press, 1966), 19.

8. Opinion is still divided as to the proper spelling of this name in *1 Henry VI* considering that Shakespeare's chronicle sources refer to the knight as 'Fastolf', 'Fastolfe' or 'Fastolffe'. George Walton Williams argues that the name was revised to capitalize on the success of the *Henry IV* plays, 'Fastolf or Falstaff', *ELR* 5 (1975), 308–12. For a defence of the Folio spelling, see *William Shakespeare: A Textual Companion*, eds Stanley Wells and Gary Taylor with John Jowett and William Montgomery (Oxford: Clarendon Press, 1987), 219.

9. See the discussion of this point by Rudolf Fiehler, 'How Oldcastle Became Falstaff', *MLQ*, 16 (March 1955), 16–28, and Robert F. Willson, 'Falstaff in *Henry IV*: What's in a Name?', *Sh. Q.*, 27 (1976), 199–200.

10. Further examples of this preoccupation include Part One, 2.2.16–20 and Part Two, 2.4.43–5 and 82–93..

11. Bernard Spivack defines this subgenre as the battle of vice and virtue for the soul of a man, characterized by its method of personification, and its intention to morally instruct. See *Shakespeare and the Allegory of Evil: The History of a Metaphor in Relation to his Major Villains* (London: Oxford University Press, 1958), 60–95.

12. St Paul's warning to the Ephesians, *Tyndale's New Testament* (1534), ed. David Daniell (New Haven, CT and London: Yale University Press, 1989), ch. 5, 286. References to this text appeared in *Lusty Juventus* (*c.* 1550) as well as in Shakespeare's *Henry IV* plays. See 'Casting off the Old Man: History and St. Paul in *Henry IV*' by D. J. Palmer, *Crit. Q.*, 12 (1970), 267–83.

13. *Lusty Juventus* in *Four Tudor Interludes*, ed. J. A. B. Somerset (London: Athlone Press, 1974), 97–127, 99.

14. *The Longer Thou Livest and Enough is as Good as a Feast* by W. Wager, ed. R. Mark Benbow (London: Edward Arnold, 1963).

15. Other banished vices include Gluttony and Riot in the remaining fragment of *Good Order* (1515), Orion and Backwinter in Thomas Nashe's *Summer's Last Will and Testament* (1592) and Flattery in *The Three Estates* (1540; rev. 1552).

16. Spivack suggests that Falstaff's banishment reinforces his identification with the Vice: 'For the banishment of Falstaff and his imprisonment in the Fleet, we have to reckon with the fact that exile, imprisonment, or hanging is the standard disposition of the vices (and the Vice) in moralities from about 1530 onward,' *Shakespeare and the Allegory of Evil*, 462, n. 69.

17. On the question of the plays' morality structure, see Alan C. Dessen, 'The Intemperate Knight and the Politic Prince: Late Morality Structure in *1 Henry IV*', *Sh. St.*, 7 (1974), 147–71 and J. A. B. Somerset, 'Falstaff, the Prince, and the Pattern of *2 Henry IV*', *Sh. S.*, 30 (1977), 35–45.

18. *King Johan*, ed. by Barry B. Adams (San Marino: Huntington Library, 1969), ll. 105–14. See also Sedition's reference to the exile of true faith, ll. 1,686–9.
19. Some lines later Civil Order urges Nobility and the Clergy: 'Of the Christen faythe playe now the true defendar, / Exyle thys monster and ravenouse devourar', ll. 2,427–8.
20. Shakespeare seems not to have used the metaphor of banishment in any clear Reformation context. For example, it occurs only once in *King John*, but without specific allusion to the Pope, and not at all in *Henry VIII*.
21. *Acts and Monuments*, vol. 5, 21. For the terms of Pope Pius V's excommunication of Elizabeth see *The Reformation in England* by Philip Hughes (London: Hollis & Carter, 1952), 3 vols, vol. 3, 418–20.
22. *The Civile Wars Between the Two Houses of Lancaster and Yorke* (1601) in *The Complete Works in Verse and Prose of Samuel Daniel*, ed. A. B. Grosart (London: Hazel, Watson & Viney, 1885), 4 vols, vol. 2, bk 6, v. 42, 2–4.
23. Jeffrey Knapp describes three central oppositional readings to the perceived weakening of England under Elizabeth: her accession has brought an end to Marian rule; the kingdom remains at peace while Europe is ravaged by war; Elizabeth's virginity defends the borders of the realm from foreign usurpation. *An Empire Nowhere: England, America, and Literature from Utopia to The Tempest* (Berkeley and Oxford: University of California Press, 1992), 4–5.
24. Sir John Davies salutes his queen: 'Exil'd Astraea is come againe', in *Hymnes of Astraea* (1599), *The Poems of Sir John Davies*, ed. Robert Krueger (Oxford: Clarendon Press, 1975), 69–86, Hymne XXIII, 84, 1. See also Frances A. Yates, *Astraea: The Imperial Theme in the Sixteenth Century* (London and Boston: Routledge & Kegan Paul, 1975), 29–87.
25. See 27 Eliz c. 2 (1585).
26. Holinshed describes how the King 'banished them all from his presence (but not unrewarded, or else unpreferred) inhibiting them upon a great paine, not once to approch, lodge, or sojourne within ten miles of his court or presence'. Hall concurs though he takes his measurement from Henry's 'courte or mansion', *Narrative and Dramatic Sources*, vol. 4, 280, 286. *The Famous Victories* is the nearest approximation to Shakespeare's terms where the King warns his followers 'not upon pain of death to approach my presence by ten mile's space', 9.46–7.
27. See *The First Part of King Henry IV*, ed. A. R. Humphreys (London and New York: Routledge, 1960; repr. 1994), 18, fn. 88.
28. *Shakespeare's Typological Satire*, 48.
29. Michael Manheim draws together the monarchs of *Woodstock*, *Edward II* and *Richard II* under the heading of 'Wanton Kings' who fall prey to courtly favourites, *The Weak King Dilemma in the Shakespearean History Play* (New York: Syracuse University Press, 1973), 15–75.
30. Quotations are taken from *The Conspiracy and Tragedy of Byron*, ed. John Margeson (Manchester: Manchester University Press, 1988) and *The Scottish History of James the Fourth*, ed. Norman Sanders (London: Methuen, 1970).
31. *The Homoerotics of Early Modern Drama*, 100–33.
32. Bagot declares his intention to travel to Ireland to join Edward in 2.2, is presumed to be at Bristol Castle in 2.3 and finally re-emerges without explanation in 4.1.
33. On the ritual sacrifice of Falstaff as a king-substitute see C. L. Barber, *Shakespeare's Festive Comedy*, 206–7, and J. I. M. Stewart, *Character and Motive in Shakespeare: Some Recent Appraisals Examined* (London: Longmans, Green & Co.,

1949), 138–9. Franklin B. Newman suggests that the banishment purges Hal and Elizabethan and modern audiences of their 'inclination toward self-indulgence and surfeit' in 'The Rejection of Falstaff and the Rigorous Charity of the King', *Sh. St.*, 2 (1966), 153–61, 157, while John Dover Wilson argues that 'what is at stake in this morality play is the salvation of England itself', *The Fortunes of Falstaff* (Cambridge: Cambridge University Press, 1943), 80. On Carnival as a structuring device, see Michael D. Bristol, *Carnival and Theater: Plebeian Culture and the Structure of Authority in Renaissance England* (London and New York: Methuen, 1985). Richard Abrams' study 'Rumor's Reign in *2 Henry IV*: The Scope of a Personification', *ELR*, 16 (1986), 467–95, and David M. Bergeron's 'Shakespeare Makes History: *2 Henry IV*', *SEL*, 31 (1991), 231–45, consider the implications of the banishment of Rumour signifying both rebelliousness and false history.

34. Falstaff's expectations of gratitude and his threats against the prince reflect the attitudes of the 'king-makers' who rebel in Part One. Further parallels are discussed by Anita Helmbold in 'King of the Revels or King of the Rebels?: Sir John Falstaff Revisited', *Upstart Crow*, 16 (1996), 70–91. It is sometimes argued that Falstaff's banishment is necessary to protect the King from his potential rebellion. This may be to read the play too much in the light of Oldcastle's treason but persuasive cases are put forward by Gary Taylor, 'The Fortunes of Oldcastle', *Sh. S.*, 38 (1985), 85–100, 95–6, and Helmbold, 88.

35. This separation Henry IV duly performs, without resorting to banishment, by sending Falstaff off to fight without Hal in Part Two, 1.2.203–4.

36. See Dover Wilson, *The Fortunes of Falstaff*, 75.

37. *A Comparative Discourse* (London, 1606), STC 11188, 32–3.

38. On the spectator's power, see David Scott Kastan, '"Proud Majesty Made a Subject": Shakespeare and the Spectacle of Rule', *Sh. Q.*, 37 (1986), 459–75, 466.

39. One context in which we might consider Falstaff's banishment is that of the player, remembering that it is in the context of play-acting that banishment is first mentioned and that this fate was frequently called for by contemporary anti-theatricalists. This point is discussed more fully in the Introduction but it may be worth recalling here the legislation of 1597 which called for the banishment of players lacking the patronage and protection of a nobleman, as later dramatized by Marston in *Histriomastix*.

40. *Francis Bacon*, ed. Brian Vickers (Oxford: Oxford University Press, 1996), 304–13, 307.

41. *The Life of Sir Walter Ralegh Based on Contemporary Documents [...] Together with his Letters*, ed. Edward Edwards (London: Macmillan, 1868), 2 vols, vol. 2, 51.

42. Jonas A. Barish, 'The Turning Away of Prince Hal', *Sh. St.*, 1 (1965), 9–17, 15.

43. The next figure to offer sustained commentary on the King is the Chorus of *Henry V* who acts as a kind of inverted double for Falstaff. Instead of the rebellious but devoted companion we have a wholly safe and impersonal eulogist who testifies to the King's affectionate relationship with his men but cannot have experienced it himself.

44. Quotations here are from the film; line references refer to the text from which they were adapted.

45. The film interpolates the plea: 'Do not, when thou art king, hang a thief' and Hal's response 'No, thou shalt' (Part One, 1.2.60–2) to the same effect. In the play, Falstaff speaks this line about hanging the thief and is followed by the Prince's assurance that he will become the hangman rather than the hanged. In

Branagh's film, Bardolph speaks this line in flashback and the film then cuts to the scene of his execution.

46. Hall and Holinshed, *Narrative and Dramatic Sources*, vol. 4, 280 and 286.

47. The influence of the morality tradition upon this double reformation is explored by H. Edward Cain in 'Further Light on the Relation of *1 Henry IV* and *2 Henry IV*', *Sh. Q.*, 3 (1952), 21–38, and Edgar T. Schell in 'Prince Hal's Second "Reformation"', *Sh. Q.*, 21 (1970), 11–16.

48. Satyrane grows up 'Emongst wild beasts and woods, from lawes of men exilde', I.VI.23.9. Similarly, when Justice decides to educate the child, Artegall: 'So thence him farre she brought / Into a cave from companie exilde', V.I.6.6–7, *The Faerie Queene*, eds Thomas P. Roche and C. Patrick O'Donnell (Harmondsworth: Penguin, 1987).

49. *Exile and Change in Renaissance Literature*, 95.

50. Ibid., 13. We find a variation of this argument at the core of Richard Helgerson's *Forms of Nationhood*: 'Self-estrangement was already the fundamental condition of national self-representation in Elizabeth's England', 16–17. Helgerson describes England as poised between two points of cultural origin: the classical and the medieval. To constitute itself as a nation required a form of self-rejection – condemning Englishness as barbarous and primitive in the Gothic vein – so as to reach for the nation's classical origins, origins from which it remained an exile but which might yet offer a pattern for self-reinvention.

51. *What is Pastoral?* (Chicago and London: University of Chicago Press, 1996), 81.

52. See also Calidore's speech on the life of the shepherd and its freedom from 'all the tempests of these worldly seas' in *The Faerie Queene*, VI.IX.19.1–5.

53. William Empson, *Some Versions of Pastoral* (New York: New Directions, 1935; repr. 1974), 27, 22, 43–6, 103–9.

54. *Shakespeare's Pastoral Comedy* (Chapel Hill: University of North Carolina Press, 1972), 179, 191–2.

55. Joseph Wittlin, 'Sorrow and Grandeur of Exile', *Polish Review* (Spring–Summer, 1957), 99–111, 105.

56. Louis A. Montrose associates the composition and reading of such pastoral fantasies with 'ambitious Elizabethan gentlemen who may be alienated or excluded from the courtly society' and argues that pastoral might even facilitate such ambitions. See 'Of Gentlemen and Shepherds: The Politics of Elizabethan Pastoral Form', *ELH*, 50 (1983), 415–59, 427.

57. Thomas Lodge's *Rosalynde*, repr. in *Narrative and Dramatic Sources of Shakespeare*, vol. 2, 181.

58. *Some Versions of Pastoral*, 11–12.

59. *Idea and Act in Elizabethan Fiction* (Princeton, NJ: Princeton University Press, 1969), 61.

60. Barish also traces the conflict between history and comedy in the plays, though without the pastoral angle I have taken here. He too focuses on the lack of any 'synthesis' between Hal and his companions: 'We would expect the dream/moment of love to have left some precious residue in the prince's spirit', 'The Turning Away of Prince Hal', 10–11.

61. This is particularly surprising given the legend, propagated by the Tudors, that Henry V first learned English in the taverns and brought it to the court on his succession. See Empson on Falstaff in *Essays on Shakespeare*, ed. David B. Pirie (Cambridge: Cambridge University Press, 1986), 29–78, 58–61.

62. For a more sustained discussion of this speech, see the previous chapter, pp. 66–71.

63. *Forms of Nationhood*, 193–246, 214. McEachern explores the shift from fellowship to estrangement in the second tetralogy in *The Poetics of English Nationhood*, 83–137.
64. *Henry V* contains 102 references to 'England', 'English' and variants as opposed to just 31 in *Henry IV* Parts One and Two. See the *Oxford Shakespeare Concordances* for these three plays (Oxford: Clarendon Press, 1971).

Chapter 4   'Hereafter, in a Better World than This': the End of Exile in *As You Like It* and *King Lear*

1. I will be using the Quarto text of the play, as included in the *Oxford Complete Works*. In doing so, I assume that the Folio is a Shakespearean revision of the Quarto text and that the Quarto was performed before these revisions were made. On this question see Stanley Wells, 'The Once and Future *King Lear*', 1–22, 11, and Gary Taylor, '*King Lear*: The Date and Authorship of the Folio Version', 351–468, in *The Division of the Kingdoms*, eds Gary Taylor and Michael Warren (Oxford: Clarendon Press, 1983).
2. From *Acastos: Two Platonic Dialogues* (London: Chatto & Windus, 1986), 61.
3. '*King Lear*, Montaigne and Harsnett', *Aligarh Journal of English Studies*, 8 (1983), 124–66, 125.
4. *Eclogues, Georgics and Aeneid I–VI* trans. H. Rushton Fairclough (London: Heinemann, 1935), 2 vols, vol. 1, 9.
5. Carol Gesner, *Shakespeare and the Greek Romance: A Study of Origins* (Lexington: University Press of Kentucky, 1970), 17. See also Margaret Anne Doody's *The True Story of the Novel* (London: Fontana Press, 1998), 33–61.
6. See *Shakespeare and the Greek Romance*, 16.
7. Leo Salingar, *Shakespeare and the Traditions of Comedy* (Cambridge: Cambridge University Press, 1974), 39.
8. See David Young's argument on the influence of the chivalric romance in *The Heart's Forest: A Study of Shakespeare's Pastoral Plays* (New Haven, CT and London: Yale University Press, 1972), 19.
9. Peter Marinelli discusses the Judaeo-Christian associations of pastoral in *Pastoral* (London: Methuen, 1971), 10.
10. *A Dialogue between Reginald Pole and Thomas Lupset*, ed. Kathleen M. Burton (London: Chatto & Windus, 1948), 27.
11. On Renaissance primitivism see E. W. Tayler, *Nature and Art in Renaissance Literature* (New York and London: Columbia University Press, 1964), Harry Levin, *The Myth of the Golden Age in the Renaissance* (London: Faber & Faber, 1970) and the useful discussion of these ideas in relation to Book VI of *The Faerie Queene* in *Spenser's Courteous Pastoral* by Humphrey Tonkin (Oxford: Clarendon Press, 1972), 192–8, 206–37.
12. *Mucedorus*, ed. Arvin H. Jupin (New York: Garland, 1987).
13. Northrop Frye identifies this pattern as a basic principle of Shakespearean comedy in *A Natural Perspective: The Development of Shakespearean Comedy and Romance* (New York and London: Columbia University Press, 1965), 73–8.
14. See David Underdown's account in *Popular Politics and Culture in England 1603–1660* (Oxford and New York: Oxford University Press, 1985), 34. Underdown notes that the problem in Somerset led one vicar, Richard Eburne, in 1624 to suggest the transportation to Newfoundland of this 'excessive multitude'.

15. Nancy R. Lindheim suggests that this scene 'unfolds within an extraordinarily civilized context' with its possible echoes of Aeneas' speech on entering the temple at Carthage, *Aeneid*, I, 446 ff., thus complicating the play's polarity between country and city, '*King Lear* as Pastoral Tragedy', in *Some Facets of King Lear*, eds Rosalie Colie and F. T. Flahiff (London: Heinemann, 1974), 169–84, 172.

16. G. K. Hunter, 'Shakespeare's Last Tragic Heroes', in *Dramatic Identities and Cultural Tradition: Studies in Shakespeare and his Contemporaries* (Liverpool: Liverpool University Press, 1978), 251–69, 252.

17. *Vagrancy, Homelessness and English Renaissance Literature* (Urbana and Chicago: University of Illinois Press, 2001), 3, 28–9, 228. Woodbridge argues for a more sympathetic reading of these lines, 228.

18. See Jo-Marie Claassen's *Displaced Persons: The Literature of Exile from Cicero to Boethius* (Madison: University of Wisconsin, 1999), 64–7.

19. On the consolation tradition see *Displaced Persons*, 85–102, and Tison's 'Shakespeare's *Consolatio* for Exile'.

20. *Seneca's Minor Dialogues*, trans. A. Stewart (London: George Bell & Sons, 1889), 325, 324.

21. *Paradoxa Stoicorum*, in *De Oratore III*, trans. H. Rackman (London: Heinemann, 1942), 254–303, 267–71.

22. 'Of Exile or Banishment', in *Plutarch's Moralia*, trans. Philemon Holland (1603), ed. E. H. Blakeney (London: J. M. Dent & Sons, 1911), 389–410, 395.

23. Plutarch's argument was paraphrased by Lyly in *Euphues: The Anatomy of Wit*, as discussed in Chapter 2.

24. *Ad Helviam*, 327.

25. Plutarch and Cicero both quote Socrates' declaration to the effect that 'he was neither Athenian nor Grecian, but a citizen of the world' in *De Exilio*, 393, and *Tusculan Disputations*, bk 5, ch. 37, 108 respectively. However, variations on this statement ('I am a citizen of the world', 'The world is my country') were also attributed to Diogenes and Theodorus (see Diogenes Laertius's *Lives of Eminent Philosophers*, vol. 2, bk 6, 63 and vol. 1, bk 2, 99 respectively) and to Seneca (*Ad Lucilium Epistulae Morales*, vol. 1, 28, 5). The repetition of the phrase recurs in sixteenth- and seventeenth-century literature in such different contexts as Bacon's essay 'Of Goodness' and Beaumont's *The Knight of the Burning Pestle* (1607), 5.149–50.

26. I am using the term 'Epicurean' in quotation marks to signify a distinction between the rather ascetic philosophy of Epicurus and Lucretius which warned against love, ambition, etc. and the more modern sense of the word which was also familiar to Renaissance England, hence Jonson's Sir Epicure Mammon.

27. *Cardanus Comforte*, 85–6. Plutarch suggests the same consolations in his *De Exilio*, 403–4.

28. *De Constantia libri duo* trans. Sir John Stradling as *Two Bookes of Constancie* (London, 1594), STC 15695, 7.

29. *Epistola de Peregrinatione italica* trans. Sir John Stradling as *A Direction for Travailers* (London, 1592), STC 15696, A4.

30. Cicero's *De Amicitia* in *De Senectute* trans. W. A. Falconer (London: Heinemann, 1923), 108–211, 159. In *The Taming of the Shrew*, Tranio tries to deflect Lucentio from his ascetic plans: 'Let's be no stoics nor no stocks, I pray, / Or so devote to Aristotle's checks / As Ovid be an outcast quite abjured' (1.1.31–3).

31. *Epistola*, A3.

32. *De Constantia*, 28.

33. *Rosalynde*, in *Narrative and Dramatic Sources of Shakespeare*, vol. 2, 189. See also Meliboe in VI.IX.19–25 of Spenser's *Faerie Queene*. He too refers to the contented humility of shepherds and to their ease of slumber.

34. For example, in *The Rare Triumphes of Love and Fortune* (Anon., 1582), Venus and Fortune try to assert their pre-eminence in a contest to determine the fate of the lovers, a contest which includes the banishment of Hermione by Fortune. In *Rosalynde*, Aliena suggests that the experiences of the banished Saladyne represent the same conflict: 'Your selfe exiled from your wealth, friends & countrey by *Torismond*, (sorrowes enough to suppresse affections) yet amidst the depth of these extreamities, Love will be Lord, and shew his power to bee more predominant than Fortune', *Narrative and Dramatic Sources*, vol. 2, 235.

35. Thus Sephestia testifies in *Menaphon* (1589). See *Menaphon by Robert Greene and A Margarite of America by Thomas Lodge*, ed. G. B. Harrison (Oxford: Basil Blackwell, 1927), 33.

36. Renato Poggioli, *The Oaten Flute: Essays on Pastoral Poetry and the Pastoral Ideal* (Cambridge, MA: Harvard University Press, 1975), 8–9.

37. *Common Conditions* in *Five Anonymous Plays*, ed. John S. Farmer (London: Early English Drama Society, 1908), 187–8.

38. Notably, Rosalynde continues to be ashamed of her father when she meets him in the forest (247–8), in contrast with Ganimede's merriment on meeting the Duke in Arden (3.4.31–4).

39. *Ovid's Metamorphoses: The Arthur Golding Translation*, ed. John Frederick Nims (London: Collier-Macmillan, 1965), bk 1, 127–8.

40. *De Providentia* in *Moral Essays*, vol. 1, 2–47, 33.

41. *Ad Helviam*, 331. On reading Nature, see Seneca's *De Otio*, 191.

42. Geoffrey Miles remarks that the 'external, self-dramatizing strain in Roman Stoicism contrasts oddly with the "inwardness" of Stoic ethics, its theoretical stress on morality as "an affair of the inner life"' in his *Shakespeare and the Constant Romans* (Oxford: Clarendon Press, 1996), 14. Alpers also refers to the difference between pastoral and tragic modes here. The Duke's speech is not 'wrenched from experience' like Gloucester's. It bears witness 'not to the individual's attempt to make sense of his own and others' suffering, but to a common condition acknowledged as obvious', *What is Pastoral?*, 73.

43. *The Maid's Metamorphosis*, ed. John S. Farmer (London: Tudor Reprinted and Parallel Texts, 1908), no page or line numbers given.

44. Similarly, in Lodge's *A Margarite of America* (1595), the courtly lover, Minecius, puts on a 'pastorall habite' to woo Philenia and carves a poem into a tree beginning, 'O desarts be you peopled by my plaints', *Menaphon by Robert Greene and A Margarite of America by Thomas Lodge*, 126. Where Orlando uses poetry to populate the forest, Minecius orders the native inhabitants to flee and leave him alone in his pose of despair.

45. In the section entitled 'Of Desart' in Stephen Batman's *Batman uppon Bartholome* (1582), he describes the 'desert' as 'a place of creeping wormes and venimous beasts, and of wilde beasts, and it is the lodges of banished men and of theeves' (London and Hildesheim: Georg Olms Verlag, 1976), ch. 52, 210–11.

46. Ibid., 308. On this strategy of metaphorical depopulation, see Greenblatt's *Marvellous Possessions: The Wonder of the New World* (Oxford: Clarendon Press, 1991), 52–85, 60.

47. *The Foure Prentises of London*, in *The Dramatic Works of Thomas Heywood*, ed. Richard H. Shepherd (New York: Russell & Russell, 1964), 6 vols, vol. 2, 183.

48. *The Downfall of Robert, Earl of Huntingdon*, ed. John C. Meagher (Oxford: Oxford University Press, 1964).

49. *Crime and Public Order in England in the Later Middle Ages* (London: Routledge, 1973), 76–7. See also Barbara A. Hanawalt, 'Ballads and Bandits: Fourteenth-Century Outlaws and the Robin Hood Poems', in *Robin Hood: An Anthology of Scholarship and Criticism*, ed. Stephen Knight (Woodbridge: D. S. Brewer, 1999), 263–84.

50. On this relationship see *As You Like It: A New Variorum Edition*, ed. Richard Knowles (New York: MLAA, 1977), 483–7.

51. *The Tale of Gamelyn*, attr. Chaucer, ed. Walter W. Skeat (Oxford: Clarendon Press, 1843), 2nd edn. Again, Bellamy notes that real-life outlaws often went on to hold local offices, even being elected to Parliament, following their reprieve, 86–7.

52. We might also compare this passage with Samuel Purchas' critique of those gentlemen travellers who attain experience only with 'the losse or lessening of their estate' in the preface to *Hakluytus Posthumus or Purchas His Pilgrimes, Contayning a History of the World, in Sea Voyages & Lande-Travells, by Englishmen & others* (London, 1625), 5 vols, vol. 1, no page numbers.

53. Maynard Mack, *King Lear in Our Time* (1965; London: Methuen, 1966), 65. Two important studies which address this issue are Colie's *Shakespeare's Living Art*, 302–16 and Lindheim's, '*King Lear* as Pastoral Tragedy'.

54. See Colie's definition of pastoral in *Shakespeare's Living Art*, 310.

55. Banishment in 1.1 needs to be understood politically in terms of James' efforts to reunite the kingdoms of England and Scotland. For examples of Jacobean anti-division rhetoric see 'A Speech, as it was delivered in the upper house of the Parliament to the Lords spirituall and temporall, and to the Knights, Citizens and Burgesses there assembled', 19 March 1603, in *The Political Works of James I*, a reprint of the 1616 edition, ed. Charles McIlwain (New York: Russell & Russell, 1965), 269–80, 271–2; and Edward Forset's *A Comparative Discourse of the Bodies Natural and Politique*, 58. As the first British king to divide his realm, with disastrous results, Brutus was often offered as the antithesis to James' policy of reunification. See Anthony Munday's pageant 'The Triumphs of Reunited Britannia' (1605) in *Jacobean Civic Pageants*, ed. Richard Dutton (Keele: Ryburn, 1995), 119–36, 129. Leah Marcus explores the relationship between Lear's division of the kingdom and James I's struggle for reunification, with particular reference to the Scots who remained outside the protection of English law and alienated within the kingdom, in *Puzzling Shakespeare*, 154.

56. In *A Knack to Know a Knave* (Anon., 1592) (Oxford: Oxford University Press, 1963). Philarcus' father condemns his son's ingratitude with a similar gesture: 'as thou hast dealt unnaturallie with me, / So I resolve to pull my heart from thee', ll. 459–60. Philarcus is eventually banished despite his father's insistence that he be put to death, ll. 491–4, 551–4.

57. Examples of the exile disguising himself as a servant to follow his friend or master may be found in *Timon* (1602) and *The Faire Maide of Bristow* (1604). In the former, Laches adopts the disguise of a soldier, commenting: 'My face I have disfigured, that unknowne / I may againe be plac'd in Timons howse', *Narrative and Dramatic Sources*, vol. 6, 297–339, 2.1–2.

58. Starvation in *The True Chronicle Historie* is partly the result of Leir's crime against Cordella. She is envisaged as a bountiful earth mother whose literal nursing Leir has forgone, turning honey to gall, grapes to sloes and sweet milk sour, 23. 2,054–62. Cordella's forgiveness of her father is signalled by the action of helping him to food and drink, 24.2,179–80.

59. 'The Dispraise of the Country in *As You Like It', Sh. Q.*, 36 (1985), 300–14, 313–14.
60. Heather Dubrow, *Shakespeare and Domestic Loss* (Cambridge: Cambridge University Press, 1999), 80–141, 109. Although Dubrow refers to the legal policy of ejectment, she does not recognize banishment as a contemporary cause for homelessness.
61. The question of *Lear's* Stoicism in general remains a matter for debate. Monsarrat has argued that neither *King Lear* nor any other Shakespearean play offers a 'representative' Stoic as found in the work of Chapman, Marston, Massinger and Ford. He concludes that there is 'little to be said about Stoicism in Shakespeare', *Light from the Porch*, 146. It seems at least perverse to suggest that Shakespeare cannot be understood to have been influenced by the popular revival of neo-Stoicism unless he produces a stereotypical character. Critics who have recognized the Stoicism of *Lear* include Hiram Haydn in *The Counter-Renaissance* (Gloucester, MA: Peter Smith, 1950), 642–51, and Arthur Kinney, 'Some Conjectures on the Composition of *King Lear', Sh. S.*, 33 (1980), 13–26.
62. Mack suggests other parallels in *King Lear in Our Time*, 64–5.
63. Cordella is cast out but wanders alone within the kingdom until discovered by the King of France who has come to Albion in the guise of a pilgrim (scene 7). Perillus is never estranged from Leir but voluntarily follows him into exile.
64. This identification is perhaps made by the 1608 Quarto title-page which juxtaposes the experiences of Lear with the 'unfortunate life of Edgar, sonne and heire to the Earle of Gloster, and his sullen and assumed humor of TOM of Bedlam'.
65. See *Jowitt's Law Dictionary*, vol. 2, 1,297.
66. After the statute of 1329 issued in the reign of Edward III, the outlaw could only be executed by the sheriff. See Maurice Keen's discussion of the outlaw's punishment in *The Outlaws of Medieval Legend* (London and Henley: Routledge & Kegan Paul, 1961), 9.
67. A more likely candidate for outlawry, I would suggest, is Gloucester himself who, after having been specifically denied a trial, is blinded and then pursued for his life. Oswald assumes that he may kill Gloucester and thus reap the reward for his 'proclaimed prize', 20.218.
68. John Breen points out that Edgar cannot have been banished because Gloucester repeatedly describes the measures put in place to capture him. He attributes this 'factual error' not to the Gentleman who makes the report (and also gets Kent's location wrong) but to Shakespeare. Breen seems to me to be labouring under two serious misapprehensions: firstly, that references to proclamation imply declarations of banishment rather than outlawry, and secondly that Shakespeare had a duty to use the term 'banished' in the most accurate 'Renaissance' sense, as Breen defines it. See 'Gloucester's Proclamation', *N & Q*, 239 (1994), 493–4. In fact, even the most famous outlaws were often mistaken for banished men in the drama of the period, if only for lexical variety. In *The Downfall of Robert, Earl of Huntingdon*, Robin Hood is described by Prince John as 'The banish'd, beggar'd, bankrupt Huntington', 2.1, p. 130.
69. It is also significant that, contrary to the pastoral tradition, Edgar's gentility does not shine through his disguise. On the liberties taken with rank in Edgar's case, see Patterson, *Shakespeare and the Popular Voice*, 110.
70. *The Countess of Pembroke's Arcadia*, ed. Maurice Evans (Harmondsworth: Penguin, 1987), bk 2, ch. 10, 278.

71. William C. Carroll, *Fat King, Lean Beggar: Representations of Poverty in the Age of Shakespeare* (Ithaca, NY and London: Cornell University Press, 1996), 180–207, 190.
72. See Peter J. Milward's *The Catholicism of Shakespeare's Plays* (Southampton: Saint Austen Press, 1997), 78–91. A more cautious allegorizing of the play along these lines is offered by Greenblatt in 'Shakespeare and the Exorcists', *Shakespeare and the Question of Theory*, eds Patricia Parker and Geoffrey Hartman (New York: Methuen, 1985), 163–87, 178–9.
73. *The Catholicism of Shakespeare's Plays*, 87.
74. For details of those banished at these times, see Richard Challoner's *Memoirs of Missionary Priests* [...] *that have Suffered Death in England on Religious Accounts* [...] *1577–1684*, rev. John Hungerford Pollen (London: Burns, Oates & Washbourne, 1924), 109, 248, 268, 274, 282, 359. This compilation gives a powerful sense of the extent of the banishment imposed upon Elizabethan and Jacobean Catholics, many of whom experienced it more than once. For a less emotive perspective on the 1585 statute, see Bellamy's *The Tudor Law of Treason*, 74–5.
75. See Introduction, 16.
76. Milward insists that the experiences of Edgar, Cordelia, Lear and Gloucester reflect 'precisely [...] the situation of English Catholics, whether in exile abroad or at home in disguise or in prison', 83–4. Yet there is nothing precise about an argument which fails to distinguish between these different kinds of exile and the various literary as well as contemporary social and political contexts which inform them. If we believe that Shakespeare encouraged his Catholic audience to identify themselves with Edgar, we might ask why he did not use the conjecture of the Gentleman at 21.88 that Edgar was 'banished' and had gone into exile abroad to extend the analogy. Rather than suggesting he was now in Protestant Germany, might not Edgar have been imagined in Catholic France or Italy – familiar destinations for the banished Catholic?
77. It may be that a potential conflation of Catholic fugitive and vagrant was suggested by Shakespeare's reading of Harsnett. In the *Declaration of Egregious Popish Impostures* (1603), he asks whether 'our vagrant devils [...] did take theyr fashion of new names from our wandring Jesuits, who [...] have alwaies three or foure odd conceited names in their budget'. See *Shakespeare, Harsnett and the Devils of Denham* by F. W. Brownlow (London and Toronto: Associated University Presses, 1993), 119, 239.
78. *Fat King, Lean Beggar*, 193–5. See also Woodbridge's discussion of *King Lear* in *Vagrancy, Homelessness and English Renaissance Literature*, 205–37, and Raman Selden, 'King Lear and True Need', *Sh. St.*, 19 (1987), 143–68.
79. On Edgar's guilt and shame with regard to Gloucester see Stanley Cavell, 'The Avoidance of Love: A Reading of *King Lear*', in *Disowning Knowledge in Six Plays of Shakespeare* (Cambridge: Cambridge University Press, 1987), 39–124.
80. The *Oxford Complete Works* dates *Timon of Athens* c.1604 and places it immediately before *The History of King Lear*, a decision endorsed by James C. Bulman in his dating of the comedy, 'The Date and Production of *Timon* Reconsidered', *Sh. S.*, 27 (1974), 111–28.
81. *Sir Philip Sidney*, 238.
82. 'The Thirteenth Discourse: In Athens, About his Banishment', *Dio Chrysostom* trans. J. W. Cohoon (London: William Heinemann, 1950), 5 vols, vol. 2, 91–121, 99.
83. 'Who Are King Lear's Philosophers? An Answer, With Some Help From Erasmus', *English Studies*, 67 (1986), 511–24. The reference to a 'learned Theban' is taken to refer to Crates, Diogenes' disciple, who might easily merge with his more famous teacher in Lear's mind.

84. Ibid., 512, 515–17. See also Jane Donawerth's 'Diogenes the Cynic and Lear's Definition of Man, *King Lear* III iv 101-109', *English Language Notes* 15 (1977), 10–14.
85. John Coates, '"Poor Tom" and the Spiritual Journey in *King Lear*', *Durham University Journal* (December 1986), 7–14, 10.
86. Roger Warren, 'The Folio Omission of the Mock Trial: Motives and Consequences', in *The Division of the Kingdoms*, 45–57.
87. *The Unnatural Scene*, 213.
88. On the Fool's exit in the Folio, see John Kerrigan's 'Revision, Adaptation, and the Fool in *King Lear*', 229. Curiously, King James I's fool, Archie Armstrong, was to be banished from the court of Charles 1 for slander. See the *DNB*, 562, and *Archy's Dream, Sometime Jester to his Maiestie: but Exiled the Court by Canterburies Malice* (1641), in *The Old Book Collector's Miscellany* (London: Reeves & Turner, 1873), vol. 3, no. 16.
89. The Folio cuts this speech entirely, perhaps suggesting Shakespeare's desire to lessen the bathos of Kent's return.
90. When Lear asks 'Am I in France?', Kent responds 'In your own kingdom, sir' (73, 75). Lear's question reflects not only his association of Cordelia with that kingdom but perhaps an echo of *The True Chronicle Historie* where Leir was reconciled with his daughter in that country.
91. Translated by T. I. (London, 1598), 127.
92. Nicholas Grene, *Shakespeare's Tragic Imagination* (Basingstoke: Macmillan – now Palgrave Macmillan, 1992), 162.
93. *Boethius' Consolation of Philosophy* trans. George Colville (1556), ed. Ernest Belfort Bax (London: David Nutt, 1897), bk 1, 24–5.
94. Ibid., bk 4, 89.
95. *The Catholicism of Shakespeare's Plays*, 91.

Chapter 5 *Coriolanus*: the Banishment of Rome

1. *Sejanus His Fall*, ed. Philip J. Ayres (Manchester and New York: Manchester University Press, 1990).
2. The one occasion when the plebeians alone represent Rome is in the anticipation of Coriolanus' invasion. Since the hero's banishment was their work, it is their city that will be destroyed (4.6.103). This positing of the city as somewhere and something else echoes Coriolanus's own alienated perspective.
3. *The Unnatural Scene*, 75–6.
4. Christopher Givan argues that Coriolanus defines himself against the plebeians with such vehemence, not merely to aggrandize himself, but because in them he recognizes what he may become, 'Shakespeare's *Coriolanus*: The Premature Epitaph and the Butterfly', *Sh. St.*, 12 (1979), 143–58. See also Janet Adelman, '"Anger's My Meat": Feeding, Dependency and Aggression in *Coriolanus*' in *Representing Shakespeare: New Psychoanalytic Essays*, eds Murray M. Schwartz and Coppélia Kahn (Baltimore, MD and London: Johns Hopkins University Press, 1980), 129–49, 135.
5. See 1.1.197, 1.6.7, 3.2.8–9. The word 'slave' was a common pejorative term which did not necessarily refer to the literal status of the recipient. Coriolanus applies it to Aufidius as well as to the plebeians. However, the repeated and unemphatic appellation of a messenger in 4.6 as 'slave' and the practice of taking Volscians as prisoners may also suggest the presence of slaves in Coriolanus' Rome.

6. Plutarch describes Coriolanus as too angry and vengeful to speak, *The Lives of the Noble Grecians and Romanes*, trans. Sir Thomas North (London, 1579), 237–59, 248. In Shakespeare's other main source, *The Romane Historie of T. Livy*, trans. Philemon Holland (1600), the protagonist does not appear at his trial but goes into exile 'menacing his own countrie as he went', *Narrative and Dramatic Sources*, vol. 5, 501. In the histories of Coriolanus available to the Jacobeans, Shakespeare's counter-banishment is unique.

7. The bad breath Coriolanus complains of may well be another symptom of the plebeians' starvation.

8. See the Queens' appeal for their unburied husbands, left strewn on the battlefield of Thebes, in *The Two Noble Kinsmen*, 1.1.39–54.

9. The extent of Shakespeare's knowledge of Cicero remains a matter for conjecture. There seems general agreement that he knew *De Officiis* and the *Tusculan Disputations* – the latter includes some references to banishment as cited in the previous chapter. See Baldwin, *William Shakspere's Small Latine & Lesse Greeke*, vol. 2, 581–610.

10. *Paradoxa Stoicorum* in *De Oratore III*, 279–83, 281.

11. See, in particular, the meeting between the Roman and Volscian spies in 4.3. In Livy, when Veturia (Volumnia) goes to plead with Coriolanus at the Volscian camp she asks: 'Let me know [...] before I suffer thee to embrace me, whether I am come to an enemie or to a sonne, whether I be in thy campe as a captive prisoner, or as a naturall mother', *Narrative and Dramatic Sources*, vol. 5, 504.

12. *'Antike Roman': Power Symbology and the Roman Play in Early Modern England, 1585–1635* (Athens and London: University of Georgia Press, 1995), 81.

13. Contemporary consolations, often based on the work of banished Romans, frequently palliate the grief of exile with reference to the city's thanklessness. Erasmus' letter to a fictional Roman exile named Canidius reminds him that Scipio, Brutus, Cato and Cicero were all 'constrained to suffer the loss of the country they had saved at great personal peril'. Rather than resent the efforts 'lavished [...] in vain upon most ungrateful fellow-citizens', these men gloried in the undying fame their deeds had brought them. See *De Conscribendis Epistolis* in *The Collected Works of Erasmus*, vol. 25, trans. and ed. J. K. Sowards (Toronto: University of Toronto Press, 1985), 148–55, 154.

14. *The Consent of Time*, STC 16619, 496–7. In *The Strategems of Jerusalem* (1602), STC 16630, Lloyd argues that Rome should have been grateful that Coriolanus changed his mind about invading the city, 312.

15. 'The Life of Aristides', *Lives*, 352–72, 356–7 and also 'The Life of Cimon', *Lives*, 528–43, 541.

16. See *The Oxford Classical Dictionary*, 762–3, and Tabori, *The Anatomy of Exile*, 45–8.

17. *The Governour* (London: J. M. Dent & Sons, 1907; repr. 1937), bk 1, ch. 2, 7.

18. *The Treasurie of Auncient and Modern Times* by Thomas Milles (London, 1613), STC 17936, bk. 8, ch. 32, 817. In his study of *Timon of Athens*, Robert S. Miola makes a similar point, arguing that according to such contemporary literature 'by a perverse but persistent logic, banishment from the corrupt Athenian city, voluntary or otherwise, was a sure sign of private rectitude', 'Timon in Shakespeare's Athens', *Sh. Q.*, 31 (1980), 21–30, 29. Although Coriolanus' banishment differs from ostracism in various ways, some association may be hinted at when he blames his exile on 'The cruelty and envy of the people', 4.5.75.

19. According to Willard Farnham, Coriolanus' pride renders him 'monstrously deficient as a human being', though this pride is also the source of his virtues,

Shakespeare's Tragic Frontier (Berkeley and Los Angeles: University of California Press, 1950), 263. A similar approach is taken by Carol M. Sicherman in 'Coriolanus: The Failure of Words', *ELH*, 39 (1972), 189–207 in her thesis that Coriolanus is incapable of using language. It is notable how often critics associate *Coriolanus* with failure, either that of the protagonist or of Shakespeare himself.

20. *Shakespeare and the Solitary Man* (London: Macmillan, 1981), 145.
21. '"There is a world elsewhere": Tragedy and History in *Coriolanus*', *SEL*, 16 (1976), 273–85, 275. Velz also suggests that Coriolanus' heroic code is anachronistic in the new city-state in 'Cracking Strong Curbs Asunder'.
22. *Shakespeare and the Solitary Man*, 145.
23. Adelman, '"Anger's My Meat"'.
24. Shannon Miller, 'Topicality and Subversion in William Shakespeare's *Coriolanus*', *SEL*, 32 (1992), 287–322, 292–3.
25. See Zvi Jagendorf, '*Coriolanus*: Body Politic and Private Parts', *Sh. Q.*, 41 (1990), 455–69, and Arthur Riss, 'The Belly Politic: *Coriolanus* and the Revolt of Language', *ELH*, 59 (1992), 53–75.
26. *De Officiis* trans. Walter Miller (London: Heinemann, 1913), 113.
27. I am indebted to Miles' *Shakespeare and the Constant Romans* here.
28. Ibid., 159–60.
29. 'Tragic Superfluity in *Coriolanus*', *ELH* 50 (1983), 485–507, 500.
30. J. L. Simmons identifies pragmatic concerns as the *raison d'être* of the myth in *Shakespeare's Pagan World: The Roman Tragedies* (Brighton: Harvester Press, 1974), 19.
31. 'The Comparison of Anniball with P. Scipio African', *Lives*, 1,173–5, 1,174. In this case, Scipio has not been officially banished but chooses exile for the sake of peace.
32. *The Wounds of Civil War*, ed. Joseph W. Houppert (London: Edward Arnold, 1969).
33. *Catiline*, eds W. F. Bolton and Jane F. Gardner (London: Edward Arnold, 1973).
34. *Coriolanus in Context* (Lewisburg, PA: Bucknell University Press, 1971), 210–11.
35. See, for example, *Timon of Athens* when Timon apostrophizes the city wall from the outside: 'Let me look back upon thee. O thou wall / That girdles in those wolves, dive in the earth, / And fence not Athens!', 4.1.1–3. Wolves have long been associated with what is savage and marginal, as Ronan notes in 'Antike Roman', 136–40.
36. Hans-Jürgen Weckermann draws attention to the similarity between Lucius' and Coriolanus' plots in '*Coriolanus*: The Failure of the Autonomous Individual' in *Shakespeare: Text, Language, Criticism: Essays in Honour of Marvin Spevack*, eds Bernhard Fabian and Kurt Tetzeli von Rosador (Zurich and New York: Olms-Weidmann, 1987), 334–50, 334.
37. Shakespeare would have found the two avengers juxtaposed in Plutarch's *Lives*, 260–2 where Alcibiades' patriotic motives in attacking Athens are contrasted with Coriolanus' 'intent utterly to destroy and spoyle his countrie, and not as though he ment to recover it, or to returne thither againe', 261. It has also been argued that the plays were linked together in their conception. Bullough speculates: 'while drafting *Timon* Shakespeare came to realize the thinness of his subject, and that Coriolanus would give a richer opportunity for a tragedy of wrath and ingratitude. I suspect that Shakespeare abandoned *Timon* to write *Coriolanus*', *Narrative and Dramatic Sources*, vol. 6, 239.

38. The editors of the *Oxford Complete Works* assert that a considerable part of the play, including 3.6, was written by Thomas Middleton in *The Textual Companion*, 501.
39. See also *Catiline* in which Cicero condemns the conspirators for lacking any cause but their own ambition, 3.2.101–2.
40. Various critics have condemned Coriolanus' volte-face as a betrayal of his own principles. For example, Givan considers that 'in attacking Rome he is violating his own constancy and oath-keeping', 'The Premature Epitaph and the Butterfly', 144. Those who have argued for Coriolanus' self-consistency include Eugene M. Waith in *The Herculean Hero in Marlowe, Chapman, Shakespeare and Dryden* (London: Chatto & Windus, 1962), 131, and Charles and Michelle Martindale in *Shakespeare and the Uses of Antiquity: An Introductory Essay* (London and New York: Routledge, 1990), 179–81.
41. Hamlet's journey into exile brings him proof of Claudius' murderous intent such that he is no longer stricken by doubt on his return. However, one might also argue that the Hamlet who returns to Denmark is merely resigned to his fate, as if exile had had a spiritual effect upon him.
42. *The Oxford Classical Dictionary*, 580.
43. Miola suggests that Coriolanus' arrival in Actium 'reenacts' Ulysses' return to Ithaca. Both men are in disguise, both meet insolent resistance to their ingress. Nevertheless, this comparison does not serve to alleviate the shame of Coriolanus' non-recognition by the servants or by Aufidius here. Ulysses has been a master of such deceptions so that disguise is in itself an expression of his identity. It can be no less than a betrayal of Coriolanus' sense of self. See *Shakespeare's Rome*, 193.
44. See also Cominius' testimony that, defying all titles, Coriolanus is now 'a kind of nothing', 5.1.14.
45. *The Civile Conversation of M. Steeven Guazzo*, trans. George Pettie and Bartholomew Young (London, 1586), bk 3, 144, quoted in an abbreviated form in *Suffocating Mothers*, 5.
46. Extended readings of the late plays in terms of maternity and the exile of both mother and child can be found in *Suffocating Mothers*, 193–238, Carol Thomas Neely's *Broken Nuptials in Shakespeare's Plays* (New Haven, CT: Yale University Press, 1985), 171–7, 191–209 and Helen Hackett, '"Gracious be the Issue": Maternity and Narrative in Shakespeare's Late Plays', in *Shakespeare's Late Plays: New Readings*, eds Jennifer Richards and James Knowles (Edinburgh: Edinburgh University Press, 1999), 25–39.
47. Helen Wilcox argues that tragicomedy is an essentially maternal genre in 'Gender and Genre in Shakespeare's Tragicomedies', in *Reclamations of Shakespeare DQR Studies in Literature*, 15th edn A. J. Hoenselaars (Amsterdam: Rodopi, 1994), 129–38.
48. Coppélia Kahn, *Roman Shakespeare: Warriors, Wounds, and Women* (London: Routledge, 1997), 150.
49. See Anna Lydia Motto and John R. Clark, 'The Development of the Classical Tradition of Exile to Seneca', *Mosaic*, 8 (1975), 109–17, 112.

Chapter 6 'A World Elsewhere': Magic, Colonialism and Exile in *The Tempest*

1. This chapter is based on my article, '*The Tempest*'s Forgotten Exile', *Shakespeare Survey*, 54 (2001). I am grateful for CUP's permission to reprint it here.

2. Shakespeare's connections with members of the Virginia Company and his possible acquaintance with William Strachey are discussed by Frank Kermode in *The Tempest* (London: Methuen, 1954; repr. 1961), xxvii–viii.
3. *The Two Noble Kinsmen* seems to have been Shakespeare's last play to feature banishment though it remains uncertain whether Shakespeare himself wrote the relevant scenes. This question is further discussed in n. 6.
4. *Love's Sacrifice*, ed. A. T. Moore (Manchester: Manchester University Press, 2002).
5. The Shakespearean and Websterian influences upon *Love's Sacrifice* are considered by A. T. Moore in his introduction, 29–30, 35–6, 40–1.
6. Act 2, Scene 3 of *The Two Noble Kinsmen* begins with Arcite's cry of 'Banished the kingdom?' It is generally thought that this scene was Fletcher's work, though a counter-argument has been proposed by T. B. Horton in 'Distinguishing Shakespeare from Fletcher through Function Words', *Sh. St.*, 22 (1994), 314–35. Whether this scene was written by Shakespeare or Fletcher, the first twelve lines of Arcite's speech seem to me to recall Romeo's speech on exile at 3.3.29–51. Arcite begins with the possibility of exile as mercy, just as Romeo does in response to the Friar. However, both men reject this association, perceiving banishment from the beloved rather as a punishment for sins and as death. Arcite's imagery of his rival 'feed[ing] / Upon the sweetness' of Emilia's beauty might recall Romeo's image of carrion flies who 'seize' on Juliet's hand or lip. Finally, Arcite's suggestion that his rival will 'stay and see / Her bright eyes break each morning 'gainst thy window' (8–9) echoes the balcony scene.
7. See *Forms of Nationhood* and Mikalachki's *The Legend of Boadicea: Gender and Nation in Early Modern England* (London and New York: Routledge, 1998), 1–17.
8. *Legend of Boadicea*, 4.
9. *Eclogues, Georgics and Aeneid I–VI*, vol. 1, Eclogue 1, l.66. This analogy is also discussed by J. P. Brockbank in 'History and Histrionics in *Cymbeline*', *Sh. S.*, 11 (1958), 42–9, 48. Brockbank suggests that when reading Holinshed's account of Brutus' banishment and founding of Britain, Shakespeare may have noticed Posthumus as the name of one of Brutus' ancestors and taken the banishment plot from here, 43–4.
10. 'Britain among the Fortunate Isles', *Stud. in Phil.*, 53 (1956), 114–40.
11. *Aristotles Politiques, or Discourse of Government. Translated out of Greeke into French, with Exposition taken out of the best Authours ... By Loys Le Roy, called Regius. Translated out of French into English. At London printed by Adam Islip Anno Domo: 1598*, 15. In *Coriolanus*, the protagonist's banishment is partly incurred through his virtues; he is both the beast and God of Aristotle's dictum. See F. N. Lees, 'Coriolanus, Aristotle and Bacon', *RES*, 1 (1950), 114–25.
12. See, for example, John Pitcher's 'A Theatre of the Future: The *Aeneid* and *The Tempest*', *E. in C.*, 34 (1984), 193–211.
13. David Sundelson suggests that Prospero is aware of his inadequacies as Duke and longs to escape his own shame and weakness, 'So Rare a Wonder'd Father: Prospero's *Tempest*', in *Representing Shakespeare*, 33–53, 36.
14. 'Miraculous Harp: A Reading of *The Tempest*', *Sh. St.*, 5 (1969), 253–84, 258.
15. Jonathan Bate, 'The Humanist *Tempest*', in *Shakespeare: La Tempête: Etudes Critiques*, ed. Claude Peltraut (1993), 5–20, 12–3.
16. Prospero's need to prove his civility may also inform the pains he takes with Miranda's education. By making her eligible for marriage with Ferdinand, this education indirectly ensures that Prospero's credentials as an Italian prince and humanist scholar will never again be in doubt.

17. On Prospero's reconstruction of past events on the island, see 'Miraculous Harp', 271, and Peter Hulme, *Colonial Encounters: Europe and the Native Caribbean 1492–1797* (London and New York: Routledge, 1986), 89–136, 121.

18. William Strachey describes the terrible reputation of the Bermudas: 'such tempests, thunders, and other fearefull objects are seene and heard about them, that they be called commonly, *The Devils Ilands* and are feared and avoyded of all sea travellers alive, above any other place in the world', *A True Reportory of the Wracke and Redemption of Sir Thomas Gates, Knight* (1610) in *Hakluytus Posthumus or Purchas His Pilgrimes*, vol. 4, ch. 6, bk 9, p. 1,737. On the identification of the natives with devils see pp. 1,708 and 1,713.

19. 'Prospero's Empty Grasp', *Sh. St.*, 22 (1994), 277–313, 297.

20. This is the 1604 A-Text as reproduced in *Doctor Faustus and Other Plays*, eds David Bevington and Eric Rasmussen (Oxford and New York: Oxford University Press, 1995).

21. Agrippa described this work as deliberately elusive: 'for we have delivered this Art in such a manner, that it may not be hid from the prudent and intelligent, and yet may not admit wicked and incredulous men to the mysteries of these secrets, but leave them destitute and astonished, in the shade of ignorance and desperation', *Three Books of Occult Philosophy* trans. J. F. (1651) (Hastings: Chthonios Books, 1986), 3 vols, vol. 3, ch. lxv, p. 555. Nevertheless, it is suggested in *Dr Faustus* that whoever possesses the magic books will be similarly empowered.

22. In *Dr Faustus*, Mephistopheles repeatedly attests to the agony that is absence from God and from heaven (1.3.78–81, 2.1.121–6). See also the account of Lucifer's banishment from heaven in *The History of the Damnable Life and Deserved Death of Doctor John Faustus* (the English Faust-book) trans. P. F. (1592), reprinted in *Christopher Marlowe: The Plays and Their Sources*, eds Vivien Thomas and William Tydeman (London and New York: Routledge, 1994), 186–238, 199.

23. *Shakespeare's Cross-Cultural Encounters* (Basingstoke: Macmillan – now Palgrave Macmillan, 1999), 160.

24. Ibid., 209–10, n. 2.

25. *Friar Bacon and Friar Bungay*, ed. J. A. Lavin (London: Ernest Benn, 1969).

26. John Dee offers an example of a 'real-life' contemporary magician whose scientific and genealogical studies were dedicated to the realization of what he considered Elizabeth's imperial destiny. His conversations with angels, like Bacon's hopes for the brazen head, were directed to the discovery of some secret that might be to England's benefit. See William H. Sherman, *John Dee: The Politics of Reading and Writing in the English Renaissance* (Amherst: University of Massachusetts Press, 1995), 14–15, 148–200. Although accounts of Dee's banishment are probably exaggerated, Dee himself referred to his exiled state in a letter to the Queen's commissioners pleading for succour in *The Compendious Rehearsal* (1597), reproduced in *John Dee: Essential Readings*, ed. Gerald Suster (Wellingborough: Crucible, 1986), 110.

27. I am indebted for the discovery of the following passages to Andrew Hadfield's study, *Literature, Travel and Colonial Writing in the English Renaissance* (Oxford: Clarendon Press, 1999), ch. 2.

28. Reprinted in *The First Three Bookes on America*, ed. Edward Arber (Edinburgh: Turnbull & Spears, 1885), Book 3, 117.

29. Martyr describes the prince's response to the contention among the Spaniards. He was seen 'commynge sume what wyth an angery countenaunce towarde hym whiche helde the balences, he strooke theym wyth his fyste, and scatered all the golde that was therein, abowte the porche, sharpely rebukynge theym with

woordes in this effecte ...' Perhaps Martyr is remembering the scene of Christ rebuking the moneylenders in the temple in *Matthew* 21:12–13.

30. Paul Brown also makes the connection between colonialism and the discourse of wandering or masterlessness. In '"This thing of darkness I acknowledge mine": *The Tempest* and the Discourse of Colonialism', he examines the identification of the native with the European masterless man and savage, both associated with a 'directionless and indiscriminate desire', *Political Shakespeare: New Essays in Cultural Materialism*, eds Jonathan Dollimore and Alan Sinfield (Manchester: Manchester University Press, 1985), 48–71, 52.

31. There were also plans for English Catholics to establish colonies in the New World. Two Catholic noblemen, Sir George Peckham and Sir Thomas Gerard, proposed such a migration in the early 1580s and found some supporters in Elizabeth's government, though their plans eventually came to nothing due to Spanish opposition. See David Beers Quinn, *England and the Discovery of America 1481–1620* (London: Allen & Unwin, 1974), 364–86.

32. Cecil's letter is reprinted in *The Other Face*, 141.

33. 'A Sermon Preached in London before the right honorable the Lord Lawarre, Lord Governour and Captaine Generall of Virginea', STC 6029.

34. *The Overthrow of the Protestants Pulpit-Babels*, STC 11111, 321.

35. See also Nicholas Canny, 'The Permissive Frontier: the Problem of Social Control in English Settlements in Ireland and Virginia 1550–1650', in *The Westward Enterprise: English Activities in Ireland, the Atlantic and America 1480–1650*, eds K. R. Andrews, N. P. Canny and P. E. H. Hair (Liverpool: Liverpool University Press, 1978), 17–44.

36. See *A True Declaration of the Estate of the Colonie in Virginia with a confutation of such scandalous reports ...* (London, 1610), STC 24833, 34.

37. This observation is also made by Ben Ross Schneider who examines Prospero's anger within a Stoic context in 'Are We Being Historical Yet?: Colonialist Interpretations of Shakespeare's *Tempest*', *Sh. St.*, 23 (1995), 120–45, 123; and by Knapp who examines English colonialism within a context of national trifling in *An Empire Nowhere*, 221.

38. L. T. Fitz notes that Prospero has progressed no further than a 'hunting and gathering economy' in 'The Vocabulary of the Environment in *The Tempest*', *Sh. Q.*, 26 (1975), 42–7, 43. Compare this with Fiedler's assumption, I think an erroneous one, that Prospero sets Caliban to the cutting down of trees because he wants to subdue and order the island rather than because he wants to survive, *The Stranger in Shakespeare*, 235–6.

39. There is a clear disjunction between Prospero's ambitions and, for example, those of the Virginia company as defined in *A True and Sincere Declaration of the purpose and ends of the plantation begun in Virginia* (London, 1610), STC 24832. These aims include the conversion of natives to the Christian faith, the creation of a 'Bulwarke of defence' against the Spanish, and the appropriation of all kinds of goods which England had previously been forced to import at great expense, 3–4.

40. Of the various challenges to this stereotypical colonialist, one of the most persuasive is that of Meredith Anne Skura who examines the multiple and dissonant expressions of 'colonialism' and their possible relationship to *The Tempest* in 'Discourse and the Individual: The Case of Colonialism in *The Tempest*', *Sh. Q.*, 40 (1989), 42–69.

41. Aristotle's beast/God dichotomy was also a feature of much contemporary colonialist literature with the European identifying himself as a god and the native

as beast, but again this opposition would not hold. See Karol Ordahl Kupperman's *Settling with the Indians: The Meeting of English and Indian Cultures in America 1580–1640* (London and Toronto: J. M. Dent, 1980), 119–40.

42. This situation also reflects the Alonso/Antonio usurpation plot. Caliban plays the Antonio role by offering to share the kingdom with Stefano/Alonso in return for his support in overthrowing the present ruler. At the same time, Caliban reminds us of Prospero when he is threatened with exile by the man he has empowered.

43. There is obviously the potential for Caliban's submission here to be seen as a kind of colonialist wish-fulfilment wherein the master is finally kneeled to voluntarily. Yet this need not preclude the possibility that Caliban responds to something higher which Prospero does not embody but might lead him towards. On Caliban's suing for grace in the Christian sense see Bate, 'The Humanist *Tempest*', 18–19.

44. We might compare the ending of *The Tempest* with that of *The Winter's Tale*. Both plays suggest the deferment of narrative with Prospero and Leontes promising that all will be explained off-stage. However, before the close of *The Tempest*, Prospero has acceded to a blatantly false narrative of events invented by Gonzalo which renders Prospero no more than a hostage to Fortune like everyone else. Prospero's identity as magus needs to be forgotten at the end if he is to be reintegrated into the human world. His narrative will be 'probable', not factually accurate, 1.252.

45. '"This Tunis, sir, was Carthage": Contesting Colonialism in *The Tempest*', in *Post-Colonial Shakespeares*, eds Ania Loomba and Martin Orkin (London and New York: Routledge, 1998), 23–42, 30.

Conclusion

1. 'Reflections on Exile' (1984), repr. in *Reflections on Exile and Other Literary and Cultural Essays* (London: Granta Books, 2000), 173–86, 173.

2. Ibid., 174.

3. On the Danvers' analogy, see Chapter 1. The Essex reading of *As You Like It* is discussed by Knowles in *As You Like It: New Variorum Edition*, 370, 537–8 and 630.

4. 'Memento', in *Minima Moralia: Reflections from Damaged Life*, trans. E. F. N. Jephcott (London: Verso, 1951; repr. 1974), 85–7, 87.

Bibliography

Primary sources

Agrippa, Henry Cornelius, *Three Books of Occult Philosophy*, trans. J. F. (1651) (Hastings: Chthonios Books, 1986), 3 vols.

Allen, William, *A True, Sincere, and Modest Defense of English Catholics* (1584), in *The Execution of Justice by William Cecil and The True, Sincere, and Modest Defense of English Catholics by William Allen*, ed. Robert M. Kingdon (Ithaca, NY: Cornell University Press, 1965).

Archy's Dream, Sometime Jester to his Maiestie: but Exiled the Court by Canterburies Malice (1641), in *The Old Book Collector's Miscellany* (London: Reeves & Turner, 1873), vol. 3, no. 16.

Aristotle, *Politica*, trans. Benjamin Jowett, in *The Works of Aristotle*, eds J. A. Smith and W. D. Ross (Oxford: Clarendon Press, 1921).

Aurelius, Marcus, *The Diall of Princes compiled by ... Don Anthony of Guevara*, trans. Thomas North (London, 1557).

Bacon, Sir Francis, *Francis Bacon*, ed. Brian Vickers (Oxford: Oxford University Press, 1996).

Bacon, Sir Francis, *The Letters and the Life of Francis Bacon*, ed. James Spedding (London: Longmans, 1868–90), 7 vols.

Bale, John, *King Johan* (*c.* 1538), ed. Barry B. Adams (San Marino, CA: Huntington Library, 1969).

Bale, John, *The Select Works of John Bale*, ed. Rev. Henry Christmas (Cambridge: Cambridge University Press, 1849).

Batman, Stephen, *Batman uppon Bartholome* (1582) (London and Hildesheim: Georg Olms Verlag, 1976).

Beaumont, Francis, *The Knight of the Burning Pestle* (1607), ed. Sheldon P. Zitner (Manchester: Manchester University Press, 1984).

Boethius, *Boethius' Consolation of Philosophy*, trans. George Colville (1556), ed. Ernest Belfort Bax (London: David Nutt, 1897).

Bullough, Geoffrey, *Narrative and Dramatic Sources of Shakespeare* (London: Routledge & Kegan Paul, 1960), 6 vols.

Cardan, Jerome, *Cardanus Comforte* (1576), trans. the Earl of Essex (Amsterdam: De Capo Press, 1969).

Cawdrey, Robert, *A table alphabeticall, contayning and teaching the true writing, and understanding of hard usuall English words* (London, 1604).

Cecil, William, *The Execution of Justice in England* (1583), in *The Execution of Justice by William Cecil and The True, Sincere and Modest Defense of English Catholics by William Allen*, ed. Robert M. Kingdon (Ithaca, NY: Cornell University Press, 1965).

Challoner, Richard, *Memoirs of Missionary Priests* [...] *that have Suffered Death in England on Religious Accounts* [...] *1577–1684*, rev. John Hungerford Pollen (London: Burns, Oates & Washbourne, 1924).

Chapman, George, *The Conspiracy and Tragedy of Byron* (1608), ed. John Margeson (Manchester: Manchester University Press, 1988).

Cicero, *De Finibus*, trans. H. Rackham (London: Heinemann, 1983).

Cicero, *De Officiis*, trans. Walter Miller (London: Heinemann, 1913).

Cicero, *De Oratore III, De Fato, Paradoxa Stoicorum, De Partitione Oratoria*, trans. H. Rackman (London: Heinemann, 1942).

Cicero, *De Senectute, De Amicitia*, trans. W. A. Falconer (London: Heinemann, 1923).

Cicero, *Tusculan Disputations*, trans. J. E. King (London: Heinemann, 1950).

Coke, Sir Edward, *The First Part of the Institutes of the Laws of England* (1628) (New York and London: Garland, 1979).

Coke, Sir Edward, *The Third Part of the Institutes of the Laws of England* (1644) (New York and London: Garland, 1979).

Common Conditions (1576), in *Five Anonymous Plays*, ed. John S. Farmer (London: Early English Drama Society, 1908).

Constable, Henry, *The Poems of Henry Constable*, ed. Joan Grundy (Liverpool: Liverpool University Press, 1960).

Coryat, Thomas, *Coryat's Crudities* (1611) (Glasgow: James MacLehose & Sons, 1905).

Crashaw, William, 'A Sermon Preached in London before the right honourable the Lord Lawarre, Lord Governour and Captaine Generall of Virginea' (London, 1610), STC 6029.

Daniel, Samuel, *The Complete Works in Verse and Prose of Samuel Daniel*, ed. A. B. Grosart (London: Hazel, Watson & Viney, 1885), 4 vols.

Daniel, Samuel, *Poems and A Defence of Ryme*, ed. Arthur Colby Sprague (Chicago: University of Chicago Press, 1930: repr. 1965).

Dante, *The Portable Dante*, trans. Mark Musa (London: Penguin, 1995).

Davies, Sir John, *A Discoverie of the True Causes why Ireland was never entirely Subdued* (London, 1612).

Davies, Sir John, *The Poems of Sir John Davies*, ed. Robert Krueger (Oxford: Clarendon Press, 1975).

'A Declaration of the Lyfe and Death of John Story' (1571), reprinted in *Somer's Tracts* (London, 1809) (New York: AMS Press, 1965), 10 vols, vol. 1, 477–87.

Dee, John, *John Dee: Essential Readings*, ed. Gerald Suster (Wellingborough: Crucible, 1986).

Devereux, Walter Bourchier, *Lives and Letters of the Devereux, Earls of Essex, in the Reigns of Elizabeth, James I and Charles I 1540–1646* (London: John Murray, 1853), 2 vols.

A Dictionary of Proverbs in England in the Sixteenth and Seventeenth Centuries, ed Morris Palmer Tilley (Michigan: University of Michigan Press, 1950).

Dio Chrysostom, *Dio Chrysostom*, trans. J. W. Cohoon (London: William Heinemann, 1950), 5 vols.

Donne, John, *John Donne: The Complete English Poems*, ed. A. J. Smith (Harmondsworth: Penguin, 1971).

Du Vair, Guillaume, *The Moral Philosophie of the Stoicks*, trans. T. I. (London, 1598).

Dyer, Sir Edward, *The Life and Lyrics of Sir Edward Dyer*, ed. Ralph M. Sargent (Oxford: Clarendon Press, 1935; repr. 1968.

Elizabethan Critical Essays, ed. G. Gregory Smith (London: Oxford University Press, 1904), 2 vols.

Elyot, Sir Thomas, *The Governour* (1531) (London: J. M. Dent & Sons, 1907; repr. 1937).

Erasmus, Desiderius, *The Collected Works of Erasmus*, vol. 25, trans. and ed. J. K. Sowards (Toronto: University of Toronto Press, 1985).

Florio, John, *A Worlde of Wordes, or Most copious and exact Dictionarie in Italian and English* (London, 1598).

Floyd, John, *The Overthrow of the Protestants Pulpit-Babels* (London, 1612), STC 11111.

Ford, John, *The Chronicle History of Perkin Warbeck* (1633), ed. Peter Ure (London: Methuen, 1968).

Ford, John, *Love's Sacrifice* (1632), ed. A. T. Moore (Manchester: Manchester University Press, 2002).

Forset, Edward, *A Comparative Discourse of the Bodies Natural and Politique* (London, 1606), STC 11188.

Four Tudor Interludes, ed. J. A. B. Somerset (London: Athlone Press, 1974).

Foxe, John, *The Acts and Monuments of John Foxe*, 4th edn, rev. Josiah Pratt (London: Religious Tract Society, 1877). 8 vols.

Froissart, Sir John, *The Chronicle of Froissart translated out of French by Sir John Bourchier, Lord Berners* (1523–5), ed. William Paton Ker (London: David Nutt, 1901–3), 6 vols.

Gascoigne, George, *The Posies* (1575), ed. John W. Cunliffe (Cambridge: Cambridge University Press, 1907).

Goodman, Christopher, *How Superior Powers Oght to be Obeyd of their Subjects* (Geneva, 1558), STC 12020.

Gosson, Stephen, *Markets of Bawdrie: The Dramatic Criticism of Stephen Gosson*, ed. Arthur F. Kinney (Salzburg: Universität Salzburg, 1974).

Greene, Robert, *The Comicall Historie of Alphonsus, King of Aragon* (1587) (Oxford: Oxford University Press, 1926).

Greene, Robert, *Friar Bacon and Friar Bungay* (1589), ed. J. A. Lavin (London: Ernest Benn, 1969)

Greene, Robert, *Menaphon* (1589), in *Menaphon by Robert Greene & A Margarite of America by Thomas Lodge*, ed. G. B. Harrison (Oxford: Basil Blackwell, 1927).

Greene, Robert, *The Scottish History of James the Fourth* (1590), ed. Norman Sanders (London: Methuen, 1970).

Guazzo, Stephen, *The Civile Conversation of M. Steeven Guazzo*, trans. George Pettie and Bartholomew Young (London, 1586).

Harington, Sir John, *The Letters and Epigrams of Sir John Harington together with the Prayse of Private Life*, ed. Norman Egbert McClure (Philadelphia: University of Pennsylvania Press, 1930), 2 vols.

Hayward, John, *The First and Second Parts of John Hayward's The Life and Raigne of Henrie IIII* (1599), ed. John J. Manning (London: Royal Historical Society, 1992).

Heywood, Thomas, *An Apology for Actors* (London, 1612).

Heywood, Thomas, *The Dramatic Works of Thomas Heywood*, ed. Richard H. Shepherd (New York: Russell & Russell, 1964), 6 vols.

Heywood, Thomas, *A Woman Killed with Kindness* (1603), ed. Brian Scobie (London: A. & C. Black, 1985; repr. 1998).

Holinshed, Raphael, *The First and Second Volumes of the Chronicles of England, Scotlande, and Irelande* (London, 1587).

James I, *The Political Works of James I*, ed. Charles McIlwain (New York: Russell & Russell, 1965).

Jonson, Ben, *Catiline* (1611), eds F. Bolton and Jane F. Gardner (London: Edward Arnold, 1973).

Jonson, Ben, *Poetaster* (1601), ed. Tom Cain (Manchester: Manchester University Press, 1995).

Jonson, Ben, *Sejanus His Fall* (1603), ed. Philip J. Ayres (Manchester and New York: Manchester University Press, 1990).

Joyce, James, *Ulysses* (London: Penguin, 1992).

A Knack to Know a Knave (1592), ed. G. R. Proudfoot (Oxford: Oxford University Press, 1963).

Kristeva, Julia, *The Kristeva Reader*, ed. Toril Moi (Oxford: Blackwell, 1986).

Laertius, Diogenes, *Lives of Eminent Philosophers*, trans. R. D. Hicks (London: Heinemann, 1925), 2 vols.

Lipsius, Justus, *De Constantia libri duo*, tr. Sir John Stradling (London, 1594), STC 15695.

Lipsius, Justus, *Epistola de Peregrinatione italica*, trans. Sir John Stradling (London, 1592), STC 15696.

Lloyd, Lodowick, *The Consent of Time* (London, 1590), STC 16619.

Lloyd, Lodowick, *The Strategems of Jerusalem* (London, 1602), STC 16630.

Lodge, Thomas, *The Wounds of Civil War* (1588), ed. Joseph W. Houppert (London: Edward Arnold, 1969).

Lusty Juventus (1550), in *Four Tudor Interludes*, ed. J. A. B. Somerset (London: Athlone Press, 1974).

Lyly, John, *The Complete Works of John Lyly*, ed. R. Warwick Bond (Oxford: Clarendon Press, 1902; rep. 1973), 2 vols.

Maid's Metamorphosis, The (1600), ed. John S. Farmer (London: The Tudor Reprinted and Parallel Texts, 1908).

Manwood, John, *A Treatise and Discourse of the Lawes of the Forrest* (London, 1598; rev. 1615).

Marlowe, Christopher, *Doctor Faustus and Other Plays*, eds David Bevington and Eric Rasmussen (Oxford and New York: Oxford University Press, 1995).

Marlowe, Christopher, *Edward the Second* (1592), eds Martin Wiggins and Robert Lindsey (London: A. & C. Black, 1997).

Marston, John, *Antonio and Mellida* (1599), ed. W. Reavley Gair (Manchester: Manchester University Press, 1991).

Marston, John, *Antonio's Revenge* (1600), ed. W. Reavley Gair (Manchester: Manchester University Press, 1978).

Marston, John, *The Malcontent* (1604), ed. G. K. Hunter (Manchester: Manchester University Press, 1975).

Marston, John, *The Plays of John Marston*, ed. H. Harvey Wood (Edinburgh and London: Oliver & Boyd, 1939), 3 vols.

Martyr, Peter, *De Orbe Novo Decades*, trans. Richard Eden (1555), repr. in *The First Three Bookes on America,* ed. Edward Arber (Edinburgh: Turnbull & Spears, 1885).

The Metaphysical Poets, ed. Helen Gardner (Oxford: Oxford University Press, 1961).

Milles, Thomas, *The Treasurie of Auncient and Modern Times* (London, 1613), STC 17936.

The Mirror for Magistrates, ed. Lily B. Campbell (Cambridge: Cambridge University Press, 1938).

Moryson, Fynes, *The Itinerary of Fynes Moryson* (Glasgow: Glasgow University Press, 1908), 4 vols.

Moryson, Fynes, *Shakespeare's Europe: Unpublished Chapters of Fynes Moryson's Itinerary*, ed. Charles Hughes (London: Sherratt & Hughes, 1903).

Mucedorus (1590, rev. 1610), ed. Arvin H. Jupin (New York: Garland, 1987).

Munday, Anthony, *The Downfall of Robert, Earl of Huntingdon*, ed. John C. Meagher (Oxford: Oxford University Press, 1964).

Munday, Anthony, 'The Triumphs of Reunited Britannia' (1605), in *Jacobean Civic Pageants*, ed. Richard Dutton (Keele: Ryburn, 1995), 119–36.

Murdoch, Iris, *Acastos: Two Platonic Dialogues* (London: Chatto & Windus, 1986).

Nashe, Thomas, *The Works of Thomas Nashe*, ed. R. B. McKerrow (Oxford: Basil Blackwell, 1958), 5 vols.

Northbrooke, John, *A Treatise against Dicing, Dancing, Plays and Interludes with other idle pastimes* (1577) (London: Shakespeare Society, 1843).

The Oldcastle Controversy: Sir John Oldcastle Part 1 and The Famous Victories of Henry V, eds Peter Corbin and Douglas Sedge (Manchester and New York: Manchester University Press, 1991).

The Other Face: Catholic Life under Elizabeth I, coll. and ed. Philip Caraman (London: Longmans, Green & Co., 1960).

Ovid, *Ovid's Metamorphoses: The Arthur Golding Translation* (1567), ed. John Frederick Nims (London: Collier-Macmillan, 1965).

Ovid, *Tristia and Ex Ponto*, trans. Arthur Leslie Wheeler (London: Heinemann, 1924).

Oxford Classical Dictionary, eds Simon Hornblower and Antony Spawforth (Oxford and New York: Oxford University Press, 1996), 3rd edn.

Parsons, Robert, *A Conference about the next Succession to the Crowne of Ingland* (Antwerp, 1594), STC 19398.

Peele, George, *The Dramatic Works of George Peele*, ed. Charles Tyler Prouty (New Haven, CT and London: Yale University Press, 1961), 3 vols.

Petrarch, Francis, *The Life of Solitude*, trans. Jacob Zeitlin (Urbana, Illinois: University of Illinois Press, 1924).

Petrarch, Francis, *Petrarch's Lyric Poems: The Rime sparse and Other Lyrics*, trans. and ed. Robert M. Durling (Cambridge, MA: Harvard University Press, 1976).

Petrarch, Francis, *Rerum familiarium libri I–VIII*, trans. Aldo S. Bernardo (New York: State University of New York Press, 1975).

Petrarch, Francis, *Rerum familiarium libri IX–XVI* (Baltimore, MD: Johns Hopkins University Press, 1982).

Plato's Republic, trans. Desmond Lee (Harmondsworth: Penguin, 1987), 2nd edn.

Plutarch, 'Of Exile or Banishment', in *Plutarch's Moralia*, trans. Philemon Holland (1603) (London: J. M. Dent & Sons, 1912), 389–410.

Plutarch, *The Lives of the Noble Grecians and Romanes*, trans. Sir Thomas North (London, 1579).

Ponet, John, *A Shorte Treatise of Politicke Power, and of the True Obedience which Subjects owe to Kings and other Civill Governours* (London, 1556), STC 20179.

Prynne, William, *Histriomastix; The Players Scourge, or Actors Tragaedie* (1633) (New York and London: Garland, 1974).

Purchas, Samuel, *Hakluytus Posthumus or Purchas His Pilgrimes, Contayning a History of the World, in Sea Voyages & Lande-Travells, by Englishmen & Others* (London, 1625), 5 vols.

Raleigh, Sir Walter, *The Life of Sir Walter Ralegh based on contemporary documents [...] together with his letters*, ed. Edward Edwards (London: Macmillan, 1868), 2 vols.

The Rare Triumphes of Love and Fortune (1582), ed. John Isaac Owen (New York and London: Garland, 1979).

Remembrancia 1574–1664, Guildhall London Records Library.

Robinson, Robert, *The Phonetic Writings of Robert Robinson*, ed. E. J. Dobson (London: Oxford University Press, 1957).

Rowe, Nicholas, 'Some Account of the Life, etc., of Mr William Shakespear' (1709), repr. in *Eighteenth Century Essays on Shakespeare*, ed. D. Nichol Smith (Glasgow: James MacLehose & Sons, 1903), 1–23.

Rushdie, Salman, *The Moor's Last Sigh* (1995) (London: Vintage, 1996).

Sanders, Nicholas, *The Rise and Growth of the Anglican Schism* (1585), trans. and ed. David Lewis (London: Burns & Oates, 1877).

Seneca, *Ad Lucilium Epistulae Morales*, trans. Richard M. Gummere (London: Heinemann, 1961), 3 vols.

Seneca, *Moral Essays*, trans. John W. Basore (London: Heinemann, 1928), 3 vols.

Seneca, *Seneca's Minor Dialogues*, trans. A. Stewart (London: George Bell & Sons, 1889).

Shakespeare, William, *As You Like It: A New Variorum Edition of Shakespeare*, ed. Richard Knowles (New York: MLAA, 1977).

Shakespeare, William, *The Complete Works*, eds Stanley Wells, Gary Taylor, John Jowett and William Montgomery (Oxford: Oxford University Press, 1986).

Shakespeare, William, *The First Part of King Henry IV*, ed. A. R. Humphreys (London and New York: Routledge, 1960; repr. 1994).

Shakespeare, William, *The First Quarto Edition of Shakespeare's Romeo and Juliet* (1597), ed. Frank G. Hubbard (Madison: University of Wisconsin, 1924).

Shakespeare, William, *King Richard II*, ed. Andrew Gurr (Cambridge: Cambridge University Press, 1984).

Shakespeare, William, *A New Variorum Edition of Shakespeare: The Life and Death of Richard II*, ed. Matthew W. Black (Philadelphia and London: J. B. Lippincott, 1955).

Shakespeare, William, *Romeo and Juliet*, ed. G. Blakemore Evans (Cambridge: Cambridge University Press, 1984).

Shakespeare, William, *Romeo and Juliet*, ed. Jill L. Levenson (Oxford: Oxford University Press, 2000).

Shakespeare, William, *The Tempest*, ed. Frank Kermode (London: Methuen, 1954).

Shakespeare, William, *The Tragedy of King Lear*, ed. Jay L. Halio (Cambridge: Cambridge University Press, 1992).

Shakespeare, William, *The Two Gentlemen of Verona*, ed. Clifford Leech (London: Methuen, 1969)

Sidney, Sir Philip, *The Countess of Pembroke's Arcadia* (1593), ed. Maurice Evans (Harmondsworth: Penguin, 1987).

Sidney, Sir Philip, *Miscellaneous Prose of Sir Philip Sidney*, eds Katherine Duncan-Jones and Jan van Dorsten (Oxford: Clarendon Press, 1973).

Sidney, Sir Philip, *Sir Philip Sidney*, ed. Katherine Duncan-Jones (Oxford: Oxford University Press, 1989).

Spenser, Edmund, *The Faerie Queene* (1590–6), eds Thomas P. Roche Jr and C. Patrick O'Donnell Jr (Harmondsworth: Penguin Books, 1987), 4th edn.

Spenser, Edmund, *A View of the Present State of Ireland* (1633), ed. W. L. Renwick (Oxford: Clarendon Press, 1970).

Spenser, Edmund, *The Works of Edmund Spenser: A Variorum Edition*, eds Edwin Greenlaw, Charles Grosvenor Osgood, Frederick Morgan Padelford and Ray Heffer (Baltimore, MD: Johns Hopkins University Press, 1943), 9 vols.

Starkey, Thomas, *A Dialogue between Reginald Pole and Thomas Lupset* (1534), ed. Kathleen M. Burton (London: Chatto & Windus, 1948).

Strachey, William, *A True Reportory of the Wracke and Redemption of Sir Thomas Gates, Knight* (1610) in Purchas, Samuel, *Purchas his Pilgrimes*, vol. 4.

Stuart Royal Proclamations, eds James F. Larkin and Paul L. Hughes (Oxford: Clarendon Press, 1973), 2 vols.

Stubbes, Philip, *The Anatomie of Abuses* (1583) (Amsterdam and New York: De Capo Press, 1972).

Student's Blackstone: Selections from the Commentaries on the Laws of England by Sir William Blackstone, ed. R. M. Kerr (London: John Murray, 1858).

The Tale of Gamelyn, ed. Walter W. Skeat (Oxford: Clarendon Press, 1843), 2nd edn.

Thomas, Vivien and William Tydeman (eds), *Christopher Marlowe: The Plays and Their Sources* (London and New York: Routledge, 1994).

The Trial of Treasure, in *A Select Collection of Old English Plays*, ed. R. Dodsley (London: Turner & Reeves, 1874), 15 vols, vol. 3.

A True Declaration of the Estate of the Colonie in Virginia with a confutation of such scandalous reports ... (London, 1610), STC 24833.

A True and Sincere Declaration of the purpose and ends of the plantation begun in Virginia (London, 1610), STC 24832.

Tudor Royal Proclamations, eds Paul L. Hughes and James F. Larkin (New Haven, CT and London: Yale University Press, 1969), 3 vols.

Two Tudor Interludes: Youth and Hick Scorner, ed. Ian Lancashire (Manchester: Manchester University Press, 1980).

Tyndale's New Testament, trans. William Tyndale (1534), ed. David Daniell (New Haven, CT and London: Yale University Press, 1989).

Vaughan, William, *The Golden Grove* (London, 1608), 2nd edn.

Virgil, *Eclogues, Georgics and Aeneid I–VI*, tr. H. Rushton Fairclough (London: William Heinemann, 1935), 2 vols.

Wager, W., *The Longer Thou Livest and Enough is as Good as a Feast,* ed. R. Mark Benbow (London: Edward Arnold, 1967).

Webster, John, *Three Plays*, ed. D. C. Gunby (Harmondsworth: Penguin, 1972).

Wood, Anthony, *Athenae Oxonienses* (1695) (London: R. Knaplock, D. Midwinter and J. Tonson, 1721), 2 vols.

Woodstock: A Moral History (1592), ed. A. P. Rossiter (London: Chatto & Windus, 1946).

Wyatt, Sir Thomas, *Sir Thomas Wyatt: Collected Poems*, ed. Joost Daalder (London: Oxford University Press, 1975).

Secondary sources

Abrams, Richard, 'Rumor's Reign in *2 Henry IV*: The Scope of a Personification', *ELR*, 16 (1986), 467–95.

Adelman, Janet, '"Anger's My Meat": Feeding, Dependency and Aggression in *Coriolanus*', in *Representing Shakespeare: New Psychoanalytic Essays*, eds C. Kahn and M. Schwartz (Baltimore, MD and London: Johns Hopkins University Press, 1980), 129–49.

Adorno, Theodor, *Minima Moralia: Reflections from Damaged Life*, tr. E. F. N. Jephcott (London: Verso, 1951; repr. 1974).

Akrigg, G. P. V., *Shakespeare and the Earl of Southampton* (London: Hamish Hamilton, 1968).

Albright, Evelyn May, 'Shakespeare's *Richard II* and the Essex Conspiracy', *PMLA*, 42 (1927), 686–720.

Alpers, Paul, *What is Pastoral?* (Chicago and London: University of Chicago Press, 1996).

Anderson, Judith H., *Words that Matter: Linguistic Perception in Renaissance English* (Stanford, CA: Stanford University Press, 1996).

Axton, Marie, *The Queen's Two Bodies: Drama and the Elizabethan Succession* (London: Royal Historical Society, 1977).

Baker, J. H., *An Introduction to English Legal History* (London: Butterworths, 1990), 3rd edn.

Baldwin, T. W., *William Shakspere's Small Latine & Lesse Greeke* (Urbana: University of Illinois Press, 1944), 2 vols.

Barber, C. L., *Shakespeare's Festive Comedy: A Study of Dramatic Form and its Relation to Social Custom* (Princeton, NJ: Princeton University Press, 1959).

Barbour, Kathryn, 'Flout 'em and Scout 'em and Flout 'em and Scout 'em: Prospero's Power and Punishments in *The Tempest*', in *Shakespearean Power and Punishment: A*

Volume of Essays, ed. Gillian Murray Kendall (London: Associated University Presses, 1998), 159–72.

Barish, Jonas A., 'The Turning Away of Prince Hal', *Sh. St.*, 1 (1965), 9–17.

Barroll, Leeds, 'A New History for Shakespeare and His Time', *Sh. Q.*, 39 (1988), 441–64.

Barroll, Leeds, *Politics, Plague and Shakespeare's Theater* (Ithaca, NY and London: Cornell University Press, 1991).

Barton, Anne, 'Shakespeare and the Limits of Language', *Sh. S.*, 24 (1971), 19–30.

Bate, Jonathan, 'The Humanist *Tempest*', in *La Tempête: Etudes Critiques* (1993), 5–20.

Bate, Jonathan, *Shakespeare and Ovid* (Oxford: Oxford University Press, 1993).

Baugh, Albert C., *A History of the English Language* (London: Routledge, 1951), 3rd edn.

Bednarz, James P., 'Representing Jonson: *Histriomastix* and the Origin of the Poets' War', *HLQ*, 54 (1991), 1–30.

Beier, A. L., *Masterless Men: The Vagrancy Problem in England 1560–1640* (London: Methuen, 1983).

Bellamy, John, *Crime and Public Order in England in the Later Middle Ages* (London: Routledge, 1973).

Bellamy, John, *The Tudor Law of Treason: An Introduction* (London: Routledge & Kegan Paul, 1979).

Belsey, Catherine, 'The Name of the Rose in *Romeo and Juliet*', *YES*, 23 (1993), 126–42.

Bennett, Josephine Waters, 'Britain among the Fortunate Isles', *Stud. in Phil.*, 53 (1956), 114–40.

Berger, Harry Jr, 'Miraculous Harp: A Reading of Shakespeare's *Tempest*', *Sh. St.*, 5 (1969), 253–84.

Bergeron, David M., '*Richard II* and Carnival Politics', *Sh. Q.*, 42 (1991), 33–43.

Bergeron, David M., 'Shakespeare Makes History: *2 Henry IV*', *SEL*, 31 (1991), 231–45.

Berry, Philippa, 'Between Idolatry and Astrology: Modes of Temporal Repetition in *Romeo and Juliet*', in *A Feminist Companion to Shakespeare*, ed. Dympna Callaghan (Oxford: Blackwell, 2000), 358–72.

Blank, Paula, 'Speaking Freely about Richard II', *Journal of English and Germanic Philology*, 96 (1997), 327–48.

Bradbrook, M. C., *Shakespeare: The Poet in his World* (London: Weidenfeld & Nicolson, 1978).

Braden, Gordon, *Petrarchan Love and the Continental Renaissance* (New Haven, CT: Yale University Press, 1999).

Breen, John, 'Gloucester's Proclamation', *N & Q*, 239 (1994), 493–4.

Breight, Curt, '"Treason doth never prosper": *The Tempest* and the Discourse of Treason', *Sh. Q.*, 41 (1990), 1–28.

Bristol, Michael D., *Carnival and Theater: Plebeian Culture and the Structure of Authority in Renaissance England* (London and New York: Methuen, 1985).

Brockbank, J. P., 'History and Histrionics in *Cymbeline*', *Sh. S.*, 11 (1958), 42–9.

Brooke, Nicholas, *Shakespeare's Early Tragedies* (London: Methuen, 1968).

Brotton, Jerry, '"This Tunis, sir, was Carthage": Contesting Colonialism in *The Tempest*', in *Post-Colonial Shakespeares*, eds Ania Loomba and Martin Orkin (London and New York: Routledge, 1998), 23–42.

Brower, Reuben A., *Hero and Saint: Shakespeare and the Graeco-Roman Heroic Tradition* (Oxford: Clarendon Press, 1971).

Brown, Paul, '"This thing of darkness I acknowledge mine": *The Tempest* and the Discourse of Colonialism', in *Political Shakespeare: New Essays in Cultural Materialism*, eds Jonathan Dollimore and Alan Sinfield (Manchester: Manchester University Press, 1985), 48–72.

Brownlow, F. W., *Shakespeare, Harsnett and the Devils of Denham* (London and Toronto: Associated University Presses, 1993).

Bulman, James C., 'The Date and Production of *Timon* Reconsidered', *Sh. S.*, 27 (1974), 111–28.

Burke, Kenneth, '*Coriolanus* and the Delights of Faction', in *Language as Symbolic Action: Essays on Life, Literature and Method* (Berkeley and Los Angeles: University of California Press, 1968), 81–100.

Butler, F. G., 'Who Are King Lear's Philosophers? An Answer, With Some Help From Erasmus', *English Studies*, 67 (1986), 511–24.

Cain, H. Edward, 'Further Light on the Relation of *1* and *2 Henry IV*', *Sh. Q.*, 3 (1952), 21–38.

Calderwood, James L., '*Coriolanus*: Wordless Meanings and Meaningless Words', *SEL* 6 (1966), 211–24.

Calderwood, James L., 'Creative Uncreation in *King Lear*', *Sh. Q.*, 37 (1986), 5–19.

Calderwood, James L., 'Richard II: Metadrama and the Fall of Speech', in *Shakespeare's History Plays: Richard II to Henry V*, ed. Graham Holderness (Basingstoke: Macmillan – now Palgrave Macmillan, 1992), 121–35.

Calderwood, James L., *Shakespearean Metadrama* (Minneapolis: University of Minnesota, 1971).

Canny, Nicholas, 'The Permissive Frontier: the Problem of Social Control in English Settlements in Ireland and Virginia 1550–1650', in *The Westward Enterprise: English Activities in Ireland, the Atlantic and America 1480–1650*, eds K. R. Andrews, N. P. Canny and P. E. H. Hair (Liverpool: Liverpool University Press, 1978), 17–44.

Cantor, Paul A., *Shakespeare's Rome: Republic and Empire* (Ithaca, NY and London: Cornell University Press, 1976).

Caputi, Anthony, *John Marston, Satirist* (Ithaca, NY: Cornell University Press, 1961).

Carroll, William C., *Fat King, Lean Beggar: Representations of Poverty in the Age of Shakespeare* (Ithaca, NY and London: Cornell University Press, 1996).

Carroll, William C., *The Metamorphoses of Shakespearean Comedy* (Princeton, NJ: Princeton University Press, 1985).

Cavell, Stanley, *Disowning Knowledge in Six Plays of Shakespeare* (Cambridge: Cambridge University Press, 1987).

Chambers, E. K., *The Elizabethan Stage* (Oxford: Clarendon Press, 1923; repr. 1961), 4 vols.

Chambers, E. K., *The Mediaeval Stage* (London: Oxford University Press, 1903), 2 vols.

Chambers, E. K., *William Shakespeare: A Study of Facts and Problems* (Oxford: Clarendon Press, 1930), 2 vols.

Cheng, Vincent J., *Joyce, Race and Empire* (Cambridge: Cambridge University Press, 1995).

Cixous, Hélène, *The Exile of James Joyce*, trans. Sally A. J. Purcell (London: John Calder, 1976).

Claassen, Jo-Marie, *Displaced Persons: The Literature of Exile from Cicero to Boethius* (Madison: University of Wisconsin, 1999).

Coates, John, '"Poor Tom" and the Spiritual Journey in *King Lear*', *Durham University Journal* (December 1986), 7–14.

Colie, Rosalie L., 'Reason and Need: *King Lear* and the "Crisis" of the Aristocracy', in *Some Facets of King Lear: Essays in Prismatic Criticism*, eds Rosalie Colie and F. T. Flahiff (London: Heinemann, 1974), 163-221.

Colie, Rosalie L., *Shakespeare's Living Art* (Princeton, NJ: Princeton University Press, 1974).

Daley, A. Stuart, 'The Dispraise of the Country in *As You Like It*', *Sh. Q.*, 36 (1985), 300–14.

Danby, John F., *Shakespeare's Doctrine of Nature: A Study of King Lear* (London: Faber & Faber, 1949).

Davidson, Clifford, '*Coriolanus*: A Study in Political Dislocation', *Sh. St.*, 4 (1968), 263–74.

Davis, Lloyd, '"Death-marked Love": Desire and Presence in *Romeo and Juliet*', *Sh. S.*, 49 (1996), 57–67.

Davis, Walter R., *Idea and Act in Elizabethan Fiction* (Princeton, NJ: Princeton University Press, 1969).

De Grazia, Margreta, '*The Tempest*: Gratuitous Movement or Action Without Kibes and Pinches', *Sh. St.*, 14 (1981), 249–67.

De Grazia, Margreta and Peter Stallybrass, 'The Materiality of the Shakespearean Text', *Sh. Q.*, 44 (1993), 255–83.

De Sousa, Geraldo, *Shakespeare's Cross-Cultural Encounters* (Basingstoke: Macmillan – now Palgrave Macmillan, 1999).

Dessen, Alan C., 'The Intemperate Knight and the Politic Prince: Late Morality Structure in *1 Henry IV*', *Sh. St.*, 7 (1974), 147–71.

Dickens, A. G., *The English Reformation* (London: B. T. Batsford, 1964).

Dickens, A. G., *Reformation and Society in Sixteenth-Century Europe* (London: Thames & Hudson, 1966).

Dickinson, Hugh, 'The Reformation of Prince Hal', *Sh. Q.*, 12 (1961), 33–46.

Digangi, Mario, *The Homoerotics of Early Modern Drama* (Cambridge: Cambridge University Press, 1997).

Dillon, Janette, *Language and State in Medieval and Renaissance England* (Cambridge: Cambridge University Press, 1998).

Dillon, Janette, *Shakespeare and the Solitary Man* (Basingstoke: Macmillan – now Palgrave Macmillan, 1981).

Dollimore, Jonathan, 'Desire is Death', in *Subject and Object in Renaissance Culture*, eds Margreta De Grazia, Maureen Quilligan and Peter Stallybrass (Cambridge: Cambridge University Press, 1996), 369–86.

Donawerth, Jane, 'Diogenes the Cynic and Lear's Definition of Man, *King Lear* III iv 101–9', *English Language Notes* 15 (1977), 10–14.

Donawerth, Jane, *Shakespeare and the Sixteenth-Century Study of Language* (Urbana: University of Illinois Press, 1984).

Doody, Margaret Anne, *The True Story of the Novel* (London: Fontana Press, 1998).

Dubrow, Heather, *Shakespeare and Domestic Loss* (Cambridge: Cambridge University Press, 1999).

Duncan-Jones, Katherine, *Sir Philip Sidney: Courtier Poet* (London: Hamish Hamilton, 1991).

Duncan-Jones, Katherine, *Ungentle Shakespeare: Scenes from his Life* (London: Thomson Learning, 2001).

Dutton, Richard, *Mastering the Revels* (Basingstoke: Macmillan – now Palgrave Macmillan, 1991).

Earl, A. J., '*Romeo and Juliet* and the Elizabethan Sonnets', *English*, 27 (1978), 99–119.

Eisenstein, Elizabeth L., *The Printing Press as an Agent of Change* (Cambridge: Cambridge University Press, 1980).

Elton, G. R., *The Tudor Constitution* (Cambridge: Cambridge University Press, 1960).

Empson, William, *Essays on Shakespeare*, ed. David B. Pirie (Cambridge: Cambridge University Press, 1986).

Empson, William, *Some Versions of Pastoral* (New York: New Directions, 1935; repr. 1974).

Evans, Bertrand, *Shakespeare's Tragic Practice* (Oxford: Clarendon Press, 1979), 154–68.

Evans, Robert O., *The Osier Cage: Rhetorical Devices in Romeo and Juliet* (Lexington: University of Kentucky Press, 1966).

Farley-Hills, David, *Shakespeare and the Rival Playwrights* (London: Routledge, 1990).

Farnham, Willard, *Shakespeare's Tragic Frontier* (Berkeley and Los Angeles: University of California Press, 1950).

Felperin, Howard, *Shakespearean Romance* (Princeton, NJ: Princeton University Press, 1972).

Fiedler, Leslie A., *The Stranger in Shakespeare* (London: Croom Helm, 1972).

Fiehler, Rudolf, 'How Oldcastle Became Falstaff', *MLQ*, 16 (March 1955), 16–28.

Finkelpearl, Philip J., *John Marston of the Middle Temple* (Cambridge, MA: Harvard University Press, 1969).

Fitz, L. T., 'The Vocabulary of the Environment in *The Tempest*', *Sh. Q.*, 26 (1975), 42–7.

Fraser, Russell, *The War Against Poetry* (Princeton, NJ: Princeton University Press, 1970).

Frey, Charles, '*The Tempest* and the New World', *Sh. Q.*, 30 (1979), 29–41.

Friedman, Donald M., 'John of Gaunt and the Rhetoric of Frustration', *ELH*, 43 (1976), 279–99.

Frye, Northrop, *A Natural Perspective: The Development of Shakespearean Comedy and Romance* (New York and London: Columbia University Press, 1965).

Garrett, Christina, *The Marian Exiles: A Study in the Origins of Elizabethan Puritanism* (Cambridge: Cambridge University Press, 1938; repr. 1966).

Gellner, Ernest, *Nations and Nationalism* (Oxford: Blackwell, 1983; repr. 1997).

Gesner, Carol, *Shakespeare and the Greek Romance: A Study of Origins* (Lexington: University of Kentucky, 1970).

Giamatti, A. Bartlett, *Exile and Change in Renaissance Literature* (New Haven, CT and London: Yale University Press, 1984).

Gildersleeve, Virginia Crocheron, *Government Regulation of the Elizabethan Drama* (Westport, CT: Greenwood Press, 1908; repr. 1975).

Gillies, John, 'Shakespeare's Virginian Masque', *ELH*, 53 (1986), 673–707.

Givan, Christopher, 'Shakespeare's *Coriolanus*: The Premature Epitaph and the Butterfly', *Sh. St.*, 12 (1979), 143–58.

Gordon, D. J., 'Name and Fame: Shakespeare's *Coriolanus*', in *Papers Mainly Shakespearian* ed. G. I. Duthie (London: Oliver & Boyd, 1964), 40–57.

Greenblatt, Stephen, *Marvelous Possessions: The Wonder of the New World* (Oxford: Clarendon Press, 1991).

Greenblatt, Stephen, *Renaissance Self-Fashioning: From More to Shakespeare* (Chicago and London: University of Chicago Press, 1980).

Greenblatt, Stephen, 'Shakespeare and the Exorcists', in *Shakespeare and the Question of Theory*, eds Patricia Parker and Geoffrey Hartman (New York and London: Routledge, 1985; repr. 1993), 163–87.

Grene, Nicholas, *Shakespeare's Tragic Imagination* (Basingstoke: Macmillan – now Palgrave Macmillan, 1992).

Gurr, Andrew, '*Coriolanus* and the Body Politic', *Sh. S.*, 28 (1975), 63–70.

Gurr, Andrew, *The Shakespearean Stage 1574–1642* (Cambridge: Cambridge University Press, 1992), 3rd edn.

Hackett, Helen, '"Gracious be the Issue": Maternity and Narrative in Shakespeare's Late Plays', in *Shakespeare's Late Plays: New Readings*, eds Jennifer Richards and James Knowles (Edinburgh: Edinburgh University Press, 1999), 25–39.

Hadfield, Andrew, '"Hitherto she ne'er could fancy him": Shakespeare's "British" Plays and the Exclusion of Ireland', in *Shakespeare and Ireland: History, Politics, Culture*, eds Mark Thornton Burnett and Ramona Wray (Basingstoke: Macmillan – now Palgrave Macmillan, 1997), 47–63.

Hadfield, Andrew, *Literature, Politics, and National Identity* (Cambridge: Cambridge University Press, 1994).

Hadfield, Andrew, *Literature, Travel, and Colonial Writing in the English Renaissance* (Oxford: Clarendon Press, 1999).

Hadfield, Andrew, *Spenser's Irish Experience: Wilde Fruit and Salvage Soyl* (Oxford: Clarendon Press, 1997).

Haigh, Christopher, *English Reformations: Religion, Politics, and Society under the Tudors* (Oxford: Clarendon Press, 1993).

Halliwell, J. O., *On the Character of Sir John Falstaff* (1841) (New York: AMS Press, 1966).

Hanawalt, Barbara A., 'Ballads and Bandits: Fourteenth-Century Outlaws and the Robin Hood Poems', in *Robin Hood: An Anthology of Scholarship and Criticism* ed. Stephen Knight (Woodbridge: D. S. Brewer, 1999), 263–84.

Harbage, Alfred, *Annals of English Drama 975–1700*, rev. S. Schoenbaum, 3rd edn rev. Sylvia Stoler Wagonheim (London and New York: Routledge, 1989).

Hastings, Adrian, *The Construction of Nationhood: Ethnicity, Religion and Nationalism* (Cambridge: Cambridge University Press, 1997).

Hawkes, Terence, *Shakespeare's Talking Animals: Language and Drama in Society* (London: Edward Arnold, 1973).

Haydn, Hiram, *The Counter-Renaissance* (Gloucester, MA: Peter Smith, 1950).

Heffner, Ray, 'Shakespeare, Hayward, and Essex', *PMLA*, 45.2 (1930), 754–80.

Helgerson, Richard, *Forms of Nationhood: The Elizabethan Writings of England* (Chicago and London: University of Chicago Press, 1992).

Helgerson, Richard, *Self-Crowned Laureates: Jonson, Spenser, Milton and the Literary System* (Berkeley: University of California Press, 1983).

Helmbold, Anita, 'King of the Revels or King of the Rebels?: Sir John Falstaff Revisited', *Upstart Crow*, 16 (1996), 70–91.

Henderson, Diana E., 'Many Mansions: Reconstructing *A Woman Killed with Kindness*', *SEL*, 26 (1986), 277–94.

Heninger, S. K., 'The Sun-King Analogy in *Richard II*', *Sh. Q.*, 11 (1960), 319–27.

Highley, Christopher, *Shakespeare, Spenser, and the Crisis in Ireland* (Cambridge: Cambridge University Press, 1997).

Hobsbawm, Eric, *Nations and Nationalism Since 1780* (Cambridge: Cambridge University Press, 1990).

Hockey, Dorothy C., 'A World of Rhetoric in *Richard II*', *Sh. Q.*, 15 (1964), 179–91.

Holderness, Graham, *Shakespeare Recycled: The Making of Historical Drama* (London and New York: Harvester Wheatsheaf, 1992).

Holderness, Graham, Nick Potter and John Turner (eds) *Shakespeare: The Play of History* (Basingstoke: Macmillan – now Palgrave Macmillan, 1988).

Holdsworth, Sir William, *A History of English Law* (London: Methuen, 1903; repr. 1973), 5th edn, 16 vols.

Holstun, James, 'Tragic Superfluity in *Coriolanus*', *ELH*, 50 (1983), 485–508.

Honigmann, E. A. J., *Shakespeare: The 'Lost Years'* (Manchester: Manchester University Press, 1985; rev. 1998).

Horton, T. B., 'Distinguishing Shakespeare from Fletcher through Function Words', *Sh. St.* 22 (1994), 314–35.

Howard-Hill, T. H. (ed.), *Shakespeare and Sir Thomas More: Essays on the Play and Its Shakespearean Interest* (Cambridge: Cambridge University Press, 1989).

Huffman, Clifford Chalmers, *Coriolanus in Context* (Lewisburg, PA: Bucknell University Press, 1971).

Hughes, Philip, *The Reformation in England* (London: Hollis & Carter, 1952), 3 vols.

Hulme, Hilda H., *Explorations in Shakespeare's Language: Some Problems of Lexical Meaning in the Dramatic Text* (London: Longman, 1962).

Hulme, Peter, *Colonial Encounters: Europe and the Native Caribbean 1492–1797* (London and New York: Routledge, 1986).

Hunter, G. K., 'Shakespeare's Last Tragic Heroes', in *Dramatic Identities and Cultural Tradition: Studies in Shakespeare and his Contemporaries: Critical Essays by G. K. Hunter* (Liverpool: Liverpool University Press, 1978), 251–69.

Ingram, Martin, *Church Courts, Sex and Marriage in England, 1570–1640* (Cambridge: Cambridge University Press, 1987).

Jagendorf, Zvi, '*Coriolanus*: Body Politic and Private Parts', *Sh. Q.*, 41 (1990), 455–69.

Jenkins, Harold, 'Kent and Alcibiades and the Dating of *Timon of Athens*', in *KM80: A Birthday Album for Kenneth Muir* (Liverpool: Liverpool University Press, 1987), 78–9.

Jones, Richard Foster, *The Triumph of the English Language: A Survey of Opinions Concerning the Vernacular from the Introduction of Printing to the Restoration* (London: Oxford University Press, 1953).

Jowitt, Earl (ed.), *The Dictionary of English Law* (London: Sweet & Maxwell, 1959).

Kahn, Coppélia, 'The Absent Mother in *King Lear*', in *Rewriting the Renaissance: The Discourses of Sexual Difference in Early Modern Europe*, eds Margaret W. Ferguson, Maureen Quilligan and Nancy J. Vickers (Chicago and London: University of Chicago Press, 1986), 33–49.

Kahn, Coppélia, 'Coming of Age in Verona', in *The Woman's Part: Feminist Criticism of Shakespeare*, eds Carolyn Lenz, Gayle Greene and Carol Thomas Neely (Urbana, Chicago and London: University of Illinois Press, 1980), 171–93.

Kahn, Coppélia, *Roman Shakespeare: Warriors, Wounds, and Women* (London: Routledge, 1997).

Kantorowicz, Ernst H., *The King's Two Bodies: A Study in Mediaeval Political Theology* (Princeton, NJ: Princeton University Press, 1957).

Kastan, David Scott, 'Proud Majesty made a Subject: Shakespeare and the Spectacle of Rule', *Sh. Q.*, 37 (1986), 459–75.

Kastan, David Scott, *Shakespeare and the Book* (Cambridge: Cambridge University Press, 2001).

Keen, Maurice, *The Outlaws in Medieval Legend* (London and Henley: Routledge & Kegan Paul, 1961).

Kerrigan, John, 'Revision, Adaptation and the Fool in *King Lear*', in *The Division of the Kingdoms*, ed. Gary Taylor and Michael Warren (Oxford: Clarendon Press, 1983), 195–246.

Kinney, Arthur, 'Some Conjectures on the Composition of *King Lear*', *Sh. S.*, 33 (1980), 13–26.

Knapp, Jeffrey, *An Empire Nowhere: England, America, and Literature from Utopia to The Tempest* (Berkeley and Oxford: University of California Press, 1992).

Kronenfeld, Judy Z., 'Social Rank and the Pastoral Ideals of *As You Like It*', *Sh. Q.*, 29 (1978), 333–48.

Kupperman, Karol Ordahl, *Settling with the Indians: The Meeting of English and Indian Cultures in America 1580–1640* (London and Toronto: J. M. Dent, 1980).

Lacey, Robert, *Robert, Earl of Essex: An Elizabethan Icarus* (London: Weidenfeld & Nicolson, 1971).

Landt, D. B., 'The Ancestry of Sir John Falstaff', *Sh. Q.*, 17 (1966), 69–76.

Lee, Arthur Gould, *The Son of Leicester: The Story of Sir Robert Dudley* (London: Victor Gollancz, 1964).

Leech, Clifford, 'The Moral Tragedy of *Romeo and Juliet*', in *English Renaissance Drama: Essays in Honor of Madeleine Doran and Mark Eccles*, eds Standish Henring, Robert Kinbrough and Richard Knowles (Carbondale and Edwardsville: Southern Illinois University Press, 1976), 59–75.

Lees, F. N., 'Coriolanus, Aristotle and Bacon', *RES*, 1 (1950), 114–25.

Leggatt, Alexander, *Shakespeare's Political Drama: The History Plays and the Roman Plays* (London and New York: Routledge, 1988).

Levenson, Jill L., 'The Definition of Love: Shakespeare's Phrasing in *Romeo and Juliet*', *Sh. St.*, 15 (1982), 21–36.

Levin, Harry, 'Form and Formality in *Romeo and Juliet*', *Sh. Q.*, 11 (1960), 3–11.

Levin, Harry, *The Myth of the Golden Age in the Renaissance* (London: Faber & Faber, 1970).

Levith, Murray J., *Shakespeare's Italian Settings and Plays* (Basingstoke: Macmillan – now Palgrave Macmillan, 1989).

Liebler, Naomi Conn, *Shakespeare's Festive Tragedy: The Ritual Foundations of Genre* (London and New York: Routledge, 1995).

Lindheim, Nancy R., '*King Lear* as Pastoral Tragedy', in Rosalie Colie and F. T. Flahiff, *Some Facets of King Lear: Essays in Prismatic Criticism* (London: Heinemann, 1974) 169–184.

Long, Michael, *The Unnatural Scene: A Study in Shakespearean Tragedy* (London: Methuen, 1976).

Loomba, Ania, *Colonialism/Postcolonialism* (London and New York: Routledge, 1998).

Loomie, Albert J., *The Spanish Elizabethans: The English Exiles at the Court of Philip II* (New York: Fordham University Press, 1963).

McCabe, Richard, 'Edmund Spenser, Poet of Exile', *Proceedings of the British Academy*, 80 (1993), 73–103.

McCoy, Richard C., *The Rites of Knighthood: The Literature and Politics of Elizabethan Chivalry* (Berkeley and London: University of California Press, 1989).

Macdonald, Ronald R., 'Uneasy Lies: Language and History in Shakespeare's Lancastrian Tetralogy', *Sh. Q.*, 35 (1984), 22–39.

McEachern, Claire, *The Poetics of English Nationhood, 1590–1612* (Cambridge: Cambridge University Press, 1996).

McFarland, Thomas, *Shakespeare's Pastoral Comedy* (Chapel Hill: University of North Carolina Press, 1972).

Mack, Maynard, *Killing the King: Three Studies in Shakespeare's Tragic Structure* (New Haven, CT and London: Yale University Press, 1973).

Mack, Maynard, *King Lear in Our Time* (London: Methuen, 1966).

MacKenzie, Clayton G., 'Paradise and Paradise Lost in *Richard II*', *Sh. Q.*, 37 (1986), 318–39.

MacLean, Hugh, 'Disguise in *King Lear*: Kent and Edgar', *Sh. Q.*, 11 (1960), 49–54.

Mahood, M. M., *Shakespeare's Wordplay* (London: Methuen, 1957).

Manheim, Michael, *The Weak King Dilemma in the Shakespearean History Play* (New York: Syracuse University Press, 1973).

Marcus, Leah S., *Puzzling Shakespeare: Local Reading and its Discontents* (Berkeley, Los Angeles and London: University of California Press, 1988).

Margolies, David, *Monsters of the Deep: Social Dissolution in Shakespeare's Tragedies* (Manchester: Manchester University Press, 1992).

Marinelli, Peter, *Pastoral* (London: Methuen, 1971).

Martindale, Charles and Michelle, *Shakespeare and the Uses of Antiquity: An Introductory Essay* (London and New York: Routledge, 1990).

Maus, Katherine Eisaman, *Inwardness and Theater in the English Renaissance* (Chicago and London: University of Chicago Press, 1995).

Mazzotta, Giuseppe, 'Dante and the Virtues of Exile', in *Exile in Literature*, ed. Maria-Ines Lagos-Pope (London: Associated University Presses, 1988), 49–71.

Mazzotta, Giuseppe, *The Worlds of Petrarch* (Durham, NC and London: Duke University Press, 1993).

Merrix, Robert P. and Carole Levin, '*Richard II* and *Edward II*: The Structure of Deposition', *Sh. Y.*, 1 (1990), 1–13.

Meszaros, Patricia K., '"There is a world elsewhere"': Tragedy and History in *Coriolanus*', *SEL*, 16 (1976), 273–85.

Mikalachki, Jodi, *The Legend of Boadicea: Gender and Nation in Early Modern England* (London and New York: Routledge, 1998).

Miles, Geoffrey, *Shakespeare and the Constant Romans* (Oxford: Clarendon Press, 1996).

Miller, Shannon, 'Topicality and Subversion in William Shakespeare's *Coriolanus*', *SEL*, 32 (1992), 287–322.

Milward, Peter J., *The Catholicism of Shakespeare's Plays* (Southampton: Saint Austen Press, 1997).

Miola, Robert S., *Shakespeare's Rome* (Cambridge: Cambridge University Press, 1983).

Miola, Robert S., 'Timon in Shakespeare's Athens', *Sh. Q.*, 31 (1980), 21–30.

Monsarrat, Gilles, *Light from the Porch: Stoicism and Renaissance Literature* (Paris: Didier Erudition, 1984).

Montrose, Louis A., 'Of Gentlemen and Shepherds: The Politics of Elizabethan Pastoral Form', *ELH*, 50 (1983), 415–59.

Montrose, Louis A., '"The Place of a Brother" in *As You Like It*: Social Process and Comic Form', *Sh. Q.*, 32 (1981), 28–54.

Motto, Anna Lydia and John R. Clark, 'The Development of the Classical Tradition of Exile to Seneca', *Mosaic*, 8 (1975), 109–17.

Muir, Kenneth, *The Life and Letters of Sir Thomas Wyatt* (Liverpool: Liverpool University Press, 1963).

Mullaney, Steven, *The Place of the Stage: License, Play, and Power in Renaissance England* (1988; Ann Arbor: University of Michigan Press, 1995).

Murdoch, Iris, *The Fire and the Sun: Why Plato Banished the Artists* (Oxford: Clarendon Press, 1977).

Neely, Carol Thomas, *Broken Nuptials in Shakespeare's Plays* (New Haven, CT: Yale University Press, 1985).

Neill, Michael, 'Broken English and Broken Irish: Nation, Language, and the Optic of Power in Shakespeare's Histories', *Sh. Q.*, 45 (1994), 1–32.

Newman, Franklin B., 'The Rejection of Falstaff and the Rigorous Charity of the King', *Sh. St.*, 2 (1966), 153–61.

Norbrook, David, '"A Liberal Tongue": Language and Rebellion in *Richard II*', in *Shakespeare's Universe: Renaissance Ideas and Conventions*, ed. John M. Mucciolo (Aldershot: Scolar Press, 1996), 37–52.

Oliver, H. J., 'Coriolanus as Tragic Hero', *Sh. Q.*, 10 (1959), 53–61.

Ouditt, Susan (ed.), *Displaced Persons: Conditions of Exile in European Culture* (Aldershot: Ashgate, 2002).

Palmer, D. J., 'Casting off the Old Man: History and St. Paul in *Henry IV*', *Crit. Q.*, 12 (1970), 267–83.

Parker, Barbara L., *A Precious Seeing: Love and Reason in Shakespeare's Plays* (New York and London: New York University Press, 1987).

Parker, Patricia, *Shakespeare from the Margins: Language, Culture, Context* (Chicago and London: University of Chicago Press, 1996).

Parker, R. B., '*Coriolanus* and "th'interpretation of the time"' in *Mirror up to Shakespeare: Essays in Honour of G. R. Hibbard*, ed. J. C. Gray (Toronto and London: University of Toronto Press, 1984), 261–76.

Paster, Gail Kern, 'To Starve with Feeding: The City in *Coriolanus*', *Sh. St.*, 11 (1978), 123–44.

Patterson, Annabel, *Shakespeare and the Popular Voice* (Oxford: Basil Blackwell, 1989).

Perry, Curtis, *The Making of Jacobean Culture: James I and the Renegotiation of Elizabethan Literary Practice* (Cambridge: Cambridge University Press, 1997).

Pitcher, John, 'A Theatre of the Future: The *Aeneid* and *The Tempest*', *E. in C.*, 34 (1984), 193–211.

Poggioli, Renato, *The Oaten Flute: Essays on Pastoral Poetry and the Pastoral Ideal* (Cambridge, MA: Harvard University Press, 1975).

Porter, Joseph A., *The Drama of Speech Acts: Shakespeare's Lancastrian Tetralogy* (Berkeley and London: University of California Press, 1979).

Potter, Nicholas, '"Like to a tenement or pelting farm": *Richard II* and the Idea of the Nation', in *Shakespeare in the New Europe*, eds Michael Hattaway, Boika Sokolova and Derek Roper (Sheffield: Sheffield Academic Press, 1994), 130–47.

Prior, Moody E., *The Drama of Power: Studies in Shakespeare's History Plays* (Evanston, IL: Northwestern University Press, 1973), 59–82.

Quinn, David Beers, *England and the Discovery of America 1481–1620* (London: Allen & Unwin, 1974).

Rhodes, Neil, *The Power of Eloquence and English Renaissance Literature* (Worcester: Harvester Wheatsheaf, 1992).

Riss, Arthur, 'The Belly Politic: *Coriolanus* and the Revolt of Language', *ELH*, 59 (1992), 53–75.

Ronan, Clifford, *'Antike Roman': Power Symbology and the Roman Play in Early Modern England 1585–1635* (Athens and London: University of Georgia Press, 1995).

Said, Edward, *Reflections on Exile and Other Literary and Cultural Essays* (London: Granta Books, 2000).

Salgado, Gamini, *The Elizabethan Underworld* (London: J. M. Dent, 1977).

Salingar, Leo, '*King Lear*, Montaigne and Harsnett', *Aligarh Journal of English Studies*, 8 (1983), 124–66.

Salingar, Leo, *Shakespeare and the Traditions of Comedy* (Cambridge: Cambridge University Press, 1974).

Sams, Eric, *The Real Shakespeare, Retrieving the Early Years 1564–1594* (New Haven, CT and London: Yale University Press, 1995).

Schell, Edgar T., 'Prince Hal's Second "Reformation"', *Sh. Q.*, 21 (1970), 11–16.

Schneider, Ben Ross, 'Are We Being Historical Yet?: Colonialist Interpretations of Shakespeare's *Tempest*', *Sh. St.*, 23 (1995), 120–45.

Schoenbaum, S., '*Richard II* and the Realities of Power', *Sh. S.*, 28 (1975), 1–13.

Schoenbaum, S., *Shakespeare's Lives* (Oxford: Clarendon Press, 1970).

Schutte, William M., *Joyce and Shakespeare: A Study in the Meaning of Ulysses* (New Haven, CT: Yale University Press, 1957).

Scoufos, Alice-Lyle, *Shakespeare's Typological Satire: A Study of the Falstaff–Oldcastle Problem* (Athens, OH: Ohio University Press, 1979).

Scragg, Leah, *Shakespeare's Mouldy Tales: Recurrent Plot Motifs in Shakespearian Drama* (London: Longman, 1992).

Selden, Raman, 'King Lear and True Need', *Sh. St.*, 19 (1987), 143–68.

Seward, James H., *Tragic Vision in Romeo and Juliet* (Washington, DC: Consortium Press, 1973).

Shaw, Catherine M., 'The Tragic Substructure of the *Henry IV* Plays', *Sh. S.*, 38 (1985), 61–7.

Shell, Alison, *Catholicism, Controversy and the English Literary Imagination, 1558–1660* (Cambridge: Cambridge University Press, 1999).

Sherman, William H., *John Dee: The Politics of Reading and Writing in the English Renaissance* (Amherst: University of Massachusetts Press, 1995).

Sicherman, Carol M., '*Coriolanus*: The Failure of Words', *ELH*, 39 (1972), 189–207.

Simmons, J. L., *Shakespeare's Pagan World: The Roman Tragedies* (Brighton: Harvester Press, 1974).

Skura, Meredith Anne, 'Discourse and the Individual: The Case of Colonialism in *The Tempest*', *Sh. Q.*, 40 (1989), 42–69.

Slater, Ann Pasternak, 'Petrarchism Come True in *Romeo and Juliet*', in *Images of Shakespeare*, eds Werner Habicht, D. J. Palmer and Roger Pringle (London and Toronto: Associated University Presses, 1988), 129–50.

Smith, Emma, 'Author v. Character in Early Modern Dramatic Authorship: The Example of Thomas Kyd and *The Spanish Tragedy*', *Medieval and Renaissance Drama*, 11 (1999), 129–42.

Smith, Peter J., *Social Shakespeare: Aspects of Renaissance Dramaturgy and Contemporary Society* (Basingstoke: Macmillan – now Palgrave Macmillan, 1995).

Snyder, Susan, *The Comic Matrix of Shakespeare's Tragedies: Romeo and Juliet, Hamlet, Othello and King Lear* (Princeton, NJ: Princeton University Press, 1979).

Snyder, Susan, 'Ideology and the Feud in *Romeo and Juliet*', *Sh. S.* 49 (1996), 87–96

Sokol, B. J. and M., *Shakespeare's Legal Language: A Dictionary* (London and New Brunswick, NJ: Athlone Press, 2000).

Somerset, J. A. B., 'Falstaff, the Prince, and the Pattern of *2 Henry IV*', *Sh. S.*, 30 (1977), 35–46.

Spivack, Bernard, *Shakespeare and the Allegory of Evil: The History of a Metaphor in Relation to his Major Villains* (London: Oxford University Press, 1958).

Starn, Randolph, *Contrary Commonwealth: The Theme of Exile in Medieval and Renaissance Italy* (Berkeley: University of California Press, 1982).

Stewart, J. I. M., *Character and Motive in Shakespeare: Some Recent Appraisals Examined* (London: Longmans, Green & Co., 1949).

Sundelson, David, 'So Rare a Wonder'd Father: Prospero's *Tempest*', in *Representing Shakespeare*, eds C. Kahn and M. Schwartz (Baltimore and London: Johns Hopkins University Press, 1980), 33–53.

Tabori, Paul, *The Anatomy of Exile: A Semantic and Historical Study* (London: Harrap, 1972).

Tayler, E. W., *Nature and Art in Renaissance Literature* (New York and London: Columbia University Press, 1964).

Taylor, Gary, 'The Fortunes of Oldcastle', *Sh. S.*, 38 (1985), 85–100.

Taylor, Gary, '*King Lear*: The Date and Authorship of the Folio Version', in Gary Taylor and William Warren, eds, *The Division of the Kingdoms* (Oxford: Clarendon Press, 1983).

Thomas, Keith, *Religion and the Decline of Magic* (London: Weidenfeld & Nicolson, 1971).

Tison, John L. 'Shakespeare's *Consolatio* for Exile', *MLQ*, 21 (1960), 142–56.

Tomlins, T. E., *The Law-Dictionary* (London: C. Baldwin, 1820), 3rd edn, 2 vols.

Tonkin, Humphrey, *Spenser's Courteous Pastoral: Book Six of the Faerie Queene* (Oxford: Clarendon Press, 1972).

Underdown, David, *Popular Politics and Culture in England 1603–1660* (Oxford and New York: Oxford University Press, 1985).

Velz, John W., 'Cracking Strong Curbs Asunder: Roman Destiny and the Roman Hero in *Coriolanus*', *ELR*, 13 (1983), 58–69.

Waith, Eugene M., *The Herculean Hero in Marlowe, Chapman, Shakespeare and Dryden* (London: Chatto & Windus, 1962).

Weckermann, Hans-Jürgen, '*Coriolanus*: The Failure of the Autonomous Individual', in *Shakespeare: Text, Language, Criticism: Essays in Honour of Marvin Spevack*, eds Bernhard Fabian and Kurt Tetzeli von Rosador (Zurich and New York: Olms-Weidmann, 1987), 334–50.

Wells, Charles, *The Wide Arch: Roman Values in Shakespeare* (London: Bristol Classical Press, 1993).

Wells, Stanley, 'The Challenges of *Romeo and Juliet*', *Sh. S.*, 49 (1996), 1–15.

Wells, Stanley, 'The Lamentable Tale of *Richard II*', *Sh. St.* (Tokyo), 17 (1982), 1–23.

Wells, Stanley, 'The Once and Future *King Lear*', in Gary Taylor and Michael Warren, eds, *The Division of the Kingdoms* (Oxford: Clarendon Press, 1983).

Wells, Stanley and Gary Taylor with John Jowett and William Montgomery (eds) *William Shakespeare: A Textual Companion* (Oxford: Clarendon Press, 1987).

Westlund, Joseph, *Shakespeare's Reparative Comedies: A Psychoanalytic View of the Middle Plays* (Chicago and London: University of Chicago Press, 1984).

Whittier, Gayle, 'The Sonnet's Body and the Body Sonnetized in *Romeo and Juliet*', *Sh. Q.*, 40 (1989), 27–41.

Wickham, Glynne, 'From Tragedy to Tragi-Comedy: *King Lear* as Prologue', *Sh. S.*, 26 (1973), 33–48.

Wilcox, Helen, 'Gender and Genre in Shakespeare's Tragicomedies' in *Reclamations of Shakespeare DQR Studies in Literature*, 15th edn, ed. A. J. Hoenselaars (Amsterdam: Rodopi, 1994), 129–38.

Williams, David, 'The Exile as Uncreator', *Mosaic*, 8 (1975), 1–15.

Williams, George Walton, 'Fastolf or Falstaff', *ELR*, 5 (1975), 308–12.

Williamson, Marilyn L., 'Romeo and Death', *Sh. St.*, 14 (1981), 129–37.

Willson, Robert F., 'Falstaff in *Henry IV*: What's in a Name?', *Sh. Q.*, 27 (1976), 199–200.

Wilson, J. Dover, *The Fortunes of Falstaff* (Cambridge: Cambridge University Press, 1943).

Wittlin, Joseph, 'Sorrow and Grandeur of Exile', *Polish Review* (Spring–Summer, 1957), 99–111.

Woodbridge, Linda, *Vagrancy, Homelessness and English Renaissance Literature* (Urbana and Chicago: University of Illinois Press, 2001).

Wraight, A. D., *The Story that the Sonnets Tell* (London: Adam Hart, 1994).

Yates, Frances A., *Astraea: The Imperial Theme in the Sixteenth Century* (London and Boston: Routledge & Kegan Paul, 1975).

Young, David, *The Heart's Forest: A Study of Shakespeare's Pastoral Plays* (London and New Haven, CT: Yale University Press, 1972).

Index

abjuration, 9–11, 13, 61
abolitio memoriae, 157
Adelman, Janet, 145, 155
Adorno, Theodor, 177
Aeneas, as exile, 114
Agrippa, Henry Cornelius, 165
Allen, William, 18–19
Alpers, Paul, 97, 201n.42
antimetabole, 77
Antipodes, 73, 193n.65
aquae et ignis intedictio, 153
Arden, forest of, 110
Aristides, 144
Aristotle, 30, 162, 163, 167, 170–1
Armstrong, Archie, as exile, 205n.88
Ascham, Roger, 121
Astraea, 87, 196n.24
Athens, 144, 206n.18
Augustus, Emperor, 157
Aurelius, Emperor Marcus, 48
Axton, Marie, 58

Bacon, Sir Francis, 93, 200n.25
    as exile, 14, 21, 182n.75
Baker, J. H., 10
Bale, John, as exile, 20
    The Image of Both Churches, 20
    King Johan, 86–7
Bandello, Matteo, 44
banishment
    definition of, 2, 8–15, 18, 180n.41
    as legal punishment of/for:
        Anabaptists, 11 (*see also* religious exile); beggars/vagabonds, 11, 12, 14, 23–4, 128–30, 175, 180n.31, 190n.25; border/shire rebels, 11, 13; Catholics, 7, 10–11, 129, 179n.25 (*see also* religious exile); duelling, 11, 93; 'Egyptians', 11, 13; illegal hunting, 8–9, 11; Irish, 11, 13; Negroes, 11, 13; prostitution, 12; sumptuary law transgressions, 11; treason, 13, 18, 61, 90, 141

distances implied, 14–15, 160; from bed (divorce), 3, 27, 86–7, 178n.6, 184n.100, 188n.51; from city of London, 12; from court/royal presence, 11, 14–15, 88–90, 93, 116; from mother (wet-nursimg), 145, 155–6; from the world, 15
    of poets and players, 5, 11, 19–24, 183n.85, 183n.89, 197n.39 (*see also* Plato)
    of theatres, 5, 19–21, 23, 182–3n.76
    volition/force implied, 13–14, 15–16, 20, 180n.41, 183n.76
    see also abolitio memoriae; abjuration; deportation; excommunication; exile; *exsilium*; extradition; outlawry; transportation; wandering
Barish, Jonas, 93, 198n.60
Barroll, Leeds, 5
Bate, Jonathan, 70, 163, 192n.55, 192n.56
Batman, Stephen, 119, 201n.45
Beaufort, Francis, 200n.25
Bedlam beggars, 129
Bellamy, John, 120
Belsey, Catherine, 43
Bennett, Josephine Waters, 161
Berger, Harry, 163
Berry, Philippa, 52
biblical exiles
    Adam, 28, 184n.98
    Cain, 83, 93
    Lucifer, 27–8, 210n.22
    Noah, 114, 121
Boaistuau, Pierre, 44
Boethius, 135, 176
Branagh, Kenneth, 94
Brooke, Arthur, 38, 44, 48–50, 54, 186n.25, 188n.41
Brotton, Jerry, 173
Brutus, 209n.9
Burbage, James 19, 21
Butler, F. G., 131

236 *Index*